In this study of Genesis 37-50, Dr. Pulse offers a unifi[ed] section of Genesis, focusing on Joseph. His research in[to] extra-biblical sources relating to it is thorough and careful. Pulse's argument that Joseph is presented as a figure exemplifying death and resurrection is based on sound and methodical research into the text. His exploration of recent approaches to interpreting the Joseph cycle is exemplary, demonstrating that while his thesis departs in some places from other interpreters, he is conversant with contrasting theories currently pursued by others. Pulse's wholistic evaluation of the text is a welcome breeze amidst the somewhat stale air of past readings that have tended to atomize the text.

—**Andrew E. Steinmann**, Distinguished Professor of Theology and Hebrew, Concordia University Chicago

In Matthew 13:52 Jesus commends God's royal scribes who bring out old and new treasures as they teach his word to his disciples. Like him I commend Dr. Pulse for bringing out treasures from the Old Testament for us who are co-heirs with people of Israel in the new covenant. In his wise and winsome study of the beautifully crafted stories of Joseph in Genesis 37-50, Dr. Pulse shows how the hope for the resurrection of the body is prefigured by Joseph and implicit in them. His careful analysis explains how the motif of death and resurrection permeates and informs each stage in Joseph's life and his life as a whole. He also correlates this motif with other similar motifs, such as descent into Egypt and ascent to the promised land. So in these stories Joseph is not presented as an example for moral instruction but as a figure for God's gracious purpose for Israel and its coming king. Like Joseph, his brothers and his father and all Israel share in the same figurative experience of death and resurrection, as they, like the embalmed bones of Joseph, await the resurrection of the body. For me the greatest value of this fine study is that it helps me to make better sense of Paul's claim that Christ "was raised on the third day according to the Scriptures" (1 Cor 15:4).

—**John W. Kleinig**, Lecturer emeritus and former head of the Biblical Department, Australian Lutheran College, University of Divinity

Second Temple Judaism restored the story of Joseph to its rightful place as one of the great dramatic narratives of Genesis. Now Jeffrey Pulse has raised up Joseph in the same way for our generation. Through the motif of death and resurrection Jeffrey Pulse uses the Joseph narrative to demonstrate his hermeneutic of reading Scripture as a unified theological narrative. He does this with clarity through the pastoral exegesis for which he is known by his colleagues and students. For those who want a refreshing and rigorous reading of a neglected portion of Genesis, Jeffrey Pulse restores Joseph to us so that even now through his delightful book the bones of Joseph cry out for resurrection.

—**Arthur Just**, professor of Exegetical Theology, Concordia Theological Seminary

Through a thick figural reading, Pulse resurrects Joseph from merely an example of Hebrew prose artistry. He shows Joseph's full canonical significance as a death and resurrection figure using multiple sub-motifs that serve the death/resurrection motif.

—**Ryan M. Tietz**, assistant professor of Exegetical Theology, Concordia Theological Seminary, Fort Wayne

When Jesus interpreted to the disciples the things concerning himself in the Scriptures (Lk 24:27) what might he have said about Genesis 37–50? Dr. Pulse opens our eyes to hermeneutical and exegetical possibilities. He advocates reading Scripture as a unified theological narrative with a Christological center. His methodology of "figuring" embraces early church hermeneutics and builds on the approaches of modern interpreters. Dr. Pulse explores no less than twelve distinct submotifs in the Joseph narrative with a "downward and upward" movement (often of a beloved son) that represent the motif of death and resurrection, which may be the most prominent motif in Scripture as a whole. He traces each of these submotifs into the Gospel narratives of Jesus Christ and the NT writers' appropriation of them for the baptismal life of the church. This comprehensive book has changed the way I shall read the OT narrative.

—**Christopher W. Mitchell**, Concordia Commentary Editor, Concordia Publishing House, Saint Louis, Missouri

FIGURING
RESURRECTION

FIGURING RESURRECTION

Joseph as a Death

& Resurrection Figure

in the Old Testament

& Second Temple Judaism

JEFFREY PULSE

STUDIES IN
SCRIPTURE
& BIBLICAL
THEOLOGY

LEXHAM PRESS

I dedicate this thesis to my wife, Sara,
who has given new definition to the phrase "Long Suffering."

Figuring Resurrection: Joseph as a Death-and-Resurrection Figure in the Old Testament and Second Temple Judaism
Studies in Scripture & Biblical Theology

Copyright 2021 Jeffrey Pulse

Lexham Press, 1313 Commercial St., Bellingham, WA 98225
LexhamPress.com

Unless otherwise noted, Scripture quotations are the author's own translation.

Print ISBN 9781683594536
Digital ISBN 9781683594543
Library of Congress Control Number 2020948482

Lexham Editorial: Derek Brown, Lisa Eary, Abigail Salinger
Cover Design: Brittany Schrock
Typesetting: Justin Marr

Contents

List of Abbreviations

B. Bat.	Baba Batra
b. Ber.	Babylonian Talmud Bekorot
b. Qidd.	Babylonian Talmud Qiddušin
b. Sanh.	Babylonian Talmud Sanhedrin
b. Sukkah	Babylonian Talmud Sukkah
Cant Rab	Canticle of Canticles Rabbah
Gen Rab	Genesis Rabbah
Jub.	Jubilees
Lev Rab	Leviticus Rabbah
LXX	Septuagint
Mek.	Mekilta
Midr.	Midrash
MT	Masoretic Text
NT	New Testament
Num Rab	Numbers Rabbah
OT	Old Testament
Roš. Haš.	Roš Haššanah
Sifra Qod.	Sifra Qodašim
Sot.	Sotah
T.Jos.	Testament of Joseph
T.Jud.	Testament of Judah
T.Sim.	Testament of Simeon
Tanh.	Tanhuma
Tg. Ps.-J.	Targum Pseudo-Jonathan
Tg. Song	Targum Song of Songs
y. Hor.	Jerusalem Talmud Horayot

Introduction

AIM AND SCOPE

The pages of this book focus on the character of Joseph as recorded in the Joseph narratives of Genesis 37–50. Specifically explored is the particular aspect of his character identifying him as a death-and-resurrection figure in the Old Testament and Second Temple Judaism. Many scholars over the centuries have engaged with Joseph and his story, and their efforts have often borne useful fruit. Some of their valuable insights and discoveries have informed the writing of this book, and they will be duly noted. One aspect of Joseph's story, however, has been somewhat neglected. I suggest that a "dying and rising" theme in Genesis 37–50 plays a prominent part in the Hebrew text as we have received it in its final form. The intention of the book, therefore, is to attempt to recapture this characteristic of the Joseph narratives and to explore it in detail, noting its impact on the canonical figure of Joseph.

PART I: BIBLICAL INTERPRETATION

In order to accomplish this, an examination of the history of biblical interpretation is required.[1] Part I explores this history. However, this history can never be seen as a straight, unadulterated line that demonstrates a logical, sequential progression. Nor can one assume clean and clear lines of

---

1. I have specifically relied on R. N. Whybray, *The Making of the Pentateuch: A Methodological Study* (Sheffield: Sheffield Academic Press, 1987); B. S. Childs, *Old Testament Theology in a Canonical Context* (Philadelphia: Fortress, 1985), J. D. Levenson, *The Hebrew Bible, the Old Testament and Historical Criticism* (Louisville: Westminster John Knox, 1993); R. Alter, *The Art of Biblical Poetry* (New York: Basic Books, 1985); R. B. Hays and E. Davis, *The Art of Reading Scripture* (Grand Rapids: Eerdmans, 2003); R. W. L. Moberly, *Old Testament Theology: Reading the Hebrew Bible as Christian Scripture* (Grand Rapids: Baker Academic, 2013); J. J. Collins, *The Bible after Babel: Historical Criticism in a Postmodern Age* (Grand Rapids: Eerdmans, 2005).

demarcation between the various hermeneutics. Too often these assumptions have encouraged the notion that the history of biblical interpretation has been a positive, progressive evolution. In reality, there is no clear, collegial adherence to one single methodology at any point on the hermeneutical timeline. Rather, there are always periods of transition with various theologians serving as bridge figures from one method to another.[2] From the beginning of the New Testament era, there have been biblical scholars who have been instructed in the current hermeneutic but have continued to explore and experiment with new approaches. They stand with one foot in the established method while the other foot explores new ground. Generally, it is their students who complete the move to the new hermeneutic; but the bridge figure has pioneered the ground.

Also important is that complete consensus in the field of biblical interpretation has never existed. This remains true today, as some still advocate a form of higher criticism with a focus on the world behind the text, while others recommend the rhetorical or narrative approaches, which tend to focus more broadly on the world within the text and the world in front of the text.[3] There is a broad spectrum represented that demonstrates a continual state of flux. On the surface this may seem a negative, but there is a positive as well. The constant experimentation, searching for the hermeneutic that best serves the text, brings new information and expands the knowledge base, and each of these hermeneutical assumptions of the past has contributed to our foundational knowledge of the text.

There are trends that may be identified in this evolution of Old Testament hermeneutics. An interesting trend and the most significant for the purpose of this book is the movement toward dissecting the text, which had its advent alongside the modern scientific approach.[4] Rather

---

2. Examples may be H. Gunkel, *Genesis* (Macon, GA: Mercer University Press, 1997); Gunkel, *The Legends of Genesis* (New York: Schocken Books, 1964); G. von Rad, *Genesis: A Commentary* (Philadelphia: Westminster, 1961); R. Alter, *The Art of Biblical Narrative* (New York: Basic Books, 1981); Childs, *Old Testament Theology*; B. S. Childs, *Introduction to the Old Testament as Scripture* (Philadelphia: Fortress, 1979).

3. For more discussion on the world behind, within, and in front of the text in relation to various textual approaches see below on Childs, Levenson, Moberly, and Brueggemann.

4. Along with J. Wellhausen, *Die Composition des Hexateuchs und der Historischen Bücher des Alten Testaments* (Berlin: G. Reiner, 1899), noted practitioners of this method of more recent times include C. Westermann, *Genesis 37–50: A Commentary* (Minneapolis: Augsburg, 1986); Westermann, *Genesis: An Introduction* (Minneapolis: Augsburg Fortress, 1992); W. Eichrodt,

than viewing the text as a whole, scholars began to take it apart to discover how it was constructed. Much information was gleaned in this process; however, the integrity of the whole was often compromised. This movement was common to all methods of historical criticism for centuries. Due to the trend toward the dissection of the text into smaller parts, little has been done in relation to the Joseph narratives, which tend to be resistant to such an approach.[5] The cohesiveness of these chapters does not fit well into the historical-critical milieu, and much has been overlooked or underemphasized in these narratives. Looking at any biblical text through a microscopic lens, while interesting, may cause one to miss the big picture. In the case of the Joseph narratives, the big picture provides elements for a balanced interpretation of the text as a whole.

Historically, the trend toward dissection has slowly reversed, moving toward a view of the text as a unified whole.[6] Scholarship has trended toward a wider view of the biblical narrative. While understanding the smallest pieces of the text is important, it is only a tool to help understand the larger narrative. Regardless of one's faith tradition and personal theology, a narrative reading allows the writings to be read in their final form, which all exegetes may engage and expound.

It is a danger to assume a simple division between those who consider the many pieces of the text and those who adhere to a more holistic approach. Again, there are no clear lines and no absolutes in approach. In some ways, the scientific methods employed belong to the academy, while the more holistic approaches continue to function in the practical realms of

Theology of the Old Testament (Philadelphia: Westminster, 1961); and J. van Seters, *Prologue to History: The Yahwist as Historian in Genesis* (Louisville: Westminster John Knox, 1992).

5. Even scholars who tend toward the dissection of the text frequently note the coherence of the Joseph narratives. Examples include M. Noth, *A History of Pentateuchal Traditions* (Englewood Cliffs, NJ: Prentice-Hall, 1972), 208–13; W. L. Humphreys, *Joseph and His Family* (Columbia: University of South Carolina Press, 1988), 6–7; and G. A. Rendsburg, *The Redaction of Genesis* (Winona Lake, IN: Eisenbrauns, 1986), 106.

6. Alter, *Art of Biblical Narrative*, 12–13; Childs, *Old Testament Theology*, xiii–1; R. W. L. Moberly, "What Is Theological Interpretation of Scripture?," *Journal of Theological Interpretation* 3, no. 2 (2009): 163–78; Moberly, "Living Dangerously: Genesis 22 and the Quest for Good Biblical Interpretation," in Hays and Davis, *Art of Reading Scripture*, 181–97; C. Seitz, *The Character of Christian Scripture: The Significance of a Two Testament Bible* (Grand Rapids: Baker Academic, 2011); G. A. Anderson, "Joseph and the Passion of Our Lord," in Hays and Davis, *Art of Reading Scripture*, 198–215.

the faith communities; but even this account presupposes a false dichotomy that no longer exists in the field of biblical interpretation—if it ever did.

In this historical analysis of biblical hermeneutics I have focused on the various trends from 1980 onward. Although this may appear to be a slim slice, it most closely resembles and informs my own recommended methodology. I have attempted to describe the current landscape of hermeneutical thought, describing more recent trends and movements in the discipline, in order to demonstrate how my own approach fits in and adds to the discussion.

The hermeneutic for interpretation that I advocate is reading the text of Scripture as a unified theological narrative. Reading the Scriptures as a unified narrative that also demonstrates a unified theology is not new, but it has suffered disuse in modern history.[7] Returning to this view of the text can reveal a rich and substantive meaning. This approach assumes the place of individual portions of Scripture, such as the Joseph narratives, as essential to the entire narrative of the biblical text. Not only are all the parts integral to the whole, but their placement within the present, final form of the received text is significant as well. Following the attempts of various methods to divide and dismantle the biblical narrative, this approach may, at first, seem counterintuitive. However, looking at the text from a grander perspective is in keeping with its canonical purpose.

The recommended method of reading Scripture as a unified theological narrative not only avoids the tendency toward the dissection of the text, but it also moves away from a wooden, literalistic approach. This flat, one-dimensional approach sees only the surface of the text and does not allow the exploration of its rich theological depths. While the Old Testament writings are historical documents filled with many interesting isagogical facts, they are so much more. It is important to take into account, as far as we are able, the way in which the canon was received by its ancient audience and by the oldest Jewish interpreters known to us.[8]

---

7. Martin Luther employed this hermeneutic in his Christocentric understanding. The earlier methods of Ambrose and Augustine also demonstrate this approach to a certain degree.

8. For example, secondary sources such as Testaments of the Twelve Patriarchs and Jubilees help demonstrate how the second-century BCE Jewish community understood their sacred writings and may give insight into an older Hebrew understanding.

The usefulness of reading Scripture in such a way may be attested to by the presence of various biblical motifs that wind their way throughout the wider narrative. These motifs reveal themselves as the threads that provide the woven fabric of the text and as the themes that speak to a unified message. The majority are first encountered by the reader in Genesis; and as they continue to appear in the rest of the canon, greater meaning and deeper import are often ascribed to them. Because they represent themes that are taken up in canonical books outside Genesis, they can present the reader with new information as they are used in new contexts.

As one might expect, these motifs also intertwine with one another as they progress through the text. In those characters and events that demonstrate a multiplicity of these motifs, there is great respect and honor often afforded by the faith community. This may well be due to the community's recognition of these important motifs and not only the way in which they hold the text of Scripture together, but also how they convey a consistent, unified theological message.

I have used this approach as the direction from which I approach the Joseph narratives. Such a reading reveals these chapters as a beautifully structured narrative that contains many and various biblical motifs. Not only can these motifs reflect the deeper character of the text, but they also tie Joseph and his story into the overall context of the narrative of Scripture.[9]

PART II: THE TEXT

Following the hermeneutic of reading Scripture as a unified theological narrative, I have examined the MT of the Joseph narratives with an eye toward the biblical motifs that define its sense and meaning. In comparison, this examination often shows efforts to portray Joseph in various ways. These variations have not been noted in any systematic way by current scholars, and yet they prove invaluable in helping establish Joseph's identity. The overriding emphasis, brought out in the MT, portrays Joseph as a death-and-resurrection figure.

---

9. Of particular significance in this discussion is Childs and his canon criticism or canonical context. This approach recommends seeing the entire canon as a united narrative, as opposed to the more technical approaches, which seek to dismantle in search of meaning. See chap. 1 below.

In the examination of the MT, the story of Joseph is unique in how the narrator uses language. Even the casual reader recognizes the distinct style incorporated. The narrator uses an inordinate amount of doubling in these chapters. Not only are various words doubled, but we also note the doubling of dreams, blessings, and even narratives. This is quite distinct, and the narrator uses this literary format to emphasize the importance of what he is relaying and to establish authority for his account.

Another aspect of the MT noted and mentioned by a fair number of scholars is the "downward/upward" movements within the story.[10] No other portion of Scripture shows such a preponderance of these movements. Joseph goes down into a pit and is lifted out; Joseph goes down to Egypt, is sold into slavery, and then is raised to second in command of Potiphar's household; Joseph goes down into the pit of prison, only to be raised to second in charge of the prisoners and then second in command of all Egypt; Joseph, Jacob, and the brothers go down to Egypt and up to the promised land; and so on. These downward/upward movements are prevalent and well noted, and they help set up and support one of the most important biblical motifs in Scripture, and the most important motif in the Joseph narratives: the death-and-resurrection motif. Following Joseph's first descent into the pit, Jacob declares that he will go down to Sheol in mourning at the loss of his son. The language does not appear to be accidental considering the downward/upward movements within the text.

A close reading of the MT unveils these textual movements and important motifs, but a careful scrutiny also unveils various issues. These issues center on Joseph and Judah and can be seen as flaws in their characters. While the Scriptures are replete with tarnished heroes, these flaws stand in the way of Joseph's and Judah's adoption as examples for later generations. The desire to use Joseph as a moral and ethical example, especially in the matters of sexual purity, is hindered by these perceived difficulties. While Joseph, on the surface, appears righteous, a deeper reading reveals more.

---

10. J. D. Levenson, *The Death and Resurrection of the Beloved Son: The Transformation of Child Sacrifice in Judaism and Christianity* (New Haven: Yale University Press, 1993), 152; D. Seybold, "Paradox and Symmetry in the Joseph Narrative," in *Literary Interpretations of Biblical Narratives* (Nashville, Abingdon, 1974), 59–73; Y.-W. Fung, *Victim and Victimizer: Joseph's Interpretation of His Destiny* (Sheffield: Sheffield Academic Press, 2000), 27–30, 151–56.

The next section of this book examines in greater detail the death-and-resurrection motif of Scripture and its many manifestations, especially Joseph's place in this motif. Death and resurrection is arguably the most prevalent theme in the biblical narrative as it now stands; yet, due to its many manifestations and its pervasiveness in the fabric of the text, it is often overlooked. Even though the first explicit references to the resurrection of the body are in Isaiah 25–26, the language of Scripture makes multiple implicit references throughout. These implicit references are often based in the submotifs of death and resurrection and may indicate an early concept of the afterlife among the Hebrews, perhaps even the belief in a bodily resurrection. Certainly, there is a distinction between those who "go down" and those who are "raised up." Given the language of the Joseph narratives, may it not be the case that ideas of resurrection are more ancient in Hebrew literature than commonly supposed? Although we do not know for certain when the Joseph narratives were written, the Torah was probably in its present form by 450 BCE at the latest. Therefore, the repeated themes of going down and coming up in these narratives can be read as extended symbols or metaphors. The language is pervasive and highly suggestive.

The manifestations of this death-and-resurrection motif in the Joseph narratives identified and expounded on in this book are:

1. separation and reunion

2. three-day/three-stage separation and restoration

3. the barren womb and the opening of the womb

4. being cast into a pit/Sheol and being raised up/lifted out

5. going down to Egypt and going up to Canaan/the promised land

6. slavery and freedom

7. thrown into prison and freed from prison

8. famine and deliverance

9. seeds/planting and growth/fertility/fruitfulness

10. going down into the water/being drowned and being brought up out of the water/new life

11. exile and return from exile

12. stripped and clothed

These submotifs, viewed separately, may not seem particularly significant. Taken together, and with so many being present in one character and his story, the cumulative evidence might well be considered impressive and suggestive, even constituting an invitation to the reader to ponder more intently the deeper sense of the whole narrative.[11] While the New Testament is beyond the scope of this thesis, it is interesting to note that the New Testament writers are capable of recognizing and adopting these same themes in their discussion of dying and rising again.

PART III: OTHER TEXTS

The final part of this dissertation examines other biblical and extrabiblical texts and their interaction and relationship to the MT. The Septuagint (LXX) is a translation from Hebrew into Greek and reveals additional concerns as compared to the MT. The context of third-century BCE Alexandria, Egypt led the translators to subtly change the text for their audience. Much of the doubling present in the Hebrew has been excluded, but in its place the LXX adds to the dramatic nature of the narrative. Word choice and placement show an intensification that presents the Joseph story in a fashion that might have well been suited for the stage. Alexandria was vying with Athens, seeking recognition as a center for the arts, especially the theater.[12] Thus, the intention was to produce a literary work that was "heard well" as it was presented.

It is also from the LXX that the notion of a second messianic figure from the house of Joseph begins to take root. In the blessings of Genesis 49:22–26,

---

11. Levenson, using the language of descent/ascent, points to the connection of death and life in Joseph's life. "Over against these three descents—into the pit, into slavery in Egypt, and into prison—stand a series of ascents: out of the pit, out of slavery, out of prison, and, ultimately, after Joseph's death, out of Egypt and up to the Promised Land in which his life began" (*Death and Resurrection*, 152).

12. P. M. Fraser, *Ptolemaic Alexandria* (Oxford: Oxford University Press, 1972), 1:618–674.

the LXX includes the idea that it is from Joseph that the one who strengthens Israel will come. We see this same idea recorded in Testaments of the Twelve Patriarchs and in Qumran materials. The LXX appears to be the earliest datable source for this idea, and it appears to have been included as an effort to bolster Joseph's character in the eyes of the third-century BCE Alexandrian community.

A significant by-product of the Septuagintal focus on Joseph's role as a salvific figure is the early church fathers' view of Joseph. While the MT does not exclude Joseph's role of saving the people of Israel from famine, it does not include any messianic language in the blessing of Joseph. Because of the early church reliance on the LXX, the salvific role of Joseph took precedence over his death-and-resurrection character, although that character was never dismissed.

In the comparison of the targumic writings, with specific emphasis on Targum Onqelos, a different focus on Joseph is discovered. While the LXX focuses on the salvific figure, Targum Onqelos focuses on Joseph as a moral and ethical figure. Joseph is chosen for this role because he resisted the advances of Potiphar's wife, but because the MT leaves some doubts as to Joseph's overall character, Targum Onqelos adjusts the text in an attempt to remove these doubts. Still, Targum Onqelos preserves the downward/upward movement and generally retains the doubling, remaining faithful to the MT.

It appears that Targum Onqelos, while not emphasizing the death-and-resurrection motif of the MT, still recognizes and maintains it. The reasons for this cautious approach are likely many. Some considered include the religious climate of the day. Targum Onqelos was written at the time when the Christian sect was making inroads among the Jewish population. To acknowledge or emphasize death and resurrection when this was a foundational teaching of the Christian sect would have been counterproductive. There were also the competing teachings within Judaism concerning death and resurrection, and Targum Onqelos may be trying to avoid the alienation of any portion of the writer's faith community. These and other issues may have come into play, and so the moral and ethical character of Joseph became the focus.

The political and religious climate of the Second Temple era may explain why Joseph was resurrected from obscurity. Since the interment of his bones by Joshua, Joseph slipped from view in the biblical text. Yet, when the southern kingdom of Judah was taken to Babylon in exile and the holy city of Jerusalem and its holy temple were destroyed, Joseph began to reemerge, not only in the pages of Scripture but also in the Second Temple pseudepigraphal writings. The reason for this will be discussed in some detail: however, when the other biblical characters who also enjoyed new popularity are considered (i.e., Enoch and Elijah), the connecting link appears to be resurrection. Joseph, because of the multiple manifestations of the death-and-resurrection motif, had always been considered a character expressive of dying and rising. When the Israelites found themselves in difficult circumstances, concerned about the loss of land, city, and temple and wondering about their relationship with God, they sought out Joseph, Elijah, and Enoch to bring clarity to their situation.

Joseph experienced such a resurgence of popularity that many of the groups and significant historical figures of Second Temple times sought to adopt him for their own agendas. These agendas varied, not always in keeping with the death-and-resurrection emphasis of the MT; however, they do point to Joseph as an important and highly respected individual. Thus, the Joseph story is frequently changed or nuanced as liberties are taken to enhance his character. The portrayal of the Joseph of the MT, therefore, has sometimes been distorted in such a way that the dying and rising themes in his story have been overlooked.

The final chapter of this dissertation deals with a rather peculiar aspect of the life of Joseph. At his death, Joseph made his brothers swear that when God visited them that they would carry his bones from Egypt up to the promised land. This request and the resulting action is unique to all of Scripture. The emphasis on the bones of Joseph leads to a consideration of the use and role of bones in the greater narrative.

When one thinks of bones, the first thought is of death, or in some relation to death. It is easy to understand the death component, but what is overlooked is the life and resurrection aspect. Strangely, scriptural references to bones being unclean are quite rare, but the situations where bones are associated with life are common. The bones of the Passover Lamb, the blood of which averts the angel of death, are not to be broken (Exod 12:46); the bones of Elisha resurrect a dead body (2 Kgs 13:21); and in Ezekiel 37, the valley of the dry bones demonstrates dead bones coming to life.

The detail of the biblical narrative that tells us that Moses remembers to procure Joseph's bones on the way out of Egypt speaks volumes on the importance of Joseph to the Hebrew people. His bones are carried for forty years as they journey through the wilderness and even throughout the conquest of Canaan. Several possible reasons for this strange occurrence are explored. One of the possibilities discussed, and for the purposes of this book the most important, is that the transportation of Joseph's bones to the promised land may represent the completion of a downward/upward move and a death-and-resurrection submotif as well. Joseph was taken down to Egypt, but in the end he will go up to the promised land.

Understanding Joseph as a death-and-resurrection figure in the Old Testament and Second Temple Judaism is helpful if one is to understand the Hebrews and their concepts of the afterlife. Approaching the text and reading it as a unified theological narrative reveals the biblical motif and helps unveil the greater reality and meaning associated with Joseph's character and story. This book is an attempt to resurrect Joseph's character and present him as he once was seen. Such an attempt may provide a new view of Joseph and may also provide insight into the Hebrew understanding of death and resurrection from ancient times.

Part I

—

Biblical Interpretation

1

Biblical Interpretation and the Joseph Narratives

No other collection of writings has received as much interpretive attention as the text of the Bible. In an attempt to decipher and understand these writings, many and various methodologies have been employed with the goal of discernment. These methodologies have particularly focused on the book of Genesis. This scrutiny is to be expected as one considers the importance of "In the beginning" and the formation and early history of the people of God.

From the early church fathers through the Middle Ages into the Enlightenment to the contemporary context of our day, there has been what some would label as a progression, even an evolution, of interpretive methodologies connected to the biblical text. While it is true that the art of interpretation has undergone many transformations, the language used to describe this process gives the impression that one method gives way to another method, or that one approach is built on the approaches that have preceded. This is true only in a very general way. It is true that each methodology has brought useful information to the table and the overall art of interpretation has benefited, but it is a mistake to assume clean lines of demarcation between these methodologies.

The academy has never totally embraced one methodology, nor has there ever been one method officially adopted as the hermeneutical rule or principle. This reality pictures an art in a continual state of flux. Some methods and approaches may have been popular at various times and in various locations, but even the most influential have never existed apart from competing and even conflicting methods.

While this reality has occasionally caused concern within the ranks of theologians, one can point to no clear, collegial adherence or adoption of one single methodology at any point on the hermeneutical time line. In fact, a lockstep agreement is not to be found even within the same faith traditions. One could argue that such a lack of agreement is normal and perhaps even useful. Where there is a lack of agreement, the conversation continues. When there is a closing of the ranks, there is then a closing of the conversation. With this ongoing dialogue each method has provided important data to the continuing discussion and helped to more clearly articulate the approaches. Thus the debate moves forward in a positive direction, a movement that can be best appreciated from the perspective of a panoramic view.

There are no clean lines of demarcation between methodologies. Rather, what one observes are periods of transitions in which various theologians have had the distinction of serving as bridge figures from one method to another. Generally, these scholars are those who have studied and been mentored in one methodology and have gone beyond in their own hermeneutical pursuits. Using their training as a foundation, they continue to explore and grow in understanding the nature of the text and the realities of the task. In turn, their students often define the next generation of interpretative tradition while continuing to do homage to those scholars and methodologies that have shaped them.

THE JOSEPH NARRATIVES

Over the course of time Genesis 37–50, the Joseph narratives, has received less attention than most portions of Genesis. This is due in part to the cohesiveness of these chapters[1] in vocabulary, style and content, in both the ancient and modern, Western sense. This is not to say that they have escaped scrutiny altogether; rather, the scrutiny of the text has focused more on the nature of the narrative and the message of the final form.

One can, however, examine the historical development of the textual hermeneutic on a broader scale and relate this to the Joseph narratives. For the purpose of this book, I will begin the historical review of the textual hermeneutical methodologies in the 1980s in an attempt to describe the current landscape of hermeneutical thought. It is important to remind the

---

1. This is the case with the exception of Gen 38 (the story of Judah and Tamar) and 49 (Jacob blessing/cursing his sons), which have caused many scholars to question their placement and authorship. Genesis 38, at first glance, seems awkward and out of place in the midst of the Joseph story because there is no mention of Joseph, nor does there seem to be any connection to Joseph apart from the familial. Genesis 49 is questioned because of the change of style from narrative to poetry, which, once again, seems oddly placed.

reader that I am not suggesting cohesion of thought or method. Rather, my attempt is to show current movement and trends in the discipline in order to demonstrate how my own approach fits in or adds to the discussion.

There are several scholars who have proved to be essential in the development of textual hermeneutics and who did much to advance the discipline toward a more perceptive analysis of biblical narrative techniques and conventions, and toward a deeper, more systematic, and ultimately more satisfying explication of the text. Three who stand out in this progression are Brevard Childs, Robert Alter, and Jon Levenson.

BREVARD CHILDS: A CANONICAL APPROACH

As mentioned above, Childs is an important figure in the arena of textual hermeneutics and biblical theology. His canonical approach is the methodology that has laid the groundwork for many of the current narrative-reading approaches being explored today. He received his doctoral education at the University of Basel, with a semester at Heidelberg in 1951, and thus was immersed in the methodologies of that era. Nevertheless, it was these methodologies and his perceived inadequacies of their approach that led him to develop his own method of interpreting and reading the text. He referred to this methodology as a canonical approach.[2]

> The approach seeks to work descriptively within a broad theological framework and is open to a variety of different theological formulations which remains the responsibility of the systematic theologian to develop. I would admit, however, that the canonical method which is here described does run counter to two extreme theological positions. It is incompatible with a position on the far right which would stress the divine initiative in such a way as to rule out any theological significance to the response to the divine Word by the people of God. It is equally incompatible with a position on the far theological left, which would understand the formation of the Bible

---

2. Others have referred to his method as canonical criticism. See J. Barr, *Holy Scripture: Canon, Authority, Criticism* (Oxford: Oxford University Press, 1983), 168. Childs objects to this designation, as he believes it gives the impression of being grounded in the historical-critical method.

in purely humanistic terms, such as Israel's search for self-identity, or a process within nature under which God is subsumed.[3]

It is important to note that Childs's canonical approach intentionally runs counter to both ends of the theological spectrum. Whereas Childs states that "one of the most difficult problems of the canonical approach to the Old Testament involves understanding the relationship between the divine initiative in creating Israel's Scripture and the human response in receiving and transmitting the authoritative Word," he sees the far theological left negating (subsuming) the role of the divine, while the far theological right negates the human response.[4] Both, then, misconstrue the relationship between divine and human in the canonical process.

Childs is concerned with the role of the community of faith in the development of the final form of the text, and yet is equally concerned for the role of the divine.

Indeed one of the central goals of emphasizing the role of the canon is to stress the horizontal dimension of the reception, collection and ordering of the experiences of the divine by a community of faith. A canonical approach would be equally critical of a stance which stressed only the vertical dimension of divine truth, as if word and tradition were always in tension.[5]

The relationship between human and divine action in the final form forms the challenge for Childs's approach. How does one distinguish each role and influence, or is it necessary to do so? What is the proper balance in this canonical formation? These are questions asked, but the answers are absent. Childs, it seems, is willing to accept the messiness of the final form of the text. This is not a crucial issue to him. Rather,

It is constitutive of Israel's history that the literature formed the identity of the religious community which in turn shaped the literature. … In my judgment, the crucial issue which produced the

---

3. Childs, *Introduction to the Old Testament*, 81–82.
4. Childs, *Introduction to the Old Testament*, 80.
5. Childs, *Old Testament Theology*, 23.

confusion is the problem of the canon, that is to say, how one understands the nature of the Old Testament in relation to its authority for the community of faith and practice which shaped and preserved it.[6]

The final form of the story is of most importance. Indeed, the final form has an integrity of its own.

The emphasis on scripture as canon focuses its attention on the process by which divine truth acquired its authoritative form as it was received and transmitted by a community of faith. Accordingly, there is no biblical revelation apart from that which bears Israel's imprint. All of scripture is time-conditioned because the whole Old Testament has been conditioned by an historical people. There is no pure doctrine or unconditional piety. Any attempt to abstract elements from its present form by which, as it were, to distinguish the kernel from its husk, or inauthentic existence from authentic expression, runs directly in the face of the canon's function.[7]

Frequently, critics on both sides of the theological divide point to Childs's canonical framework as unhistorical, or as ignoring the historical development of the final form altogether. From Childs's perspective this is far from the truth or his intention.

First of all, it should be incontrovertible that there was a genuine historical development involved in the formation of the canon and that any concept of canon which fails to reckon with this historical dimension is faulty. Secondly, the available historical evidence allows for only a bare skeleton of this development.[8]

Childs considers the history of the text and its development and transmission as quite important. The difficulty lies with the lack of evidence, and Childs is unwilling to allow speculation concerning this history to hold

6. Childs, *Introduction to the Old Testament*, 41.
7. Childs, *Old Testament Theology*, 14.
8. Childs, *Introduction to the Old Testament*, 67.

sway over the final form. Ultimately, canon and its final form trumps all, although there is great significance in the process.

> It is a basic tenet of the canonical approach that one reflects theologically on the text as it has been received and shaped. Yet the emphasis on the normative status of the canonical text is not a denial of the significance of the canonical process which formed the text. The frequently expressed contrast between a "static" canonical text and a "dynamic" traditio-historical process badly misconstrues the issue. Similarly, to claim that attention to canon elevates one specific historical response to a dogmatic principle utterly fails to grasp the function of the canon. Rather, the basic problem turns on the relationship between text and process.[9]

It appears that Childs is not uninterested in the history behind the text and how the text developed over the course of time. He seems eager to embrace this history. However again, it is the canon in its final form that holds first place—a place he believes some scholars of the past have not fully appreciated. This does not mean that Childs abandons a critical approach to the text. Rather, his concern seems to be to bring the matter of the canon into full dialogue with other concerns of the academy. Thus he sets out his position:

> The effect of this history on the concept of the canon was clear. Those scholars who pursued historical criticism of the Old Testament no longer found a significant place for the canon. Conversely, those scholars who sought to retain a concept of the canon were unable to find a significant role for historical criticism. This is the polarity which lies at the centre of the problem of evaluating the nature of Old Testament Introduction.
>
> In my judgment, the crucial task is to rethink the problem of Introduction in such a way as to overcome this long established tension between the canon and criticism. Is it possible to understand

---

9. Childs, *Old Testament Theology*, 11.

the Old Testament as canonical scripture and yet to make full and consistent use of the historical critical tools?[10]

Childs is clear: proper appreciation of the canon directs the reader's attention to the sacred writings rather than to their editors.[11] He even considers it basic to the canonical process that those responsible for the actual editing of the text did their best to obscure their own identity.[12] How the text was edited or reworked lies in almost total obscurity. Also obscured in this process were various sociological and historical differences within the people of Israel. Thus, a religious community emerged that found its identity in terms of sacred Scripture.[13] The evidence for those elements in the text most sought after by modern historical criticism was thus blurred and, Childs would agree, was blurred deliberately.

For Childs the Bible, in the context of the church's confession, is the instrument of encounter with the living God.[14] The canonical process made the tradition accessible to each successive generation by means of "canonical intentionality," which is coextensive with the meaning of the biblical text.[15] His later insistence that a theology of the entire Christian Bible must have a christological center caused him several challenges.[16] However, Childs strongly holds to what constitutes the "inner unity" of the text. Daniel Driver writes:

Childs is quite frank about what constitutes the "inner unity," and it is far from the old enthusiasm for universal religion: a biblical theologian has to do with "inner unity because of ... the one gospel of Jesus Christ." At the center of Childs's approach, then, is a startlingly specific confession of the lordship of Jesus Christ.[17]

---

10. Childs, *Introduction to the Old Testament*, 45.
11. Childs, *Introduction to the Old Testament*, 59.
12. Childs, *Introduction to the Old Testament*, 78.
13. Childs, *Introduction to the Old Testament*, 78.
14. D. R. Driver, *Brevard Childs, Biblical Theologian* (Grand Rapids: Baker Academic, 2010), 4.
15. Childs, *Introduction to the Old Testament*, 79.
16. Driver, *Brevard Childs, Biblical Theologian*, 93.
17. Driver, *Brevard Childs, Biblical Theologian*, 9.

While this assertion seems provocative on the surface, especially considering his own historical time frame, Childs believes that this understanding of inner unity is essential to successful ecumenical discussion between the Jewish faith community and the Christian. Jon Levenson, a noted Jewish biblical scholar, agrees. "Founded upon a historical particularity—the Protestant canon—Childs's method harbors a potential for respect for other historically particular traditions."[18] Levenson's comment on Childs's approach is quite generous and shows the great respect he holds for Childs's work. He has obviously carefully studied Childs and come to an understanding that demonstrates the breadth and depth of his own learning. The intersection of the approaches of Childs and Levenson greatly informs my own approach, as will be demonstrated later.

Childs writes,

Yet the canonical approach differs from a strictly literary approach by interpreting the biblical text in relation to a community of faith and practice for whom it served a particular theological role as possessing divine authority. For theological reasons the biblical texts were often shaped in such a way that the original poetic forms were lost, or a unified narrative badly shattered. The canonical approach is concerned to understand the nature of the theological shape of the text rather than to recover an original literary or aesthetic unity.[19]

Childs never held to the idea of an aesthetic unity. To do so would have begun the historical process of discovering this unity, and that would run counter to his canonical approach. The question that comes to the fore in regards to Childs's assertion of an "inner unity based on the gospel of Jesus Christ" is, How does one see this in the final form of the text? For Childs this question is answered with allegory. Allegory itself was on the decline in Childs's day but certainly was a dominant feature in the early church fathers. As with all terminology of this age, a definition is required.

---

18. Levenson, *Hebrew Bible*, 122.

19. Childs, *Introduction to the Old Testament*, 74. Here Childs is not attacking a unified theological narrative approach to the text but some putative process in the formation of texts that make up the canon.

"Allegory, for Childs and Barr in different ways, means locating the meaning of scripture at another level than the textual. For Childs, Christian allegory (as opposed to Jewish midrash) moves biblical interpretation to a 'level beyond the textual.'"[20] Childs claims that there is something behind the text, that there is another dialectic between the reality and the text. In order to understand Christ as the inner unity of both Testaments and the entire canon as witness to Christ, allegory is required. Driver, using a paper Childs delivered at St. Mary's College, University of St. Andrews, titled, "Allegory and Typology within Biblical Interpretation," lays out Childs's understanding:

> There are four points. First, the distinction between allegory and typology is a recent invention without roots in the tradition. Distinctions were made and can still be appreciated, but the relationship is more subtle. Allegory is not necessarily fanciful or arbitrary. Instead—here Childs, following Louth, speaks more programmatically—"the function of allegory is related to the *struggle to understand the mystery of Christ*. It is a way of relating the whole of Scripture to that mystery." Second, a "distinction between the so-called literal sense and the figurative/allegorical cannot correctly be defined in terms of historicity. ... Rather, the heart of the problem of allegory turns on the nature of referentiality of the biblical text." Origen, for example, saw that multiple senses means multiple referents. Third, allegory has a context. "The appeal to allegory is not a device by which to avoid difficulties in the text, as often suggested, or to allow unbridled use of human imagination. Rather, its use functions within a rule of faith (its *theoria* in Greek terminology) as the language of faith seeks to penetrate into the mystery of Christ's presence." It is "a means of appropriation" by which "the Holy Spirit continued to address each new generation." Finally, the old contrast between Antiochene and Alexandrian exegesis has needed reevaluation. The Antiochenes were not literalists per se, much less historicists. They "resisted a type of allegory that destroyed textual coherence, that is to say, which distorted the

---

20. Driver, *Brevard Childs, Biblical Theologian*, 210.

overarching framework (its *theoria*) and thus failed to grasp its true subject matter, its *hypothesis*."[21]

As indicated by Childs's paper, there is the possibility, perhaps even the likelihood, that allegory will be misappropriated and wander off into the fanciful. How does one govern allegory to avoid this difficulty? Childs does address this by suggesting that allegory can only properly function within a rule of faith. For Childs this rule of faith is canon. It is the canon as rule of faith that guides Childs's multileveled meanings and governs allegory.

Childs's canonical approach to the text made a large impact on textual hermeneutics over the course of his lifetime. The responses were both positive and negative, as one would expect. However, there is little doubt that Childs is advocating a fresh and different approach.[22] Childs notes the inadequacies of the higher-critical approach, but also believes that the rhetorical approach has not advanced far enough, although it was his students who moved the approach from its moorings in rhetorical and form criticism to a new methodology.[23]

ROBERT ALTER: A POETIC READING

Another critical figure who moved this discussion forward in a somewhat different manner is Robert Alter. Alter proposes a literary approach to the text, but is advocating literary criticism in a new and genuine sense.

It is a little astonishing that at this late date literary analysis of the Bible of the sort I have tried to illustrate here in this prelimi-nary fashion is only in its infancy. By literary analysis I mean the

---

21. Driver, *Brevard Childs, Biblical Theologian*, 233–34.

22. Childs's approach has no shortage of critics, including Barr, who considers Childs's canonical approach too simplistic (*Holy Scripture*, 168). See also J. Barton, *Reading the Old Testament: Method in Biblical Study* (Louisville, Westminster John Knox, 1998). Others main-tain that Childs is difficult to understand; for example, R. Rendtorff, who claims Childs is so invested in source criticism that he barely manages to give a "canonical" reading of the text at all. See Rendtorff, *The Canonical Hebrew Bible: A Theology of the Old Testament* (Leiderdorp, Germany: Deo, 2005), 722. Driver successfully sorts and separates this criticism in a fair and honest manner in his book *Brevard Childs, Biblical Theologian*.

23. Some have suggested that Childs fails to completely loose his moorings from Karl Barth (Barr, *Holy Scripture*), while Childs contends they never understood what Barth was doing. See B. S. Childs, "Karl Barth as Interpreter of Scripture," in Karl Barth and the Future of Theology: A Memorial Colloquium Held at Yale Divinity School January 28, 1969, ed. D.L. Dickerman (New Haven: Yale Divinity School Association, 1969), 34

manifold varieties of minutely discriminating attention to the artful
use of language, to the shifting play of ideas, conventions, tone,
sound, imagery, syntax, narrative viewpoint, compositional units,
and much else; the kind of disciplined attention, in other words,
which through a whole spectrum of critical approaches has illumi-
nated, for example, the poetry of Dante, the plays of Shakespeare,
the novels of Tolstoy. The general absence of such critical discourse
on the Hebrew Bible is all the more perplexing when one recalls
that the masterworks of Greek and Latin antiquity have in recent
decades enjoyed an abundance of astute literary analysis, so that
we have learned to perceive subtleties of lyric form in Theocritus
as in Marvell, complexities of narrative strategy in Homer or Virgil
as in Flaubert.[24]

Alter argues that the depth and vision of the Bible has been ignored,
lost by scholars' failure to address it in a literary and narrative fashion. He
sees his approach as a practical direction warranted by the nature of literary texts in general and of the Bible in particular.[25] In regards to Alter's
approach, R. N. Whybray states:

Drawing on a wide knowledge of both ancient and modern literature, Alter approached the subject from a point of view which is
precisely the opposite of the documentary critic: he regarded the
repetitions in biblical narrative not as indications of literary insensitivity or ineptitude (on the part of redactors) but of consummate
literary skill.[26]

It could also be argued, and Alter would argue, that his approach is
more of a poetic reading of the text, although he does so with caution.

For the moment, at any rate, it would seem that literary studies at
large have branched off into two divergent directions, one involving the elaboration of formal systems of poetics that have only a

---

24. Alter, *Art of Biblical Narrative*, 12–13.
25. Alter, *Art of Biblical Narrative*, 178.
26. Whybray, *Making of the Pentateuch*, 81.

hypothetical relation to any individual literary work, the other, dedicated to performing on the given text virtuoso exercises of interpretation which are in principle inimitable and unrepeatable, aimed as
they are at undermining the very notion that the text might have any
stable meanings. Throughout this study, I have tried to follow a third
path, not really between these two alternatives but rather headed in
another, more practical direction, one which I believe is warranted by
the nature of literary texts in general and of the Bible in particular.[27]

He does see poetic analysis as a valid path—his suggested third path—in
understanding various textual difficulties.

On this issue, I would only observe that some supposed textual inco-
herencies or anomalies in fact make perfect sense in the light of certain general (and generally ignored) principles of biblical poetics.
Readers familiar with these scholarly questions will note a few points
along the way where poetic analysis of the sort I propose ought to
be carefully weighed before conclusions are drawn about the need
to amend the text.[28]

Alter understands this method as extending beyond the traditional poetic
and wisdom books of Scripture. He identifies Genesis 2:23 as the first example of poetic discourse, and he also argues that the poetic style of a culture
influences and bears a relationship to the literary prose of the same culture.[29] The entire narrative of the Scriptures is influenced by the poetic style,
structure, and principles. Therefore, a poetic analysis of the text will reveal
much, especially as one considers the various uses of parallelism and structures of intensification.

How the poetics influence the narrative becomes the significant question. Alter argues that the Hebrew writers of biblical poetry seem to avoid
narrative. While this avoidance of narrative may be caused by negative reaction to the pagan mythologies, Alter points out other, positive reasons for
the style, pointing to the suppleness and subtlety of prose, which "made

---

27. Alter, *Art of Biblical Narrative*, 178.

28. Alter, *Art of Biblical Poetry*, x.

29. Alter, *Art of Biblical Poetry*, 6.

possible a more nuanced and purposefully ambiguous representation of human character."[30]

> The perception, however, of this decisive shift of narration from poetry to prose should not lead us to conclude that biblical verse is chiefly a poetry of assertion and reassertion, "purified" of narrative elements. On the contrary, I would contend that the narrative impulse, for the most part withdrawn from the prominent structural and generic aspects of the poems, often resurfaces in their more minute articulations, from verset to verset within the line and from one line to the next. Recognizing the operation of such a narrative impulse in the poems may help us see their liveliness more fully, may help us understand the links in modes of expression between the typical nonnarrative poems and the occasional poems with explicit narrative materials.[31]

For Alter, what he claims for the biblical poets is not "narrative but narrativity," by which he means the narrative development of metaphor.[32] And, he continues:

> It makes sense that divine speech should be represented as poetry. Such speech is directed to the concrete situation of a historical audience, but the form of the speech exhibits the historical indeterminacy of the language of poetry, which helps explain why these discourses have touched the lives of millions of readers far removed in time, space, and political predicament from the small groups of ancient Hebrews against whom Hosea, Isaiah, Jeremiah, and their confreres originally inveighed.[33]

Alter sees poetry, and thus a poetic reading of Scripture, as a particular way of imagining the world employed by the Hebrew poets and that the faith community would do well in restoring this method. Such a restoration

---

30. Alter, *Art of Biblical Poetry*, 28.
31. Alter, *Art of Biblical Poetry*, 28.
32. Alter, *Art of Biblical Poetry*, 39.
33. Alter, *Art of Biblical Poetry*, 141.

has much to overcome. Much has happened in the course of time that has prevented readers from recognizing this poetic structure. So, his aim is to point out the essential connection between poetic form and meaning that has most often been neglected by scholarship.[34]

While Childs and Alter have differing approaches brought about by their unique circumstances and backgrounds,[35] together they proved to be key figures in the next significant development of textual studies.

JON LEVENSON

Another scholar who continues to have great impact in the area of textual hermeneutics is Jon Levenson. Levenson received his theological education at Harvard University, graduating with a PhD in 1975. He was able to study under Frank Cross and others who influenced his understanding of the relationship between traditional methods of biblical interpretation and modern historical criticism. It was, however, his faith community that helped inform his own method of approaching the biblical text. As an observant Jew, who teaches Hebrew Bible at a liberal Protestant divinity school in a university of Puritan origins,[36] Levenson observed firsthand the problems and difficulties in the conflict in the relationship between two modes of biblical study, the traditional and the historical critical.

> Liberal Protestantism, which has always dominated the distinctively modern study of scripture, tends to advocate the *replacement* of traditional interpretation with the historical-critical method. My claim is that this is unsound in both theory and practice. The theoretical deficiency is a blindness to the inability of a self-consciously universalistic and rationalistic method to serve as the vehicle of any particularistic religious confession. The practical consequence has been the development of a host of historical-critical interpretations that are really only rewordings or recastings of traditional Christian views. This, in turn, has meant that the continuity of the Hebrew

---

34. Alter, *Art of Biblical Poetry*, 205.

35. Alter is Jewish, while Childs came from a Christian background; Childs was also a student of Karl Barth.

36. Levenson, *Hebrew Bible*, 34.

Bible with the ongoing Jewish tradition (and not with the church alone) has been denied or, more often, simply ignored.

Awareness of the problem moves us in two seemingly opposite directions. On the one hand, it requires us to view with suspicion any unqualified claim of continuity between the Hebrew Bible and the religious traditions that derive from it, Jewish as well as Christian. In the name of intellectual honesty and a sense of historical change, we are compelled to adopt an interpretive stance that is rigorous in its resistance to religious tradition. On the other hand, in privileging *historical* context the historical-critical method shortchanges the *literary* context defined by the completed Bible, Jewish and Christian. Having decomposed the Bible into its historically diverse constituent sources, its practitioners lack the means to do justice to the Book currently in our possession as a synchronic, systemic unity.[37]

The world behind the text is given precedence in the historical-critical method, and, as Levenson notes, this shortchanges both the world of the text and the world in front of the text. R. W. L. Moberly comments on this:

Levenson has no doubts as to the value of rigorous historical work; yet context of origin is not the only context. There is also a context constituted by the formation of the literature into a larger whole, a context that is literary and/or canonical. ... Levenson recasts a familiar preoccupation of biblical scholars, concerning the difference between what the text meant in its ancient context and how it is to be understood now, into the issue of differing contextualizations of the biblical text.[38]

Like Childs, Levenson sees danger on both ends of the spectrum and argues that the extremes need each other and should work together in the task of textual hermeneutics. Neither the religious traditionalist nor the modern rationalist can dispense with the other. However, he views their

37. Levenson, *Hebrew Bible*, xiii–xiv.
38. Moberly, *Old Testament Theology*, 156.

cooperation as being highly unlikely.[39] A Christian exegete who recognizes
a "historical sense" to the Old Testament without relinquishing a christocentric interpretation of it would be the ideal. However,

> Historical critics take the text apart more ruthlessly than traditional
> *pashtanim*, and, qua historical critics, they lack a method of putting
> it back together again. They reconstruct history by concentrating
> on contradictions, which they then allow to stand. The traditions,
> of course, often recognize the same contradictions. The difference
> is that traditionalists had a method that could harmonize the con-
> tradictions and, in the process, preserve the unity of the text and
> its religious utility.[40]

Levenson understands the two methods as having different starting
points as they approach the text. The traditionalist assumes a unity of the
text, while the historical critic instead assumes a disunity from the start.
The historical critic begins his task with no assumption of stability and
continuity, but with a commitment to restore the texts to their historical contexts.[41] This produces a significant impasse. Levenson argues that
the price of recovering the *historical* context of sacred books has been the
erosion of the largest *literary* contexts that undergird the traditions that
claim to be based on them.[42]

Levenson makes note of other scholars who have been asserting the
same. He especially points to Childs and his canonical approach, also referring to it as the literary context. "Some have sought to develop a hermeneutic that respects the integrity of the received text for the purpose of
literary analysis or theological affirmation, without in the process slipping
into a fundamentalistic denial of historical change."[43] There is a certain
respect for Childs that is expected. On the other hand, Levenson, while
seeing this as a reasonable move for the Christian faith community, stills
finds it lacking for the Jewish community.

---

39. Levenson, *Hebrew Bible*, xiv.
40. Levenson, *Hebrew Bible*, 2.
41. Levenson, *Hebrew Bible*, 4.
42. Levenson, *Hebrew Bible*, 4.
43. Levenson, *Hebrew Bible*, 5.

I have argued that the essential challenge of historical criticism to book religion lies in its development of a context of interpretation, the *historical* context, which is different from the *literary* (or canonical) contexts that underlie Judaism and Christianity, in their different ways. In one fashion or another, these religions presuppose the coherence and self-referentiality of their foundational book. These things are what make it possible to derive a coherent religion, *one* religion, (one's own), from the Book.[44]

How then does Levenson describe his own method as an observant Jew, well versed in rabbinic midrash? Before we move to this discussion, it is important to note another aspect of Levenson's context and background. Levenson has joined his voice to others in the Jewish scholarly community in claims that the historical-critical method has anti-Semitic consequences, if not motivated by anti-Semitic doctrines. Levenson points out that this is a partial reason for the lack of interest among Jewish scholars to engage in biblical theology. Past efforts of the historical-critical method have left the sacred text of the Jews broken and lying piecemeal. Levenson maintains that even though the higher-critical efforts of Julius Wellhausen were not a racial anti-Semitism of the kind that flowered in Nazism, his work "made a modest contribution" and steered Jewish scholarship away from textual hermeneutics even to this day.[45]

One reason is that the critical study of the Hebrew Bible is itself often seen by Jews as inherently anti-Semitic. The method and the uses to which it is put are not always adequately distinguished, and the fact that historical criticism has undermined Christianity no less than Judaism, as any Christian fundamentalist knows all too well, is too often ignored.[46]

These are strong assertions and an attitude that has its effect on Levenson and other Jewish scholars. And while Levenson notes the negative

---

44. Levenson, *Hebrew Bible*, 28.
45. Levenson, *Hebrew Bible*, 42.
46. Levenson, *Hebrew Bible*, 43.

effect for the Christian community as well, his is not the common consensus in Judaism. Still, he is adamant in his critique:

> No critical scholar of the Hebrew Bible believes in its *historical* unity
> or in the *historical* unity even of the Pentateuch. If Leviticus and
> Galatians cannot be accommodated in one religion, then neither,
> perhaps, can Exodus and Deuteronomy, and certainly Isaiah and
> Qohelet cannot. Jews need their harmonious midrash no less than
> Christians need theirs, for it is midrash that knits the tangled skein
> of passages into a religiously usable "text" (from Latin, *texo*, "to
> weave") and continues the redactional process beyond the point of
> the finalization of the text. The pulverizing effects of the histori-
> cal-critical method do not respect the boundaries of religions: the
> method dismembers *all* midrashic systems, reversing tradition.[47]

As Levenson moves forward to describe his own approach or model,
he does so by way of discussing the eighth principle of Judaism as laid out
by Maimonides in the eleventh century CE: "The eighth of these reads: 'I
believe with perfect faith that the entire Torah presently in our possession is the one given to Moses our master (may he rest in peace).'"[48] As
Levenson continues, he argues that for Maimonides and the tradition that
continued after him, it is divine origin rather than Mosaic authorship that
is at point.[49] Levenson describes the foundation of his own approach to
the Hebrew Bible:

> The chief objective of this essay is to argue that although in his-
> torical-critical discourse the notion of Mosaic authorship of the
> Pentateuch is indefensible, the underlying and antecedent ideas
> of the unity and divinity of the Torah must remain relevant con-
> siderations for Jewish theologians, and whether these are affirmed
> or denied makes a larger difference than most of their Christian
> colleagues wish to concede. In that difference lies the enduring

---

47. Levenson, *Hebrew Bible*, 30.
48. Levenson, *Hebrew Bible*, 63.
49. Levenson, *Hebrew Bible*, 64–65.

importance of the eighth principle of Judaism, properly understood, and an essential constraint on traditional Jewish biblicists
that not all their Christian counterparts will feel.[50]

What is most important is not how the Torah came to be in its current
shape (history), but rather that the text as we have it is considered one
and from God, the unity and divinity of the Torah. This is not so different from Childs's canonical approach, although it seems that Levenson is
more interested in considering the history of the text as long as the inquiry
stays within the boundaries established. Levenson notes that because this
model of interpretation allows for freedom of inquiry while at the same
time respecting and preserving the traditional, theocentric Jewish life, it
has found favor across a wide spectrum of Jewish thought.[51] There are, however, dangers if the historical research is not restricted in its role. Levenson
points to James Barr's argument against Childs's canonical approach as an
example of the problem.

> James Barr, in his fusillade against Brevard S. Childs' "canonical
> method" of biblical interpretation, has recently been at pains to
> argue against the view that "under biblical criticism the science
> of history and its methods were given control over the Bible." "On
> the contrary," Barr insists, "the criterion for biblical criticism is,
> and always has been, *what the Bible itself actually says.*"[52] There is
> something to this, but it must still be noted that when the Bible is
> perceived in the modern categories, the simultaneity of all parts
> of the Bible with all the others is undone—the Bible is, if you will,
> "decomposed"—and the unity of *"what the Bible itself actually [said]"*
> to the premodern exegete is fractured into a historical succession
> of messages, all from the past and without a clear, internal signal
> as to which is normative now. The application of a historical, or
> diachronic, perspective—even when it is denied a controlling role—
> severely undermines the principle that the Bible is a unity. It is

50. Levenson, *Hebrew Bible*, 65.
51. Levenson, *Hebrew Bible*, 66.
52. Barr, *Holy Scripture*, 37.

precisely in opposition to this decomposition, this undoing of the traditional simultaneity of biblical literature, this fracturing of the message, that Childs devised his controversial hermeneutics.[53]

Levenson is very concerned with preserving the simultaneity of the text and sees the historical-critical approach as the enemy. Historical investigation, while useful, must be relativized. To place at risk the literary context with the historical context is completely unacceptable. But again, he does not go so far as to say there is no place for this historical investigation, although with strict and careful usage.

> The efforts to take the text apart would not cease; they are informative and, as we shall soon see, not without precedent in the premodern tradition of biblical interpretation. They would, however, be dialectically checked by a continual awareness of the need to put the text back together in a way that makes it available in the present and in its entirety—not merely in the past and in the form of historically contextualized fragments.[54]

There is a certain balance in Levenson's approach that is not found within fundamental Christianity. There is no fear of contradictions within the text, nor is there a need for lockstep agreement for the text to be the foundation for the community of faith. This may well be the result of his Jewish background and being comfortable with rabbinic midrashic discussions.

> The authority of the Torah does not require faithful exegetes to deny the contradictions within it, but the frank recognition of the contradictions does not allow them to base religious life and practice on something less than the whole. I argue that if either of the

---

53. Levenson, *Hebrew Bible*, 70–71.
54. Levenson, *Hebrew Bible*, 79.

two halves of this paradox is omitted, something essential in the heritage of medieval Jewish biblical study will be lost.[55]

However:

What I believe I have here demonstrated is that no Jewish theology consonant with the classical rabbinic tradition can be built on a perception of the biblical text that denies the unity of the Torah of Moses as a current reality, whatever the long, complex, and thoroughly historical process through which that Torah came into being.[56]

For Levenson and others in his faith tradition, the Torah of Moses is the ultimate document of revelation from God. Because of this Levenson realizes that his model is not and cannot be a Christian reading of the text. This is not to say he does not respect Christians reading the Hebrew Bible as Christian literature and as God's revelation, but it is to say that this is a different reading from the Jewish community of faith. "You will recall, however, that I have argued ... Christians must ultimately aim for another sense as well, one that upholds the idea that their two-volume Bible is a meaningful whole, lest their scripture decompose before their very eyes."[57]

Perhaps Levenson is here recommending an approach such as Childs's canonical method. Certainly, he speaks well of Childs and his approach. Regardless, Levenson sees the danger that historical criticism poses not only to the Scriptures of Judaism but also to the Scriptures of Christianity. Interestingly, Levenson is favorable to reading Scripture with Christian biblical scholars as long as the particularities are maintained. In fact, it is in recognition of the differences where agreement can be found. Levenson's model for reading the Torah of Moses is one he describes as uniquely Jewish. In respect to the eighth principle of Judaism, the text as approached is viewed as having unity and divinity—unity of form and with God as divine

---

55. Levenson, *Hebrew Bible*, 80.
56. Levenson, *Hebrew Bible*, 81.
57. Levenson, *Hebrew Bible*, 103.

author. This simultaneity of Scripture must be upheld because it is the tradition of the community of faith and the foundation of its practice. All of this is distinctively Jewish because of its moorings in rabbinic Judaism.

The similarities between Childs and Levenson cannot be ignored. While Childs speaks of the community of faith and its role in developing the canon, Levenson refers to the rabbinic midrashic tradition. Both argue against the higher-critical method and its atomizing effect on the text—Levenson uses the term "decomposing," a more organic word. However, both see the usefulness of historical analysis as long as the text is not left dissected and the historical process does not take precedence over the final form. The specific difference between the two, which Levenson points to, is the community of faith and the underlying foundational beliefs. This reality must focus on their particularities, and thus a platform for agreement and disagreement can be laid.

A NARRATIVE READING

The narrative reading of Scripture is well established. Childs and Alter are two influential supporters of this approach, and they are by no means alone.[58] This methodology engages questions such as, "Is the Bible authoritative for the faith and practice of the church and synagogue? What practices of reading offer the most appropriate approach to understanding the Bible? How does historical criticism illumine or obscure Scripture's message?"[59]

There is also a strong movement toward reading the narrative of Scripture, both Old and New Testaments, in a unified manner. The dividing of books into various sources and accounts, indeed, the dividing of the narrative into books, is met with suspicion.

---

58. I am especially thinking of Levenson and his *The Hebrew Bible, the Old Testament, and Historical Criticism.* Levenson argues that "the price of recovering the *historical* context of sacred books has been the erosion of the largest *literary* contexts that under gird the traditions that claim to be based upon them" (4). This negates the theological foundation and pushes the text into the past and leaves it with no voice in the present or future. He goes so far as to equate higher criticism with an effort to destroy the veracity of the OT, an anti-Semitic move. He also contends that one of the greatest flaws of biblical theologians, as a whole, is their lack of self-awareness on the issue of context, "acting as though the change of context makes no hermeneutical difference. In point of fact, it makes all the difference in the world" (57).

59. Hays and Davis, *Art of Reading Scripture*, xiv.

One group that has emerged through the evolution of this method identifies itself as the Scripture Project.[60] This group of fifteen scholars from various theological disciplines joined together to read Scripture.[61] In the course of time they came to the conclusion that reading Scripture is an art, and they developed "Nine Theses on the Interpretation of Scripture." These nine theses are helpful in understanding and defining the narrative reading methodology:

---

60. Hays and Davis, *Art of Reading Scripture*, xv.

61. Included are such scholars as G. A. Anderson, professor of Old Testament at the University of Notre Dame, whose works include *The Genesis of Perfection* (Louisville: Westminster John Knox, 2001); R. Bauckham, professor of New Testament studies and Bishop Wardlaw Professor at the University of St Andrews, whose works include *The Testimony of the Beloved Disciple: Narrative, History and Theology in the Gospel of John* (Grand Rapids: Baker Academic, 2007), *Jesus and the Eyewitnesses* (Grand Rapids: Eerdmans, 2006), and *Bible and Mission: Christian Witness in a Postmodern World* (Grand Rapids Baker Academic, 2004); B. E. Daley, SJ; Catherine F. Huisking, Professor of Theology at the University of Notre Dame, whose works include *The Hope of the Early Church: A Handbook of Patristic Eschatology* (Peabody, MA: Hendrickson, 2003) and *The World of the Early Christians* (Collegeville, MN: Liturgical Press, 1997); E. F. Davis, associate professor of Bible and practical theology at Duke Divinity School, whose works include *Scripture, Culture and Agriculture: An Agrarian Reading of the Bible* (Cambridge: Cambridge University Press, 2008), *Proverbs, Ecclesiastes and the Song of Songs* (Louisville: Westminster John Knox, 2004), and *Getting Involved with God: Rediscovering the Old Testament* (Lanham, MD: Cowley, 2001); R. B. Hays, George Washington Ivey Professor of New Testament at Duke Divinity School, whose works include *The Conversion of the Imagination* (Grand Rapids: Eerdmans, 2005), *The Faith of Jesus Christ: Narrative Substructure of Galatians 3:1–4:11* (Grand Rapids: Eerdmans, 2002), and *Echoes of Scripture in the Letters of Paul* (New Haven: Yale University Press, 1993); J. C. Howell, senior minister at Myers Park United Methodist Church, Charlotte, NC, whose works include *Conversations with St. Francis* (Nashville: Abingdon, 2008) and *The Beatitudes for Today* (Louisville: Westminster John Knox, 2005); R. W. Jenson, senior scholar for research at the Center for Theological Inquiry, Princeton, NJ, whose works include *Canon and Creed* (Louisville: Westminster John Knox, 2010), *Ezekiel* (Grand Rapids: Brazos, 2009), and *Song of Songs* (Louisville: Westminster John Knox, 2005); W. S. Johnson, Arthur M. Adams Associate Professor of Systematic Theology at Princeton Theological Seminary, whose works include *Crisis, Call, and Leadership in the Abrahamic Traditions* (New York: Palgrave Macmillan, 2009); L. G. Jones, dean and professor of theology at Duke Divinity School, whose works include *Theology and Scriptural Imagination: Directions in Modern Theology* (Malden, MA: Wiley-Blackwell, 1998) and *Why Narrative? Readings in Narrative Theology* (Eugene, OR: Wipf & Stock, 1997); C. McSpadden, priest at the Episcopal Diocese of California; R. W. L. Moberly, professor of theology at the University of Durham, whose works include *Old Testament Theology, Prophecy and Discernment* (Cambridge: Cambridge University Press, 2006), and *The Bible, Theology, and Faith: A Study of Abraham and Jesus* (Cambridge: Cambridge University Press, 2000); D. Steinmetz, Amos Ragan Kearns Professor of the History of Christianity at Duke Divinity School, whose works include *Calvin in Context* (Oxford: Oxford University Press, 1995), *Luther in Context* (Grand Rapids: Baker Academic, 1986), and *Reformers in the Wings* (Grand Rapids: Baker, 1981); and M. M. Thompson, professor of New Testament interpretation at Fuller Theological Seminary, whose works include *Colossians and Philemon* (Grand Rapids: Eerdmans, 2005) and *1–3 John* (Downers Grove, IL: InterVarsity Press, 1992).

1. Scripture truthfully tells the story of God's action of creating, judging, and saving the world.

2. Scripture is rightly understood in light of the church's rule of faith as a coherent dramatic narrative.[62]

3. Faithful interpretation of Scripture requires an engagement with the entire narrative: the New Testament cannot be rightly understood apart from the Old, nor can the Old be rightly understood apart from the New.

4. Texts of Scripture do not have a single meaning limited to the intent of the original author. In accord with Jewish and Christian traditions, we affirm that Scripture has multiple complex senses given by God, the author of the whole drama.

5. The four canonical Gospels narrate the truth about Jesus.

6. Faithful interpretation of Scripture invites and presupposes participation in the community brought into being by God's redemptive action—the church.

7. The saints of the church provide guidance in how to interpret and perform Scripture.

8. Christians need to read the Bible in dialogue with diverse others outside the church.

9. We live in the tension of the "already" and the "not yet" of the kingdom of God; consequently, Scripture calls the church to ongoing discernment, to continually fresh re-readings of the text in light of the Holy Spirit's ongoing work in the world.[63]

These theses help distinguish not just this group, but also the basic tenets of the narrative-reading approach. First, there is a "high view" of

---

62. R. E. Longacre: "If we approach Joseph as theists and as believers in divine providence we get ourselves inside the hermeneutical cartouche along with the writer and message that we are studying." See Longacre, *Joseph: A Story of Divine Providence* (Winona Lake, IN: Eisenbrauns, 2003), 16.

63. Hays and Davis, *Art of Reading Scripture*, 1–5.

the text. The Scriptures are approached with respect and in view of God's hand in authorship. Second, the unity of the Scriptures is highly held and valued. Portions of the text are not to be interpreted in isolation from Scripture as a whole. Third, the role of these texts in the life of the church past, present, and future is strongly considered. Finally, a wooden or literalistic approach to Scripture is discouraged. Such a view would neglect the depth and various levels of meaning interwoven within the text.

Moberly, a member of the Scripture Project, provides additional commentary on this narrative approach: "Theological interpretation is reading the Bible with a concern for the enduring truth of its witness to the nature of God and humanity, with a view to enabling the transformation of humanity into the likeness of God."[64] While the Scripture Project helps define the narrative approach, it does not claim to be a solitary voice representing this methodology. There are a number of scholars who have adopted this approach to biblical interpretation. As one might suspect, this narrative reading of Scripture has opened up a wealth of studies, articles, and books on the Joseph narratives. Fresh readings of these chapters with an eye toward the literary aspects abound and have led to a deeper understanding of the text. Some of the scholars represented include Alter and his treatment of various segments of these narratives, Gary A. Anderson, James Kugel, Ron Pirson and his commentary on the Joseph narratives, Yiu-Wing Fung, and so on.[65] The list continues to grow as more and more scholars return to Genesis and the Joseph story for a new reading.

These new readings are far from unified in their approach and method. By way of example, Pirson approaches the text in a narrative fashion, considering the Torah to be one book, and therefore the context of the reading. However, while he considers the reader to play a prominent part in the process of attaching meaning, he understands context in a literary sense,[66] the Torah, and is much more focused on a literary analysis and linguistic signs.

---

64. Moberly, "What Is Theological Interpretation," 163.

65. Alter, *Art of Biblical Narrative*; Anderson, "Joseph and the Passion of Our Lord"; J. L. Kugel, *In Potiphar's House: The Interpretive Life of Biblical Texts* (Cambridge: Harvard University Press, 1990); R. Pirson, *The Lord of the Dreams: A Semantic and Literary Analysis of Genesis 37–50* (London: Sheffield Academic Press, 2002); Fung, *Victim and Victimizer*. Alter is not advocating the dissection of the text; rather, he is using various portions to illustrate the art of narrative reading.

66. Pirson, *Lord of the Dreams*, 3, 9.

One has to look for the presence of any "regularities" or "nuances" when the same word is encountered in several texts (e.g. the Torah), in other words one has to ask: Is there a typical usage? These nuances may give the word a special connotation in certain contexts. And if there are any nuances to be discerned, one must ask whether these are applicable to the text under consideration: Do the contents allow for the "newly uncovered" alluvial meaning?[67]

Fung's narrative approach varies from Pirson in that he is more focused on characterization. He states that characterization in narrative theory suggests that a portrait is constructed primarily through the actions, speech, and external appearance of a character.[68] He follows the basic principles of narrative theory in constructing a portrait from the textual elements.[69] In his book *Victim and Victimizer: Joseph's Interpretation of His Destiny*, he states: "My aim in this thesis is to provide a portrayal of Joseph from a different perspective by scrutinizing his speeches (rather than focusing mainly on his actions) in order to expose the problematic nature of his ideology. I suggest his ambiguous behavior stems from his belief."[70]

Both Pirson and Fung follow the basic principles of a narrative approach; however, they are unique in their focus. My approach is more holistic. Reading Scripture as a unified theological narrative with an eye focused on the biblical motifs that unite both the theology and the narrative incorporates both the literary and characterization approaches as important interpretive tools for the narrative.

R. W. L. MOBERLY: A THEOLOGICAL INTERPRETATION

Moberly, a member of the original Scripture Project, subscribes to its "Nine Theses on the Interpretation of Scripture."[71] However, his personal approach toward the interpretation of Scripture has a unique focus, which he terms as a theological interpretation and which bears mention.

---

67. Pirson, *Lord of the Dreams*, 17.
68. Fung, *Victim and Victimizer*, 11.
69. Fung, *Victim and Victimizer*, 16.
70. Fung, *Victim and Victimizer*, 12.
71. See footnote p. 37 n 61.

Moberly reads the Old Testament as both philologist and theologian[72] and is concerned about the relationship between text and reader. He sees this as an issue of context and recognizes the importance of establishing "whose" and "which" context.[73] In his discussion he delineates among "the world behind the text," "the world within the text," and "the world in front of the text."[74]

He has relied heavily on the world in front of the text, and his approach seeks to bring a shift toward recognizing the importance of the reader in the processes of interpretation.[75] To accomplish this he suggests a recontextualization of the text that is more reader focused with a message that is reader driven.

In my discussions I have made use of the conceptuality of the world within, the world behind, and the world in front of the text. Almost all interpreters are interested, in one way or another, in the world within the text. The question becomes how one contextualizes this world within the text, which relates also to the nature of the imaginative moves that are brought to bear upon it. The dominant move in modern biblical scholarship has been to relate the world within the text to the world behind the text—to look backward, as it were, from the Old Testament to the world that gave rise to it, the immediate world of Israel and also the wider world of the ancient Near East. This means, for the most part, a focus on times and places before ever there was an Old Testament, when at most there were incipient collections and compilations of material that only over time became Israel's scriptures. My approach, by contrast, has been to focus primarily upon the world within the text in relation to the world in front of the text—to look forward from Israel's scriptures toward those enduring faiths, both Jewish and Christian.[76]

---

72. Moberly, *Old Testament Theology*, 287.

73. Moberly, *Old Testament Theology*, 145.

74. Moberly, *Old Testament Theology*, 18.

75. Moberly, *Old Testament Theology*, 286.

76. Moberly, *Old Testament Theology*, 283.

As a result, he sees and focuses on what may be called a practical application of the text in the life of the community of faith. He concludes: "So too I would argue that the crowning achievement of a theological interpretation of Scripture should be performance, that is ways of living, on the part of believers and those sympathetically interested, who are enabled to realize more fully that wholeness of life to which God calls."[77]

WALTER BRUEGGEMANN: A POSTMODERN INTERPRETATION

One final scholar to consider is Walter Brueggemann and his postmodern interpretation. While Childs, Alter, and Levenson represent great moves—departures—from former foundations, none can be considered postmodern in their approach. Brueggemann is distinct:

> The great new fact of interpretation is that we live in a pluralistic context, in which many different interpreters in many different specific contexts representing many different interests are at work on textual (theological) interpretation. The old consensus about limits and possibilities of interpretation no longer holds. Thus interpretation is no longer done by a small, tenured elite, but interpretive voices and their very different readings of the texts come from many cultures in all parts of the globe, and from many subcultures even in Western culture.[78]

In describing this pluralistic context and the postmodern culture, William Dever lays out the main features of postmodernism in general:

> (1) rebellion against all authority; (2) distrust of all universal, "totalizing" discourse; (3) the assumption that "social constructs" determine all knowledge; (4) it is only "discourse" and "realms of discourse" that manner; (5) all truth is relative; (6) there is no intrinsic "meaning," only that which we supply; (7) there is no operative "consensus" view, so that everything becomes ideology,

---

77. Moberly, *Old Testament Theology*, 288.
78. W. Brueggemann, *Theology of the Old Testament* (Minneapolis: Fortress, 1997), 61–62.

ultimately politics; (8) one ideology is as appropriate as another (sometimes the more "radical" the better); (9) ideological discourse need not be rational or systematic, but may be intuitive or even eccentric, representing the neglected "peripheries" of society rather than the center.[79]

Dever is concerned about this approach specifically and its pluralistic nature in general, and his opinion of this agenda is not positive; however, he does list the basic tenets accurately. This is the contemporary situation that Brueggemann appeals to as he lays out his postmodern approach.

It appears that Brueggemann sees this movement as a natural progression from Paul Ricoeur's "the world in front of the text." This is described as the "life-world" generated by the text and mediated to the hearers of the text as they receive it.[80] Now that our world has moved forward from "interpretive privilege granted to certain advantaged perspectives," the interpretive conversation is opened to every voice.[81] Brueggemann states:

> We now recognize that there is no interest-free interpretation, no interpretation that is not in service of some interest and in some sense advocacy. Indeed, it is an illusion of the Enlightenment that advocacy-free interpretation can exist. Interpretation as advocacy is an ongoing process of negotiation, adjudication, and correction. This means, most likely, that there can be no right or ultimate interpretation, but only provisional judgments for which the interpreter is prepared to take practical responsibility, and which must always yet again be submitted to the larger conflictual conversation.[82]

There no longer exists any common or universal assumptions at the beginning of the interpretive task, and every voice and every agenda has equal footing and voice. Although this is the stated purpose and goal of

---

79. W. G. Dever, *What Did the Biblical Writers Know and When Did They Know It?*, 25.
80. Brueggemann, *Theology of the Old Testament*, 58.
81. Brueggemann, *Theology of the Old Testament*, 61.
82. Brueggemann, *Theology of the Old Testament*, 63.

Brueggemann, John Collins in his *The Bible after Babel* notes several difficulties and inconsistencies:

> One can only admire the scope and courage of Brueggemann's
> undertaking and the irenic spirit in which it is carried out. There
> are, however, some problems with the project, both in regard to
> its relationship to postmodernism and in regard to its own coher-
> ence. One cannot fail to be struck by the frequency with which he
> appeals to "the text itself" as if this were unproblematic. ... There
> is no recognition here that any reading of a text involves a con-
> strual, whether one construes the text as history or as testimony,
> and Brueggemann seems to have forgotten his own declaration that
> no construal or interpretation is innocent or interest-free. It is note-
> worthy in this context that he never declares his own interest.[83]

Collins goes on to contend that Brueggemann's appropriation of postmodernism is partial and has a familiar Protestant, Barthian look because
he wants to exempt the text from the suspicion to which all other metanar-
ratives are subjected.[84] Perhaps it is best said that Brueggemann adopts a
pluralistic, postmodern approach in a desire to be antifoundational, but he
does not quite accomplish his stated goal to let all voices be heard equally
without constraints. Nevertheless, the postmodern interpretive approach
is a strong voice in current biblical hermeneutic circles.

CONCLUSION

The current state of scholarship in textual hermeneutics by no means
demonstrates a unified approach. As has always been the case, there
remains a broad variety of methodologies that themselves are in continual flux. This does not need to be a negative reality, but should present a
positive picture for the future of textual hermeneutics. Each movement
and methodology brings its own strengths and weaknesses to the table,
and when the day is over, each contributes to the feast.

---

83. Collins, *Bible after Babel*, 143–44.
84. Collins, *Bible after Babel*, 145.

While I have restricted my coverage of the vast history of biblical interpretation to the 1980s and beyond, much of what precedes this had obvious effect, as discussed in the cases of Childs and Levenson in particular. Whether negatively or positively, past methodologies have led to the current trends of today. This is instructive as one considers the various ways of approaching the Joseph narratives. These approaches, and the hermeneutics they represent, reveal certain attitudes and understandings in regards to the last fourteen chapters of Genesis, attitudes and understandings that reflect differing and shifting views of Joseph and his story.

Reading Scripture as a Unified Theological Narrative: A Recommended Methodology

When we look at the current trends in biblical hermeneutics, we observe a direction and certain identifiable characteristics. As explored in the previous section, reading Scripture as a unified narrative is a methodology that is employed by a growing number of scholars.[1] This narrative reading is generally accompanied by a high view of the text. A narrative reading also proposes a unified text, viewing the entirety of Scripture, Old and New Testaments, as one continual, flowing narrative.[2] Another characteristic of a narrative reading is a consideration of the role of the church, or religious community, as it used the text in its community and worship life. Many keys to the deeper meaning of the text are provided as the role of its religious community is explored.

A literalistic approach, while still popular and practiced by many in the faith community, does not allow the text to "breathe" and exhibit the life with which it has been infused. This one-dimensional view sees only the surface of Scripture and does not allow a probing of the depth of the writing and the levels of meaning. Too often, this wooden approach relegates the biblical text, especially the Old Testament writings, to historical documents filled with interesting and pertinent isagogical facts. While the historicity of the text is important, along with the history of its transmission and the isagogical components, it is not to be seen as the totality

---

1. The synchronic approach: J. Barr, "The Synchronic, the Diachronic and the Historical: A Triangular Relationship," in *Synchronic or Diachronic? A Debate on Method in Old Testament Exegesis*, ed. Johannes C. De Moor (Leiden: Brill, 1995), 1–14; J. P. Fokkelman, "Structural Reading on the Fracture between Synchrony and Diachrony," *Jaarbericht van het Voorasiatisch-Egyptisch Gezelschap (Genootschap) Ex oriente lux* 30 (1989): 123–36.

2. In the case of this form of reading within the conservative Jewish community, the text considered is most generally the Torah of Moses. See Levenson, *Hebrew Bible*, 62–66, 78–81.

of its purpose or revelation. Such an approach is frequently in danger of collapsing the world behind the text into the world within the text.[3]

Another approach addressed to a greater or lesser extent by viewing Scripture as unified is the widely adopted methodology of breaking down the biblical text into grammatical forms and parts in order to uncover meaning, structure, and origin. While examples of this hermeneutic are found throughout history, it began to be practiced in earnest in the 1600s and became popular as higher criticism became the methodology de jour in the Age of Enlightenment.[4] Both the supporters and opponents of this methodology employed an even more intense historical, and later sociological, scrutiny of the text to prove or disprove the method. The result was a fractured, dissected text with little thought given as to how all these parts worked together to deliver a coherent message. Rhetorical criticism began to respond to this problem, but it is the narrative reading of the text—seeing Scripture as a unified narrative—that more fully trends away from this approach.

A RECOMMENDED METHODOLOGY

Growing up, I remember an occasion when I discovered my father's watch laying on the table. Being a curious sort, I wondered what exactly made this watch tick. Simply wondering would not suffice; I took the watch apart. Piece by piece I dismantled the watch until I had a rather fascinating array of wheels, cogs, and little screws. It was all very interesting to my young mind, and I did learn much about the inner workings of a watch; however, I had absolutely no idea how to reassemble the pile of pieces.

All the pieces of the watch were present—every piece proved to be an integral part for the watch to work—but a pile of pieces does not a watch make. Unassembled, the watch was interesting from a scientific point of view, yet totally worthless from a practical standpoint.

---

3. Moberly, *Old Testament Theology*, 17.

4. Also called the Age of Reason, the eighteenth century saw the emergence of several influential biblical scholars who worked with the text in a "modern scientific" way. Of note are J. S. Semler (1725–92), J. G. Eichhorn (1752–1827), A. Dillmann (1823–94), and J. Wellhausen (1844–1918). Examples from the seventeenth century include Benedict Spinoza (1632–77), a Dutch Jew; Jean Astruc (1684–1766), a French Roman Catholic. Each scholar has been referred to as the father of higher criticism; however, it was the Age of Enlightenment that saw the adoption of this method in a significant way.

This is an unfortunate illustration of how the Old Testament text, as it has been received in its final form, has been handled. In an effort to discover the various aspects of its origin and history, scholars have dismantled the text to see what makes it tick. This scientific dissection is all well and good, and properly handled can reveal a great deal of useful information. I have no objections to utilizing any productive insights that may result from these methods of interpreting the text. However, if the text is not properly reassembled and allowed to convey its message, it has no practical value. There is no good reason to dispense with the use of the various disciplines used to examine the text. However, they must be seen as tools to be used, not as methodologies in and of themselves. No hermeneutic is complete without the use of these tools, but the method and the tools should support the received text.

READING SCRIPTURE AS A UNIFIED THEOLOGICAL NARRATIVE

The methodology I employ in dealing with the biblical text falls in the category of narrative reading. I have built on this basic methodology by approaching the text as a unified theological narrative. As Levenson has argued, the present canonical setting of the various strands of traditional material that constitute Scripture provides the reader with the possibility of explicating these strands as part of a larger unity.[5]

When the Jews of antiquity came before God, they had certain feelings, assumptions, and expectations. They based these feelings, assumptions, and expectations on what was written in the Old Testament canon, especially the Torah. While these basic beliefs have many integral parts, they are fundamentally based on the understanding that the Hebrew people—Israel—were in a relationship with God. From early on this is often defined as a covenantal relationship, but even this is understood from the perspective of a marriage relationship. The Israelites believed that God created them and they, as a people, were married to God. Thus, we encounter marriage imagery and language when the relationship between God and his people is described. For example, idolatry was considered a major problem because it was equated with adultery—cheating

---

5. Levenson, *Hebrew Bible*, 63.

on God. So we find the phrases "Israel went a whoring after other gods," and "They played the whore," and "my covenant that they broke, though I was their husband, declares the LORD" (Jer 31:32).[6] There are also extended examples of this relationship in the prophet Hosea, whose own marriage is used as a dramatic object lesson, acted out to illustrate God's relationship to Israel (Hos 1–3),[7] and the Song of Songs, where Solomon's erotic love poem is actually describing the love relationship of the Lord (Bridegroom) with Israel (bride).

Thus, the community viewed their relationship with God as a very intimate one, and their relationships with one another as a picture of this holy relationship. This is also reflected in New Testament writings, especially Paul's, where he refers to the marriage relationship of husband and wife as an example of the marriage relationship of Christ and the church (Eph 5:22–23). It is also true that in both the Old and New Testament Israel's relationship with God is viewed as one of community. God is married to the entire people of Israel, not to individual believers. This corporate mindset is important to understand as one engages the text of Scripture.

The Israelites considered their Scriptures to be one, a unified message and revelation from God.[8] These writings were to be read and understood

6. Here Jeremiah is delivering the word of the Lord to Judah concerning the new covenant, which he points out will not be like the old covenant "that they broke" even though they were married; the Lord is the husband in the relationship. Ezekiel 16 especially details the marriage relationship the Lord entered into with Israel and how they whored after other gods and other nations, becoming an unfaithful bride. This is also spelled out clearly in Ezek 23, where Samaria and Jerusalem (Oholah and Oholibah) are called sisters who played the whore in Egypt and Assyria. The Israelites were warned against whoring after the desires of their eyes and their hearts as well (Num 15:39).

Leviticus 20:1–9 provides an excellent example of the first phrase. The Lord through Moses warns against whoring after other gods such as Molech and includes mediums and wizards in verse 6: "If a person turns to mediums and wizards, whoring after them, I will set my face against that person." It is important to note contextually that immediately following is a description of punishments for adultery and immorality (vv. 10–21) and then the importance of being holy (vv. 22–27).

7. Hosea takes a wife by God's command, and they have three children, whose names are less than complimentary, illustrating Israel's unfaithfulness and God's reaction. Then Gomer, Hosea's wife, leaves him for others, illustrating Israel's marital unfaithfulness. Finally, the Lord commands Hosea to redeem his wife—buy her back—which illustrates the Lord's actions in redeeming his people.

8. On this important matter, which is linked indissolubly to the idea entertained by Jews in antiquity of the coherence, completeness, and relevance of Scripture, see the detailed study of Alexander Samely, *The Interpretation of Speech in the Pentateuchal Targums*, Texte

as a whole—one God—one people; one Bridegroom—one bride; one unified revelation—one receiver; one message—one unified, consistent theology. My methodology attempts to reflect, as best as possible, this approach
toward Scripture and toward the God of Israel. It recommends viewing
the text as a unified theological narrative.

It would be disingenuous to recommend this approach as if it represented something new. Perhaps it would best be considered a return to
a method previously employed by scholars such as Martin Luther and,
to a greater or lesser extent, some of the early church fathers. Although
Luther's own methodology is termed Christocentric, he had a unique way
of approaching the final form of the text that reflected more of an early
church understanding. My approach is a simple incorporation of a narrative reading of the text with an Old Testament, covenantal understanding
that God's revelation is unified and consistent to his people throughout
history.

The question, Does Holy Scripture (canon) inform the life and culture
of Israel, or, does the life and culture of Israel impact the formation of
the canon? is certainly a both/and reality. Gunkel, with his form-critical
approach, leaned more heavily on the life and culture of Israel guiding
the formation of the canon, while Childs focused more on the canon's
influence on the life and culture of Israel. Childs's desire to look at the
whole of the canon and not an atomized version is in line with my recommended methodology. However, his reading of the canon as a unified
narrative did not focus strongly on the theological unity. Childs viewed
the gospel of Jesus Christ as the unifying referent of the final form of the
text. I do not disagree with this. However, Childs does not discuss and
little demonstrates how this unifying referent is shown in the text. Using
biblical motifs, I will demonstrate how this unifying referent is revealed.
In regards to Levenson and his approach to the text, one must first understand that his "unity and divinity" method is focused on the Torah of
Moses and not the rest of the Old Testament canon, and most clearly not
on the New Testament. While Levenson speaks of the simultaneity of the

---

und Studien zum antiken Judentum 27 (Tübingen: Mohr Siebeck, 1992), 107–23, 171–73. The
coherence of Scripture seems to have been a fundamental presupposition of Jewish interpreters from the time of the LXX onwards.

Torah and how rabbinic midrashic tradition has presented this final form, he strongly states that finding one great idea that pervades and unifies the Hebrew Bible is unlikely to interest Jews. He goes on the state: "The effort to construct a systematic, harmonious theological statement out of unsystematic and polydox materials in the Hebrew Bible fits Christianity better than Judaism."[9]

One would not expect his unifying principle to be the gospel of Jesus Christ; however, in true rabbinic fashion, finding one principle that provides the unity he speaks of is not a search that interests him. It is that unity exists because of the tradition, not a principal unifying factor. This leads to the "particularity" of how rabbinic Judaism approaches and understands its text. Reading Scripture as a unified theological narrative places emphasis on both the unity of the narrative and the theology therein. The unifying principle is similar to Childs. Like Childs and Levenson, my adoption of this unified theological narrative approach does not mean that I am stifling the various and different voices in the text. Rather, I am providing a platform for these different voices to speak and contribute.

BIBLICAL MOTIFS AND THE TEXT

Biblical motifs (themes) provide evidence of a unified theology present within each page of the text. Childs uses the idea of allegory in this regard, but his definition is far different from most modern understandings. Basically, he claims that the distinction between allegory and typology is a recent invention and that the difference is far more subtle. Allegory is not necessarily fanciful or arbitrary. Rather, the function of allegory is related to the struggle to understand the mystery of Christ. It is a way of relating the whole of Scripture to that mystery.[10] Andrew Louth writes:

> If we look back to the Fathers, and the tradition, for inspiration as
> to the nature of theology, there is one thing we meet which must
> be paused over and discussed in some detail: and that is their use
> of allegory in interpreting the Scriptures. We can see already that

---

9. Levenson, *Hebrew Bible*, 51.
10. Driver, *Brevard Childs, Biblical Theologian*, 233.

for them it was not a superfluous, stylistic habit, something we can fairly easily lop off from the trunk of Patristic theology. Rather it is bound up with their whole understanding of tradition as the tacit dimension of the Christian life: allegory is a way of entering the "margin of silence" that surrounds the articulate message of the Scriptures, it is a way of glimpsing the living depths of tradition from the perspective of the letter of the Scriptures.[11]

Using motifs, a way is shown to move from one book to the next, even from one Testament to the next, in what may be viewed as an allegorical fashion. There is a cohesive nature to these motifs, whose steady accumulation may point to the kind of "grand narrative" discerned by scholars such as C. J. H. Wright.[12] The motifs themselves must be critically analyzed.[13] However, the cohesion of the motifs is an important factor underlying the use of allegory by the church fathers, on which Louth remarks as follows: "but whatever *language* the Fathers use to describe their exegetical practice (and there is no great consistency here), they all interpret Scripture in a way we would call allegorical, and *allegoria* is the usual word the Latin Fathers use from the fourth century onward to characterize the deeper meaning they are seeking in the Scriptures."[14] My use of motif is related to the use of allegory, but in a classical rather than the modern sense, drawing on the practice of the early church.

---

11. A. Louth, *Discerning the Mystery: An Essay on the Nature of Theology* (Oxford: Clarendon, 1983), 96.

12. C. J. H. Wright understands the unifying nature of the themes of Scripture: "I have tried to identify some of the underlying themes that are woven all through the Bible's grand narrative—themes that are the foundational pillars of the biblical worldview and therefore also of biblical theology: monotheism, creation, humanity, election, redemption, covenant, ethics, future hope." See Wright, *The Mission of God: Unlocking the Bible's Grand Narrative* (Downers Grove, IL: InterVarsity Press, 2006), 17.

13. Kugel also recognizes the importance of these motifs and discusses how they should be dealt with. "Treat each exegetical motif separately. Once individual exegetical motifs are isolated, one can then go on to treat each separately—that is, to focus on motif X as embodied in texts A, B, and C, or to analyze text A as embodying three separate exegetical motifs, X, Y, and Z. To treat each motif *separately* is simple enough, but it is nonetheless immensely important; numerous studies have gone astray precisely because they fail to isolate each individual motif" (*In Potiphar's House*, 8).

14. Louth, *Discerning the Mystery*, 96.

There are a multitude of these motifs in the Joseph narratives; however, I will focus on one for the purpose of example.[15] This motif is the garment motif, which is central to the Joseph narratives. The garment motif makes its first canonical appearance in the Genesis narrative about the garden of Eden and appears again and again in Genesis and elsewhere. When Adam and Eve eat of the fruit of the tree of the knowledge of good and evil, they suddenly realize that they are naked, and, in their shame, they sew together fig leaves to cover themselves (Gen 3:7). Then, when God comes to the end of his confrontation with Adam and Eve, even as he sends them out of the garden, he replaces these fig-leaf garments with those he has made from animal skins (Gen 3:21). The provision of these garments requires the shedding of blood; thus we see the birth of the garment motif and its connection to blood being shed.

Already in the text of Genesis the motif reappears with the patriarch Jacob as he uses the garment of his brother, Esau, and animal skins to deceive his father, Isaac, and to steal his brother's blessing (Gen 27). Interesting to note is the use of בגד for "garment" in several Old Testament texts. The root of this Hebrew word contains the idea of deception, to act faithlessly, or treacherously, especially in the context of a marriage or covenantal relationship.[16] So, Jacob deceives his father with garments and skins from a recently killed animal. In the Joseph narratives, garments are frequently used to deceive.

> Here it bears mention again that it was through two goats of the flock (*gedaye 'izzim*) that Jacob had deceived his own father, Isaac. Rebekah it will be recalled, used the goats for the tasty dish that the blind old man mistook for Esau's venison, and she clothed her smooth-skinned son in the hides of the same animals in order to perpetrate the same momentous act of impersonation (Gen. 27:5–17). It is as though some strange karmic force keeps this act of deception

---

15. Later I will use the death-and-resurrection motif to argue for understanding Joseph as a death-and-resurrection figure.

16. G. J. Botterweck, H. Ringgren, and H.-J. Fabry, eds., *Theological Dictionary of the Old Testament* (Grand Rapids, 1974), 1:470–479. There is some disagreement concerning this root and its connection to "clothing." This verb occurs in South Arabic with the meaning "to deceive," which can be traced back to two different roots.

in continual ricochet, dooming the chosen family to re-experience it in succeeding generations and even within the same generation.[17]

In Genesis 37, Joseph's special tunic is bloodied by his brothers in order to deceive their father, Jacob. This tunic is not "many colored" but most likely white and of exceptional quality.[18] Genesis 38 contains the account of Tamar exchanging her widow garb for the dress of a prostitute in order to deceive Judah. Again in Genesis 39, Potiphar's wife uses Joseph's abandoned cloak to deceive her husband and convict Joseph.

The correlation between deceiving and garments is found at the beginning of Genesis and appears throughout the Hebrew Bible. The covering, or clothing, to cover humanity's shame is understood as hiding the reality of its sinfulness, its unholiness, from a holy God. Thus we see the priestly garments carrying out the same function. It is interesting to note this in the special white linen garments worn by the high priest on the Day of Atonement (Lev 16:4, 23). These are significant in that they are worn into the holy of holies before the presence of the Holy One.[19] Note also that the high priest brings the blood of a goat into the holy of holies.

The prophet Isaiah builds on the garment motif as he speaks of humankind's deeds and actions as "filthy rags" (Isa 64:6)—unclean and unholy. The Lord is not fooled by humankind's attempt to present itself as holy or righteous. Significantly, the same canonical writing looks forward to the days when human beings will be clothed in garments of salvation, the robes of righteousness (Isa 61:10), replacing the shame and unholiness of humanity with his imputed righteousness. Here Isaiah, along with other prophets and writings (Song of Songs), also speaks of the bridal garments with which the coming Bridegroom will clothe his bride.[20] The use of the

---

17. Levenson, *Death and Resurrection*, 159.

18. The LXX and Vulgate read "a robe of many colors," while Targum Onqelos reads "a robe with stripes."

19. Some scholars, especially in the early church, have noted the relationship between Joseph's special tunic, the Day of Atonement priestly linen garment, and the linen garment of Christ for which the soldiers cast lots.

20. Isaiah 61:10: "I will rejoice greatly in the LORD; my soul shall exult in my God, for he has clothed me with the garments of salvation; he has covered me with the robe of righteousness, as a bridegroom decks himself like a priest with a beautiful headdress and as a bride adorns herself with her jewels."

garment motif, the clothing of humanity in garments of salvation, and the adorning of the bride with bridal garments prophesy and point to the great reversal that is to come in this garment motif. For the Christian reader, this motif comes to fruition with the advent of the Messiah.

The New Testament Scriptures continue the garment motif as the Christ is born and wrapped in "swaddling clothes" (grave clothes) and laid in a manger (Luke 2:7). Note the reversal when the tomb is found open and empty apart from the grave clothes, which remain (Luke 24:12). This reversal is but a microcosm of the great reversal as seen on the cross. Christ is stripped of his seamless white linen garment, and his nakedness is uncovered. However, the shame that is revealed is not his own but that of humanity, for he bears humanity's sins and carries humanity's sorrow (Isa 53, the fourth servant song). Accordingly, Christ is stripped bare on the cross, and, by means of his sacrifice, the shedding of the blood of the Lamb, the sins of humanity are covered, cleansed, and atoned for, and now humanity is clothed in the garments of salvation and the robes of righteousness.[21] It is an alien righteousness, but these are the garments provided that humanity might be found properly clothed at the wedding feast (Matt 22:11–14). It is also important to see the stripping of Joseph's garment as connected to Christ's stripping.[22]

Finally, in the last pages of the Scriptures we see the eschatological fulfillment of this motif as John records his revelation. John speaks of the great multitude gathered before the throne of the Lamb in heaven, who have washed their robes in his blood (Rev 7:13–14). These are Isaiah's garments of salvation and robes of righteousness, about which he prophesies in Isaiah 61. Revelation also speaks of the marriage feast of the Lamb (Rev 19:7–8),[23] where the proper attire will be these same robes of righteousness—white linen garments. From Genesis to Revelation, Scripture may be read as providing a consistent and unified theological message by means of the garment motif.

---

21. Note the return to Gen 3 and the theme of covering shame, Lev 16 and atonement, and Isa 53.

22. See chap. 5.

23. Note again these robes are of white linen, as was the high priest's robe on the Day of Atonement.

This treatment of the garment motif is far from complete. However, it is clear that the simple presence of the garment in each account is operating only on the surface of the text. In all these related verses, there are deeper senses at work—a combination of echoes of other scriptural passages, allusion, allegory, deeper themes—all working together to support the motif. A reading of the garment motif in such a manner is ultimately more compelling than any purely historical or sociological interpretation. These interpretations can only rightly investigate the garment as a marker of personal status, or as expressive of joy or sorrow or some other emotional state, or as appropriate for particular occasions, rituals, or places.

Treatment of Scripture as a unified theological narrative allows us to discern the operation of the various motifs within the canon. It also helps one to observe the consistency and the continuity of the text, a reality that was understood by the community of faith as they considered the final form of the text of which they were in possession. These motifs are not only interwoven throughout all the Scriptures, but they are also woven into one another, thus providing a text that is not unlike a tapestry. Woven together and seamless, they provide a unified message and theology.

A UNIFIED THEOLOGICAL NARRATIVE
AND THE JOSEPH NARRATIVES

Before we proceed, we should note two chapters that require special attention because of their contents. These are Genesis 38, the story of Judah and Tamar, and 49, the poetic section known as the blessing of Jacob.

The account of Judah and Tamar in Genesis 38 has proven perplexing. The common question following a quick reading is, Why has this account been included in the Joseph narratives? There is no mention of Joseph, and there appears to be no logical connection, apart from familial, to the Joseph story. The events described do not appear to have any bearing on what follows.

Critical scholarship has tended to take the easy way around by reading it as an addition to the text by another source.[24] This explanation fails to address the question of placement, as well as failing to consider the

---

24. Von Rad, *Genesis*, 351; E. A. Speiser, *Genesis*, Anchor Bible (Garden City, NY: Doubleday, 1983), 299.

reasoning behind its inclusion. Others have suggested that Genesis 38 marks the end of the Genesis story and that 39–50 were a later addition.[25] Once again, placement and reason for inclusion are not adequately addressed. Instructive in this regard are the words of Childs:

> Certainly one of the keys to the canonical interpretation is given in the place assigned to the story of Judah (ch.38). In the large majority of commentaries (cf. Gunkel, von Rad, etc.) the chapter is summarily dismissed as an unfortunate interpolation into the Joseph story. At best it serves a secondary literary role of marking the passage of time when Joseph journeyed into captivity. Only Benno Jacob, among modern commentators, reflects more seriously on the purpose of the chapter.[26]

The textual placement of Genesis 38 has not been significantly dealt with in a manner that recognizes its pivotal position within the narrative. Not only are there words and phrases in common between Genesis 38 and the other chapters of the Joseph narratives, but they also share the same style of writing, and most significantly, they share many of the same biblical motifs. These motifs connect the narratives and provide the key to unlocking the mystery of this unusual chapter and its purpose. Thus, Alter writes:

> I should like to discuss, then, the story of Tamar and Judah (Genesis 38), which is set in between the selling of Joseph by his brothers and Joseph's appearance as a slave in the household of Potiphar. This story is characterized by E.A. Speiser, in his superb Genesis volume in the Anchor Bible series, as "a completely independent unit," having "no connection with the drama of Joseph, which it interrupts at the conclusion of Act I." The interpolation does, of course, as Speiser and others have recognized, build a sense of suspense about the fate of Joseph and a feeling of time elapsed until

---

25. Westermann claims that Gen 38 and 49 are not additions to the Joseph story, but rather belong to the conclusion of the Jacob story (*Genesis 37–50*, 22). Speiser says that this chapter is a completely independent unit with no connection to the Joseph drama (*Genesis*, 299).

26. Childs, *Introduction to the Old Testament*, 156.

Joseph shows up in Egypt, but Speiser's failure to see its intimate connections through motif and theme with the Joseph story suggests the limitations of conventional biblical scholarship even at its best.[27]

Alter identifies the limitations of conventional biblical scholarship. The motifs and themes that are missed with this view of Genesis 38 result in a lack of understanding of the unified nature of the final form of the text. Levenson builds on Alter:

> For purpose of our investigation, another element of narrative analogy, one to which none of these midrashic observations points, is, however, preeminent. Alter comes close to it when he observes that the tale of Judah and of Joseph both are "about the election through some devious twist of destiny of a younger son to carry on the line."[28] What he has in mind is Joseph's status as the "next to the youngest" and Judah's as "the fourthborn" of Jacob's brood. This is indeed important, and the emergence of kings from precisely these two tribes is a point of no small consequence in the interpretation of the story of Joseph.[29]

The view, demonstrated here, is that these chapters present a classic story with all the necessary dramatic elements. The style and language are unique in many ways and therefore point strongly to a unified authorship with little or no redacting. As a result, the Joseph narratives provided little fodder for higher critics and their art.[30] As critical scholarship moved

---

27. Alter, *Art of Biblical Narrative*, 3–4.

28. Alter, *Art of Biblical Narrative*, 6.

29. Levenson, *Death and Resurrection*, 161.

30. Much could be said concerning historical critical efforts to separate the J (Yahwist) and E (Elohist) sources within the Joseph narratives due to the interesting use of the names for God. However, there is little consensus to be found in these efforts, although the language often persists in various summaries. While O. Eissfeldt clearly states that "as far as Genesis is concerned, the two strands (J and E) may also be differentiated by the divine names (Yahweh and Elohim)," he goes on to claim that "it is very clear that the Yahwistic sections ... do not fit with J Joseph story, but noticeably disturb it." He notes this is particularly true of Genesis 38. See Eissfeldt, *The Old Testament: An Introduction*, trans. P. R. Ackroyd (New York: Harper & Row, 1965), 190–92. G. Fohrer assigns the bulk of the Joseph novella to J but especially excludes

toward rhetorical criticism, attention to these chapters increased and continued to increase with the narrative-reading approach. There still appears
to be resistance in regards to Genesis 38 and 49, but this too is weakening
as more scholars reconsider these chapters and their place in the text's
final form.

There is a general inadequacy in terms of interpreting the Joseph story
simply within historical-critical, form-critical, or traditional-historical categories. This is a long narrative that has not been taken up by other biblical
writers in any systematic manner. Why is this so? Why was this narrative
preserved and preserved in the form which it has come to be possessed?
The story line could have been abbreviated and simplified for greater dramatic effect. It could have been more explicitly theologized. The matter
of Israel being resident in a foreign land could have been built up into a
major thematic concern. None of this is the case. My purposed approach
and interpretation of this narrative goes some way in accounting for the
story being as it is—a point in the narrative of Genesis where certain key
themes come to the surface and receive an airing, before being pursued
later in the wider context of the canon.

From the beginning, the primary purpose of biblical criticism was of
a practical nature. The text was studied in order that its message might
be understood and therefore proclaimed. As time progressed, the genre
of biblical criticism took on a more academic nature. No longer was the
study of the text exclusively for the practical purpose of preaching and
teaching the faith. Now came the advent of the study of the text for the
sake of textual study. With the advent of the academy and its study of the
text of Scripture outside the walls of church and synagogue came various
difficulties and challenges. Louth's judgment on this is penetrating:

Gen 38 and 49. However, he understands the Joseph novella as a primary addition in "second
groundwork" (G2), a source followed largely by J. He views E as also coming from G2, following
Noth, which renders the division of sources by use of the divine names too simplistic. See
Fohrer, *Introduction to the Old Testament* (London: SPCK, 1968), 131–60. S. R. Driver claims:
"The narrative of Joseph cannot be judged entirely by itself; it must be judged in light of the
presumption derived from the study of JE as a whole." He subscribes to the view that these
sources are distinguished by the use of the names for God. See Driver, *Introduction to the
Literature of the Old Testament* (Edinburgh: T&T Clark, 1898), 13–20. Westermann describes
this lack of cohesive thought in regards to the sources of the Joseph story in detail (*Genesis:
An Introduction*, 234–42).

But the case with theology is in some respects different: the crack and divisions go deeper and have been there longer, and it might even be argued that it is the collapse of the centre in theology that has led to the spreading of the cracks throughout our culture. In any case, it is certain that much of the division in theology is simply a reflection of the division in our culture; the specialization in theology, the remoteness of theologians—often complained of—from the Church and the believing Christian, and indeed the remoteness of theologians from one another.[31]

This disconnect between theologian and church and synagogue has led to a separation of academy from the faith community. Is the reading of Scripture and the study of the text art or science? While it may be a mistake to state that the genre of biblical criticism strictly belongs to one or the other, it is true that the approach one adopts as one's prevailing philosophy will color one's understanding.

In advocating the more holistic approach of reading Scripture as a unified theological narrative, I must concede that the pieces are the important building blocks of the narrative. Unfortunately, when the scientific approach has been fully employed, the disconnect from the humanities is disturbing.[32] The text is dissected into its numerous pieces, but in themselves the pieces tell us little. They cannot convey the message of the narrative; they cannot provide the revelation, the purpose for which the text exists.

In reading these fourteen chapters as a unified theological narrative, it is essential to consider them in the context of the final form of the canon—part of the overall narrative of Scripture—as well as to recognize their unique structure as a dramatic presentation. Throughout history these chapters and Joseph's character have been presented again and again in teaching, in story, and even on the stage.[33] The Joseph narratives are to

---

31. Louth, *Discerning the Mystery*, 2.

32. Louth, *Discerning the Mystery*, 27.

33. B. Lang, *Joseph in Egypt: A Cultural Icon from Grotius to Goethe* (New Haven: Yale University Press, 2009). Lang chronicles the various approaches and usages of Joseph, not only helping to illustrate his popularity as an iconic figure but also revealing how the structure of the story begs to be told.

be approached as a beautifully structured narrative that presents a historical transition from Israel's patriarchal era into the tribal era. At the same time, this account uses several brilliant biblical motifs that reflect the christological character of the final form of the text as they tie the Joseph story into the overall narrative of Scripture.[34] Thus the theological message reflected in these chapters resonates with themes apparent in both Old and New Testaments.

Reading all of Scripture, and thus the Joseph narratives, as a unified theological narrative helps to preserve the integrity of both text and theology. It also most closely reflects the manner in which the faith community of the Old Testament approached their sacred writings, especially the Torah. With such an approach, the various narratives, prophecies, writings, and stories of the Old Testament are seen in a unified manner, and they convey a common message. Even though there may be disagreement concerning said message, honest scholarship looks at the world behind, the world of, and the world in front of the text and allows the final form of the text to fulfill its intended purpose and deliver its theological point regardless. This approach finds its roots in textual scholarship pre–higher criticism, and has returned in some fashion with the canonical approach of Childs and the work of Levenson. As it is my adopted approach, I have modified and built on these others in only a small way.

---

34. Biblical motifs: garment, covenantal, death and resurrection, etc.

Part II

—

The Text of Genesis 37–50

3

The Masoretic Text of the Joseph Narratives

INTRODUCTION

The MT of Genesis 37–50 is written in narrative form, with the exception of Genesis 49. The faith communities who received this text heard it as a unified narrative, a coherent story that relayed certain truths through its characters and situations. It is important to read these chapters as a unified theological narrative lest we miss the forest for the trees as we attempt to sort through the disassembled pieces.[1]

Within the Joseph narratives there are various motifs and themes woven into the tapestry of the text. These motifs provide the connecting threads that bind together the greater tapestry of the narrative. It is also in these motifs that a close reading of the text may perceive aspects of the narrative that a surface reading might fail to identify. These motifs provide the key to how the Joseph narratives are interwoven into the greater narrative of the book of Genesis and thereby the Torah and all of Scripture. Levenson writes:

> The story of Joseph in Genesis 37–50 is not only the longest and most intricate exemplar of the narrative of the death and resurrection of the beloved son, but also the most explicit. In it is concentrated

---

1. J. S. Kaminsky writes in relation to an election motif and the Genesis brotherly struggles: "The larger framework that binds these stories together consists of recurring themes, motifs, word patterns, and wordplays. The use of shared literary patterns among the stories of brotherly struggle in Genesis and between these stories and certain other narratives elsewhere in the Hebrew Bible raises an issue that will come up periodically in this book: when should one limit oneself to the immediate narrative frame of a given passage and when should one utilize pieces from elsewhere in the Hebrew Bible to clarify textual and/or exegetical issues under discussion? Clearly, one must strike the right balance between recognizing that each of the stories of brotherly struggle is unique while they are also connected to one another as part of a canonical whole." See Kaminsky, *Yet I Loved Jacob: Reclaiming the Biblical Concept of Election* (Eugene, OR: Wipf & Stock, 2016), 16.

almost every variation of the theme that first appeared in the little tale of Cain and Abel and has been growing and becoming more complex throughout the Book of Genesis. The story of Joseph thus not only concludes the book and links the Patriarchal narratives to those of the people Israel in Egypt for which they serve as archetypes; it is also the crescendo to the theme of the beloved son, which it presents in extraordinarily polished literary form. It is arguably the most sophisticated narrative in the Jewish or the Christian Bibles.[2]

The challenge in studying such a text in detail is to look carefully at the details of the text without losing sight of the narrative's character. As a friend so aptly said, "It depends on which end of the telescope one looks through." A study such as this must look through both ends of the telescope. I will seek to clarify as far as possible the theological aims of the Joseph narrative in its final, canonical form, as the Masoretic Hebrew text presents it to us.

THE JOSEPH NARRATIVES

While the book of Genesis is filled with many narratives, no other character has a longer narrative than Joseph. No other character, Abraham included, has as much material devoted to him.[3] The Joseph narratives form the final תלדות of Genesis—often referred to as the Jacob *toledoth*. These fourteen chapters bring to conclusion the book of Genesis in a very intriguing and dramatic way. Not only is there an obvious change in style and form, but there is also the clear sense that these last chapters are preparing for something more. In no way is the impression given that this is the end of the story. Rather, we begin to realize that as we are ushered to the end of Genesis, we have been artfully brought to the beginning of something new.

---

2. Levenson, *Death and Resurrection*, 143.

3. B. Vawter claims that Joseph's career was more intimately connected with the Israelites than any of his predecessors, referring to his role in preserving them and forming them as a people in Egypt. See Vawter, *A Path through Genesis* (New York: Sheed & Ward, 1956), 241.

GENESIS 37

The Joseph narratives begin with the final *toledoth* (אלה תלדות; "These are the generations") of Genesis.[4] As the final *toledoth*, it may also indicate that this is the end of an era—the patriarchal era—as the sons of Jacob and their descendants transition into the tribal era of the Hebrew people. Thus we see in this final narrative both an ending and a beginning. The original narrator of this *toledoth* immediately distinguishes himself by adopting a style of writing unique from the other narratives. The writer employs various techniques that are not as evident in the rest of Genesis. We see a broader vocabulary, which should be expected considering the Egyptian setting of the bulk of the narratives; however, much of the new vocabulary is not so much related to the Egyptian context as to underlying theological messages. The writer also employs an extensive use of doublets in his writing style. Much of this is for emphasis and dramatic effect. Alter observes that doublets are a recurrent principle of organization in the Joseph story.[5]

Following the introducing *toledoth*, the narrator begins with seventeen-year-old Joseph, one of the twelve sons of Jacob, pasturing the flock with his brothers. The narrator is careful to point out that these are his brothers from the mothers Bilhah and Zilpah, the maidservants of Jacob's wives, Leah and Rachel. From the beginning we are given a window into the family dynamics of the house of Jacob. There is a definite hierarchy among these sons; of first importance are the sons of Rachel, then the sons of Leah, and last the sons of Bilhah and Zilpah.[6] As the story unfolds, the distrustful nature of this family will play a crucial role in the account.

Most English versions translate נער as "boy." Considering Joseph's age of seventeen years, it would be better to use a secondary meaning for נער, "assistant, apprentice."[7] Joseph was learning the shepherding vocation from the sons of Bilhah and Zilpah. Jacob may have also sent Joseph to work with them as a means by which to keep an eye on them. This would encourage

---

4. Genesis is divided into twelve patriarchal narratives, with all but the first beginning with אלה תלדות . The Joseph narratives actually begin at 37:2.

5. R. Alter, *Genesis* (New York: Norton, 1996), 210.

6. See also the group arrangements Jacob made when preparing to encounter his brother Esau in Gen 33:1–2.

7. Pirson, *Lord of the Dreams*, 32–33; Alter, *Genesis*, 208.

the animosity resulting from the "bad report" (דבתם רעה) that Joseph made to his father.[8] Gordon Wenham notes:

> It is not clear whether Joseph's report about his brothers was true or not, but the term דבה "tales" is always used elsewhere in a negative sense of an untrue report, and here it is qualified by the adjective "evil" (cf. Num 13:32; 14:36–37). So it seems likely that Joseph misrepresented his brothers to his father, his father believed him, and his brothers hated him for his lies.[9]

However, Levenson points out another important aspect of this apprenticeship:

> In a mere two and a half verses, the narrator here sets up the problematic of Joseph's status, which is, in turn, the force that sets the story—and its hero—on its uncertain way. Joseph is not only one of the youngest of the brood but the son given the most menial task—to assist the sons of his father's wives, the slaves Bilhah and Zilpah. The narrative thus begins with a curious and suspect inversion: the son of a free woman—nay, Jacob/Israel's son by his favorite wife and the only one he is ever said to love (29:18)—has been relegated to a rank beneath even that of his half-brothers by the slave-women. Contradicting this humiliation, however, is the exalted implication of Joseph's pastoral livelihood. "Shepherd" is in fact, a term that in the ancient Near East often denoted the ruler. Long before this narrative was composed, Mesopotamian kings has already described themselves as "shepherds" of their people.[10]

Levenson goes on to make comparison of Joseph as shepherd with Moses and David, who are noteworthy for their transition from the literal to the metaphorical forms of their vocation. He especially points out the similarity of the language of Exodus 3:1 that introduces Moses

---

8. See also Num 14:36–37. Joseph may very well have been playing the role of a spy.

9. G. J. Wenham, *Genesis 16–50*, Word Biblical Commentary (Dallas: Word Books, 1994), 350.

10. Levenson, *Death and Resurrection*, 143–44.

and his divine call to leadership—"Now Moses, tending the flock of his father-in-law Jethro ..."—to the introduction of Joseph to the narrative bearing his name—"At seventeen years of age, Joseph tended the flocks with his brothers" (37:2).[11] Once again, this was a bad report concerning the sons of Bilhah and Zilpah.

In verse 3 we begin to understand Joseph's standing among his brothers. This family hierarchy and the resulting favoritism toward one son over another/others has been seen before in the book of Genesis. Jacob himself experienced it in his relationship with Esau. However, the first example takes place when the Lord favors Abel's offering over Cain's. In past accounts conflict and confrontation result, and this story will be no exception.

In this verse the narrator uses the term "Israel" for Joseph's father, while in the preceding verse "Jacob" is used. This begins an interesting pattern throughout the Joseph narratives, albeit a difficult one to understand. There seems to be no explanation without exceptions, but perhaps this is another indication of the transition from the patriarchal to the tribal era. Wenham writes:

> Since Jacob is the normal form, it is the exceptional appearance of Israel that needs to be explained. Second, whereas in prose Jacob always refers to the historical individual, Israel sometimes refers to the people (46:8; 47:27; 48:20). Third, when Israel is used of the individual, it seems to allude to his position as clan head (43:6, 8, 11; 46:1; 48:2), whereas Jacob seems to be used where his human weakness is most obvious (e.g., 37:34; 42:4, 36; 47:9). This fits in with the etymology of the names ("Jacob"="struggler, deceiver" and "Israel"= "prevailer with God") given earlier in Genesis. So Jacob turns into Israel when his strength revives (45:28; 48:2). Finally, in those scenes where Joseph is present, Israel seems to be preferred (37:3, 13; 46:29, 30; 48:2, 8, 11, 14, 20, 21; 50:2).[12]

---

11. Levenson, *Death and Resurrection*, 144.
12. Wenham, *Genesis 16–50*, 351.

Joseph is referred to as being more loved by Israel than all his brothers because he was בֶן־זְקֻנִים הוּא לוֹ, "a son of his old age." Was not Benjamin
a son of his old age? In Genesis 44:20 the brothers refer to Benjamin as
יֶלֶד זְקֻנִים, "a child of (his) old age." While this may seem a difficulty, both
Joseph and Benjamin are sons/children of his old age, and since Benjamin
plays no part in the early stages of the narrative, he is not mentioned.
Clearly, Benjamin replaces Joseph when Jacob presumes him dead.

Verse 3 also introduces us to the famous garment of Joseph. When most
people recall Joseph, they immediately think of his "coat of many colors."
However, the Hebrew כְּתֹנֶת פַּסִּים is more correctly translated as a "sleeved
tunic" or a "tunic reaching to the extremities (wrists and ankles)." "Coat of
many colors" originates from the LXX and then the Latin Vulgate, and they
were followed by Martin Luther in his German translation.[13] Regardless,
the point is that this garment set Joseph apart from his brothers in an obvious way, demonstrating Jacob's preference for him over his brothers (Gen
49:26). Verse 4 clearly shows the depth of emotion this garment creates.[14]

This is the first encounter with the garment motif in the Joseph narratives. It is one of the most significant motifs in these chapters and throughout all Scripture.[15] The gift of a special tunic not only shows his father's great
favor; it also brings Joseph great grief.[16] However, when taken in context

---

13. Luther spoke of this in his Genesis lectures at great length, acknowledging that he
does not know what sort of robe it was but that, in the end, it was a cloak that honored Joseph
above his brothers. See *Luther's Works*, American ed. (St. Louis: Concordia, 1965), 6:322–24. For
discussion of the evidence of the ancient versions and medieval Jewish exegetes, see important note in *Biblia Hebraica Quinta* (Stuttgart: Deutsche Bibelgesellschaft, 2015), "Commentary
on the Critical Apparatus," 168*, prepared by A. Tal.

14. Westermann points to 2 Sam 13:18, where such a garment is the apparel of a princess.
Thus he notes that the garment sets Joseph apart from his brothers, saying, "The consequence
of predilection is preference" (*Genesis 37–50*, 37). Speiser translates as "an ornamented tunic"
(*Genesis*, 287).

15. For more on this see chs. 2, 5.

16. Kaminsky is referring to the "motif of the endangered child." He writes: "Many times
the parents themselves contribute to the endangerment brought about through sibling rivalry,
and sometimes they appear to endanger their children independently. Here one thinks of
characters like Abraham, who endangers Ishmael and Isaac in Gen 21 and 22 respectively
(albeit both times following God's command); Rebekah, whose plot to steal Esau's blessing
endangers Jacob's life, which is only spared through an extended exile from the Holy Land
and his immediate family (Gen 27:41–45); or the father Jacob, who openly dotes on Joseph
and then sends him all alone to check on his brothers who hate him (Gen 37:1–14)" (*Yet I
Loved Jacob*, 36–37).

with the overall garment motif in Scripture, Joseph and his special tunic take on deeper theological significance.

These first three verses set the stage for what is to come. The jealousy and envy of Joseph's brothers toward him is established, and the rest of this drama builds on what we have learned. The narrator has wasted no time apprising us of the situation, preparing us for the escalation that is coming.

"Joseph dreamed a dream" (ויחלם יוסף חלום)—this doubling of חלום is unique to the Joseph narratives and is found four times in Genesis 37 alone (37:5-6, 9-10). It is also the first of many doublets in these chapters. Not only is חלום doubled, but the three dream narratives also occur in pairs; Joseph dreams two dreams; the chief cupbearer and the chief baker dream the same night; and Pharaoh dreams two dreams. This consistent dream pattern in the Joseph narratives recommends a unified reading of the story. Jonathan Grossman writes: "It is generally agreed that the three pairs of dreams featured in the Joseph narrative (Joseph's dreams [ch. 37]; the ministers' dreams [ch. 40]; and Pharaoh's dreams [ch. 41]) testify not to a fusion of sources or traditions but to a unity of composition."[17]

God does not appear, nor does he speak in any of the dreams of these narratives. Thus far in Genesis, God has spoken or appeared in all dreams (20:3-7; 28:12-15; 31:10-13, 34). The dreams of the Joseph narratives are also the first to be symbolic in nature and the first to require interpretation. The pairing of these dreams also appears to require both dreams to provide a full interpretation. The greater meaning seems to lie in seeing the dreams as one, as Joseph states in 41:25, "The dreams of Pharaoh are one."[18]

Verse 5 uses the *hiphil* form of the verb נגד for the telling of the passing on of information (also 37:16). This is in contrast to verse 9, which uses the *piel* form of ספר (ויספר; "and he told"). Joseph's first dream does not involve numbers or counting, while his second dream does. The *piel* form of ספר is used eight times in Genesis, six times in combination with a dream in the Joseph narratives (37:9-10; 40:8-9; 41:8, 12). The other two occurrences in Genesis 24:66 and 29:13 also have the meaning "to tell." All the uses of ספר

---

17. J. Grossman, "Different Dreams: Two Models of Interpretation for Three Pairs of Dreams," *Journal of Biblical Literature* 135, no. 4 (2016): 717.

18. N. Sarna notes: "Throughout the Joseph narratives, dreams come in pairs in order to demonstrate their seriousness, as noted in 41:32." See Sarna, *The JPS Torah Commentary: Genesis* (Philadelphia: Jewish Publication Society, 1989), 257.

in the *piel* form combined with the dreams have a counting or numbering aspect. The *qal* and *niphal* forms of ספר occur five times in Genesis, with the meaning "to count."[19]

Joseph's first dream causes his brothers to hate him even more. In this dream Joseph's sheaf rises up (קמה, from קום), and the sheaves of his brothers gather around it and bow down (ותשתחוין, from חוה). The verb חוה is used 170 times in the Old Testament and 23 times in Genesis, and while the common meaning is "to bow down," the connotation is not one of submission but rather the idea of respect, or sometimes fear. The combination of קום/חוה is an example of the downward/upward motif in the Joseph narratives, although in reverse order, perhaps reflecting not only the future of Joseph, but also the ultimate reversal of his fortunes. Joseph's brothers respond with, "Are you indeed to reign [המלך תמלך] over us?" Or are you indeed to rule [משול תמשל] over us?" The doubling of מלך indicates reigning over as a king, while the doubling of משל suggests ruling over as a tyrant. Joseph's brothers are quick to interpret his dream, but Genesis does not record Joseph doing so. Is this the correct interpretation?

Joseph's second dream, in verse 9, includes the first occurrence of ירח, "moon," in Genesis. Joseph recounts (ספר) this dream to his father and brothers, while his first dream is told (נגד) to his brothers alone. Jacob interprets this dream to include both him and Joseph's mother, but once again, Joseph provides no interpretation. Again, is this the correct interpretation?[20]

Jacob rebukes Joseph, and in his rebuke he adds to the dream הבוא נבוא, "must we come."[21] While Jacob assumes the sun and the moon refer to him and his wife Rachel, this does not appear to be the correct interpretation. Rachel, Joseph's mother, has already died (Gen 35:19), and Jacob never bows down to Joseph in these narratives, or even to Pharaoh. All

---

19. *Qal*: 15:5; 32:13; 41:49; *niphal*: 16:10. Genesis 16:10 and 32:13 concern the covenant and the counting of the seed of Abraham and Jacob respectively; 15:5 is the covenant and the counting of the stars; 41:49 is "could not count all the grain."

20. Pirson: "As for Joseph's first dream, it has become evident that there are some serious doubts regarding the correctness of the brother's interpretation. The same goes for the interpretation of Joseph's second dream. For a start, there is the observation that Israel's reading of the dream deviates from the brothers'. They interpret it in terms of kingship and domination. This element is lacking in Israel's exegesis" (*Lord of the Dreams*, 50). Pirson continues here at some length.

21. Infinitive absolute construction; note the doubling.

the interpreting has been provided by Joseph's brothers and father and is most likely incorrect.

> In contrast to the narrative's other pairs, no interpretation scene is devoted to Joseph's dreams. Rather, these visions are deciphered over the course of the plot, their solutions implied through the characters' reactions. Through the brothers' angry words, the reader learns how they have interpreted the first dream: "Do you mean to reign over us? Do you mean to rule over us?" (37:8); and Jacob's chiding of Joseph reveals his reading of the second dream: "Are we to come, I and your mother and your brothers, and bow low to you to the ground?" (37:10). The fact that these readings are not presented as actual solutions but rather as the characters' reactions, leads the reader to question their accuracy.[22]

Joseph's brothers do bow down to him, but not as their ruler. They bow down to Joseph first as a sign of respect (Gen 42:6; 43:28) and later perhaps out of fear (43:26; 44:14), but never to Joseph as one who rules over them. Jacob's interpretation of the second dream is likewise incorrect. The stars most likely refer to the brothers, who represent the people of Israel, but the sun and the moon are more likely a reference to all the foreign nations who also came to Egypt to escape death by famine (41:57; 47:13–14). Both sun and moon may be references to the pagan deities of those who bow before Joseph, as many foreign nations worshiped sun or moon or both.[23]

The first section of the Joseph narratives (37:1–12) serves as an introduction and prepares us for what takes place next. The depth of the brothers' animosity and jealousy toward Joseph has been well established and is seen as a simmering pot ready to boil over.

The brothers are pasturing the flocks near Shechem, so Israel sends Joseph to check on them and the condition of his flocks and instructs Joseph to return with a report. Considering the deterioration of Joseph's relationship with his brothers, this task again places him in the role of spy in

---

22. Grossman, "Different Dreams," 720.

23. Pirson postulates that the stars, sun, and moon might indicate the passing of time, and points to the use of numbers and the passage of time in all the dreams recorded in the Joseph narratives (*Lord of the Dreams*, 45, 52–59).

his brothers' eyes.[24] Joseph goes from the Valley of Hebron, where Israel
has his base camp, to Shechem.[25] He does not find his brothers there and
appears to be wandering around lost and confused when a man directs
him to Dothan. Dothan was located on the trade routes used by merchants
traveling to and from Egypt. In the verses that follow, we see the garment,
the dream, and the downward/upward motifs woven together.

When the brothers see Joseph in the distance, they conspire to kill
him. The title they give to Joseph, בעל החלמות, is translated as "the lord of
the dreams."[26] This is followed with the uncommon Hebrew form הלזה:[27]
"Behold, the lord of the dreams approaching." The plan is to kill Joseph and
throw him into one of the pits. Apparently, there is more than one pit from
which to choose, as Reuben suggests they chose one "in the wilderness"
(37:22). The word for "pit" (בור) is first used here in this context and used
a total of seven times in this chapter. The word בור, "pit, cistern," is not to
be confused with באר, "well." In this context, בור indicates a cistern or pit
that would be empty, perhaps used for storage waiting for a trade caravan,
or used for collecting water in the rainy season. The only previous use of
בור in Genesis is found in 14:10 in reference to "bitumen pits."

Joseph's brothers are still troubled by the dreams of Joseph and by their
interpretation, as evidenced by their statement "And we will see what will
become of his dreams." This concern appears repeatedly in the Joseph narratives, even following the death of Jacob (50:15–21). Reuben convinces his
brothers not to shed Joseph's blood, rescuing him (ויצלהו) from being killed
with the plan to rescue him from the pit (בור) later.[28]

Reuben seeks to save Joseph with the plan to cast him into the pit in the
wilderness, off the beaten path, that he might return to rescue him later
and restore him to his father. This is the first example of the restoration
motif in the Joseph narratives, although the plan fails to accomplish its
purpose. Either Reuben is attempting to fulfill his role as the eldest among

---

24. For more on this see chap. 4.

25. A distance of approximately sixty miles.

26. Westermann translates this as "dream-addict," or "master dreamer" (*Genesis: An Introduction*, 40).

27. Perhaps a reinforced demonstrative.

28. Vawter sees the interplay between Reuben and Judah and their striving for the leadership role among the brothers as evidence of two versions of the same story, "Reubenite
and Judaite versions of the history" (*Path through Genesis*, 246).

the brothers, or he has devised a plan by which he might restore himself to favor in his father's eyes after his affair with Bilhah (35:22). Judging from his reaction at finding Joseph missing from the pit in 37:29–30, Reuben's main concern seems to be himself and his restoration. He has lost his standing with his father and now his brothers. The narrator has included this piece of information as a sign of a realignment of leadership among the brothers.[29] As the text begins to unfold, we note the ascendancy of Judah as leader. It is interesting to note Reuben's use of imperatives when speaking to his brothers (also 42:21) contrasted to Judah's approach, as seen in 37:26–27.[30]

There is no mention of Joseph making any response to his brothers and their actions in these verses, but in 42:21 it says that Joseph begged his brothers. The brothers, minus Reuben, sit down to eat and discuss Joseph's fate. It is then that they see one of the caravans of merchants traveling the trade route to Egypt. Genesis 37:25 identifies it as a caravan of Ishmaelites. They are traveling from Gilead "down to Egypt" (להוריד מצרימה). Genesis always references traveling to Egypt as "going down" to Egypt, and when one leaves as "going/coming up" from Egypt. This is not a mere geographical notation.[31] This occurs first in 12:10 and then 13:1 as Abram goes down (ירד) and comes up (עלה) from Egypt. This is another example of the downward/upward motif of these narratives as well as one of the significant themes of the death-and-resurrection motif.

The narrator has deemed it important to make mention of the trade goods being carried to Egypt, gum (נכאת), balm (צרי) and myrrh (לט), which are similar to the items in Jacob's later gift to Joseph (43:11). Perhaps more interesting is the use of these trade goods in the embalming process. The narrator has established a definite downward/death theme in these verses.

---

29. Levenson comments, "At all events, the documentary source that has Reuben, the first-born, planning 'to save [Joseph] from [his other brothers] and restore him to his father' (v 22) shows Reuben distraught upon returning to find the pit empty (vv 29–30). His plan, more daring but also more responsible, as befits the first-born, fails altogether, and Judah's strategy, more modest but also less moral, may have failed as well. In the redacted text that now confronts us, all the brothers can be said to know for sure is that the favored son has disappeared and is unlikely ever to be restored to his loving father" (*Death and Resurrection*, 147–48).

30. Apparently this approach works well, as the brothers listen to Judah, and Reuben's voice is no longer heard. This is also seen as Reuben and Judah speak to Jacob in 42:37–38 and 43:3–14.

31. See chap. 5.

The brothers desire to kill Joseph; Joseph is thrown down into a pit; the merchants are going down to Egypt; the trade goods mentioned are used in the embalming process. Levenson notes:

> The son's descent into Egypt is a kind of death; his ascent to ruler- ship, a kind of resurrection. Whereas the pit is a metaphor of Sheol in the case of Joseph's first descent, in the case of his second, the metaphor is Egypt, or, to be more precise, slavery in Egypt. Each descent is a manifestation of his symbolic death, and with each, Joseph moves farther away from the source of his vitality—his family and his native land.[32]

Judah, seeing the Ishmaelite traders, devises a plan to save Joseph's life, while at the same time removing the nuisance from their presence. He says, "What profit is it if we kill our brother and conceal his blood?" מה-בצע, "what profit," from the root בצע, is used thirty-nine times in the Old Testament, with the primary meaning of "cut off." Derivations include "to cut off someone's lifeline, to do well, to make a profit." The original meaning was value indifferent, and it is unlikely that Judah is suggesting that he and his brothers should profit monetarily, but rather is pointing out that cutting off Joseph's life might indeed cost them in the long run. וכסינו, "and conceal/cover up," from the root כסה, "to make the covered invisible," illustrates Judah's concern. Hiding Joseph's body in a cistern might be a messy business best avoided. Judah's approach in dealing with his brothers is markedly different from Reuben's. While Reuben takes a more demanding, authoritative tone with his use of imperatives, Judah's word choices, "our brother," "his blood," "our flesh," show a friendly, less authoritative approach. Reuben attempts to use his position of preem- inence as firstborn, but it is the smooth, reasonable voice of Judah that distinguishes him and wins the day. This pattern will be repeated, and Judah will continue to move up into the role of leader among the broth- ers, as well as spokesman to Jacob.

Judah convinces his brothers to follow his plan, but one is faced with a difficulty in the narrative. In 37:25, 27, and 28 the Ishmaelites are

---

32. Levenson, *Death and Resurrection*, 152.

referenced, but in verse 28, the Midianites are spoken of, while in verse 36 it is the Medanites. The question is, Who sold whom to whom? Medanites or Midianites; Joseph's brothers; Ishmaelites—Who sold Joseph to whom? Pirson writes:

> I will start with the latter. The easiest solution, as seen in most translations, commentaries and exegetical studies, is to insert a yod, and turn Medanites (מדנם) into Midianites (מדנים). In that case Gen. 37:36 reads "the Midianites had sold Joseph to Egypt ... ," which is supposed to mean "the actions of the Midianites made Joseph arrive in Egypt (because of the trading activities of the Ishmaelites)." This solution not only looks nice, but it is also in accordance with the text: Midianite traders pull Joseph out of the cistern (v.28b), sell him to the Ishmaelites (v.28c-d), who take him to Egypt (v. 28e). So, in the end, the Midianites did cause Joseph to arrive in Egypt and be sold to Potiphar. In Gen. 39 the story of the sale is continued by the statement that Potiphar bought Joseph out of the Ishmaelites' hands—the perspective having changed from the selling to the buying party.[33]

This explanation makes sense and follows the text, but how did Joseph's brothers get cut out of the sale? It appears that the brothers, contemplating a sale, moved too slowly. The pit, located "in the wilderness," some distance from their campsite in order to serve Reuben's purpose for rescue, was hidden from sight. While the brothers talked over a possible sale with Judah, the Midianites carried out the transaction.[34] Even Joseph does not understand exactly what transpired, or the full, deadly intentions of his brothers. Later, in Egypt, as he hears his brothers talking about their deed (42:22-24), the puzzle is solved. It is ironic that the brothers' attempt to be rid of Joseph because of their concern

---

33. Pirson, *Lord of the Dreams*, 76; see also G. W. Coats, *From Canaan to Egypt: Structural and Theological Context for the Joseph Story*, Catholic Biblical Quarterly Monograph Series (Washington, DC: Catholic University of America Press, 1976), 17.

34. Wenham disagrees: "The alternative possibility that the Midianites pulled Joseph out of the pit and then sold him to the Ishmaelites, though favored by many Jewish exegetes, seems less probable" (*Genesis 16–50*, 355).

about his dreams coming to fruition is frustrated by the Midianites. This frustrating of their plans will result in the dreams' fulfillment.

In verse 28 we again see the doubling frequently employed by the narrator: וימשכו ויעלו, "they drew up and lifted up," Joseph from the pit. This is the first use of משך, "to draw, drag, lift out of," in Genesis, and used along with עלה, "to go up, ascend, climb," it completes a downward/upward action. Joseph is cast down into a pit and then drawn up and lifted up out of the pit. This first completed downward/upward motif cycle also provides a submotif of the death-and-resurrection motif—being cast down into a pit/raised up, lifted out.[35] When Reuben returns to the pit to rescue Joseph, he finds it empty and is distraught. He goes to his brothers and says: "The boy is gone, and I, where shall I go?" One can interpret הילד איננו as "the boy is gone; the boy is not there; the boy is no more (dead)." The word איננו is used each of these ways in the narratives (Gen 42:13, 36; 44:26, 30, 34). Note also the alliteration in Reuben's short, dramatic speech: הילד איננו ואני אנה אני־בא. Reuben does not know of the sale of Joseph, and the other brothers may be unaware as well, but again, for whom is Reuben most concerned? "Where shall I go?" may be a reference to facing his father, as the oldest son would be expected to deliver the news concerning Joseph, or this phrase may illustrate Reuben's despair, as his hopes of restoring his relationship with his father have been dashed.[36]

The brothers resort to deception as the way to deal with their problem. The garment motif comes into play as they take Joseph's tunic and dip it in the blood of a slaughtered goat: וישלחו...ויביאו, "and they sent ... and they brought" the tunic to Jacob. Some commentators treat the וישלחו... ויביאו as another example of the narrator's use of doubling and translate the phrase as "and they took ... and they brought."[37] However, the clearer meaning of שלח is "to send," with the implication of sending with someone. It appears that the brothers send the bloody tunic with servants to their father, and, after the initial shock had worn off, they arrive to

---

35. See chap. 5.

36. Pirson notes Reuben's apparent concern only for himself (*Lord of the Dreams*, 81).

37. Gunkel, *Genesis*, 355; Hamilton, *Genesis*, 2:426.

check on Jacob's reaction. This is not the last time they handle a delicate situation in this manner.[38]

The brothers leave the identification of the bloody tunic up to their father, הכר־נא, "please identify." Rather than lie to their father, they let him draw his own conclusions. The same phrase is employed by Tamar in 38:25 when she presents the signet, cord, and staff of Judah. Jacob comes to the conclusion Joseph's brothers are hoping for, and he proclaims that Joseph has been devoured by a wild animal; he has been torn to pieces (טרף טרף). The Hebrew טרף usually signifies meat of an animal improperly or violently killed, thus rendering it unfit for consumption or sacrifice.

In 37:34 we read of the mourning practices of the ancient Hebrews, which are repeated throughout the Old Testament. Jacob tears his garment or mantle and puts sackcloth (שק) on his loins and engages himself in the act of mourning many days. Apparently, Jacob's mourning exceeds what is considered to be customary, as his sons and daughters (daughters-in-law) rise up to comfort him (ויקמו). "They rose up to raise up his spirit." Jacob refuses to be confronted—raised up—saying: "For I will go down to my son to Sheol, mourning."[39]

This is the first occurrence of שאול, "Sheol," in the Old Testament Scriptures, which is significant to the death-and-resurrection motif. Here we now find the association of "Sheol" with "pit," which later in the Psalms and Prophets are used synonymously as references to going down to eternal death.[40] Note that "going down to Sheol" has no positive connotation, only negative. Whenever death is mentioned in a positive way, the phrase "gathered to one's people" or "sleep with one's fathers" is employed. Later in these narratives, when Jacob is preparing to die a peaceful death, he says: "Let me lie with my fathers" (Gen 47:30) and: "I am to be gathered to my people" (49:29, 33) and makes no mention of Sheol. Going down to Sheol is reserved for the godless, or those who

---

38. In Gen 50:16–18 the brothers send a message to Joseph at the death of Jacob by way of servants, and when they hear of a favorable reaction, they come in person.

39. Levenson: "To be separated from Joseph is, for Jacob, to be dead, and to be together with him is to live again" (*Death and Resurrection*, 151).

40. See chap. 5.

refer to the tragic circumstances of their lives as a going down to Sheol and a separation from God.

Jacob refuses to be comforted and weeps for Joseph. The verb בכה, "to weep," occurs fifteen times in Genesis, with ten of these occurrences taking place in the Joseph narratives.[41] As Jacob mourns for his son, Joseph is transported to Egypt and sold as a slave to Potiphar, a סריס, "royal official," of Pharaoh, שר הטבחים, "the captain of the guard"; סריס is a loanword from the Akkadian *sa resi*. Being sold into slavery is another downward movement and will be complemented with an upward move later in the narratives. Being sold into slavery is also the beginning of another important submotif of the death-and-resurrection motif.[42]

GENESIS 38

We now come to Genesis 38, which, at first reading, seems to have nothing to do with Joseph.[43] Neither Joseph nor any of the other brothers are mentioned in this account of Judah. The placement of this chapter appears problematic. It seems incongruent with the surrounding material, so some have attempted to explain its presence by suggesting that Genesis 38 was added by a later redactor of the Genesis text. Such an explanation does not properly address the question why the story of Judah and Tamar was included in the Joseph narrative in the first place; nor does it account for the peculiar positioning of the chapter within the larger narrative.[44] Others postulate that Genesis 38 is the end of the

---

41. Jacob: 37:35; Joseph: 42:24; 43:30; 45:14, 15; 46:29; 50:1, 17; Benjamin: 45:14.

42. See chap. 5.

43. Wenham: "The sudden switch of focus from Joseph on his way to Egypt (37:36) to Judah's marriage (38:2) has thrown many readers, who see chap. 38 as an irrelevant digression. This is because they have forgotten that chaps. 37–50 are not headed 'this is the story of Joseph' but 'this is the family history of Jacob' (37:2)" (*Genesis 16–50*, 369). Alter: "Many readers have sensed this tale of Judah and Tamar as an 'interruption' of the Joseph story, or, at best, as a means of building suspense about Joseph's fate in Egypt. In fact, there is an intricate network of connections with what precedes and what follows, as close attention to the detail of the text will reveal" (*Genesis*, 217).

44. See von Rad, *Genesis*. Speiser, indeed, views Gen 38 as an independent unit, having no connection to the Joseph drama (see *Genesis*, 299). Westermann, on the other hand, claims that Gen 38 and 49 are not additions to the Joseph story but form a conclusion of the Jacob story (see *Genesis 37–50*, 22). A quite different account is provided by Sarna, who invokes the midrash, commenting: "This digression heightens the reader's suspense at a critical moment in the Joseph Narrative, but the skillful blending of the chapter into the larger story shows

traditional material of Genesis and the following chapters, 39–50, were an addendum to the original. While there may be some reason and evidence to support these suggestions, they do not adequately address the questions of why this material is included in the narrative and why it is positioned in such a peculiar place.

Following Childs's focus on the canonical context and the text we have received, I consider Genesis 38 to be in its intended place and will examine the narrator's intent in placing it so.[45] The narrator has provided interesting clues. Of first significance is the use of similar biblical motifs in both Genesis 38 and the rest of the Joseph narratives. Within Genesis 38 we observe the garment motif, the restoration motif, the barren-womb motif, and the seed/fertility motif—all motifs that play an important part in the rest of the narratives. Present also is much of the same language and similar contexts. Both Judah and Joseph marry a foreign wife; both are deceived or are the victims of deception via a garment; both fulfill levirate law with their two sons; both have left or been removed from their father's household; and both prove to be leaders in their own context. There is also similar language, including the phrase הכר־נא, "please identify," in 37:32 and 38:25. E. M. Menn notes:

> Regardless of this narrative's prehistory, the final redaction of Genesis 38 in its present context is intentional and artful. The numerous verbal and thematic links between Genesis 38 and the larger Joseph story in which it is embedded, especially the chapters that immediately precede and follow it, point to this conclusion. These links integrate Genesis 38 into its current context and emphasize certain motifs through repetition. They also stimulate intertextual comparisons and contrasts that can serve as the starting points for creative biblical exegesis.[46]

---

that the digression is deliberate and the result of careful literary design, as noted in Genesis Rabba 85:3" (*Genesis*, 263).

45. Longacre, in dealing with the placement of Gen 38 and 49, speaks of the Joseph narratives as "two interwoven strands: the Joseph story and the broader concerns of Jacob and his family" (*Joseph*, 21).

46. E. M. Menn, *Judah and Tamar (Genesis 38) in Ancient Jewish Exegesis* (Leiden: Brill, 1997), 75–76.

It appears that the narrator purposefully sets up two interacting and interconnected stories by using two distinct introductions—one for each character.[47]

We have already noted in Genesis 37 Judah's ascendance over his elder brother Reuben. Reuben, the oldest, is the natural choice to influence and lead the twelve brothers, but it is Judah and his disarming ways that cause the brothers to rely on his guidance.[48] We see this trend continue in these narratives. In addition, there is another ascendance taking place. Joseph, the main character in Genesis 37, 39–50, begins these accounts as the father's favorite, the lord of the dreams, and the instrument God uses to interpret dreams and rescue his covenantal people from famine, but as the story continues, we see Joseph descend to a lesser position. He marries a pagan wife, the daughter of a pagan priest; even though he is the second-most powerful man in all of Egypt, he makes no attempt to find his father or reunite with him, and he puts his brothers through unnecessary tests. While Joseph descends, Judah ascends—another example of the downward/upward motif. Judah begins at the bottom: he plays a vocal part in Joseph's being sold into slavery; his two oldest sons die because of their godlessness; he loses his wife and seeks the company of a cult prostitute; and he has two sons through his own daughter-in-law, Tamar. Judah is not a heroic figure in these two chapters. However, Judah slowly ascends: he emerges as the leader of his brothers; he offers himself to take the place of Benjamin to his father (Gen 43:8–9), Jacob; he offers himself to take the place of Benjamin to Joseph (44:32–34); and, most notable, he receives the blessing of carrying the covenantal, messianic, and kingly line (49:8–11). Genesis 44:33, as indicated in the diagram below, is the precise point in the narratives that Judah and Joseph exchange positions.[49]

---

47. "Another distinct possibility is that with a true instinct for suspense in storytelling, the writer deliberately ran in this incident concerning Judah in order to leave his reader dangling for a while" (Longacre, *Joseph*, 24). "Yet, chaps. 38 and 46–50 are more coherent if one understands this to be a story of the emergence of the tribal groups of Israel more than that of an individual." See T. E. Fretheim, *The Pentateuch* (Nashville: Abingdon, 1996), 87. "Gen. 38 is a curious story, unrelated to its context. It must be treated independently." See W. Brueggemann, *Genesis: A Bible Commentary for Teaching and Preaching* (Atlanta: John Knox, 1982), 289.

48. See R. Syrén's discussion of Reuben and Judah in *The Forsaken First Born: A Study of a Recurrent Motif in the Patriarchal Narratives* (Sheffield: Sheffield Academic Press, 1993), 130–35.

49. Levenson, *Death and Resurrection*, 163–64.

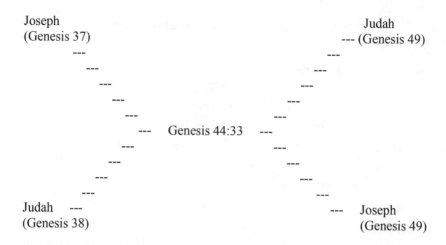

The Joseph narratives appear to be the tale of two brothers.[50] The narrator appears to use this chiasm as a way to show the transition from the patriarchal era (Joseph) to the tribal era (Judah). Later in Israel's history, we see this trend reversed when the Israelites return from the Babylonian exile. The rise of patriarchalism and the decline of tribalism would appear to be the cause. This provides one explanation for the sudden resurgence of Joseph and his reputation in Second Temple literature. Thus, the first two chapters of the Joseph narratives can be understood as two introductory chapters, one for each brother, which are then cleverly set up and woven into the rest of the narrative.

Genesis 38 begins with Judah "going down" (ירד) from his brothers and "turning aside" (ויט) to an Adullamite named Hirah. The combination of these verses shows a separation between Judah and his brothers. While the text does not identify the reason for this separation, if Genesis 38 is chronological to 37, Judah moves away from his brothers and father following the rebellion against Joseph. One can only speculate on the family dynamics following such an event, but the emotional state of Jacob and the hidden deceit of Judah and his brothers most likely brought about this separation.

In verse two, Judah follows the path of his uncle Esau and takes for himself a Canaanite wife. The Hebrew reads ויקחה ויבא אליה, "and he took her and went into her." Some have suggested that she was not his wife in

---

50. This title is not a reference to the Egyptian Tale of Two Brothers, although it is interesting that Gen 39 is often considered to be patterned after this Egyptian writing.

the proper sense, claiming that in early times the union was only temporary. If this is true, it calls into question Judah's period of mourning at
her death in verse 12, which refers to the daughter of Shua as Judah's wife.
Supportable or not, the result is three sons, Er, Onan, and Shelah. In verse
6 Judah takes a wife for Er, whose name is Tamar—meaning "date palm"—
and who is, in all probability, a Canaanite.

The text says that Er is the firstborn of Judah twice in as many verses
(Gen 38:6–7) in order to set up what follows. Er is wicked in the sight of the
Lord (יהוה), and the Lord puts him to death. This is the first time the tetragrammaton, יהוה, is used in the Joseph narratives. In fact, it is the first use
of any name for the Divine. This is also why some suggest that this chapter
was an addition by the Yahwist (J) into the original text,[51] or that Genesis
39 and following are a later addendum to Genesis.

There is no mention of what this wickedness of Er was, or by what
manner he was put to death by the Lord. As a result of Er being put to death,
Judah calls on Onan, his next son, to perform the duty of his brother in
order that Er will have offspring. Levirate law—brother-in-law marriage—
is only specifically referred to three times in the Old Testament (Gen 38;
Deut 25:5–10; Ruth), although I argue that Genesis 48 provides another,
unusual example.[52] Levirate law (Latin: levare, levis, "to raise up")[53] states
that the firstborn son of the union of Tamar and Onan, the brother-in-law,
would belong to the deceased Er and would therefore preserve his name
and preserve his property rights.[54] The Hebrew root ויבם is found only three
times in the Pentateuch, and the story of Onan is one of a very restricted

---

51. Speiser, *Genesis*, 1983.

52. I am referring to Jacob's adoption of Joseph's sons Ephraim and Manasseh. It appears
from the text that Jacob is taking the sons of Joseph to replace his sons Reuben and Simeon
(Gen 48:5).

53. Sarna provides another etymology: "When brothers dwell together and one of them
dies and leaves no son, the wife of the deceased shall not be married to a stranger, outside
the family. Her husband's brother shall unite with her: take her as his wife and perform
the levir's duty. This institution is known in Hebrew as *yibbum*, or 'levirate marriage' (from
Latin *levir*, 'a husband's brother'). The basic root meaning of the Hebrew is uncertain, but it
is believed to be 'procreate'" (*Genesis*, 266). Alter points to the connection to the "raising up
seed" of the original Hebrew (*Genesis*, 218).

54. Westermann: "The meaning of the custom is explained in Deut. 25:6: 'that his name
may not be blotted out of Israel.' It is only a secondary purpose of the levirate that the property of the deceased passes on to the one who is heir to his name, and is probably a later
accretion" (*Genesis 37–50*, 52).

number of narratives in the Hebrew Bible that depicts application of the law of levirate marriage (see Deut 25:5-10).[55] Levenson explains:

> In this way, the late brother can beget a child even after his death, and one of the most dreaded aspects of his own demise, the extinction of his name through the lack of a son, can be reversed. By a kind of legal fiction, his family brings something of their dead kinsman back to life, birth reversing death. Levirate marriage is a mode of redemption of the dead.[56]

Judah's command to והקם זרע לאחיך, "raise up offspring/seed for your brother," does not please Onan. Perhaps the wickedness of Er was repulsive to Onan, who felt no need to preserve his lineage. More likely, Onan realized he would inherit the firstborn portion of Er if there were no descendant. So, Onan ושחת ארצה, "spilled/wasted semen on the ground," in order to prevent offspring for his brother. This action is also wicked in the sight of the Lord, and Onan is also put to death. Note the opposite reality later in the Joseph narratives when the Egyptian people ask Joseph for seed that they and their ground might live, producing life (Gen 47:13-26).

Judah is in a difficult position. The proper thing to do according to levirate law would have been to have Shelah go to Tamar in order to produce offspring for Er and Onan; however, Judah is concerned that Shelah will also die (38:11). Perhaps Judah was unaware of the wickedness of his two oldest sons and thinks Tamar to be the common denominator in their deaths. So Judah sends Tamar to her father's house to live as a widow until Shelah grows up and can carry out his brother-in-law duties. However, when he does come of age, Tamar is forgotten (38:14). Not only did Onan withhold his seed from Tamar, but Judah is guilty of withholding Shelah's seed from her as well.

After a time, Judah's wife, the daughter of Shua, dies—the fourth use of מתה in six verses. When he is comforted, or after the time of mourning is past, Judah "went up to" (ויעל) Timnah. The verb עלה, here and in verse

---

55. See discussion of this institution in J. H. Tigay, *The JPS Torah Commentary: Deuteronomy* (Philadelphia: Jewish Publication Society, 1996), excursus 23, 482-83.

56. J. D. Levenson, *Resurrection and the Restoration of Israel* (New Haven: Yale University Press, 2006), 120-21.

13, is used in opposition to ירד, "to go down," in verse 1. The downward/upward movement continues and argues for the same author for Genesis 38 as the rest of the Joseph narratives. The purpose of this going up is to join in the shearing of his sheep. When Tamar hears that Judah is traveling in her direction, and because she sees that he has no intention of sending Shelah to fulfill the levirate law, she decides to take matters into her own hands. She takes off her widow garments, covers herself with a veil, and waits for Judah to pass by.

This provides an important addition to the garment motif as seen in these narratives. In Genesis 37, Joseph's garment was used to deceive his father, and now a garment is used to deceive one of the deceivers.[57] The motif provides a connecting unity in the text.

When Judah sees this woman at the entrance of Enaim, he assumes her to be a prostitute.[58] More precisely, he thinks she is a cult prostitute, as this is how he identifies her to Hirah, who is sent back to seek her out and deliver the promised payment in verse 20.[59] In verse 15, Judah uses זונה, "prostitute," and in verse 21, Hirah uses הקדשה, "sacred woman." It is unlikely that Hirah makes this assumption on his own.

Tamar asks Judah what he will pay her if she lets him "come in to her."[60] She is able to see that Judah is traveling with Hirah but with no other servants or flocks. This gives her an opportunity to ask for a pledge (ערבון) of his promised payment of a young goat. ערבון, found in verses 17, 18, and 20, is a loanword from Akkadian and is also found in 43:9 and 44:32. When Judah asks what she wants, she asks for his signet, his cord, and his staff, the insignia of a man of importance in Babylon, Canaan, and Israel (38:25).[61]

---

57. Note also that Jacob used the garment of Esau and the skin of a kid goat to deceive his father as well in Gen 27.

58. Alter, considering the meaning of the word Enaim, says: "If, as is quite likely, this place name means 'Twin Wells,' we probably have here a kind of wry allusion to the betrothal type-scene: the bridegroom encountering his future spouse by a well in a foreign land" (*Genesis*, 220).

59. Vawter, while agreeing that Tamar disguised herself as a temple prostitute, says that Judah's sin was simply one of lust and not against faith (*Path through Genesis*, 249).

60. Verse 2, ויבא אליה, "went in to her"; v. 16, הבה–נא, "please let me come in (to you)," and, כי תבוא אלי, "that you may come in to me"; v. 18, ויבא אליה, "he went in to her."

61. Levenson notes the connection here with Joseph in reverse (garment motif): "For just as it is Judah's seal, cord, and staff that serve to indict him (Gen. 38:18, 25), so it is Joseph's cloak that Pharaoh's wife employs as evidence for her false charge against the chaste steward of her

Judah agrees, the deal is done, the deed is done, and Tamar conceives by Judah and returns to her life of widowhood. When Hirah is sent back to Enaim with the young goat, no cult prostitute (sacred woman) can be found, and when he reports this to Judah, they agree to let things be lest Judah be laughed at. Obviously, a man of Judah's stature and lineage should not be consorting with a "holy woman."

Three months later, Judah receives the news that his daughter-in-law, Tamar, has been immoral, and not only this, she is pregnant as a result of her immorality. The length of three months is significant not because it has taken this length of time to show her pregnancy, but rather it is generally after a time of three (days, months, years) that a new life/resurrection occurs. Joseph is in prison three years before he is raised up; it is three days before the chief cupbearer is restored; and Joseph imprisons his brothers for three days before they are restored. The verb זנתה, "to be immoral," shares the same root as לזונה in verse 15, where Judah misidentifies Tamar as a prostitute. The verse could also be translated: "Tamar your daughter-in-law has committed prostitution. Moreover, she is pregnant by prostitution." Judah's response is to bring her out and burn her. The choice of punishment for prostitution is interesting. Later Levitical law required her to be stoned, but Judah calls for her to be burned. Perhaps this represents an earlier punishment for the immorality, although it is the prescribed punishment for the immoral daughter of a priest in Leviticus 21:9.

As Tamar is brought out, she sends word to Judah that she is pregnant by the man who owns this signet, this cord, and this staff. As in Genesis 37:32, we read הכר-נא, "Identify please." Tamar spares Judah humiliation by sending the items ahead of her. She could have waited until all were assembled but chose not to do so. Note the similarities to the events of Genesis 37 and 50. Items and reports are sent ahead with the words of "please identify" or just "please" (נא). Judah recognizes his belongings, understands what has happened, and declares Tamar to be more righteous (צדקה) than he because he withheld his son Shelah from her. This is the first use of צדק in Genesis, which occurs once more in 44:16, again spoken by Judah.

---

husband's estate (39:11–18). Whereas Judah's articles of attire testify to his moral and religious laxity, Joseph's cloak witnesses to his probity and his fear of sin" (*Death and Resurrection*, 160).

The narrator makes certain the reader knows that Judah and Tamar have no more sexual relations, ולא–יסף עוד לדעתה, "he did not know her again." Judah's previous relationship with Tamar fulfilled the levirate obligation and provided a son, Perez, for Er, as well as a son, Zerah, for Onan.[62] Any further relationships between the two would have been regarded as incest. Later, as the Hebrews established the lineage of Judah, traced back from the Messiah, Perez is in the line. Levenson tracks the story:

> Judah, ancestor of Boaz and thus of royal line from which David would hail, loses two sons, the second because of a refusal to fulfill the levirate requirement, "to provide offspring for his brother" (38:9; see Deut 25:5–10). Having refused to release his third son for fear the same fate would befall him, too, and mistaking his widowed daughter-in-law for a prostitute, Judah inadvertently fulfills the requirement himself. In the end of this strange and disquieting tale, full of odd twists and unexpected reversals, the man who lost two sons gains twins, as the widow whose in-laws neglected her gives birth to the boys who will carry on her father-in-law's tribe and her husband's name.[63]

This brings us to another significant death-and-resurrection submotif: the barren womb/opening of the womb.[64] This is another submotif shared by the brothers Joseph and Judah. Joseph is born from the barren womb of Rachel;[65] Judah's sons, Perez and Zerah, are effectively born from a barren womb as well. Because a barren womb in Judah's line would have brought an end to messianic hope, Perez's birth is of great importance. It is also important to realize the birth of Joseph from the barren womb of Rachel provided one who would save the people of Israel from destruction by

---

62. Kaminsky notes other patterns in this dual birth: "Often such patterns run even deeper. For example, the twin births of Jacob and Esau and of Peretz and Zerah involve an extremity, the color red, and a reversal of primacy between the children. ... Such repetitive patterns create a haunting effect in which narratives keep rubbing up against one another" (*Yet I Loved Jacob*, 73).

63. Levenson, *Resurrection and the Restoration*, 116–17.

64. See chap. 5.

65. Genesis 30:1: "Give me children, or I am as good as dead."

famine, thereby preserving the messianic line along with its hopes and promises.

GENESIS 39

The narrator returns focus to Joseph by reiterating how Joseph arrived in Egypt in the household of Potiphar (Gen 37:28, 36). He also continues his use of doubling by making two references concerning Joseph being "brought down" to Egypt already in verse 1 (הורדה/הורדהו). This next section of the narratives can be viewed as three main episodes: (1) in the house of Potiphar (39:2–20), (2) life in prison (39:21–40:23), and (3) the journey to the house of Pharaoh (Gen 41).

The first episode begins by emphasizing Joseph's separation from his father's house and being sold as a slave into the house of Potiphar. This is a threefold separation, similar to that of his great-grandfather Abram in Genesis 12.[66] Joseph is forced to leave his father, his father's household, and his homeland. We see here the beginning of two themes of the death-and-resurrection motif. The first is the separation/reunion, or three-stage separation/restoration submotif, and the second is the slavery/freedom submotif. At the beginning of this section we therefore make note of three downward movements that reflect the death portion of this major motif: (1) down to Egypt, (2) separation, and (3) slavery.[67] It appears that Joseph has arrived at the lowest point of his blessed life. The text, however, continues to make note that the Lord is with him and blessing him in all his endeavors.

Both 37:36 and 39:1 identify Potiphar as an officer of Pharaoh, the captain of the guard, with 39:1 adding that he is an Egyptian. There is much discussion linking Potiphar, the captain of the guard, with Potiphera, the priest of On in 41:45, 50; 46:20. פוטיפר (37:36; 39:1), which means "the one whom Re gives," and פוטי פרע (41:45, 50; 46:20) is another form of the same name.[68] Some suggest this is the same person, and various Second Temple writings

---

66. Abram is called by God to leave his father's house, his kinsmen, and his homeland.

67. Sarna contends, "The national identity of Joseph's master is repeated three times for emphasis (vv. 1, 2, 5), probably because the sale of Joseph into Egyptian slavery sets the stage for the looming enslavement and subsequent redemption of Israel" (*Genesis*, 271).

68. Westermann, *Genesis: An Introduction*, 61.

have encouraged this. There remains the question of job title—captain of the guard versus priest of On—which is difficult to resolve.

Being brought down to Egypt and sold as a slave represents a definite downward movement for Joseph. From being a favored son to being stripped and cast into a pit, to being lifted up from the pit and taken down to Egypt, we have already seen strong evidence of the downward/upward motif. Now, Joseph has been sold as a slave (downward), but the text shows an upward movement. The narrator relates that the Lord (יהוה) was with Joseph, and five times in the next five verses the Lord is named as the force that ensures Joseph is successful in all that he does.[69] Interestingly, only the narrator refers to the Divine as יהוה, "LORD"; Joseph always refers to him as אלהים, "God" (39:9).

The narrator continues to use the literary device of doubling with מצליח, "to be successful; to succeed," in verses 2–3, and ויפקדהו, "made him overseer," in verses 4–5. Joseph's status immediately rises from common slave to the overseer of Potiphar's household. The text reiterates three times (39:4–6) "and all that he had he gave into his hands," and by this repetition the narrator drives home the point that Joseph became more than a slave. Joseph is the steward of Potiphar's household, and Potiphar has no household concerns apart from the food he eats. All of this the Lord does for the sake of Joseph.

Joseph's upward mobility is about to be threatened. The second part of verse 6 notes that Joseph is handsome in form and appearance.[70] The narrator is setting up the story, for the good looks of Joseph do not escape his master's wife's notice, and she says to him: שכבה, "Lie with me" (39:7, 12). Joseph refuses, pointing out that the master has placed great trust in him and has entrusted everything in his household to him, apart from her.[71]

---

69. Wenham: "'The Lord was with Joseph.' It is a characteristic feature of the Jacob cycle that God promised to be with Isaac and Jacob (26:3, 24, 28; 28:15, 20; 31:3). Now the same thing is said about Joseph, twice here and twice in the introduction to the next section (39:21, 23). These remarks help to put the unfortunate events into perspective. Despite all the setbacks Joseph was about to face, God was on his side" (*Genesis 16–50*, 374).

70. Wenham notes that Joseph's mother, Rachel, is also described as having a lovely figure and a beautiful face (29:17). They are the only two people in the OT given this double accolade (Wenham, *Genesis 16–50*, 374; also see Alter, *Genesis*, 225).

71. Kugel notes that it is Joseph's refusal to succumb to Potiphar's wife's advances that distinguishes him from others in the OT (David, Judah, etc.). Therefore, this incident is often taken as the defining moment of these narratives (Kugel, *In Potiphar's House*, 24).

Joseph's position in the house of Potiphar is very similar to the position he is later to have in prison (39:22) and then in the land of Egypt (41:40). He is second only to Potiphar, as he will be second only to the jailer, as he will be second only to Pharaoh. I also argue that when the Joseph narratives come to a close, Joseph is second to his brother Judah as well. This "second position" is noted by the rabbis, who write that this is to remind Joseph, and us, that there is always one who is above us—God himself.[72] Joseph remains faithful and virtuous, asking, "How can I do this great wickedness and sin against God?"[73]

Potiphar's wife is persistent, continually encouraging him to lie with her.[74] One day, when all the men are absent from the household, Joseph goes in to do his work. Why?[75] Potiphar's wife has been forthright in making her desires and intentions known, and with all the male servants gone from the house, Joseph is placing himself in a very dangerous and compromising position. It is possible that Joseph is so faithful and dedicated to his work that he thinks it worth the risk, or perhaps Joseph is beginning to weaken, falling prey to temptation, desiring to give in to the woman's advances.[76]

---

72. Levenson also notes this: "The pattern reappears too many times to be coincidental. In each situation, Joseph rapidly ascends to the rank of second in command and enjoys in practice the powers of his superior denied him in theory. In Potiphar's house and in Pharaoh's palace, only one thing differentiates his master from Joseph, the wife in the first instance (Gen. 39:9) and the throne in the second (41:40). Indeed, it is precisely Joseph's stout refusal to yield to the wife's seductions that sets in motion the chain of events that brings him near the throne. The threefold pattern of ascent to the rank of second in command is a reenactment of the situation at the opening of the tale, when Joseph is presented in the role of the beloved son of Jacob (37:3)" (*Death and Resurrection*, 153–54).

73. The similarities to the Egyptian Tale of Two Brothers are interesting. In this tale the two brothers, Anubis and Bata, live together. Anubis is married, while his brother is not. Anubis' wife seeks to seduce Bata, but, like Joseph, he was virtuous and resisted. The wife then slanders Bata with false accusations in order to cover her own guilt. Bata is forced to flee from his brother, but in the end Anubis believes his brother and slays his wife and throws her into the river. Due to the antiquity of this document (1225 BCE), many believe the narrator of the Joseph story borrowed heavily from it. See J. Pritchard, ed., *Ancient Near Eastern Texts Relating to the Old Testament*, 11–14.

74. There are some who argue that Potiphar was a eunuch, which led to his wife's advances toward Joseph. For more on this see Kugel, *In Potiphar's House*, 75.

75. Sarna states: "A rabbinic tradition (Sot. 36b) interprets the phrase as a euphemism: Joseph actually succumbed to the woman's blandishments, but at the critical moment a mental image of his father inhibited him from sinning" (*Genesis*, 273).

76. Kugel: "But the second, represented in our passage by R. Yohanan and one half of the Rab-Samuel dispute, sees Joseph as something of a willing participant, a man given in to temptation. Now one support for this approach is adduced from the biblical narrative itself; it is the innocent looking phrase in 'Joseph went to the house *to do his work*'—which,

Joseph would be well aware of the lack of male servants, as he is in charge of everything, so it certainly seems strange that he could walk into this situation unawares.[77] Regardless, when she catches hold of Joseph's garment, he immediately reconsiders his location and his actions and he "fled and got out of the house" (ויצא החוצה וינס). This emphasis is also seen in verses 15 and 18 as Potiphar's wife tells her story.

As has been noted with Joseph's special tunic and Tamar's veil, once again, Joseph's garment becomes a means of deception. Just as his bloody tunic conveyed a false story, so also his cloak in the hands of Potiphar's wife is used to reinforce her lie.[78] Garments used to hide and deceive are a pivotal part of the garment motif in Scripture, and especially in the Joseph narratives. Potiphar's wife tells her story twice (doubling). Apparently, she has decided that if Joseph is not going to lie with her, he will not lie with anyone else. Her desire is not that Joseph should go to prison, but rather that he be executed. Death would have been the traditional and accepted punishment for a crime of such magnitude. Why then does Potiphar send Joseph to prison? Concerning this question, Wenham writes:

> This is a somewhat unexpected punishment, because convicted rapists were executed when both parties were free citizens (Deut 22:23–27). A slave assaulting his master's wife would certainly expect no better fate. But for some reason Joseph escaped the death penalty. Presumably his protestations of innocence, though unrecorded, were sufficient to convince Potiphar that his wife might not be telling the whole truth, so Joseph was given a lighter sentence.[79]

It appears that Potiphar is not convinced of Joseph's guilt.[80] Perhaps there have been similar difficulties with his wife in the past. For whatever reason, Joseph does not receive the death penalty as his punishment for

---

this second school of thought holds, is merely a euphemism for 'to satisfy his desires'" (*In Potiphar's House*, 95).

77. For more on this see chap. 4.

78. Westermann, *Genesis 37–50*, 67.

79. Wenham, *Genesis 16–50*, 377.

80. Sarna asks the same question. "19. he was furious. The text does not say at whom, an omission that may hint at an underlying ambivalence in his reaction. He must also have resented losing the services of so accomplished an administrator as Joseph" (*Genesis*, 275).

the accusation.[81] Potiphar delivers Joseph to prison. This term for "prison," אל־בית הסהר, is used twice in this account but nowhere else in Genesis. There were no prisons in ancient Israel's nomadic culture.

Joseph, who had risen to chief of Potiphar's household, again descends into the depths. This time the downward movement is to prison. This is also the beginning of another death-and-resurrection submotif: thrown into prison/released from prison.[82] So begins episode two of this section.[83] Joseph finds himself in the depths of prison, but once again "the LORD was with him and showed him mercy and gave him favor." The word חסד, "faithfulness, mercy, lovingkindness, loyalty, fidelity, upholding one's end of the relationship," is especially employed concerning the Lord's support for Israel and her leaders. Humphreys notes: "Rarely in the entire Genesis narrative is the very particular covenantal term 'hesed' used."[84] Because of the Lord's favor Joseph rises up once again, and the keeper of the prison places him in charge of all the prisoners. "Whatever was done there he was the one who did it" (כל־אשר עשים שם הוא היה עשה).[85] As in verses 2–5, the narrator states in verses 21–23 that it is the Lord who makes Joseph successful. Again, only the narrator actually uses the term יהוה in Genesis 37–50. Some scholars have suggested that this links Joseph with the patriarchs, with whom the Lord was also present. This may also explain the use of חסד in verse 21. The narrator sees Joseph as part of the patriarchal and not the tribal era.

GENESIS 40

Joseph's life in prison continues into Genesis 40 as two servants of the king of Egypt (מלך־מצרים) join him. The chief cupbearer and the chief baker have angered Pharaoh in some way, although the text does not specify. The captain of the guard appoints Joseph to be with them and attend to them.

---

81. "What or who is the object of his (Potiphar's) anger is an open question, and must remain so. In any case he is angry because he has been put into such a situation. ... The nature of the punishment is a sign that he is not convinced of Joseph's guilt" (Sarna, *Genesis*, 67). Speiser also makes note of the "surprisingly mild punishment of Joseph" (*Genesis*, 304; also see von Rad, *Genesis*, 361).

82. See chap. 5.

83. Life in prison: Gen 39:21–40:23.

84. Humphreys, *Joseph and His Family*, 211; see Gen 32:11; Ps 40:2.

85. The last three words are missing in the LXX.

One might speculate that the title "captain of the guard" (Gen 40:3–4) identifies the head of the prison as Potiphar, who was previously referred to as the "captain of the guard." This might add understanding to Potiphar's reaction to his wife's charge. Perhaps he simply removed Joseph from his house and took him to work.

One night, both of these prisoners "dream a dream" (ויחלמו חלום), each his own dream with its own "interpretation" (כפתרון). The narratives return us to the dream motif begun in Genesis 37, and once again the dreams occur in pairs. Joseph inquires of the two men as to why their faces are downcast, to which they reply that each of them dreamed a dream, but there is no one to interpret these dreams (פתר). The dreams were stirring enough that they realize, or at least suspect, they are a message of some sort. Joseph claims that interpretations (פתרנים) belong to God and offers to make the interpretations for them. Note the use of ספר with these dreams because they have the number three incorporated within them.[86]

This is Joseph's first time to interpret dreams. As previously noted, he never interpreted his own dreams.[87] In 40:9–11 the chief cupbearer recounts (ויספר) his dream. He tells of a vine with three branches. The vine budded, blossoms burst forth, and clusters ripened into grapes, which the chief cupbearer pressed into Pharaoh's cup, then placed the cup in Pharaoh's hand. Joseph identifies the three branches with three days and proceeds to tell the cupbearer that in three days Pharaoh will lift up (ישא) and restore (והשיבך) him to his former position of responsibility. Note the return to the restoration motif, which frequently finds its climax after a time period of three. Sarna, commenting on the use of three, says: "The recurrence of the number three indicates specifically three days, three branches, three stages of growth, three actions performed; and both 'Pharaoh' and his 'cup' are mentioned three times. It is quite likely that Joseph actually has knowledge of Pharaoh's impending birthday celebration, as Bekhor Shor and Ibn Ezra suggest."[88]

---

86. See 37:5 and also 38:24 for a brief discussion of the number three. Note also chap. 5.

87. Pirson: "From the dream-episodes as told in Gen. 40 and 41, it becomes clear that during his imprisonment Joseph has both acquired the art of reading dreams and the art of making people see things the way he does" (*Lord of the Dreams*, 90).

88. Sarna, *Genesis*, 278.

We see more of the downward/upward motif, but this time it is not Joseph but rather the cupbearer. It is interesting how Joseph, not directly involved in the chief cupbearer's dream, attempts to use it as a means to escape his life of imprisonment. This is the first time the text mentions Joseph taking any action on his own behalf, relying on his own skill to provide a personal rescue. Later rabbinical sources believe this is the reason that Joseph is initially forgotten and remains in prison two more full years. He did not trust exclusively in God, who had thus far protected and prospered him.[89]

The fact that Joseph relays גנב גנבתי, "I was indeed stolen" (40:15), out of the land of the Hebrews, is interesting. This may provide a clue that better explains the chain of events that led to his being brought down to Egypt. While Joseph was thrown into the pit by his brothers, he was stolen from the pit by the Midianites and sold to the Ishmaelites, who in turn sold him into slavery in Egypt.[90] Joseph also maintains his innocence in regard to his prison sentence, which he equates with the pit (בבור). It is likely that the prison was built below ground level and thus referred to as a pit.

Joseph has interpreted the chief cupbearer's dream, and the interpretation has been favorable; now the chief baker is anxious to have his dream interpreted as well. He tells Joseph about three cake baskets on his head, and in the top basket there were all manner of baked goods for Pharaoh. However, birds were eating the bread goods out of the top basket on his head. Joseph quickly provides an interpretation; however, this time it is less than favorable. Joseph tells the chief baker that the three cake baskets represent three days, and in three days Pharaoh will lift up (ישא) his head—from him—and hang him on a tree, where the birds will eat his flesh.[91] While the chief baker also shows a downward/upward motif, it is certainly not positive. He goes down to prison only to have his head lifted

---

89. Targum Pseudo-Jonathan: Genesis 40:14. Here the Targum adds, "Joseph abandoned his trust in heaven and put his trust in a human being." See also chap. 4.

90. See notes on 37:25–28.

91. Sarna here discusses a possible alternate reading: "However, since verse 20 uses a single phrase to indicate the fate of both officials, and since the 'removal of the head' is expressed in Hebrew by a different verb (cf. I Sam. 17:46), and verse 22 indicates that his punishment was not decapitation but impalement (41:13), many scholars regard the preposition 'off' (Heb. me'-aleikha) as a dittograph, an unintentional scribal insertion influenced by the last word of the verse. As a matter of fact, the word does not appear in all Hebrew manuscripts or in the Vulgate translation. ... Impaling, and not hanging, was a widely used

off and be raised up and hanged from a tree. On the third day, Pharaoh's birthday, Joseph's interpretations came to fruition, but the chief cupbearer forgets him (וישכחהו).

GENESIS 41

Genesis 41 begins with the third episode of this section—Joseph's journey to the house of Pharaoh. Verse 1 notes the passage of time. Since the dreams of the chief cupbearer and chief baker, Joseph has spent "two entire/whole years" in prison (ויהי מקץ שנתים ימים). It is unusual for the Hebrew to be so specific in marking two "entire/whole" years. This makes Joseph's stay in prison a duration of three years and is the narrator's way of pointing to another restoration after a specific time of three. Again, a pair of dreams will play a significant role in Joseph's destiny.

This time it is Pharaoh who dreams dreams, and there are two dreams, and each is recounted (ספר) twice: first by the narrator and then by Pharaoh himself. As before, when ספר is used in connection with dreams, there are numbers involved. This time it is the number seven (שבע). In each of the dreams in the Joseph narratives, those who dream the dream are themselves present in the dream, as active participants or as observers.

In Pharaoh's first dream (vv. 1–4) he was standing by the Nile, when behold, seven cows, "attractive and plump," came up out of the Nile and fed in the reed grass. Then, behold, seven cows "after (them) came up after them" from the Nile, ugly and thin, and stood beside the other cows on the bank of the Nile. The ugly, thin cows ate up the seven attractive, plump cows.

At this point Pharaoh woke up, then fell asleep and dreamed a second time. The narrator makes sure we understand that these are two separate dreams as he preserves the doubling style. In this dream (vv. 5–7) seven ears of grain, plump and good, were growing on one stalk. And behold, after them sprouted up seven ears, thin and blighted by the east wind. And the thin ears swallowed up the seven plump, full ears.

In the morning Pharaoh's spirit is troubled (ותפעם רוחו), and he calls out and sends for his magicians and wise men and recounts (ויספר) his

---

mode of execution in the ancient Near East. (Cf. Deut. 21:22f; Josh. 10:26; I Sam. 31:10)" (*Genesis*, 279–80); see also Wenham, *Genesis 16–50*, 384; Alter, *Genesis*, 232.

dreams, but none can interpret (פותר) them. Finally, after forgetting for two whole years, the chief cupbearer says to Pharaoh: "My sins I remember today" (41:9; את-חטאי אני מזכיר היום). The chief cupbearer goes on to explain to Pharaoh that when he and the chief baker were in the house of the captain of the guard—in custody in prison—they each "dreamed a dream," and a young Hebrew interpreted their dreams for them, and it came to pass just as he said.

Pharaoh sends for and calls Joseph, and they quickly bring him out of the pit (ויריצהו מן-הבור). This is the second time that prison is referred to as "the pit" (40:15). When Joseph has shaved and changed his clothes, he comes before Pharaoh. Joseph was in no shape to stand before Pharaoh coming straight up from the pit of prison. Egyptian culture preferred being clean shaven, and an exchange of his prison garments for garments suitable to stand before the king was necessary. This appears to be a continuation of the garment motif. Elsewhere in the Old Testament we read of the exchange of garments of sackcloth (mourning) for robes of rejoicing (Ps 30:11), which usually refers to a restoration of one's status in the eyes of God. Therefore, this garment exchange could be understood as another downward/upward movement, as is Joseph's being brought up from the pit of prison. The reversal of Joseph's fortunes is seen in the garment exchange. He has been stripped of his beautiful garment and thrown down into the pit, but now he is raised up from the pit of prison and clothed in new, clean garments. This ascending is preparing the reader for what follows.

Pharaoh says: "I have dreamed a dream and there is no one who can interpret it." He says he has heard of Joseph's ability to give an interpretation. Again, Joseph gives credit to God (אלהים) as the one who will give a favorable answer to Pharaoh. Since Joseph has not yet been told of the dreams, how does he know that the interpretation will be favorable? Perhaps he means that God will indeed favor Pharaoh with an answer, which has eluded him thus far, or maybe those who brought Joseph out of the pit and cleaned him up have already recounted the dreams to Joseph. By this time the entire household of Pharaoh was aware of the dreams and the lack of interpretation.

In verses 17-21 Pharaoh recounts his first dream to Joseph. There are some additions in his recounting compared to the narrator's version. In verse 19 we see the addition of "such as I have never seen in all the land of Egypt," in reference to the poor, ugly, thin cows. It seems that Pharaoh added this for the benefit of the Hebrew, Joseph. The Hebrews were known to be herders and shepherds of livestock. Pharaoh wanted to make clear that Egypt has better-looking stock than the second set of seven cows in his dream. He also gives more information about the dream than the narrator. In verse 21 he tells how the seven ugly, thin cows ate the seven plump cows: "But when they had eaten them no one would have known that they had eaten them, for they were still as ugly as before." Pharaoh has been playing this dream over and over in his head and has either imagined more or fleshed out the details in order to encourage an interpretation. He then recounts his second dream, after the text makes it clear that he awoke after the first (41:4). His recounting of the second dream follows that of the narrator. Pharaoh then informs Joseph that no one has been able to explain his dreams.

Joseph tells Pharaoh that his dreams "are one" (41:25) and that God has revealed to Pharaoh what he is about to do. Each pair of dreams in the Joseph narratives is interpreted "as one" in order to arrive at the greater meaning. "Are one," אחד הוא, is repeated again in verse 26 but does not indicate there is one dream; rather, it indicates to Pharaoh that there is one meaning—they share the same interpretation. As in verse 15, Joseph asserts that God has done something. It is God who gives the interpretation of dreams (v. 15). It is God who is telling you what he is about to do (v. 25), and the same again in verse 28.

Joseph interprets that seven plump cows and seven good ears of grain represent seven years of plenty, and the seven lean and ugly cows as well as the seven empty ears are seven years of famine. First come the seven years of plenty in the land of Egypt, but then will arise seven years of famine that will cause all to forget the years of plenty. "The famine will consume" (וכלה הרעב) the land (41:30).

Joseph continues in verse 32 saying that the "doubling" (השנות) of Pharaoh's dreams means that the thing is "fixed" (נכון) by God, and God will bring it to pass shortly. "The doubling fixes it" may well be the narrator's way of explaining the use of doubling throughout these narratives.

He employs doubling as a means to fix the authority and prove the veracity of his writing.[92]

Having provided the interpretation to Pharaoh's dreams, Joseph volunteers advice on how to deal with the next fourteen years. This is unsolicited advice, but since Joseph has shown his wisdom in the area of interpretation, Pharaoh is likely to listen to his suggestions. Joseph presses his advantage and uses this opportunity to further his situation. He has nothing to lose. At worst, he will be sent back to the pit of prison. Following the interpretation of Pharaoh's dreams no one asks, Why? Why is God sending a famine? Why is he angry with us? These common responses, found elsewhere in Scripture, are missing.

Joseph tells Pharaoh to choose (ירא, "raise up, select) a man discerning (נבון) and wise (וחכם). Joseph knows that he is in a position to fill the job description. The excitement and amazement at his interpretation may not last, so he moves quickly. He encourages Pharaoh to choose a man, discerning and wise, set him over the land of Egypt, appoint overseers, take one-fifth of the produce, and store up grain for food. This grain will be a reserve "so the land may not perish in the famine" (ולא־תכרת הארץ ברעב). The verb כרת, "to cut," gives the idea of being "cut off": "so the land may not be cut off in the famine." Famine/deliverance is another of the death-and-resurrection submotifs. As is evident here in Genesis 41, famine does not just result in the death of people; it is also seen as the death of the land. When the rain returns and the seed sprouts, a new life, a resurrection, takes place.[93]

A brief excursus on the prophet Daniel is in order. Much has been said concerning the similarities between the lives and times of Joseph and Daniel, and, since the accounts of Joseph and Daniel feature in two different sections of the canon, in the Torah and in the Writings, we should pay some attention to the latter character.

The similarities are too striking to have been missed by the people of Israel in Second Temple times and beyond. Both Joseph and Daniel were

---

92. See Sarna and footnote 53. Wenham writes: "Doubling also shows that 'God is in a hurry to do it.' In the immediate context, Joseph's remark refers to the forthcoming famine, but in the context of the book as a whole, it has a deeper significance. Some years earlier Joseph had dreamed a pair of dreams announcing that one day his father and brothers would bow down to him. That prophecy too is established, and God is hurrying to do it. So once again the narrative is hinting at the next development within the story" (*Genesis 16–50*, 394).

93. See chap. 5.

taken to a foreign land against their will—Joseph to Egypt and Daniel to Babylon. Both are noted for their faithfulness and reliance on God in their difficult circumstances. Joseph and Daniel interpret dreams for the rulers of these foreign lands, giving credit to God. Both are raised up in stature and esteem as a result. Daniel is thrown into a pit of lions as Joseph is thrown into a pit, although the placement in the narratives is distinct in each case. The text says Joseph is "a man in whom is the spirit of God," (Joseph), and of Daniel "you have the spirit of the gods in you." There are other similarities, but in Daniel 7 we see a departure as Daniel begins to have apocalyptic visions. However, in the end Daniel and his explicit death-and-resurrection character is well recognized.[94]

It is possible that the Daniel account helped resurrect Joseph's character in Second Temple times. The similarities are striking, and the explicit death-and-resurrection nature of Daniel 12 would have drawn attention to the figure of Joseph and the downward/upward movement of his life.

Having examined the six dreams of these narratives, there is one aspect yet to be considered. All of the dreams involve either food or time, in some cases both. Joseph's first dream involves sheaves of grain bowing down, and the chief cupbearer's and the chief baker's dreams have both food and time elements, as do the dreams of Pharaoh. This leaves only the second dream of Joseph. If it follows the pattern of the other dreams, its interpretation may become clear. Jacob thought Joseph's dream meant that Joseph's brothers, he himself, and Joseph's mother would bow down before him one day, but this is not the correct interpretation. When we consider the food and time aspects, the meaning changes. The eleven stars are indeed Joseph's brothers, but the sun and moon represent other nations associated with the sun and moon (e.g., Mesopotamia: Saba—moon; Egypt—sun). All of these will bow down before Joseph, not because he rules over them, but because they have come before him seeking food during the famine. When we add the numbers together, 11+1+1=13, thirteen is the number of years from the time of the dream until Joseph begins his work of collecting the grain, which

94. These similarities have been noted by several scholars, including A. Steinmann, *Daniel*, Concordia Commentary Series (St. Louis: Concordia, 2008), 37–39; J. J. Collins, *A Commentary on the Book of Daniel*, Hermeneia (Minneapolis: Fortress, 1993), 39–40.

will be distributed to the starving nations.[95] Thus, we have a more plausible interpretation of the first pair of dreams since Joseph does not provide one.[96]

Verse 37 represents the beginning of a new stage in Joseph's life. While this new stage is exciting and paramount to the story, it is also disturbing. This section begins Joseph's transition from a Hebrew to an Egyptian.[97] Joseph's proposal as how to deal with the upcoming famine pleases Pharaoh, and he says to his servants: "Can we find a man like this, in whom is the spirit of God?" Pharaoh says that since God has shown Joseph these things and because there is no one as discerning and wise, "You shall be over my house, and all my people shall order themselves as you command" (literally: "and according to your command, all my people shall kiss the ground"). "Only as regards the throne will I be greater than you" (רק הכסא אגדל ממך).

Joseph has experienced a dramatic reversal, the greatest of his life. He has been raised up out of the pit of prison to the position of second in command of all Egypt. Again we see the downward/upward motif in the life of Joseph. This is also the fulfillment of the death-and-resurrection submotif of thrown into prison/released from prison.[98] As mentioned, in each reversal or upward movement in these narratives, there is always someone greater than Joseph. His father, Jacob; Potiphar; the captain of the guard in prison; Pharaoh; and, in the blessings, Judah.

Joseph has received his appointment, and Pharaoh takes his signet ring from his hand, clothes him in garments of fine linen, puts a gold chain around his neck, and makes him ride in his second chariot. This is the earliest suggestion of horses in the Old Testament (see also Gen 46:29; 47:17; 49:17). Note also the garment motif as representing Joseph's rise to favor. Once again, a special robe designates his special status. As Joseph rides in this second chariot, dressed in his robe, servants go before him and call out אברך, "bow the knee." This is most likely an Egyptian word similar to the Hebrew meaning "to kneel."[99]

---

95. See Pirson for a discussion on the numbers and the passage of time (*Lord of the Dreams*, 57).

96. For more on this see Pirson, *Lord of the Dreams*, 50–52, 55–59.

97. See chap. 4.

98. See chap. 5.

99. Hamilton, *Genesis*, 506; von Rad, *Genesis*, 372. Sarna: "Abrek! An exclamation found nowhere else. Its meaning was already lost by rabbinic times. A fanciful interpretation, ab rek

Pharaoh gives Joseph an Egyptian name, צפנת פענח (Zaphenath-paneah).
There is much discussion concerning Joseph's new name and not a little
disagreement. Sarna writes:

> **Zaphenath-paneah** Traditional exegesis connects the name with
> Joseph's penchant for interpreting dreams, seeing in the first ele-
> ment a derivation from the Hebrew stem *ts-f-n*, "to hide," and ren-
> dering the second, contextually, "elucidate." The name would thus
> mean "revealer of hidden things." However, an Egyptian origin
> is evident, and a widely held view regards it as the transcription
> of *ḏd-p',-nṯr-'iw.f-'nḫ*, "God speaks; he lives." The Septuagint tran-
> scribed it *psonthomphanech*, which seems to represent the Late
> Egyptian word *psontenpa'anḫ*, which means, "the creator/sustainer
> of life." This latter interpretation has the advantage of being appro-
> priate to Joseph's mission as vizier.[100]

Among many of the suggestions there is a general theme of life held in
common.[101] I prefer the translation "God speaks and he lives," which also
holds to the life theme.[102] This aspect would certainly be in keeping with
the ongoing death-and-resurrection motif, but also reflects more specifically Joseph's role in saving and preserving the lives of many. Following
his name change, Joseph is given a wife, אסנת, "Asenath," the daughter of

---

(=rex), 'father of the king' (cf. Gen. 45:8), is found in the targums (cf. BB 4a) and is reflected
in the Peshitta, 'father and ruler.' Medieval Jewish commentators took the term to be a verb
formed from the noun berekh, 'knee,' meaning 'bend the knee!' In Akkadian, abarakku is the
term for a steward of the temple and the chief steward of a private or royal household. The
word may well be Egyptian, and 'b-r.k, meaning 'attention!' has been suggested" (Genesis, 287).
Alter identifies this as of Egyptian origin with the likely meaning of "make way" (Genesis,
240). On the range of meanings proposed for this word, see F. Brown, S. R. Driver, and C. A.
Briggs, *A Hebrew and English Lexicon of the Old Testament*, rev. and corrected ed. (Oxford:
Clarendon, 1968), 7–8; L. Koehler and W. Baumgartner, *The Hebrew and Aramaic Lexicon of the
Old Testament*, rev. ed. (Leiden: Brill, 1994), 1:10; Botterweck, Ringgren, and Fabry, *Theological
Dictionary of the Old Testament*, 279–81; *Biblia Hebraica Quinta*, 177*–78*.

100. Sarna, *Genesis*, 287–88; Brown, Driver, and Briggs, *Hebrew and English Lexicon*, 861;
Biblia Hebraica Quinta, 178*; Koehler and Baumgartner, *Hebrew and Aramaic Lexicon*, 1046–47;
W. A. VanGemeren, ed., *The New International Dictionary of Old Testament Theology and Exegesis*
(Grand Rapids: Zondervan, 1997), 3:839–40.

101. Josephus: "hiding discoverer"; Steindorff (1905): "the god has said 'he will live.'"

102. On this translation see von Rad, *Genesis*, 373; Vawter, *Path through Genesis*, 264. The
Vulgate renders his name as *Salvatorem mundi*.

Potiphera, the priest of On.[103] Joseph is becoming more Egyptian, a reality that raises difficult questions in the minds of his fellow Hebrews. Not only has Joseph married a foreigner: she is also the daughter of a pagan priest.[104]

Joseph goes about the work of preparing for the upcoming famine by collecting grain during the years of bounty. Verse 49 says the grain was "like the sand of the sea" (כחול הים), "and he ceased to count it (measure it) for it could not be counted (measured)" (כי חדל לספר כי–אין מספר). Note the similarities to the covenantal language used in describing Abraham's descendants.[105]

Before the famine arrives, Joseph and Asenath have two sons. Joseph names the firstborn מנשה, "Manasseh," which is derived from the verb נשה, "to forget." This verb occurs only once again in the Torah (Deut 32:18).[106] Joseph chooses the name Manasseh because "God has made me forget all my hardship and all my father's house." Joseph's name choice for his first-born son is a difficulty. How could a good Hebrew dismiss his father and family from his life?[107] We understand the issues with his ten brothers, but Benjamin and his father, Jacob, have not participated in Joseph's hardship. Perhaps Joseph, not having all the information surrounding his sale into Egypt, is upset that Jacob made no effort to search for him. Joseph has no idea that Jacob thinks he is dead. Nevertheless, this name choice will be a problem for Joseph in the future (Gen 48:13-20). The Jewish rabbis will also struggle with its implications.[108]

Joseph names his second son אפרים, "Ephraim," which comes from the verb פרה, "to be fruitful, to make fruitful." Joseph's message through Ephraim's name is, "God has made me fruitful in the land of my affliction." The names of Joseph's sons indicate a reversal of fortune and point to an

---

103. See notes on Gen 39:2.

104. Targum Pseudo-Jonathan deals with this difficulty by claiming that Asenath was the daughter of Dinah and only raised in the household of Potiphera.

105. In Gen 16:10 the *niphal* form of ספר is used, while the *qal* form is used in 32:13 and here in verse 49. See also Wenham, *Genesis 16–50*, 397.

106. Here in Genesis is the only *piel* conjugation of נשה.

107. Pirson: "This remark on forgetting his father's house sheds a not entirely favourable light upon Joseph. All the more so, since Joseph has been the man in charge for at least a year now (and perhaps even more)—and he has not made any attempt yet to contact his family in the land of Canaan. Nor will he for years to come!" (*Lord of the Dreams*, 92).

108. See chap. 7.

upward trend. Joseph can now forget all his troubles (i.e., family problems, slavery, prison) because he has been blessed and raised above them to a position of power. Even in the land of Egypt, the land of his slavery, the land of his imprisonment, a foreign land away from his people, God has made him fruitful.[109]

Why did Joseph not use his new power, position, and authority to go and search for his family—especially Jacob and Benjamin? He had the resources available to him, and the reigning Pharaoh looked on him with favor. Why did he choose not to seek his family? The names of Manasseh and Ephraim may be Joseph's way of officially forgetting his past life and family. It appears that Joseph has forsaken his Hebrew roots and has adopted the Egyptian culture and context.

Verse 53 begins by announcing that the seven years of plenty have come to an end. Now, the seven years of famine begin. The narrator points out that this famine occurred "in all the lands" (בכל-הארצות), but in Egypt "there was bread" (היה לחם). When the people of Egypt are "famished," Pharaoh sends them to Joseph. "Go to Joseph. What he says to you, do." Joseph sells grain from the storehouses to the Egyptian people. Soon "all the earth/all the land" (וכל-הארץ) came to Egypt to buy grain, "because the famine was severe" in all the land/over all the earth. When these people of other lands came before Joseph, they would have prostrated themselves, bowing down before him—a partial fulfillment of his second dream.

GENESIS 42

The end of Genesis 41 sets up the events of 42–47. The severe famine spreads far beyond the borders of Egypt, as indicated by the end of Genesis 41 (Gen 41:53–57) and certainly to the land of Canaan and to Joseph's Hebrew family. In verse 1, Jacob learns that there is grain for sale in Egypt, and he says to his sons, "Why do you look at one another?" Apparently, there has been much discussion over what to do in the midst of the famine, and Jacob, having learned of grain in Egypt, calls them to action. "Go down to there [Egypt] and buy grain for us from them so that we may live and not die." The irony of "going down" to Egypt to "be saved" should not be lost on the

---

109. Longacre: "Perhaps the names given to his sons indicate a certain disposition on Joseph's part to settle down in Egypt and forget all the unpleasant and painful past" (*Joseph*, 47).

reader. Egypt was often thought to be a dangerous, even evil place. Thus, going down to Egypt seeking life is a strange reality. Yet, each of the patriarchs faced famine and gave thought to "going down to Egypt" to escape death. Abraham "went down" (Gen 12:10), Isaac was told not to go down to Egypt (26:1–2), and Jacob sends his sons down and will later journey there himself (46:1–7). All of this sets up the life-giving, or salvific, role of Joseph for the household of Jacob; famine is the beginning of one of the death-and-resurrection submotifs.[110]

Ten of Joseph's brothers go down to Egypt. Jacob is unwilling to send Benjamin for fear he will be harmed and lost to Jacob. Benjamin would have been a grown man. It has been twenty-two years since Joseph disappeared, and Jacob has moved Benjamin into his place as favored son, and because of what happened to Joseph, he is overprotective of his youngest. Nowhere in the Joseph narratives do we discover any animosity toward Benjamin by the other brothers. Perhaps they have learned their lesson and amended their ways—this appears to be of interest to Joseph as well. So, the sons of Israel (בני ישראל) come to buy grain among the others who come from Canaan. This picture brings to mind the multitudes who come to the holy mountain for a great banquet feast of Isaiah 25. The explicit death-and-resurrection theme of Isaiah 25 points back to Joseph and his salvific role as the provider of food for many nations.

Joseph's brothers come before him and "bowed themselves before him, faces to the ground" (וישתחוו–לו אפים ארצה). Genesis 42:7–8 says that Joseph recognizes them (v. 7); "he recognized them, but treated them like strangers" (ויכרם ויתנכר אליהם), and then in verse 8: "Joseph recognized his brothers but they did not recognize him" (ויכר יוסף את–אחיו והם לא הצרהו). The narrator uses doubling once again to emphasize that the brothers are unaware of with whom they are dealing, while Joseph knows immediately they are his brothers. His brothers, bowing before him, cause Joseph to "remember" (זכר) the "dreams which he had dreamed" (42:9). However, in each dream there had been eleven brothers who had bowed down before him (eleven sheaves, eleven stars). Thus, Joseph devises a way to discover what has become of his other brother. He may be concerned that

---

110. See chap. 5.

his brothers have acted against Benjamin in some way, considering their past actions against him.

Demonstrated here in Genesis 42 is the motif of forgetting/remembering. While most readers are quick to make note of a forgiveness theme in the Joseph narratives, the forgetting/remembering motif is much stronger and more prevalent. Joseph, who has "forgotten" his past (41:51), is forced to "remember" (זכר) when he sees his brothers bowing, and he remembers his dreams. This motif will continue throughout the narratives and help tie these narratives to the rest of the Torah. Exodus, after bringing us up to date with the sons of Israel in Egypt, connects us to the Joseph narratives with these words: "And God heard their groaning, and God remembered His covenant with Abraham, with Isaac and with Jacob. God saw the sons of Israel—and God knew" (Exod 2:24–25).

Joseph accuses the brothers of being spies sent to "uncover the nakedness of the land."[111] This is the same concern the sons of Bilhah and Zilpah had in Genesis 37:2 and the feelings of all the brothers when Jacob sent Joseph to them in 37:14. Joseph turns this back on them, as he will do with other past remembrances. The phrase לראות את-ערות הארץ, "to see the nakedness of the land," is very powerful. Such language used elsewhere in the Bible, including the expression "uncover the nakedness of" (also 42:12), most commonly refers to incest (Lev 18; 20). Here, in a spying context, the brothers are being accused of looking for the weaknesses of the land, the country, and the people, with the implied accusation that they intend to attack Egypt, capitalizing on these weaknesses.[112] Upon this accusation, the brothers proclaim their innocence, saying: "We are honest men" (נחנו כנים אנחנו). This is repeated in verses 19, 31, 33, and 34. Joseph continues to accuse them, forcing them to identify themselves further. In verse 13 they respond: "We your servants are twelve brothers, the sons of one man in the land of Canaan: behold, the youngest is with our father this day, and the one is no more." The brothers do not identify Joseph as being dead, as Jacob does in verse 38.

---

111. Pirson: "In his youth he himself was the messenger (or provider?) of slander: he used to be a spy himself. Now, Joseph appears to be accusing his brothers of an act he was not unfamiliar with himself" (*Lord of the Dreams*, 95).

112. Sarna, *Genesis*, 293.

In verse 15, Joseph begins to reveal his plan. Using the word בחן, "test," Joseph tells them their younger brother must come before him in order to prove their claims. While בחן is used only twice in the Torah (42:15–16), it occurs thirty-two times in the Old Testament, chiefly in the poetical and prophetic books. Generally, it is the Lord (יהוה) who does the testing. While there is often concern expressed because Joseph seems too harsh in the testing of his brothers, Joseph is not only seeking information; he wants to see a change of attitude and heart among his brothers.

"As the Pharaoh lives/by the life of the Pharaoh," this is what must happen to prove their innocence and the truth of their words. One of them must go to Canaan and return with Benjamin while the rest remain in Egypt. Joseph then confines them together, in custody/prison, for three days. As Joseph was unjustly imprisoned in Egypt for three years, so his brothers are placed in custody on false charges for three days. Here we see the submotifs of three-stage separation/restoration, as well as the motif thrown in prison/released from prison.[113] Both demonstrate the downward/upward movement of these narratives.

After the third day, the brothers have had plenty of time to think, wondering why they have been accused of being spies (42:5). Joseph shows he is a reasonable man by giving them another option. "Do this and you will live, I fear God/I fear the gods." One of the brothers must remain in custody while the others may carry grain to their households. Then they must bring the younger brother back to verify their story and free the imprisoned one, "and you shall not die" (ולא תמותו). This prompts an immediate discussion among the brothers, who speak in Hebrew, unaware that Joseph can understand them (42:23), because there was an interpreter (המליץ) between them.

In their conference (vv. 21–22) the brothers associate their current situation with their misdeeds of the past. It seems their actions concerning Joseph twenty-two years previous have haunted them. They refer to their guilt (אבל אשמים אנחנו), "truthfully we are guilty"; they speak of ignoring Joseph's begging in "the distress of his soul" (צרת נפשו); and they think this is why "this distress" (הצרה הזאת) has come on them. This is the first indication that Joseph protested during the events that transpired long ago in

---

113. See chap. 5.

Canaan, although it is reasonable to assume that he did not go quietly into
the pit.[114] As Joseph listens to his brothers argue, he picks up information
that he likely did not previously possess. Reuben, unknowingly, reveals
to Joseph that he had made an attempt to save him. While we note that
Reuben's attitude toward his brothers and his self-absorption have not
changed in twenty-two years (37:21–22, 29–30), he may have unwittingly
saved himself from being the one chosen to remain behind in prison in
the land of Egypt.[115] Joseph chooses Simeon, the second born, to be bound
before their eyes and remain behind. Reuben summarizes the thoughts
of all the brothers when he says: "So now there comes a reckoning for his
blood" (ותם–דמו הנה נדרש).

Joseph is moved to tears by their words, but he hides his emotions in
order to continue his plan for testing his brothers. He chooses Simeon,
binds him before their eyes—a stern object lesson and reminder—and
gives orders to fill their bags with grain and replace each man's silver in
his sack. The word for "sack" changes from שק in verse 27 to אמתח in verse
28, back to שק in verse 35, and back again to אמתח in 43:12. When the brothers find the silver in their sacks, they are afraid and say: "What is this that
God has done to us?" (42:28, 35; מה–זאת עשה אלהים לנו). This is the question
Pharaoh did not ask when warned of the famine that was coming. The
brothers' devotion to Simeon is being tested. There will be a greater risk in
returning to Egypt under such circumstances. Will the brothers set aside
their personal safety and well-being to return with Benjamin and restore
Simeon? Again we see an example of the separation/reunion submotif.[116]
As for the brothers, they are beginning to wonder when this will all come
to fruition and what will result.

Upon the brothers' arrival in Canaan, they relate all that has happened
to their father, Jacob. The only addition is "you shall trade in the land"
(42:34). The brothers may be trying to convince Jacob—and themselves—
that this might turn out to be a good thing. Jacob is far from convinced
and points out that they have bereaved him his children. "Joseph is no

---

114. Alter, *Genesis*, 247.

115. Speiser, *Genesis*, 322, notes that Simeon was imprisoned because he was the next in
seniority to Reuben, who was spared because Joseph remembered him as his protector. See
also Sarna, *Genesis*, 295.

116. See chap. 5.

more, Simeon is no more, and now you would take Benjamin. All this has come against me." This language, similar to Reuben's in Genesis 37:30, is immediately responded to by Reuben. He responds in accordance with his personality—a bit dramatically—"Kill my two sons if ... ," "Put him (Benjamin) in my hands." Again, Reuben is ignored as Jacob refuses to let Benjamin go down to Egypt. Alter notes that perhaps Reuben means well but completely misjudges the situation: to his father who has lost two sons, he offers the prospect of killing two grandsons.[117]

Jacob's words are, "His brother is dead, and he is the only one left." Jacob means the only one left of Rachel's sons; nevertheless, the words must have been painful to the other nine. Jacob says if Benjamin "goes down" and is harmed on the way it will "bring down" his gray hairs to Sheol (שאולה). Note the downward movement as Jacob uses the term "Sheol" with its negative connotation once again (37:35).

GENESIS 43

The famine remains heavy (כבד) on the land, as Joseph warned, and the family of Jacob eats all the grain they bought in Egypt. Even Jacob realizes that another journey to Egypt is imminent, and he tells his sons to "Go again, buy" (שבו שברו). This time it is Judah, not Reuben, who speaks. The narrator makes abundant use of doubling to emphasize the importance of his speech.[118] Judah reminds his father of Joseph's words and then stands firm, saying: "If you will send our brother with us, we will go down and buy you food. But if you will not send our brother with us, we will not go down." The narrator uses ישראל instead of יעקב for the father, who in verse 6 laments: "Why did you treat me so badly as to tell the man that you had another brother?" It is ironic to see Israel being tricked time and time again—by his sons and now by Joseph—when one considers the deeds of his younger years and the meaning of his name יעקב.[119]

---

117. Alter, *Genesis*, 250.

118. Verse 3: העד העד, "spoke solemnly"; v. 7: שאול שאל, "questioned carefully"; v. 7: הידוע נדע, "could we know."

119. יעקב, "Jacob," meaning "deceiver, supplanter, heel grabber." In living up to his name, Jacob tricks Esau and Isaac in the matter of his birthright and then engages in a cyclical battle of trickery with his uncle Laban.

Judah's words in verses 8–10 show how much he has matured and taken over the role of leader among the brothers. Judah takes full, personal responsibility for Benjamin and his safety. "Send the boy with me"; "We will arise and go that we may live and not die" (ונקומה ונלכה ונחיה ולא נמות). Again the irony; they must go down to Egypt in order to live and not die. Note the significant difference in the offers of Judah and Reuben. While Reuben offers the lives of his two sons, Judah pledges (ערב) himself, promising to bear the blame/sin forever.[120] The first time that ערבון occurs in Scripture is Genesis 38:17, 18, 20, with Judah and Tamar as the main characters. The repeated use of ערב shows the connection of Genesis 38 with the rest of the Joseph narratives. Note the change of circumstances as they coincide with Judah's change of stature. Judah is beginning his upward trend. In verse 10, Judah scolds his father for not relenting sooner, and Jacob does not rebuke him. We see Judah's growing authority and respect within the family.

Jacob gives in to Judah, but also shows his own authority by telling them what to bring "the man" in Egypt. The list of balm, honey, gum, myrrh, pistachio nuts, and almonds is similar to the list of items the Ishmaelite traders were carrying to Egypt (37:25), choice fruits of the land. Israel also instructs them to take double the money to replace that which was found in the mouths of their sacks. Finally, he says: "Take also your brother" (ואת־אחיכם קחו). He also says, "May God Almighty ..." (ואל שדי); this is the third name used to identify the Divine in the Joseph narratives. It is a common patriarchal term and was last used by Isaac in his blessing of Jacob (35:10–12). While Israel calls on God Almighty to grant mercy before "the man," it appears he does not have a positive outlook. He expects the worst. "If I am bereaved, I am bereaved" (שכלתי שכלתי). Then, the brothers "arose and went down"; again the downward/upward motif.

When they arrive in Egypt in verse 16 and Joseph sees Benjamin with them, he tells the stewards of the house to bring them into his house and slaughter (טבח טבח) an animal and make ready for them to dine with him at noon. Note the difference between טבח טבח, "slaughter," and the טרף טרף, "devoured, torn" of 37:33. Once more, the brothers are fearful, for they have

120. Vawter, *Path through Genesis*, 271, who once again sees this as evidence of two different accounts (Reuben's and Judah's) of the same event.

been separated out and brought to Joseph's house. They imagine only evil design, so they approach the steward, saying: "We came down" (ירד ירדנו) the first time to buy food. They go on to say they found "the full weight," the entire amount in their sacks, and have returned it along with more in order to purchase food. The steward assures them: "Peace to you, do not be afraid" (שלום לכם אל–תיראו), "your God has put this treasure in your sacks." At this point Simeon is returned and reunited with them—the separation/reunion submotif.[121] This gesture seems to calm them, and "they washed their feet" (וירחצו רגליהם; 43:31),[122] and prepare the gift for Joseph.

When Joseph arrives, the brothers "bowed down to him to the ground" (וישתחוו ארצה). Again, in verse 28, "They prostrated themselves" (ויקדו וישתחו). Finally, Joseph sees the fulfillment of his dreams as all eleven brothers are bowing down before him. Joseph immediately asks concerning the welfare of their father, and when he is assured of his health, he looks to Benjamin—"He lifted up his eyes." Benjamin is referred to as "his mother's son," a bond that Joseph and Benjamin share. Benjamin was also the only one of the brothers not involved in the trials and tribulations of Joseph. Joseph proclaims: "God be gracious to you, my son" (אלהים יחנך בני). Joseph is overwhelmed by the emotions of the moment and leaves their presence to find a place to weep. This weeping may be more than brotherly love for Benjamin. It could also signify that the other brothers have passed the first portion of the test. After weeping, he washes his face and comes out. "Controlling himself, refraining himself" (ויתאפק) is first used here and once again in 45:1.[123]

Genesis 43:32 then expounds on the eating arrangements. Egyptians do not eat with Hebrews because it is "an abomination" (תועבה הוא). We see this phrase again in 46:34, where it is further explained that every shepherd is an abomination to Egyptians. Sarna writes:

> Joseph eats alone undoubtedly because of his exalted status; but the segregation of the Hebrews was due to the Egyptian feeling of racial and religious superiority that engendered contempt for foreigners,

---

121. See chap. 5.

122. Joseph washes his face.

123. From the verb אפק, which always occurs in the *hithpael* form.

who were regarded as unclean. Herodotus (Histories, 2.41) reports that because the cow was taboo to Egyptians but eaten by Greeks, no native of Egypt would kiss a Greek. ... It is therefore likely that Egyptian particularism asserted itself here because the Hebrews were shepherds—an abhorrent profession (46:34)—and because they ate sheep—an abomination to Egyptians (Exod. 8:22).[124]

There were three distinct tables: (1) Joseph by himself, (2) Joseph's brothers, and (3) the Egyptian servants. The seating arrangement for the brothers was "the first-born according to his birthright and the youngest according to his youth." The brothers are amazed at the order, for no one had explained or instructed Joseph in this matter.[125] There are several sub-motifs at play in this event. The separation/reunion and the three-day/three-stage separation-and-restoration submotifs are evident.[126] We also see an example of the meal motif, which is common in the Old Testament. Even with the shock of finding themselves seated in proper order, the brothers are finally at ease, even though Benjamin's portion is five times greater than each of theirs. This may be another test as Joseph continues to ascertain the attitude among his siblings. The text says: "They drank and were merry with him" (וישתו וישכרו עמו). The Hebrew should be taken to read: "They drank and became intoxicated with him."

GENESIS 44

Genesis 44 begins with Joseph preparing the next part of his brothers' test. He commands his steward to fill the men's sacks with food and put their silver in the mouths of the sacks. Then he adds: "And put my cup, the cup of silver [גביעי גביע הכסף], in the mouth of the sack of the youngest."[127] This

---

124. Sarna, *Genesis*, 302.

125. Sarna, *Genesis*, 302. "It is likely, in fact, that the Egyptians, too, are amazed that the vizier should invite foreigners, especially shepherds, to dine at his house."

126. See chap. 5.

127. Sarna notes that the composition of the goblet—silver—is not to indicate its worth; rather, the main point is that Hebrew כסף, "silver, money," is a key word reiterated twenty times in the accounts of Joseph and his brothers in Egypt (Gen 42–45). The brothers sold Joseph for twenty pieces of silver (Gen 37:28); now he harasses and tests them with silver (Sarna, *Genesis*, 303; also Alter, *Art of Biblical Narrative*, 173).

is the first occurrence of the noun גביע, "goblet, cup."[128] After the brothers leave, Joseph sends his steward after them with instructions to speak these words: "Why have you repaid evil for good?" "Is it not from this that my lord drinks, and by this he practices divination?" (נחש ינחש; also 44:15). The *piel* form of נחש means "to seek, give an omen, practice divination." According to Leviticus 19:26 and Deuteronomy 18:10, the sons of Israel are not allowed to practice divination, and when they do so it is considered an act of great evil (2 Kgs 17:17; 21:6; 2 Chr 33:6). Whether Joseph is using this language as a means to conceal his true identity or he has become a true Egyptian, either choice raises concern among the rabbis, as evidenced in the targums. For example, Targum Onqelos reads for 44:5: "And moreover he carefully tests with it."[129]

When the steward overtakes them, the brothers are amazed at the accusation. So certain are they of the innocence of their party they say: "Whichever of your servants is found with it shall die, and we will also be my lord's servants." The steward agrees: "Let it be according to your words" (גם-עתה כדבריכם), and yet, when he repeats the words they reflect the words of Joseph in 44:17 and not the words of the brothers. He says: "He who is found with it shall be my servant, and the rest of you shall be innocent" (נקים). The plan has been set up in detail, and the cup is found in Benjamin's sack. Each part of Joseph's plan has in some way reflected his own life's tribulations at the hand of his brothers. They have been deceived; they have been forced to go down to Egypt; they have been imprisoned; and now they may be enslaved. In all of these things Joseph is testing to see how they will respond to unjust trials, the same that he has endured.

The response of the brothers is to rend their garments as their father Jacob did when he believed Joseph to be dead (37:34). Then everyone loads up his donkey and returns to the city. They could have left Benjamin with the steward according to the agreement, but they all return to the city together—another part of the test passed. Verse 14 begins with: "When Judah and his brothers ..." Judah is now recognized as the leader, not

---

128. Also found in Exod 25:31–34; 37:17–20; Jer 35:5. It is frequently coupled with divination, as in Gen 44:5, 15.

129. According to Westermann, the question of whether Joseph actually practiced divination is not appropriate to the text. The purpose is merely to give force to the accusation (*Genesis 37–50*, 132).

Reuben—the transition appears to be complete. When they arrive at the house of Joseph, he is there, and once again they fall to the ground before him. Joseph asks: "What is this doing you have done?" or "What deed is this you have done?" It is Judah who responds in verse 16. Note in particular ומה נצטדק, "Or how can we justify ourselves?" The Hebrew צדק, used here in the *hithpael* form, is found only one other place in Genesis—38:26, when Judah declares Tamar to be more righteous than he is. Here again we see Genesis 38 and its place in the Joseph narratives justified.

What of the guilt, the misdeed (עון) that Judah says God has found out? Is he referring to the theft of the goblet, or perhaps the previous sin of the brothers against Joseph? Judah clearly states that all the brothers are Joseph's servants because of this event, even though Joseph protests and says that only the man in whose hand the cup was found shall be his servant. His words to the rest, "But as for you, go up in peace to your father" (עלו לשלום אל–אביכם), are no comfort to them. Even though Joseph has shown grace by offering servanthood/slavery instead of death to the guilty one, there is no way they can go to their father in peace if Benjamin is left behind in Egypt.

In 44:18–34, Judah addresses Joseph. This is the second-longest human speech recorded in Genesis, with the longest being Jacob's delivering of the blessings to his sons in Genesis 49.[130] Judah begins by asking permission to speak to Joseph because Joseph is as Pharaoh himself. It appears that Judah delivers his speech to Joseph out of the hearing of the rest of the brothers. Judah carefully chooses the direction he wants his speech to go.[131] Judah inserts the idea that Joseph asked about their father in the beginning, but this is not in 42:13, 16, 20. However, this is the direction he wants his monologue to follow, arguing from what he perceives as the point of greatest strength. It is not coincidental therefore that the word אב, "father," occurs fourteen times in Judah's speech. Judah is manipulating the facts from all the previous dialogues in order to influence the outcome. He demonstrates a keen understanding of human nature and uses this ability

---

130. For Judah's speech, 223 words, and 268 for Jacob's.

131. Wenham: "Aspects of earlier dealings that could annoy Joseph are not mentioned, while Judah includes fresh details of his father's reactions that he hopes will soften Joseph's stance; in fact, he mentions his father fourteen times" (*Genesis 16–50*, 425; see also Alter, *Art of Biblical Narrative*, 174–75).

to convince. Jacob's well-being is Judah's main concern, and he senses that this somehow goes along with Joseph's interest in the father.

Judah, in verse 20, refers to Benjamin as "the child of his [Jacob's] old age" (וילד זקנים קטן).[132] The first mention of Jacob's love for Benjamin, ואביו אהבו, "his father loves him," shows that Benjamin has taken Joseph's place as most loved among the sons. Note the distinct downward/upward—upward/downward movements in this speech. Verse 21, הורדהו, "bring him [Benjamin] down"; verse 23, ירד, "come down [to Joseph]"; verse 24, עלינו, "we went up [to Jacob]"; verse 26, לרדת, "go down," and וירדנו, "we go down"; and verses 29 and 31, in reference to bringing down to Sheol. Thus far, there have been four references to being brought down to Sheol, with two of them in this speech of Judah. All four occurrences are in reference to Jacob being brought down to Sheol, but the condition in which he will be brought down varies. Genesis 37:35, אבל, "mourning"; 42:38, ביגון, "grieving"; 44:29, ברעה, "in evil"; 44:31, ביגון, "grieving." These conditions cannot be cast in a positive light.

Beginning in verse 30, Judah starts to draw conclusions for Joseph. "His soul (Jacob's) is tied up with his soul (Benjamin's)." On their return, when Jacob sees the boy is not with them, he will die. Note the connection between death and Sheol. Now, Judah tells of the pledge for the safety of Benjamin he made to Jacob.[133] Judah connects himself back to the Tamar incident once again (38:18–26). This time he intends to act justly. He insists that he be kept as slave in the place of Benjamin, saying: "How can I go up to my father if the boy is not with me? I fear to see the evil that would find my father." There are several significant points that come together in this last part of Judah's speech. First, there is a substitutionary motif shown, as Benjamin has taken Joseph's place, and also in Judah's pledge and offer to take Benjamin's place. This motif continues throughout the narratives. Second, the brothers, and especially Judah, have passed the final portion of Joseph's test.[134] Instead of trying to rid themselves of the most loved

---

132. Genesis 37:3 refers to Joseph as "the son of his old age."

133. ערב; see 43:9; also 38:17–18, 20.

134. Longacre notes that Judah's reaction in particular removes all doubt in Joseph's mind concerning the integrity of his brothers. Their actions in the past will not dictate their present and future actions (Longacre, *Joseph*, 48–49). Kaminsky writes, "Although Judah may think that Jacob's favoritism is unfair, he has come to recognize that it is a fact of life he must respect.

son, they stand up and defend him. It appears the brothers have changed dramatically.[135]

More important, at the finish of Judah's speech, when he offers himself as a substitute for Benjamin, we see the transformation of Judah. In Genesis 37, Judah desires to be rid of Joseph, and in 38 he learns the hard way to be responsible for his family—via Tamar. Then, in Genesis 43, Judah, the leader among the brothers, pledges to Jacob that he will be responsible for Benjamin's safety. Now, in Genesis 44, Judah actually takes responsibility for Benjamin, even insisting he take his place.[136] In his speech to Joseph, Judah gradually emerges as the second hero in these narratives, and in fact, he has become the central hero as we see the crossing over in 44:33 of Joseph and Judah.[137]

Whether Judah suspects the identity of Joseph is debatable:[138] (1) the brothers are treated according to their ages twice (43:33; 44:12); (2) Joseph insists on their bringing back their younger brother; (3) Joseph is excessively interested in the well-being of the brothers' father; (4) when Joseph sees Benjamin, he says: "My son, God be gracious to you"; (5) the brothers knew that Joseph was on his way to Egypt after his sale.[139] Is this the reason for Judah's emphasis on the suffering of his father in his speech?

GENESIS 45

Judah's speech delivers a passing grade to the last portion of Joseph's test, and Joseph can no longer "control/restrain" himself (להתאפק; see also 43:31). Joseph clears the room and then "makes himself known" (בהתודע) to his

---

This surely shows some growth in Judah's character, even if the brothers still exhibit certain character deficiencies at the end of the narrative" (*Yet I Loved Jacob*, 68).

135. Westermann also notes that this is the first time that Joseph hears what happened at home when the brothers came back without him (*Genesis 37–50*, 136).

136. Sarna: "The one who had been responsible for the sale of Joseph into slavery (37:26f.) now unwittingly offers to become the slave of his own victim! The story has come full circle, and the stage is set for the dramatic denouement, brought on by Judah's noble gesture of self-sacrifice and the moving image of his father's misery" (*Genesis*, 307). Westermann rightly points to this as the turning point of the Joseph story. He also claims that this is the first time the Bible speaks of vicarious suffering (*Genesis 37–50*, 137). This claim is arguable when one considers Gen 22 and God's provision of a ram to take the place of Isaac as sacrifice.

137. See figure on page 83.

138. Pirson, *Lord of the Dreams*, 107–8; though he argues that the language of Judah's speech indicates Joseph as dead, he then lays out the possibility that the brothers suspect his identity.

139. Pirson, *Lord of the Dreams*, 107–8.

brothers. The first question he asks: "Is my father still alive?" Joseph still does not completely trust his brothers, who are so dismayed by this turn of events (נבהלו) that they cannot even respond. In verse 4, Joseph once again identifies himself, with the addition אֲשֶׁר-מְכַרְתֶּם אֹתִי מִצְרָיְמָה, "whom you sold to Egypt."[140] Is this an assumption on Joseph's part? The facts, as he knows them, might lead to this conclusion. Joseph continues by telling his brothers that it was not they who sent him to Egypt, but rather, it was God's plan to preserve life, to keep alive many survivors, to preserve a remnant.[141] The remnant motif begins early in Genesis with Noah and his family (7:1, 23) and carries through all Scripture. This motif is significant because it shows the preservation of the people of Israel and especially the messianic line. Joseph was called to play an integral role in this preservation. The brothers deserved death for what they had done to Joseph, but what they received was life—and the life of many others. This is the first time the idea of God turning evil into good, or using evil to bring about good, is set forth in Scripture (see also Gen 50:19-20).[142] This is also the only overt, explicit theological teaching in these narratives.[143]

Joseph's brothers are skeptical, and this skepticism never really subsides. After the death of Jacob in 50:15-17, the brothers are still fearful that Joseph will take his revenge. The Hebrew word לְמִחְיָם, "to preserve life," used in verse 5, is repeated again in 50:20 as Joseph repeats his belief that God used their evil deeds to accomplish good. Verse 7: "And God sent me before you to preserve for you a remnant on earth and to keep alive for you many survivors." This is the first time שְׁאֵרִית, "a remnant," is used as a noun in the Old Testament and the second use of לִפְלֵיטָה, "survivors," in

---

140. See discussion on Gen 37.

141. Alter notes that Joseph's speech is a "luminous illustration of the Bible's double system of causation, human and divine" (*Genesis*, 45).

142. Brueggemann interprets this: "Based on the two explicit statements of 45:5-8 and 50:19-20, theological exposition is concerned with the providential ways of God's leadership. God's way will triumph without the contribution of any human actor, including even Joseph himself" (*Genesis*, 292). Sarna: "The brothers had indeed acted with evil intent; yet behind it all had been the hidden, guiding hand of Divine Providence investing the base deeds of men with meaning and benign purpose. Joseph reiterates this conviction to his brothers after his father dies (50:20)" (*Genesis*, 308-9). Kaminsky: "Joseph makes clear that the purpose of his election was not so that he could lord it over his brothers, but so that he could be in a position to save their lives" (*Yet I Loved Jacob*, 69).

143. This statement and its echo in Gen 50:20 provides Longacre with the title of his book, *Joseph: A Story of Divine Providence*.

Genesis. The first is in 32:9 in reference to Jacob "surviving/deliverance/escape" from Esau. There is a distinct sound of covenantal language to these words. Joseph does not say "to preserve for *us* a remnant"; instead, he continues to separate himself from his brothers. Perhaps he considers the new life illustrated in the names of his sons, Manasseh and Ephraim, his new direction—his Egyptian identity.

Joseph continues his claim that it was God who sent him to Egypt in verse 8. He points to his position of authority, saying God has made him "as a father to Pharaoh" (לאב לפרעה), meaning that he has become a source of life for Pharaoh, and not only Pharaoh but all of Egypt. There is another explanation for this phrase. It may be that Joseph is older than Pharaoh. This is generally overlooked because Joseph himself is young, but considering how easily Pharaoh installed Joseph as second in command after hearing his advice (41:37–40) and his dismay at the age of Jacob (47:8–9), it remains a possibility. Note that Joseph uses the term משל, "ruler," in speaking to his brothers. This is the same word used in 37:8 when his brothers respond to his first dream, "Are you indeed to rule over us?"

In verses 9 and 13, Joseph is now in a hurry to see his father. Much is evident from the imperatives, which follow in quick succession: מהרו, "hurry up"; אל-תעמד, "do not tarry"; ועלו, "go up"; רדה, "come down"; considering his lack of initiative in searching out his father over the last nine years, this urgency is interesting. Joseph tells them they will dwell in the land of Goshen, and they will be near him: "you and your sons and the sons of your sons" (ובניך ובני בניך). Joseph promises to provide for them (כלכלתי) because the famine will continue for five more years. He will not let them come to poverty. In saying "Behold, your eyes and the eyes of my brother Benjamin," Joseph continues to distinguish between and separate the two groups. This began with the extra portions of food at the previous meal (43:34) and will continue with extra gifts in 45:22.

Joseph falls on his brother's Benjamin's neck and weeps, and Benjamin weeps as well. Then Joseph kisses all his brothers and weeps on them,[144] but there is no mention of weeping by the other brothers. The other brothers talk with him.

---

144. Genesis 45:14, ויבך טבן ובנימן בכה; v. 15, ויבך.

Pharaoh is pleased by the report that Joseph's brothers have come, and he wants them to settle in Egypt. It appears that he is more concerned that Joseph may want to return to Canaan while Pharaoh still has need of his services. If the family of Joseph settles in Egypt, then Joseph will stay and continue to prosper Pharaoh. Because of this, Pharaoh is generous in offering the best land and "the fat of the land" (ואכלו את-חלב הארץ). He even provides the mode of transportation for the wives and the "little ones"[145] and tells them to have "no concerns for your goods," literally "let your eye not pity for your possessions" (ועינכם אל-תחס על-כליכם), because the best of the land of Egypt is theirs.

Joseph gives his brothers gifts—much more for Benjamin[146]—and he also sends a gift to his father, along with provisions for the journey. As he sends them to Canaan, he says: "Do not quarrel on the way." Joseph does not think that his brothers have had a complete change of heart, and perhaps the large gift for Benjamin is another test. The only brother who has noticeably changed in these narratives is Judah.[147]

The brothers return to "go up" to Canaan once again, and when Jacob hears the news that "Joseph is alive" (עוד יוסף חי), at first he does not believe, and "his heart became numb" (ויפג לבו), but eventually, with all the evidence before him, Jacob believes, and his spirit is revived (ותחי רוח). Note the connection between Joseph being חי, "alive," and Jacob's spirit being ותחי, "revived, made alive." We see a similar connection in verse 28; Joseph is חי, "alive," and Jacob says that he will see him "before I die," אמות. Levenson writes:

To be separated from Joseph is, for Jacob, to be dead, and to be together with him is to live again. The point is nicely brought home by the sequence of events in Gen 45:26b–27. First, Jacob's heart goes numb, recapitulating his response to the evident demise of Joseph in 37:34–35, when he refuses to be comforted and speaks only of his

---

145. לטפכם; also Gen 46:5.

146. Three hundred shekels of silver and five changes of clothes.

147. Alter disagrees, stating, "But the primary meaning of the verb is to quake or to shake either physically (as a mountain in an earthquake) or emotionally (as a person trembling with fear), and it is the antonym of being tranquil or at peace. In all likelihood, Joseph is reassuring his brothers that they need not fear any lurking residue of vengefulness on his part that would turn the journey homeward into a trap" (*Genesis*, 271).

own approaching death. But then, in 45:27, the sight of the wagons that have come with his older sons reverses the sight of the bloody ornamented tunic they brought him in chapter 37, and Jacob, emotionally dead these many years, comes back to life, for he knows that Joseph remains alive after all.[148]

The death-and-resurrection imagery associated with the character of Joseph is difficult to miss. He who was dead is now alive. Jacob, who was dead in spirit, is made alive/revived by the living presence of Joseph.

GENESIS 46

As Jacob begins his journey down to Egypt, the narrator connects this journey with his previous journey following the death of Rachel in Genesis 35 in two ways. First, he uses the phrase ויסע ישראל, "and Israel set out," which was last used in Genesis 35. Second, Genesis 35 was the last time that God spoke to someone—Jacob—and 46:2-4 is the only place in the Joseph narratives where God speaks to someone—Jacob. This is in sharp contrast with the stories of Abraham, Isaac, and Jacob in the previous narratives, yet the narrator wants to connect the Joseph narratives with them.[149] Although God is referenced in Genesis 37-50, he is seldom noted as present and speaks just this once. Even יהוה, "Lord," is mentioned only twelve times (Gen 38:7 [2×], 10; 39:2, 3 [2×], 5 [2×], 21, 23 [2×]; 49:18).

When Jacob comes to Beersheba, "he offered sacrifices" (ויזבח זבחים), and God speaks to him "in visions of the night" (במראת הלילה). This is in contrast to the dreams, in which God does not speak or even appear. Beersheba was a dwelling place of the patriarchs and a place where the patriarchs historically called on the name of the Lord.[150] It is no surprise that Jacob would go there to inquire of the Lord concerning his journey down to Egypt. At his advanced age, he doubts he will return to the land of Canaan, and considering the covenantal promise, this concerns him.[151] Verse 3, אנכי האל אלהי אביך, "I am God, the God of your father"; כי–לגוי גדול

---

148. Levenson, *Death and Resurrection*, 151–52.

149. Jubilees 44.3 records that Jacob decided to invite Joseph to visit him in Canaan.

150. Abraham—Gen 21:33; 22:19; Isaac—26:23-33; Jacob—28:10.

151. Wenham points out that to fail to secure God's blessing and approval for this trip out of the promised land might be construed as unbelief (*Genesis 16–50*, 440).

אשימך שם, "for there I will make you into a great nation." Jacob will be made into a great nation as promised in the covenant, but in Egypt (compare Gen 15:13–14). God tells Jacob not to be afraid to "go down" to Egypt because God will "go down" with him, and God will also "bring him up again" (אעלך גם־עלה). Jacob never returns to Canaan alive, but this appears to be a reference to 50:7 14, where Joseph and his brothers bury him in the cave of Machpelah. It may also be a reference to the exodus from Egypt by the people of Israel, as also anticipated by Joseph in 50:25 at the end of his life.[152] Here is a glimpse of the transition from the patriarchal to the tribal era. God finishes his address with "and Joseph's own hand will close your eyes" (ויוסף ישיב ידו על־עיניך). The death-and-resurrection submotif of down to Egypt/up to Canaan is seen twice referring to Jacob, but also to God.[153] With its connection to the death of Jacob and an allusion to God "bringing/raising up," it is more significant. Jacob is told not to be afraid of going down to Egypt, nor should he fear death itself.

Israel then sets out from Beersheba with all his family and all the "goods which they gained" (רכושם אשר רכשו). The narrator uses the next section (vv. 8–27) to list the descendants of Israel who settled together in Egypt. In verse 12 we are reminded that Er and Onan, Judah's sons, died in the land of Canaan—another reference that connects back to Genesis 38. In verse 26 the number belonging to Jacob is sixty-six, not including Jacob's sons' wives. However, in verse 27, the number is seventy. The sixty-six of verse 26 did not include Jacob, Joseph, Manasseh, or Ephraim.[154]

Jacob sends Judah ahead of him to Joseph. Judah is once again given the leadership role among Israel's sons, this time by Jacob. Joseph goes to meet his father in the land of Goshen, where it is anticipated that the family will be settling. Seeing his father, "Joseph fell on his neck and wept on his neck a good while" (46:29; ויפל על־צואריו ויבך על־צואריו עוד).[155]

---

152. Coats, *From Canaan to Egypt*, 91.

153. See chap. 5.

154. Sarna says since this is not a typological or symbolic number in the Bible, it must therefore represent a genuine calculation based on the data just recorded. The key phrase is "who came to Egypt." Accordingly, Er and Onan must be omitted because they died in Canaan. Verse 27 indicates that Manasseh and Ephraim are not included among the sixty-six. They were born in Egypt and cannot be said to have come there. The computation then would be: Leah 31 + Zilpah 16 + Rachel 12 + Bilhah 7 = 66 (Sarna, *Genesis*, 317).

155. For the theme of weeping, see also Gen 45:2, 14, 15.

Jacob's response is, "Now let me die, since I have seen your face and know that you are still alive" (אמותה הפעם אחרי ראותי את–פניך כי עודך חט).[156] The narrator provides a connection of death and life, חי, life for Joseph and death, אמותה, with Jacob (45:28). Joseph tells his brothers and his father's household that he will go up to Pharaoh and tell him that his family has arrived from the land of Canaan. "The men are shepherds for they have been keepers of livestock," והאנשים רעי צאן כי–אנשי מקנה היו. This is the message Joseph says he will deliver to Pharaoh, but he suggests that his brothers approach it differently. When Pharaoh says: "What is your occupation?" they are to tell him they are keepers of livestock. This certainly is true, but it also clearly avoids the word רעה צאן, "shepherd," which is an abomination to the Egyptians (43:32).[157] Later, in Genesis 47, we see the brothers do not listen to Joseph. They give almost the exact opposite reply to Pharaoh's question (47:3–4).[158]

GENESIS 47

Joseph approaches Pharaoh as said (Gen 46:31) and tells him that his father and brothers have arrived and are currently in the land of Goshen. By approaching Pharaoh in this way, Joseph encourages agreement to the request to allow them to dwell in Goshen. Again, Joseph is masterful in dealing with the Pharaoh and receives the desired result. Then Joseph takes from among his brothers five men and presents them to Pharaoh.[159] Although we are given no indication here in the text as to which brothers are chosen for this presentation, it is likely that they are from the sons of Leah and Rachel, not from the sons of Bilhah and Zilpah.

When Pharaoh asks the five brothers their occupation, they do not follow the advice of Joseph in 46:34 but instead choose to say רעה צאן עבדיך, "your servants are shepherds," even though this may cause offense to Pharaoh and

---

156. Longacre refers to this as Jacob's *nunc dimittis* (Joseph, 38; also Wenham, *Genesis 16–50*, 445).

157. Speiser notes, "The taboo cannot apply to shepherds as such. In all likelihood, the term shepherds is here a play on the popular interpretation of the Hyksos as 'shepherd kings' whose temporary domination of Egypt dealt a severe blow to national pride" (*Genesis*, 345).

158. Pirson, *Lord of the Dreams*, 113–14.

159. Vawter: "Five seems to have been a number dear to Egyptian hearts as seven was to Hebrew." He then refers to the fivefold portion of food for Benjamin and the five festal garments. He also points to the fact that income taxes in Egypt were counted by fifths (Vawter, *Path through Genesis*, 285–86).

jeopardize their request for Goshen. They continue in verse 4, saying: "We have come to sojourn in the land" (לגור בארץ באנו), which gives the impression of residing as aliens or sojourning as nomads. This is an abomination to Egyptians; however, they finish their short discourse by returning to the script provided by Joseph in 46:34. "Now, please let your servants dwell in the land of Goshen." This may indicate the brothers' ongoing resentment toward Joseph, or just pride in their occupation and heritage. Even though the brothers demonstrate their independence by not following Joseph's advice, it does not damage their cause. Pharaoh responds by addressing Joseph, not his brothers. This should not be construed as Pharaoh showing his distaste at being in the presence of shepherds, but rather as addressing the figure of authority—Joseph—who represents their request. Note in verse 8 the great respect Pharaoh affords Jacob by addressing him directly. Pharaoh's response is the desired one, with the addition of asking Joseph to put his brothers in charge of his livestock. This is an important task that will soon grow in its importance (47:16–17).

With the family of Jacob settled in the land of Goshen, the people of Israel are essentially separated from the Egyptians. Not only does this aid in their preservation as a unit, but it also sets up the separation/reunion submotif.[160] We have witnessed this in action as Joseph and Jacob are reunited, and now the sons of Israel are separated out as a distinct people in a distinct region in order that they might be preserved as a people from which the messianic hope and covenantal promise might be fulfilled.

Joseph now brings Jacob before Pharaoh, and ויברך יעקב את-פרעה, "Jacob blessed Pharaoh." Pharaoh appears impressed with Jacob and asks him: "How many are the days of your life?" Jacob replies twice using the same base word his sons have previously used, גור, "my sojourning" (מגורי); "their sojourning" (מגוריהם). Again, the nomadic lifestyle is intimated by this word. In his response, Jacob continues with his "woe is me" attitude, as seen on previous occasions (37:35; 42:36, 38; 43:14), with "few and evil have been my days" (מעט ורעים היו ימי), and points out—laments—that the days of his years have not attained the days of the years of the life of his fathers.

Jacob then blesses Pharaoh again as he leaves his presence, and Joseph settles them/gives them a possession "in the land of Egypt, in the best of

---

160. See chap. 5.

the land, in the land of Ramses," and provides them with food.[161] Again, the age of Pharaoh comes into question. Earlier, Joseph says that he is as a father to the Pharaoh (45:8), and now we see how amazed the Pharaoh is at Jacob's age, and he allows Jacob to bless him twice as Jacob stands and does not bow before him.

The famine remains severe in the land, and Joseph gathers all the money in the land of Egypt and the land of Canaan in exchange for grain. In relation to the separation/reunion submotif,[162] note that Joseph carries out his task in a region apart from his brothers and father and does not make his dwelling in Goshen with his family. There is no indication this ever changes, even when his work as grain distributor comes to an end. Although the famine extends beyond Egypt and Canaan and encompasses many other countries and regions, the narrator singles out Canaan in 47:13–15 to remind us that the Lord had delivered the household of Jacob and rescued them from destruction using Joseph as his instrument to preserve the remnant (remnant motif). When the money is all spent, all the Egyptians—Canaan is not mentioned again—come to Joseph, saying: "Give us food. Why should we die before your eyes?" (ולמה נמות נגדך). Since there is no more money, Joseph demands their livestock in exchange for food. The Egyptians bring "their horses" (בסוסים), the flocks, the herds, and the donkeys.[163] Since this livestock now belongs to Pharaoh, it means the brothers of Joseph have greater responsibility as they care for it (47:6). The next year the Egyptians came to Joseph with no money and no livestock, having only their bodies and their land. "Why should we die before your eyes?" (למה נמות לעיניך).[164]

"Why should we die before your eyes, both we and our land?" Famine is also seen as the death of the land, for there appears to be no life in the soil. We see that famine and deliverance is a death-and-resurrection submotif, and it plays a strong part in the Joseph narratives.[165] When the land

---

161. Wenham: "Whereas Jacob's sons had come to Pharaoh requesting favors, here Pharaoh is being done a favor by the old man visiting him. It is Jacob who blesses Pharaoh, i.e., prays for Pharaoh's welfare, both on his arrival and his departure. Pharaoh simply asks respectfully, 'How many years have you lived?' Jacob's great age demands respect from the all-powerful ruler of Egypt" (*Genesis 16–50*, 446).

162. See chap. 5.

163. This is the first use of סוס, "horse," in Genesis.

164. Note the use of לעיניך as opposed to נגדך in v. 15.

165. See chap. 5.

dies, it results in the death of the people. They offer to sell their land and themselves into slavery for food. Joseph is then cast in the role of savior and resurrector of the land and its people in verse 19 as the people ask for seed in anticipation that the land will be brought back to life (47:25). Joseph holds their lives in his hands. "Give us seed that we may live and not die" (ותן־זרע ונחיה ולא נמות) shows another submotif of the death-and-resurrection motif, seed and growth.[166] The seed is dead and goes into the dead soil in order that life may be resurrected and fertility restored. Again, the narrator contrasts חיה, "to live," and מות, "to die": another downward/upward movement.

Verse 21 continues to reflect an ironic turn of events, which continues to the time of Moses and the exodus. Joseph, sold into slavery in Egypt, now is the enslaver of the Egyptians to Pharaoh. Later, the Egyptian people will enslave the Israelites after the death of Joseph and the emergence of a Pharaoh who does not know him (Exod 1:8-11). Joseph "removed them to the cities until" (העביר אתו לערים) the famine draws to an end. Some translators regard as superior the reading of the Samaritan Pentateuch (compare also LXX) at this point and read והעביד אתו לעבדים, "he made servants of them."[167] However, the idea of removing the people to the cities where they would be able to carry out acts of servitude and readily receive grain makes sense.[168] After all, there was nothing left to plant or tend in the fields. Joseph provides seed for the people, telling them to plant and that one-fifth of the harvest belongs to Pharaoh. The people respond: "You have saved our lives" (החיתנו; 47:25). Again, the death and life of the people are wrapped up in the seed and the soil; "dead" seeds and barren soil will soon return to life/resurrect life to the land, and the people will be saved as a result.[169]

Joseph's task of dealing with the famine has come to an end, and the narrator returns to Jacob and his family in the land of Goshen in 47:27-28. They settle in the land, "and they were fruitful and multiplied greatly" (יפרו

---

166. See chap. 5.

167. See Speiser, *Genesis*, 352, and discussion in *Biblia Hebraica Quinta*, 190*-91*.

168. Sarna, while asserting the meaning is unclear, follows the literal translation, "the populace, he removed it to/by cities." He understands it as a large-scale population transfer, probably carried out to oust farmers from nationalized lands (Sarna, *Genesis*, 322).

169. Westermann, *Genesis 37-50*, 176. Here is both the submotif of seed/growth and the submotif of famine/deliverance. See also chap. 5.

48:4 ;וירבו מאד)[170] according to God's original command to Adam and Eve in the garden of Eden (1:28). Then we move forward to the life and death of Jacob in the land of Egypt—a foreshadowing of this event in Genesis 50. Jacob lived in Egypt 17 years, and the days of the years of his life were 147 years. Note the 17 years of Jacob's sojourning in Egypt equals the age of Joseph when he was sold into slavery to Egypt (Gen 37:2).[171] Verse 27 uses "Israel" as a reference to the whole family, while verse 28 uses "Jacob" when speaking of the patriarch. Verse 29 returns to the use of "Israel" for the patriarch, as it refers to his upcoming death (למות).[172]

"Place your hand under my thigh and promise to deal kindly and truly with me. Do not bury me in Egypt" (24:2, 9), ושכבתי עם–אבתי, "but let me lie with my fathers," וקברתני בקברתם, "bury me in their burying place." Israel makes Joseph promise to return his body to be buried with his fathers, Abraham and Isaac, as God promised it would be (46:4), in the cave of Machpelah. In addition to Joseph's promise Jacob also tells him to "swear to me" (השבעה לי). This appears to be another example of the lack of trust in these narratives. Perhaps this distrust is warranted, as we have seen multiple examples of deceit. Yet, this time it is Jacob who does not trust Joseph's promise—or God's—in 46:4. It may be that Jacob has considered Joseph's position and that he did not seek to return and search Jacob out. Placing one's hand under the thigh was viewed either as a swearing by the original Abrahamic covenant by touching the circumcision, or a swearing by touching the source of life itself. "Then Israel bowed himself upon the head of the staff" (וישתחו ישראל על–ראש המטה). Both the MT and the LXX agree on "staff" and continue to follow this decision in 48:2, where the context might better suggest "bed."[173]

Note the contrast in Jacob's reference to his death and the previous mentions in Genesis 37 and 42 of going down to Sheol. This is a much more

---

170. Compare the situation of the Israelites described in Exod 1:9–12.

171. Alter notes, "The symmetry with Joseph's seventeen years until he was sold into Egypt was aptly observed in the Middle Ages by Kimhi: 'Just as Joseph was in the lap of Jacob seventeen years, Jacob was in the lap of Joseph seventeen years'" (Genesis, 285).

172. Westermann makes note of the constant anticipation of Jacob's death throughout the Joseph narrative (Genesis 37–50, 181).

173. Westermann understands Jacob as seated on the bed during his conversation and now inclines "toward the head(s) of the bed" (Genesis 37–50, 183).

peaceful death than the one Jacob describes taking place in mourning and
sorrow. Wenham notes:

> Jacob is overwhelmed when he sees Joseph in all his glory; he
> appears to him as if in a vision. But Joseph turns out to be com-
> pletely real, as he falls on his father's neck and weeps over him again
> and again. And because Joseph is alive, Jacob's attitude to death is
> revolutionized. Twice Jacob had declared that the loss of his sons
> would bring him in mourning to Sheol, the realm of the hopeless
> dead (37:35; 42:38). Now Joseph's resurrection allows Jacob to die in
> peace, just as the resurrection of a greater Joseph has allowed many
> to face death with courage and hope (1 Pet 1:3; cf. Phil 1:21–26).[174]

GENESIS 48

Following the conclusion of Genesis 47, with Israel securing Joseph's promise and oath to bury him with his fathers in Canaan, Joseph is told that his
father is ill (חלה). Joseph goes to him, taking his two sons, Manasseh and
Ephraim. Genesis 48 has two major themes: the elevation, by adoption,
of Joseph's two sons to the status of Israelite tribes, and the advance in
status of Ephraim over the firstborn Manasseh.[175] When Jacob hears that
Joseph has come, "he summoned his strength" (ויתחזק) and sat up "in bed"
(המטה; see 47:31). Jacob relates to Joseph the events of 28:10–22 when אל שדי,
"God Almighty" (43:14), addressed him in Luz (בלוז), later called Bethel. The
blessing he received was the covenantal promise. The narrator alternates
between יעקב, "Jacob," and ישראל, "Israel," throughout this section. There
appears a loose connection with the use of Jacob for patriarchal times and
issues, and Israel for the upcoming tribal era, even using Israel to name
all twelve tribes (47:27). The Joseph narratives can be seen as representing
the transition between these two eras.

Jacob tells of God Almighty's covenantal promise to make fruitful and
multiply (47:27) and to make of him a company of people (ונתתיך לקהל
עמים) and to give this land (Canaan) to "his offspring/seed" (זרעך) for an

174. Wenham, *Genesis 16–50*, 451; see also Sarna, *Genesis*, 323.
175. Sarna, *Genesis*, 324.

everlasting possession (אחזת עולם). The word עולם, "everlasting," is not found in the Genesis 28:10–22 text, but it does appear again as Jacob blesses Joseph in 49:26.[176] The use of זרע, "seed," links the words of Jacob to the covenantal promise as well as to the death-and-resurrection submotif of seed and growth.[177] Note the death side of this motif in the term "seed" and the life side in the words "fruitful and multiply."[178]

In verse 5, Jacob claims Ephraim and Manasseh as his own sons. לי–הם אפרים ומנשה כראובן ושמעון יהיו–לי, "They are mine, Ephraim and Manasseh shall be mine as Reuben and Simeon are." Note first the order Jacob uses for the sons of Joseph. He places Ephraim, the younger, first and the older, Manasseh, second. This is reversed from Joseph's order in verse 1, and we see the reason in verses 17–19. Ephraim will be greater than his brother, according to Jacob's blessing. Second, note that Jacob is adopting the sons of Joseph.[179] By doing so he in essence gives a double portion of the inheritance to Joseph, the right of the firstborn, which may explain why Rachel is brought up in verse 7, as Joseph was her firstborn. Jacob appears to be replacing Reuben and Simeon with Ephraim and Manasseh. In a sense, Joseph has exercised the levirate law on Jacob's behalf—another way in which Genesis 38 is connected. Jacob is unhappy with both Reuben and Simeon, Reuben for his actions with Jacob's concubine, Bilhah (Gen 35:22), and Simeon for his actions against the men of Shechem (34:13–31). This displeasure will show itself again in the blessings of Genesis 49. Ephraim and Manasseh no longer belong to Joseph; only the sons born to him after this (מולדתך אשר–הולדת, "the children that you father"), of whom there is no mention of in Genesis, shall belong to him.

In verse 8 Israel sees Joseph's sons and asks: "Who are these?" (מי–אלה), and Joseph replies: "My sons whom God has given me here" (בני הם אשר–נתן לי אלהים).[180] Is this the correct response considering Jacob's words of verses 5–6, or does the official change of possession take place following the blessing

176. Genesis 49:26: "The blessings of your father are mighty beyond the blessings of my parents, up to the bounties of the everlasting hills."

177. See chap. 5.

178. See also Gen 3:15, Adam; 15:5; 24:7, Abraham; 26:4, Isaac; 28:13–14; 35:12, Jacob.

179. Speiser, *Genesis*, 357: "The act of placing a child on the father's knees signifies acceptance of the child as legitimate; the same act also serves to formalize adoption." Also see von Rad, *Genesis*, 410.

180. Von Rad and Westermann consider that Joseph's answer presupposes that Jacob has not yet seen the sons of Joseph (Westermann, *Genesis 37–50*, 186).

in verse 16? There appears to be a tension between Jacob and Joseph in these latter chapters. It finds its origin in the time period when Jacob did not seek after Joseph and when Joseph failed to search for his father, choosing Egypt as his new homeland. Israel's eyes are "heavy with age" (כבדו מזקן), so Joseph brings them close to him, and Israel "kissed them and embraced them," saying: "I never expected to see your face; and behold, God has let me see your offspring/seed [זרעך] also." Joseph is the one who once was dead and is now alive, and even more, he has descendants. Then Joseph "bowed himself with his face to the earth" (וישתחו לאפיו ארצה). In light of his earlier dreams and Jacob's interpretation, it is ironic that Joseph bows before his father, but Israel never bows before Joseph. Jacob's interpretation of Joseph's second dream in Genesis 37 is called into question. Then Joseph placed his sons before Israel so that the eldest, Manasseh, will be at the right hand of Israel and Ephraim at his left hand, but as Israel stretches out his hands he crosses his arms (שכל את-ידיו) so that his right hand is on Ephraim's head and his left hand on Manasseh's. He proceeds to bless Joseph and his sons.

The blessing begins by referencing the God of his fathers, Abraham and Isaac, the God who has been his Shepherd (הרעה אתי מעודי) all the days of this (life), המלאך, the angel who redeemed him from all evil. This is the first use of God as Shepherd in the Old Testament (Gen 49:24; Pss 23:1; 28:9).[181] It may be a reminder to Joseph of his roots as a shepherd, with which he has shown signs of being uncomfortable. Then, Israel makes the first angel reference in the Joseph narratives and uses it to identify God as "the Angel who has redeemed me from all evil" ("delivered me from all harm"; see also Job 19:23; Ps 19:5). This appears to be the same "angel of the LORD" who appears in other places in the Old Testament Scriptures (Exod 3:2, etc.), who is the Lord God himself and not simply an angel/messenger from God.[182] The term גאל, "to redeem," is used as a legal term for redeeming. Israel continues his blessing by saying: "In them let my name be carried on. ... Let them grow into a multitude" (וידגו לרב). Literally, this unique phrase, used only once in the Old Testament, is translated "Let them be like fish for multitude," or "multiply

---

181. Sarna points out that the image for the deity as a shepherd is common throughout ancient Near Eastern literature and expresses the idea of God as provider, protector, and guide (*Genesis*, 328; see also Wenham, *Genesis 16–50*, 465).

182. C. A. Gieschen, *Angelomorphic Christology: Antecedents and Early Evidence* (Leiden: Brill, 1998), 57–69, 138.

like fishes."[183] Ephraim and Manasseh each receive a portion when the land of Canaan is divided (Josh 14:2; 15:1–19; Num 2), and in 1 Chronicles 4–8 the descendants of Jacob's sons are listed, but Joseph is not mentioned: rather, we hear of Ephraim and Manasseh and their children.

Joseph notices that his father's hands are crossed, with his right hand on the head of Ephraim and his left on Manasseh, and is not pleased. He attempts to correct his father (Gen 48:18), but his father refuses, saying: "I know my son, I know" (ידעתי בני ידעתי), "Manasseh will become great, but his brother, Ephraim, will become greater and his offspring/seed [זרע] shall become a multitude of nations" (מלא-הגוים, literally, "a fullness of nations"). Israel places Ephraim before Manasseh, much to Joseph's surprise.

There are several things to note. First, we see the ongoing biblical motif of choosing and blessing the second born over the firstborn. Jacob should have been quite familiar with this, as he too received such a blessing when he tricked his father, Isaac, and stole his brother, Esau's, blessing (Gen 27). Second, it is possible that this switching of the blessings might have something to do with Manasseh's name, which means "God has made me forget my father's house." Jacob may be repaying Joseph for forgetting him when he rose to power. After all, Joseph never went looking for Jacob when he had the ability. Instead, he chose to forget his past and move on with his new life. Third, there are two blessings in this chapter, which continues the doubling style.

Israel tells Joseph that he is about to die, but he assures him that "God will be with you and return you to the land of your fathers." This phrase may have a dual reference, first pointing to Joseph's trip to Canaan to bury his father (Gen 50:12–14), and second to Joseph's bones being carried back to the promised land (50:25; Exod 13:19). Both provide the fulfillment of a downward/upward motif, and both reflect the death-and-resurrection submotif of down to Egypt/up to Canaan.[184] Israel also gives Joseph the only piece of land he has ever acquired with his own hand. This "mountain slope" (שכם) he took from the Amorites with his sword and bow. This is the only portion of ground that we hear Joseph receiving or possessing in

---

183. "Hebrew ve-yidgu, a unique verb apparently formed from dag, 'fish,' a symbol of proliferation and multiplicity" (Sarna, Genesis, 328).

184. See chap. 5.

Scripture. The translations "Shechem, mountain slope, mountain shoulder" may all be accurate.[185]

In Joshua 24, Joshua addresses all of Israel from Shechem, from the slope of a mountain at Shechem. Shechem is in the land of the Amorites, and this piece of ground "became an inheritance of the descendants of Joseph." There is an apparent conflict of texts. In Genesis 48:22, Jacob claims he took the area from the Amorites with his sword and bow, while in Joshua 24:32, Joshua says Jacob bought the piece of ground from the sons of Hamor, the father of Shechem, for a hundred pieces of silver. This conflict may be resolved if one considers the sword and bow of Jacob to be the same as that of his sons Simeon and Levi, who put the entire male population of Shechem to the sword after the incident with Dinah (Gen 34:13–31). Even if Jacob had purchased the land previously, the annihilation of the men of Shechem assured him of its possession. Israel's mention of this piece of ground in the context of the blessing given to Ephraim and Manasseh may support this understanding, as Jacob mentions replacing Reuben and Simeon with Ephraim and Manasseh. He has given that which was taken by Simeon—and Levi—to Joseph because he was displeased with his sons for their actions at Shechem. One could attribute the conflict between Genesis 48 and Joshua 24 as another example in a long line of Jacob's history of duplicity. Finally, the idea of this piece of ground being high up on a mountain slope is Jacob's final message to all his sons, that he considers Joseph above them all. Since this piece of ground becomes Joseph's burial place (Josh 24:32), Jacob's implied message is established forever, a raising up of Joseph above them.

GENESIS 49

Genesis 49 contains the longest speech in the book of Genesis. Jacob gathers his sons together to bestow his blessings on them and their descendants. His speech contains many lexical, syntactical, literary, and structural challenges. Jacob's blessings to his sons are filled with allusions, double entendres, alliterations, and other literary devices with which to struggle. Add

---

185. Botterweck, Ringgren, and Fabry, *Theological Dictionary of the Old Testament*, 10:681–88. Speiser sees this as a reference to Mount Gerizim (*Genesis*, 358).

to this a great number of *hapax legomena*, and the challenge of this chapter is readily apparent.[186]

The designation "the blessings of Jacob" comes from the verses following (49:28), where the narrator tells us: "This is what their father said to them as he blessed them, blessing each with the blessing suitable to him." This title is supported by the close association with the blessing bestowed by Moses on the twelve tribes in Deuteronomy 33.

Jacob begins by calling his sons together, telling them to assemble themselves and listen. Note the movement in verse 2 from "O sons of Jacob" (יעקב) to "Israel [ישראל] your father." Then Jacob addresses his firstborn son, Reuben: "the first fruits of my strength." He says he is preeminent (יתר) in dignity and preeminent (ויתר) in power, but he shall not have preeminence (תותר) because he went up to his father's bed and defiled it. This is a reference to Reuben's affair with his father's concubine, Bilhah (Gen 35:22). Jacob has not found resolution concerning this breach of trust. Reuben has repeatedly sought to restore himself in his father's eyes and to preeminence among his brothers. Jacob's blessing signals the end of Reuben's hope to regain what was lost—authority and the firstborn blessing of the covenant. Note the language Jacob uses—"You went up to your father's bed," "He went up to my couch!" Reuben ascended to an unrightful place, and Jacob's blessing brings him low.[187]

Jacob turns his attention to Simeon and Levi. These are the only brothers presented as a pair, and Jacob's reference to their swords as weapons of violence points to the other time they are mentioned as a pair—the destruction of all the males in the city of Shechem (34:20). Once again, Jacob has not forgotten the incident that took place following the rape of Dinah. Jacob says: "In their anger they killed men" (באפם הרגו), and "In their willingness they hamstrung oxen" (וברצנם עקרו–שור). Then he delivers a concluding curse, ארור, in the imperative—they will be divided in Jacob and scattered in Israel. The same structure is evident in verse 2; however, "Jacob" and "Israel" in verse two refer to the father, whereas these two names in verse 7

---

186. Longacre sums up the structure of these blessings: "The backgrounded macrostructure can be summarized as follows: *Among the descendants of Jacob, Joseph and Judah are to be preeminent both as individuals and as tribes—with some ambiguity as to the precise preeminence of each*" (*Joseph*, 51).

187. Upward/downward motif.

reference the country. Some see this division and scattering as a separation from one another,[188] but as we look at the history of Israel and how the division of tribes was carried out, there is a better interpretation. In Numbers 18:1 the tribe of Levi is tasked to serve in the tabernacle and later the temple, so they receive no specific land inheritance and are "scattered" throughout the land. Simeon's inheritance is in the midst of Judah (Josh 19:1–9) and, in the course of time, is completely absorbed. Excluding Chronicles, the tribe of Simeon is mentioned only five times in the Old Testament (Josh 21:4, 9; Ezek 48:24–25, 33). Another irony concerning Simeon shows itself when his people are absorbed by Judah. With the need to have twelve tribes, the two half-tribes of Ephraim and Manasseh become full tribes. Not only has Simeon been replaced (Gen 48): Joseph has effectively received the double portion belonging to the firstborn, Reuben.

Verses 8–12 speak about Judah, as he is lavishly praised and blessed. Sarna writes:

> The slow, almost imperceptible, rise of Judah has already been subtly insinuated into the Joseph story. Here it receives formal recognition and confirmation. In the wilderness Judah is, by far, the largest tribe: its population increases during the wanderings, as shown by the censuses of Numbers 1:26 and 26:22. The tribe encamps in front of the Tent of Meeting and heads the march (Num. 2:3, 9; 10:14). Its chieftain is the first to bring gifts for the Tabernacle (Num. 7:12), and its representative is listed first among those designated to apportion the land (Num. 34:19).[189]

Judah's blessing contains fifty-five words—more than any of his brothers with the exception of Joseph, the two eventual heroes of the Joseph narratives.[190] The blessing of Judah shows his stature among the brothers

---

188. For example Benno Jacob, *Das erste Buch der Tora*, 898–99.

189. Sarna, *Genesis*, 335.

190. Those scholars who hold to a postexilic date for this chapter see this as evidence of a southern (Judah) kingdom verses northern (Joseph) kingdom influence. See Brueggemann, *Genesis*, 288; D. B. Redford, *A Study of the Biblical Story of Joseph (Genesis 37–50)* (Leiden: Brill, 1970), 189–243. Joseph's blessing contains sixty-one words in Gen 49:22–26.

and his place in the covenant.[191] "Judah, your brothers shall praise you; your hand shall be on the neck of your enemies." Note the יהודה–יודוך–ידך construct chain. The narrator makes frequent use of alliterations in these blessings. Jacob says: "Your father's sons shall bow down before you" (ישתחוו לך בני אביך). The bowing down and praise of the brothers is given to Judah rather than Joseph, in spite of the dreams of Joseph that Jacob kept in mind (Gen 37:11). Since the narrator specifically notes that Jacob kept these dreams in mind in Genesis 37, it appears that he is reacting against the same dreams in his blessing of Judah. Jacob establishes Judah's status among his sons and proclaims him the leader in this blessing. The blessing also completes Judah's rise to preeminence, eclipsing not only Reuben but Joseph as well. The position to which Joseph rose in Egypt is now seen in Judah's position in Israel. This leadership role continues to be reinforced with the lion metaphor: גור אריה, "a lion's cub"; כאריה וכלביא, "as a lion and as a lion"; both לביא and אריה mean "lion," although some have translated לביא as "lioness" (e.g., ESV). This provides us the phrase "Lion of Judah." Jacob elevates Judah's position even further by declaring, "The scepter shall not depart from Judah, nor the ruler's staff from between his feet." The "scepter," שבט, and מחקק, "ruler's staff," that shall not depart from Judah are references to a kingly, royal line to come from Judah.[192]

In both Jewish and Christian tradition, verses 10–11 have been interpreted as reference to a messianic figure descended from Judah via the future King David. Targum Onqelos of Genesis 49:10, for example, explicitly expounds the verse with reference to a Messiah: commenting on this verse, Bernard Grossfeld lists an abundance of rabbinic texts that offer a similar interpretation. In the process, Grossfeld draws attention to the widespread understanding among Christians that these verses refer to Jesus, supplying a host of patristic references.[193] Both traditions, Jewish

191. According to Longacre, Judah accomplishes this stature among his brothers in Gen 43–45 when he offers himself as surety for Benjamin (43:3–10) and then when he offers to stay as a slave in Benjamin's place (44:33ff.) (*Joseph*, 52–53). I concur with his opinion (see comments on Gen 38 and its place in the Joseph narratives).

192. Wenham: "Historically, the military successes of King David from the tribe of Judah may be seen as the fulfillment of this blessing, which also gave rise to the messianic title 'Lion of Judah'" (*Genesis 16–50*, 476).

193. See Bernard Grossfeld, trans., *The Aramaic Bible*, vol. 6, *The Targum Onqelos to Genesis: Translated, with a Critical Introduction, Apparatus, and Notes* (Edinburgh: T&T Clark, 1988), 163–64.

and Christian, were able to perceive in Genesis 49:10–11 a prophecy of future events that could be portrayed in the light of a mighty descendant of Judah.[194] In verse 11 the words עירה, "foal," and ולשרקה, "donkey's colt," are seen again in Zechariah 9:9. Note that the narrator uses the words חוה, "bow down" (v. 8); טרף, "tear" (v 9); אסר, "bind" (v. 11); and גפן, "vine" (v. 11), which, when used previously, have referred to Joseph. Again, we see a shift of hero/leader in these narratives.

Jacob's blessing of Zebulun begins and finishes in verse 13. Note the placement of Zebulun before Issachar. Their birth order is reversed. Zebulun's blessing speaks of dwelling on the shore of the sea, of being a haven for ships (לחוף), and his border being at Sidon. None of these statements come to fruition when the land is allotted by Joshua (Josh 19:10–16). Zebulun is a landlocked tribe, but it has been noted that "in historical times the tribe migrated northward to the sea, in the vicinity of modern Haifa."[195]

Issachar's blessing is contained in verses 14–15. He is referred to as a "strong donkey" (חמר גרם), a beast of burden that stubbornly lies down between its saddlebags or between the sheep pens. He sees that the land is a good place to rest, and "he bowed his shoulder to bear" (ויט שכמו לסבל) and become a "servant at forced labor." Von Rad explains: "Later it pushed into the western plains. The move was a bad one, however, because the tribe lost its political independence and became a vassal of the Canaanites, into whose sovereign territory it had entered."[196]

Dan's blessing (Gen 49:16–17) is next, and Jacob begins with another alliteration: דן ידין, "Dan shall judge." Dan shall be a "serpent" (נחש) in the way, a "viper" (שפיפן) by the path that bites the horse's heels (עקב; also v. 19) and causes the rider to fall backward. Although not certain, "Dan shall

194. Westermann: "It is not a messianic prophecy in the sense that it promises a king of salvation at the end-time (against J. Wellhausen, H. Gunkel)" (Genesis 37–50, 232). Westermann argues instead that it is a reference to the kingly line coming forth from Judah and does not include messianic tones.

195. Von Rad, Genesis, 426. Sarna writes, "The associations of some tribes with the sea can probably be explained in two ways. It is quite likely that Philistines and Phoenicians employed Israelite labor. Coastal cities of the Near East always featured mixed populations, so that the above-cited verses may not refer to Israelite occupation of the area but, rather, to the presence of considerable numbers of Israelites engaged as stevedores, in the servicing of ships, and in commerce (cf. 2 Sam. 24:6–7). Another possibility, complementary to the first, lies in the Israelite exploitation of convenient anchorage sites for very small ships at the points where more important wadis drain into the sea" (Genesis, 338).

196. Von Rad, Genesis, 426.

judge" may be a prophecy concerning the judge who came from the tribe of Dan, Samson, and who caused great harm to the Philistines.[197]

"I wait for your salvation, LORD," לִישׁוּעָתְךָ קִוִּיתִי (v. 18), does not appear to be connected to any of the blessings, although it may be connected to the judging in verse 16. Why is this phrase inserted at this point? Is the first use of ישׁעה, "salvation," being related to the covenantal aspect of the blessings? If so, why does it not follow Judah's blessing? Perhaps Jacob calls on the name of יהוה, "the LORD," as a reminder to his sons to be faithful. This is the first use of יהוה in the Joseph narratives by anyone other than the narrator (39:2–3, 21) and the first reference to the Divine in these blessings (49:24–25). Wenham reflects that within the context of a divine prophecy about the nation's future, this prayer of Jacob appears to be a reflection of the difficulties he sees the tribes facing: he prays to the Lord that he will deliver his descendants in the future.[198]

Verse 19 is the blessing of Gad and has a strong alliteration; גָּד גְּדוּד יְגוּדֶנּוּ, "raiders shall raid Gad," but he shall raid (יגד) at their heels. This is followed by the blessing of Asher (v. 20) and the blessing of Naphtali (v. 21).

The blessing of Joseph, beginning in verse 22, is the longest by six words compared to Judah's blessing. It begins with a difficult set of phrases: בנות צעדה עלי–שׁור/בן פרת עלי עין/בן פרת יוסף. A common translation of this verse is, "Joseph is a fruitful bough/a fruitful bough by a spring/his branches run over the wall."[199] However, בן is not typically used with plants, so a better translation may be, "Joseph is the foal of a wild ass/the foal of a wild ass at a fountain/the foal of wild asses by a rocky rim (wall)."[200] The "rocky rim," שׁור, may be a reference to his land inheritance in Genesis 48:22. In defense of the first translation, there seems to be stronger life references in the fruitful bough and fountain/spring. This may be Jacob's way of referencing Joseph's naming of his second son, Ephraim, and the name's "fruitful"

---

197. Vawter speculates that the trade routes from Tyre and Sidon had to pass through Dan. Control of trade routes meant taxes and tolls, often collected by force (Vawter, *Path through Genesis*, 298).

198. Wenham, *Genesis 16–50*, 482.

199. Vawter follows the "fruitful bough" translation, citing it as a reference to Joseph's most blessed son, Ephraim (*Path through Genesis*, 299–300; also Targum Onqelos).

200. Gunkel follows the animal metaphor (cow/ox), while Speiser translates "wild colt" (Speiser, *Genesis*, 367).

connection.[201] As we have noted, the Joseph narratives are uniquely focused in this direction.[202]

Verses 23–24 are also difficult. The reference to archers attacking and harassing Joseph is puzzling, although the statement that the "offspring/seed of his arms" (זרעי ידיו) were made agile by "the hands of the Mighty One of Jacob" (מידי אביר יעקב) is certainly pointing to the help that God has afforded Joseph in the midst of all the difficulties and struggles of his past. It also points to the downward/upward movements of his life. משם רעה אבן ישראל is "from there is the Shepherd, the Stone of Israel," or "by the name of the Shepherd, the Stone of Israel." This is the second use of the shepherd metaphor in the Joseph narratives (48:15). This is the first use of אבן, "stone," in these narratives and the first time it is used in reference to God in Genesis. Also interesting are the similarities in language of Joseph's blessing to references to Ishmael in 16:12 and 21:18–21.[203]

Jacob speaks directly to Joseph in verse 25. The MT of Jacob's words about Joseph is at times ambiguous, vague, and complex, invoking rare words and expressions that demand careful thought and reflection from the reader. The LXX and the Targum Onqelos give a great deal of direction in these matters, and I will focused on them in subsequent chapters.

The presence of God in Joseph's blessing continues and sets it apart from the other blessings. Only in Joseph's blessing is the Divine mentioned in connection to the one being blessed. "By the God of your father," מאל אביך, connects this part of the blessing to the previous: "The Mighty One of Jacob" שדי ויברכך, "The Almighty who will bless you." This is the first of six uses of ברך in verses 25–26. In "May He bless you with the blessings of heaven above," שמים is most likely a reference to the sky as opposed to the dwelling place of

---

201. Alter: "22. *A fruitful son.* The morphology of the reiterated noun in this line is so peculiar that some scholars have imagined a reference to branches, others to a wild ass. There is little philological warrant for the former, and the connection between the term used here, *porat*, and *per'e*, 'wild ass,' seems strained. (The main argument for the wild ass is that it preserves the animal imagery, but there are several other tribes in the poem that have no animal icons.) A link between *porat* and the root *p-r-h*, to be fruitful, is less of a grammatical stretch, and is encouraged by Joseph's play on that same root in naming his son Ephraim" (*Genesis*, 299).

202. Both Wenham (*Genesis 16–50*, 484–85) and Sarna (*Genesis*, 343) follow the "wild ass" translation.

203. Pirson: "The narrator suggests a relationship between Ishmael and Joseph by words and motifs that appear in his description of Ismael and Joseph as well as in Jacob's blessing of Joseph. Both characters have several things in common. Could the implication be that both will follow a similar route?" (*Lord of the Dreams*, 132).

God because of its use in tandem with ברכת תהום רבצת תחת, "blessings of the
deep that lies beneath." Note the continued contrasting of low and high—a
downward/upward example. "The blessings of the breast and of the womb"
is another life reference, and since Joseph was born from a "barren womb"
(30:1–2, 22–24), this may be another example of the death-and-resurrection
submotif of barren womb/opening of the womb.[204] Jacob says (49:26): "The
blessings of your father are greater than the blessings of my parents, up to
the bounties of the everlasting hills." Again, bounty, fruitfulness, and an
upward motif are linked.

Jacob closes with, "May they [all these blessings] be on the head of
Joseph, on the brow of him who was set apart from his brothers [נזיר אחיו]."
"All these blessings" is amplified by the inordinate use of ברך. This is the
first use of נזיר in Genesis and indicates "the one singled out; the one of
high rank; the one consecrated."[205] As Joseph was set apart in his life, beginning with a special tunic and ending with his rank of prominence among
the Egyptians, so Jacob also sets him apart in his blessing.[206] Here the
death-and-resurrection submotif of separation/reunion is noted.[207] Jacob
also sets apart Joseph in another way. The only use of ברך, "to bless," in
these twenty-seven verses is in the blessing of Joseph. Six times Jacob uses
"bless" or "blessing" in Joseph's blessing, while it is absent in the rest of the
verses. It appears that Jacob is again pointing to Joseph's favored status. It
is also important to consider the similarities of the Abrahamic blessing of
Genesis 12:2–3 and the blessing of Joseph here in Genesis 49.[208] In Abram's
blessing there is also an inordinate use of ברך, "to bless" (5×), and the blessing is strongly connected to earth and land, as we see in Joseph's blessing.
There is also the understanding that those who stand against Abram or
Joseph will not succeed and will not be blessed.

---

204. See chap. 5.

205. Deuteronomy 33:16, Moses' blessing for Joseph; also Lev 15:31; 22:2; 25:5, 11; Num
6:2, 5, 6, 12, 18, 21.

206. Longacre claims this blessing of Joseph shows Jacob's intention to designate Joseph
as firstborn. He points to Jacob's adoption of Ephraim and Manasseh, Jacob's gift to Joseph of
Shechem, the repeated use of "blessing" (more even than Judah), and the reference to Joseph
as "the one consecrated (especially set apart) among his brothers" (*Joseph*, 54).

207. Joseph is also set apart in his burial place; see chap. 5.

208. Kaminsky, in his treatment of election, makes note of the blessing of Abram and the
inordinate use of ברך. He also discusses this in relationship to Joseph as a special, set-aside,
elected one (*Yet I Loved Jacob*, 82–85).

Throughout the blessing of Joseph it appears that Jacob is again distinguishing between Joseph and his brothers. That Jacob uses a plant rather than an animal analogy (LXX, Targum Onqelos, etc.); the only reference to the Divine connected to the blessing; the only use of ברך, "to bless," and then six times; and the similarity between Joseph's and Abram's blessing—these are indications that perhaps Jacob still desires to give Joseph the greatest blessing, but because this belongs to Judah, he does everything short of it.

The final words are for Benjamin (49:27), and they are short and negative for a "loved" son (44:30). Benjamin is called a ravenous wolf in the morning devouring (יטרף; see 37:33) the prey and at evening dividing the spoil. Perhaps this is a reference to the future warlike character of this small tribe.[209] The men of Benjamin were renowned for their skill with the sling and the ability to wield it with both right and left hands (1 Chr 12:1–2).

This is the end of the blessings of the twelve tribes of Israel.[210] Five of the sons received the vast majority of the words of blessing—Reuben, Simeon, Levi, Judah, and Joseph—while the rest are briefly included. The Judah and Joseph blessings make up 40 percent of the material, which points the reader back to Genesis 37 and 38 and the prominence of these two sons. Note that the blessings do not follow the birth order of the sons. Then Jacob commands all of the sons as he commanded Joseph in 47:29–31: אני נאסף אל־עמי, "I am to be gathered to my people"; קברו אתי אל־אבתי, "Bury me with my fathers." Jacob is specific as to where—"in the cave that is in the field of Ephron the Hittite, in the cave that is in the field of Machpelah, to the east of Mamre, in the Land of Canaan, which Abraham bought with the field from Ephron the Hittite to possess as a burying place" (23:8–20). Jacob is very specific, reminding his sons that this is where Abraham and Sarah, Isaac and Rebekah are buried, and where he buried Leah. Previously, Jacob told Joseph of the burial place of Rachel (48:7). Now, not only does he tell where Leah is buried, but he also commands his sons to bury him in the same place. The narrator may be showing another separation of Judah from Joseph, noting the different burial places of their mothers. Then ויאסף רגליו אל־נמטה ויגוע ויאסף אל־עמיו, "he drew up his feet into the bed and breathed

209. Sarna, Genesis, 345; Wenham, Genesis 16–50, 487.
210. This is the first biblical reference to the twelve tribes of Israel.

his last and was gathered (up) to his people." Note the use of יאסף, "draw up," and יאסף, "gathered (up)," to describe Jacob's passing.

GENESIS 50

At the death of Jacob, Joseph falls on his father's face and weeps over him and kisses him (see Gen 45:14–15; 46:29). None of the other brothers are recorded as having any emotional reaction to the death of their father, apart from the fear of what Joseph may now do to them (50:15). Joseph commands "the physicians" (הרפאים) "to embalm" (לחנט) his father. The word for physicians, הרפאים, is used only twice in Genesis, and both times are in 50:2. Jacob's is the first recorded "embalming" in Scripture, the second being Joseph in verse 26. We are also told that this embalming process takes 40 days and that the Egyptians weep for Jacob 70 days. This is not a period of 110 days—40 plus 70—but rather 40 days for embalming plus another 30 days of mourning, for a total of 70 days. The children of Israel are not mentioned in this weeping and mourning, so this activity probably reflects a tradition of the Egyptian culture. The Hebrew tradition is likely noted in verse 10—a mourning of seven days—however, the Israelites are later recorded as mourning for Aaron and Moses for thirty days.[211] It is possible that in the course of the ensuing four hundred years that the Israelites adopted a custom more in line with the Egyptian culture.

In spite of Joseph's high position in the land of Egypt, it was still necessary for him to be invited into the presence of the Pharaoh to speak, and to receive permission to leave the land and bury his father. Pharaoh's quick and positive response again calls into question why Joseph did not seek permission to go find his father when Joseph first rose to power in Egypt. "To bury," קבר, is used five times in three verses in several forms. Note the frequent use of עלה, "to go up," with קבר, "to bury."[212] The downward/upward motif is illustrated in reverse by "going up to the land of Canaan" and "going down" as in burial; however, it is important to note that the death-and-resurrection submotif of going down to Egypt/going up to Canaan is also fulfilled by Jacob's return to the promised land as he

---

211. Aaron—Num 20:29; Moses—Deut 34:8.

212. ועתה אעלה-נא ואקברה, "Now, therefore, let me please go up and bury"—Joseph speaking; עלה וקבר, "Go up and bury"—Pharaoh speaking; ויעל יוסף לקבר, "Joseph went up to bury"; ויעלו, "they went up."

was assured by God himself at Beersheba in Genesis 46:1–4. Wenham states that Jacob's insistence on being buried in Canaan is a statement of where Israel belongs. The burial procession from Egypt up to Canaan is seen as a pledge or acted prophecy of the nation's future move.[213]

Due to Joseph's high position, the group that accompanies him to Canaan is impressive. "All the servants of Pharaoh, the elders of his household, and all the elders of the land of Egypt, as well as all the household of Joseph, his brothers, and his father's household … chariots and horsemen." As the narrator notes: ויהי המחנה כבד מאד, "It was a very great company." When they arrive at the threshing floor of Atad, "They lamented there with a very great lamentation," and he, Joseph, makes "a mourning" (אבל). This same word is used when Jacob mourned for Joseph in 37:35, and just as the brothers did not mourn for Joseph, they are not mentioned as personally mourning for their father. Perhaps the strained relationship caused by his show of favoritism never healed, or perhaps they are still stinging from the blessings, which for most of them resembled curses. When the Canaanites see this great display of mourning by this great company of people, they name the threshing floor אבל מצרים, "Abel-mizraim," the mourning of the Egyptians. Note that קבר is used nine times in verses 1–14, and עלה six times. Jacob's life has ended in Egypt, but he is brought up to the promised land.

Jacob's sons faithfully carry out the commands of their father, yet Joseph is more compelled to do so because he swore an oath (47:29–31). When they have completed the time of mourning and returned to Egypt, the brothers begin to worry. Their father is no more, and the protective buffer between them and Joseph is no more. Will this be the time Joseph seeks his revenge? In verse 15 the narrator uses the consonants ויראו, which can mean "they saw" or "they feared," to illustrate the point. "It may be that Joseph will hate us [bear a grudge] and pay us back for all the evil that we did to him" (לו ישטמנו יוסף והשב ישיב לנו את כל–הרעה אשר במלנו אתו). The brothers are so fearful that they send a message to Joseph rather than go in person, saying that their father gave a command (צוה) before he died. "Please forgive the transgression [פשע] of your brothers and their sin [וחטאתם], because they did evil [רעה] to you. And now, please forgive the transgression of the servants of the God of your father." פשע, "transgression, crime," is a word

---

213. Wenham, *Genesis 16–50*, 488.

whose use originated in the political realm. It was a reference to a rebellion of a vassal against an overlord. The use of this term by the brothers may indicate that they consider their transgression to be against their father for not accepting Joseph, and that their sin and evil are against Joseph. By using פשע they may be acknowledging Joseph's position of authority over them. Note also that the brothers recall how Joseph mentioned God as the one who turns evil into good (45:4–8), and so they include "the God of your father" in their message.

Upon hearing the message, Joseph weeps, and when the brothers hear of his reaction, they come to him in person. This is a repeat of the same pattern in Genesis 37, when they sent the bloody tunic of Joseph to their father, and then, when things had calmed down, they went in person. The narrator even uses the נא, "please," as he does in 37:32, "please identify." This same pattern is seen in 38:25, when Tamar sent Judah's signet, cord, and staff to him, saying: "Please identify."

When the brothers come to Joseph, "They fell before him [ויפלו לפניו] saying, 'We are your servants.'" In order to indicate submission, נפל is used. Perhaps the brothers feel guilt and sorrow over their past actions. Perhaps they remember Joseph's dreams. Most probable is that the dreams' fulfillment and their repentance or submission is suddenly not as important as their survival. Joseph says: "Do not fear, for am I in the place of God?" (כי התחת אלהים אני). Then Joseph repeats his words of 45:4–8: "As for you, you meant evil against me, but God meant it for good, to bring it about that many people should be kept alive as they are today." Only in the Joseph narratives is the idea of evil being turned to good by God found in Genesis; elsewhere, God averts evil but does not turn it to good. Joseph repeats the only explicit theological teaching in these narratives. Note how Joseph refers to his own salvific role as life giver, life preserver. He who was thrown down, cast down, sent down was raised up that others might be saved.

Joseph's brothers seem less inclined to accept Joseph's explanation of God's role in using evil to accomplish good. His brothers still do not acknowledge him or believe him to be an instrument of God. Since Joseph sees this as his divine mission and destiny, it would have been difficult to have his family not believe it. Nevertheless, Joseph "comforted" (וינחם) and "spoke kindly to them" (וידבר על–לבם).

The Joseph narratives conclude with Joseph's death. He lived to be 110 years old and saw Ephraim's sons to the third generation, and the sons of Machir, son of Manasseh, were born on Joseph's knees.[214] Ephraim is mentioned first according to the blessing given by Jacob in 48:17–20. As he prepares himself for death, Joseph tells his brothers that "God will surely visit (remember) you" (ואלהים פקד יפקד) and bring you up out of this land to the land he swore to Abraham, to Isaac, and to Jacob. Joseph is prophesying the fulfillment of another downward/upward cycle. All the children of Israel, who came down to Egypt to escape death by famine, will be brought back up to the promised land of Canaan—at least their descendants. Joseph, like his father in 47:31, makes his brothers swear, saying: "God will surely visit (remember) you, and you shall carry my bones from here." Joseph wants to be assured that he too will complete this death-and-resurrection submotif and return to Canaan. It is possible to see this statement by Joseph as a confession. He who has become an Egyptian in life, in every way, even forsaking his father's house, does not want to remain an Egyptian in death. He wants to return to the land of his fathers, even if only in death.[215] It may also reveal a serious deterioration in the situation of the Israelites in Egypt. It has been fifty-four years since the death of Jacob, and the intervening period has seen an eroding of Israelite and Egyptian relationships.[216]

Joseph does not want his bones to remain in Egypt, but why are they carried out and up by Moses (Exod 13:19)? Why are they not returned by his brothers, as Jacob's remains were returned? Is it possible that Joseph was so revered by the Egyptians that they would not allow it? Perhaps Joseph and his family no longer enjoyed the favor of Pharaoh (Exod 1:8). Perhaps it was important for the final death-and-resurrection motif to be fulfilled in the presence of the people of the exodus. This seems to be consistent with Joseph's own words: "God will surely visit (remember) you." When God does hear their cries from slavery and remembers his

---

214. The perfect age for an Egyptian was 110; see Speiser, *Genesis*, 376. Vawter states, "The Egyptians, who probably kept no real records of their ages, repeatedly in their documents that have come down to us use the number of one hundred and ten years to stand for a full, well-rounded lifespan, a complete life" (*Path through Genesis*, 305).

215. For more on the bones of Joseph, see chap. 10.

216. Sarna, *Genesis*, 351.

covenantal people (Exod 2:23–25), sending Moses to bring them out and up, then Joseph's bones also leave the land of Egypt.

Joseph "died" (וימת) and "they embalmed him" (יחנטו) and placed him in a "coffin" (בארון)—the only use of this word in Genesis.

CONCLUSION

The Joseph narratives demonstrate their unique character in comparison to the other Genesis narratives and the rest of Scripture. The narrator's continual use of doubling, as noted in the pairing of dreams, the repetition of vocabulary, and the doubling of accounts—two blessing accounts, for example—is excessive enough to capture the reader's attention. No other narrative portion of Scripture demonstrates doubling with such frequency. While this literary device shows the continuity of these narratives, there are more methods employed to accomplish this task. The use of biblical motifs not only connects these fourteen chapters to one another: it also connects the Joseph narratives with many other parts of the canon of Scripture. These motifs encourage us to see Scripture as one grand narrative and to read these writings as a unified theological narrative.

Various biblical motifs that begin in Genesis and continue into Revelation wind their way through the Joseph narratives. Although there are many motifs, the most prevalent is the death-and-resurrection motif, as demonstrated by a downward/upward movement. This constant descending/ascending trend is used to draw the reader's attention to the multiple manifestations of the death-and-resurrection motif. The submotifs of this theme number at least twelve and will be discussed in greater detail in chapter 5. What sets the Joseph narratives apart in regard to this motif is the sheer numbers that weave their way through the chapters. No other character or portion of Scripture has such a predominance of these various death-and-resurrection manifestations. When one considers this reality coupled with the downward/upward movement of the text, one wonders why this is so. What message is the narrator sending? How does he want us to see Joseph?

Considering these questions along with the first appearance of שְׁאוֹל, "Sheol," and its proximity to בור, "pit," it is not casting too far afield to see Joseph portrayed as a death-and-resurrection figure. Those who have struggled with the early Hebrews having a developed sense of the afterlife will find difficulty with this assertion. However, if we approach Scripture with the view of seeing it as a unified theological narrative and do not attempt to dismantle it, it appears the narrator wants us to see Joseph as more than a moral and ethical figure who abstains from sexual temptations and forgives his brothers in spite of their unworthiness. The life of Joseph, with all its ups and downs, is an account interwoven with example after example of death and resurrection. Even Joseph recognizes this as he states to his brothers: "As for you, you meant evil against me (even death), but God meant it for good, to bring it about that many people should be kept alive, as they are today" (Gen 50:20). Joseph sees himself as a preserver and saver of life, and thus he was understood by the Old Testament people and beyond. The people of Israel credit Joseph with preserving the messianic line.

Of course, this is not the singular message of these narratives, although I would argue it is the greatest. While the downward/upward movements of these verses might be construed, in very general terms, as applicable to Israel's exile from her homeland and eventual restoration at the start of the Second Temple period, the death-and-resurrection themes are not so easily moved to the sidelines. Here we should take seriously the words of Levenson in his observations on Ezekiel's vision of the valley of dry bones:

> The vision of dry bones resurrected is, by way of contrast, one of the prophet's oracles of restoration and thus appropriately speaks of the people of Israel's future obedience to God who has revived them and restored them to their own land (Ezek 37:13–14). To ask whether he restores them from hopelessness, slavery, exile, estrangement from God and his righteous will, or, rather, from death is excessively academic and misses the way Israel conceives these things. Most seriously, it misses the deep inner connection between the substance of the symbol (resurrection from death) and its decoded message (a return to the land, to the knowledge of God, and to obedience to him).[217]

---

217. Levenson, *Resurrection and the Restoration*, 162.

Disconnecting restoration from resurrection, or resurrection from restoration, is not a proper reading of the text. Joseph is a death-and-resurrection figure in the same way and at the same time that he is an exile and restoration figure, and if one asks whether the ups and downs of the Joseph narratives point to death and resurrection or exile and restoration, the answer is yes. Levenson closes his book with this paragraph:

> To the rabbis, resurrection without the restoration of Israel, including its renewed adherence to Torah, was incomprehensible. And without the expectation of resurrection, the restoration of Israel would be something less than what the rabbis thought the Torah had always intended it to be—the ultimate victory of the God of life.[218]

Another dominant movement in this story is the dramatic reversal of Judah and Joseph. This tale of two brothers shows the gradual rise of Judah from the pit to the role of preeminence over all his brothers. In the end, we have two heroes, but Joseph is relegated to a supporting role.[219]

Many difficulties reveal themselves as the story progresses, difficulties that have caused considerable concern among those seeking to adopt Joseph to further their agenda. These difficulties of text and inferred character flaws will be explored in the next chapter.

---

218. Levenson, *Resurrection and the Restoration*, 229.

219. Brueggemann understands the story in a different way: "While we cannot be sure, a plausible locus for the narrative is the royal, urban ethos of Solomon which imitated international ways and which sharply critiqued the claims of the old tribal traditions. Its presuppositions suggest a cool detachment from things religious that is contrasted with the much more direct religious affirmation of the Abraham and Jacob stories. This narrative appears to belong to a generation of believers in a cultural climate where old modes of faith were embarrassing. The old idiom of faith had become unconvincing. Thus, the narrative should be understood as a sophisticated literary response to a cultural, theological crisis" (*Genesis*, 288). Brueggemann focuses on the perceived cultural, sociological, and political contexts of the tenth century BCE, the Solomonic period, while at the same time claiming that questions of historicity are inappropriate (291).

4

Joseph and His Character: Perceived Problems and Difficulties

A quick reading of the text of the Joseph narratives provides a story with intense drama along with all the excitement and angst expected from such a narrative. However, while this cursory reading does not disappoint, there is much more to be gained from a thorough, careful reading of the text. Under the surface there are levels of meaning and complexity of structure and language easily missed in a quick survey. In the pursuit of such an examination the reader will discover some rather uncomfortable and questionable character traits in reference to the heroes of the story. These problems and difficulties, some perceived and others valid, have frequently been glossed over by faith communities.[1]

It is deemed unacceptable to point to the heroes of one's faith only to uncover deficiencies in their characters. Especially in relation to Joseph, who has historically been considered one of great moral virtue and stalwart character, such a deficit of character would compromise the various attempts to use him to further faith-based agendas. Yet, those who have engaged in a close reading, especially those with an intimate knowledge of Biblical Hebrew, have frequently been placed in an uncomfortable situation in regards to the hero, or heroes, of these narratives. Reactions to these problems and difficulties have been varied, some of which will be pointed out as we examine the LXX and the Targum Onqelos translations of the Joseph narratives. However, it will prove helpful to discuss these issues before we examine how the translators and interpreters have struggled to overcome the grittiness of the Joseph story.

---

1. Kugel: "In the view of some scholars, then, the Joseph of this story is something of an idealized figure, one whose life is meant to mirror the virtues of the wisdom philosophy" (*In Potiphar's House*, 14). Kaminsky, following the theme of election, notes the interconnection of Israel and Joseph's election in spite of their shortcomings: "The notion that the Israelites are God's elect but have not yet demonstrated their right to the title by acts of obedience is a nice counterpoint to the Joseph story in which Joseph's tendency to misuse his elect status leads to his suffering but in no way means he is less elect" (*Yet I Loved Jacob*, 102).

It is worth noting the work of R. W. L. Moberly in *The Old Testament of the Old Testament*. In this writing he argues that the Pentateuch more or less consistently portrays patriarchal religion as distinct from Mosaic Yahwism. He states: "Generally speaking, patriarchal religion lacks moral content or at least moral emphasis in a way that contrasts with the strong moral content enjoined on Israel by the covenant at Sinai."[2] This has the potential to cast a different light on several of the issues perceived in the Joseph narratives. For example, in the discussion concerning Joseph's cup of divination, the moral mandate against such practice is recorded in Deuteronomy 18. Does this statute of Mosaic law hold sway over the patriarchs? Moberly argues that patriarchal religion must first be seen as in some way a coherent religious system before it can be validly compared with Mosaic Yahwism.[3]

This is a strong point but is seldom considered as readers struggle with the various character issues of all the patriarchs.[4] In the discussion that follows, the flaws identified are those recognized by various readers in a range of faith communities. One must take into account the lack of engagement with distinct patriarchal religion, and the appropriation of the material within both Christian and Jewish faith communities.

GENESIS 37: A BAD REPORT—JOSEPH THE SPY

It does not take the narrator long to set up the strange family dynamics and reveal the animosity of Joseph's brothers toward the favored one. In the first verse (37:2) of the narratives, we are introduced to seventeen-year-old Joseph, who is learning to tend flocks under the tutelage of the sons of Bilhah and Zilpah, and "Joseph brought a bad report of them to their father." This does not bode well for the relationships of the brothers, and the text clearly indicates a jealousy beginning to simmer, soon to boil over in outright hatred. Jacob is either unaware or uncaring, because in verse 14 he sends Joseph out to where all his brothers are pasturing the flocks with

---

2. R. W. L. Moberly, *The Old Testament of the Old Testament* (Eugene, OR: Wipf & Stock, 2001), 97.

3. Moberly, *Old Testament of the Old Testament*, 85–86.

4. The bulk of the Torah's commandments were unknown to the patriarchs, as the rabbis attest. However, the patriarchs were aware of some basic laws. Certain commands were given to Noah—a sort of "natural law" given to all people—and Abraham is credited with a knowledge of divine instruction (Gen 18:19).

the order to "Go now, and see if it is well with your brothers and with the flock, and bring me word." Jacob is asking Joseph to play the spy and keep him updated on the doings of his brothers. With emotions already running high, nothing good can come of this.

The brothers, seeing Joseph from a distance, conspire to kill him (37:18) because they know full well why he has been sent. Their words in verses 19–20 betray their anger: "They said to one another, 'Behold the Lord of the Dreams. Come let us kill him and throw him into one of the pits.'" The bad report, the special robe, the dreams, and now Joseph being sent to check up on them, or spy them out and make another bad report to Jacob, are too much for them, and into the pit Joseph goes (37:24).

Joseph's role as his father's spy is not lost on his brothers or other early sources.[5] Even Joseph recognizes this perception among his brothers. When Joseph has risen to power in Egypt and is dispensing grain during the famine, his brothers come before him. His words in dealing with them are instructive: "You are spies; you have come to uncover the nakedness of the land" (42:9, 14, 16, 30–31, 34). A close look at the tests and trials that Joseph inflicts on his brothers shows a plan to put them through the same kind of agony he has endured. In calling them spies he is repeating their thoughts, if not their words, directed toward him at an earlier time.

This may all seem innocuous. Name calling among brothers is hardly unique to the Joseph narratives. However, the text allows one to see that these accusations of the brothers and the actual actions of Joseph have a degree of validity. While Jacob places Joseph in this role of spy, Joseph seems all too eager to carry out the work (37:13). This is a rather inauspicious beginning for Joseph and calls into question his character or his ability to perceive the effect his actions and attitudes have on others.

GENESIS 37: A SPOILED SON AND AN ARROGANT BROTHER

Continuing in the same vein, Joseph and his father, Jacob, do little to diffuse the volatility building among the sons. In fact, Jacob's actions push the tensions to the breaking point. If it were not enough that Jacob used Joseph to spy on his other sons, he also makes it clear that Joseph is the favored one. The narrator makes certain we do not miss this: "Now Israel loved Joseph

---

5. See chaps. 6–7.

more than any other of his sons" (Gen 37:3). Jacob not only makes this reality clear in his attitude, but he goes so far as to reinforce it with his actions:
"And he made him a special robe" (37:3). The result is predictable: "But when
they saw that their father loved him more than all his brothers, they hated
him and could not speak peacefully to him" (37:4). Jacob has done no favor
for Joseph.

Joseph only makes matters worse. While he has no control over his
dreams, he certainly is responsible for the manner in which he speaks of
them.[6] God is the giver of dreams, but Joseph is rather blunt in the recounting. One might expect Joseph to contemplate his dreams carefully, thinking long and hard about how to speak of them to his brothers.[7] Perhaps he
should have wrestled with the idea of whether to relay them at all. This is
not the case, and "They hated him even more" (37:5). This is borne out by the
narrator: "So they hated him even more for his dreams and for his words"
(37:8). Even Jacob rebukes Joseph for his second dream and, with his words,
gives the impression that Joseph has portrayed an arrogant attitude in the
telling: "His father rebuked him and said to him, 'What is this dream you
have dreamed? Shall I and your mother and your brothers indeed come to
bow ourselves to the ground before you?'" (37:10).

Jacob is guilty of playing favorites and spoiling his son Joseph, and the
result appears to be an arrogant attitude on the part of Joseph. Kaminsky
writes:

> Joseph begins the story as someone who understands his father's
> tendency to favor him and the special gifts he has received from God
> primarily as signs that he will rule over his brothers, as evidenced

---

6. S. Greidanus notes that at the beginning of the narrative, young Joseph is sketched
as immature, unwise, boastful, and extremely talkative. See Greidanus, *Preaching Christ
from Genesis* (Grand Rapids: Eerdmans, 2007), 338. Kaminsky: "However, even though Joseph
eventually exhibits all of these gifts, initially he misunderstands and misuses his chosen
status. Only after a lengthy period of tribulation does he come to maturity and grow into
his elect status. His brothers, too, grow and change over the course of the narrative" (*Yet I
Loved Jacob*, 59).

7. Moberly: "For the youthful Joseph clearly interprets his dreams egotistically: His
exaltation is, pleasingly, at his brothers' expense, hence their resentment. It is only later,
when he realizes that the dreams are fulfilled as he sees his brothers bowing before him
(42:6–9), that he shows that he has learned (at least, on our preferred reading) that power is
for responsible action toward the saving of lives during famine and reconciliation, not for
an ego trip" (*Theology of the Book of Genesis*, 242).

by his rather immature conduct in relation to them. Not only does he bring back a negative report about how poorly some of them are doing their job (Gen 37:2), but he also taunts his brothers with his dreams, which he and they immediately understand as an adumbration of his future elevation over them, a rise in fortune that the brothers wrongly interpret as having only negative consequences for their lives. Of course, his brothers' hatred is further deepened by Jacob's favoritism and particularly by Joseph's tendency to flaunt his favored status.[8]

Does Joseph speak of his dreams with a tone that is bound to incite anger? Apparently, for the brothers hate him not only for his dreams, but also for his words. This does not speak well of Joseph's character. One could argue that he is young and immature, a son of seventeen years.

GENESIS 37: CLUELESS

The narrator is not finished with his portrayal of Joseph. Jacob sends Joseph to "see if it is well with your brothers and with the flocks, and bring me word." Joseph eagerly sets out for Shechem, where the brothers are supposed to be; however, they are nowhere to be found. "A man found him wandering in the fields. The man asked him, 'What are you seeking?' 'I am seeking my brothers,' he said. 'Tell me, please, where they are pasturing the flock'" (Gen 37:15–16). These two verses may seem nothing more than a way for the narrator to get Joseph to Dothan, but the way they are delivered seems to cast Joseph in a strange light. The impression is that Joseph is wandering around the fields and pastures of Shechem in a clueless manner, lost, with no sense of direction or plan. Perhaps a small thing, but taken with the rest of this chapter it does give one pause.

GENESIS 37: UNCLEAN

The last problem in Genesis 37 is different in nature. Joseph has been thrown into a pit and sold into slavery. It now is paramount that the brothers devise a plan that will conceal what they have done. They slaughter a goat, dip Joseph's robe in the blood, and have it brought to their father (Gen 37:31–32).

8. Kaminsky, *Yet I Loved Jacob*, 59.

They ask Jacob to "please identify whether it is your son's robe or not"
(37:32). Jacob complies and makes his own assumptions with the evidence
he is presented: "It is my son's robe. A fierce animal has devoured him.
Joseph is without a doubt torn to pieces" (37:33). This is exactly the conclusion the brothers wanted Jacob to draw. Without lying, their cover story has
been provided. The problem is in the words of Jacob's declaration, "Joseph
is without a doubt torn to pieces." The narrator employs doubling to add
emphasis to Jacob's words, טָרֹף טֹרַף, "torn to pieces." This is an unseemly
death for one viewed as highly as Joseph. Even though Joseph is not truly
dead, it is disrespectful to speak of him and his demise with these words.

The Hebrew, טָרֹף טֹרַף, not only indicates a grisly death, but it also renders any animal that dies in such a manner unfit for sacrifice or consumption. In effect, it is unworthy and unclean. To speak this way concerning
Joseph, one of the twelve sons of Jacob, is a difficulty not lost on Jewish
readers.[9]

GENESIS 38: JUDAH AND CANAANITE WOMEN

Genesis 38 is dedicated to Judah and his escapades following the incident
with Joseph and his sale into Egypt. While our main focus is on Joseph,
the difficulties and problems with Judah cannot be ignored. They must
be addressed in some detail because they reappear, manifested in the life
of Joseph.

The first problem is with Judah and Canaanite women. Judah has put
some distance between himself and his family, perhaps due to the ugly
scene with Joseph and the deception of his father. He goes to dwell with
an Adullamite named Hirah, and there he sees the daughter of a certain
Canaanite whose name is Shua (Gen 38:1-2). Judah marries Shua, and they
have three sons. Judah has married a foreigner, a Canaanite woman. As
is noted in various places in the Genesis patriarchal narratives, marrying
into the pagan, foreign people of the surrounding area brings displeasure
to one's parents and one's God (24:2-4; 27:46; 28:6-9; etc.). Judah has done
that which is frowned on and later expressly forbidden.

If this were not enough, when it is time for his firstborn son to be married, Judah chooses another foreign woman to be his wife. Er is married

---

9. See chap. 7.

to Tamar. Twice Judah has ignored the separation between the people of Israel and the other nations as established by God when he called Abram out of the land of Ur and then Haran (12:1–3).

GENESIS 38: SEXUAL LIAISON

The greatest problem with the account of Judah is his sexual liaison with his own daughter-in-law. Many have argued that he has been duped by Tamar and that this somehow changes the perception of guilt. However, seeking the attentions of a prostitute, especially a temple or cult prostitute, is wholly unacceptable as well. The Israelites are commanded to be sexually pure in their relationships (Lev 18) because the relationship between man and woman reflects the relationship between God and Israel. Engaging the services of a cult prostitute is twice as bad in that not only is this an impure relationship, but it also takes place in the context of the worship of false gods.

GENESIS 38: WHO IS MORE RIGHTEOUS?

Judah's illicit act with Tamar is a sin that keeps on multiplying. Three months later, Tamar is found to be with child, and the report is made to Judah. "Tamar your daughter-in-law has been immoral (committed prostitution). Moreover, she is pregnant by immorality (prostitution)" (Gen 38:24). Judah shows indignation at this news and demands she be brought out and burned. Is Judah still harboring ill will toward Tamar, who is the only visible connecting link between the death of Judah's first two sons, Er and Onan? His call to have her burned is heavy handed when stoning would have been the common practice.

Judah's indignation is soon squelched when Tamar sends him the signet, cord, and staff that he had given her as a pledge of future payment for their sexual act. "By the man to whom these belong I am pregnant.' And she said: 'Please identify'" (38:25). Judah immediately recognizes his property and identifies it. Then, he says a disturbing thing: "She is more righteous than I" (38:26).

Such a statement by one of the twelve sons, one of the founding patriarchs, would be difficult for an Israelite. The Hebrew people have deep respect for these founders of their people, a respect that only deepens as time goes on. For Judah to confess that a Canaanite woman who has played the role of a temple prostitute is more righteous than he is of great concern and provides a stumbling block to Jewish readers.

GENESIS 39: AN ILL-ADVISED RETURN

The narratives return to their namesake, Joseph. Joseph has arrived in Egypt and been sold into slavery into the house of Potiphar, a man of some importance to the Pharaoh, as he is referred to as the captain of the guard (Gen 39:1). Joseph immediately distinguishes himself: "for the LORD was with him and that the LORD caused all that he did to succeed in his hands" (39:3). Seeing this, Potiphar wisely places Joseph in charge, making him the overseer of his entire household. This is pointed out by the narrator twice (39:4-5) and reiterated twice more (39:6-8). One can sense the plot thickening.

Not only has the Lord blessed the work of Joseph's hands, but he has also made him handsome in form and appearance. This is a problem because he attracts the attention of his master's wife. She is determined that Joseph should lie with her (39:7), but Joseph is firm in his refusal, even though the text notes that she speaks to Joseph concerning this day after day (39:10). Thus far, Joseph has remained pure and steadfast, providing a singular example of moral character.

"But one day, when he went into the house to do his work and none of the men of the house were there in the house ..." (39:11). It is the ill-advised return to the house that proves to be Joseph's downfall.[10] The master's wife catches him by his garment and attempts to force herself on him, but Joseph runs away, leaving his garment behind (39:12). This is a familiar account, and the outcome is familiar as well. Lost in all of this is the question, Why did Joseph return to the house? Kugel begins the discussion:

> Was Joseph entirely innocent in the events of that fateful day in Potiphar's house? We have already seen ... that the tendency of the earliest exegetes was to celebrate Joseph's virtue to almost super-human proportions: he is "Joseph the Righteous" or "the Virtuous,"

---

10. Sarna: "Early exegesis, as reflected in the Targums, has Joseph attending to his master's accounts. A rabbinic tradition (Sot. 36b) interprets the phrase as a euphemism: Joseph actually succumbed to the woman's blandishments, but at the crucial moment a mental image of his father inhibited him from sinning" (*Genesis*, 273).

and, according to 4 *Maccabees* or *Jubilees* or *Wisdom of Solomon*, his resistance to the temptation and wiles of Mrs. Potiphar was unambiguous and altogether exemplary.[11]

The narrator has made it clear that Joseph is in charge of the household. Nothing goes on without his oversight and knowledge, so why does Joseph enter the house when he knows that none of the men of the house are in the house? He would know what a difficult position in which this could place him. Again, the narrator has been clear about Potiphar's wife's desires and intentions.

There is a sense in the text, underlying the narrative, that Joseph may have entered the house at this opportune time to make himself available to his master's wife.[12] The scenario is too well set up to ignore the possibility.

GENESIS 40: A SUDDEN SELF-RELIANCE

Following Joseph's episode with Potiphar's wife, he is relegated to prison, but once again "The LORD was with Joseph and showed him steadfast love and gave him favor in the sight of the keeper of the prison" (Gen 39:21). Again, Joseph is placed in charge, given a position of authority over the other prisoners. "And whatever he did, the LORD made it succeed" (39:23).

Thus, when the chief cupbearer and the chief baker of the Pharaoh are brought into the prison, it is Joseph who is appointed to attend them. What follows is the second set of dreams of the Joseph narratives, and this time Joseph provides interpretations for the chief cupbearer and chief baker. Although Joseph makes it clear that interpretations belong to God, when he hears and then interprets the chief cupbearer's dream, Joseph pleads his own cause. His interpretation includes the restoration of the chief

---

11. Kugel, *In Potiphar's House*, 94.

12. Kugel says that Rabbi Yohanan and "one half of the Rab-Samuel dispute" see Joseph "as something of a willing participant, a man who has given in to temptation. Now one support for this approach is adduced from the biblical narrative itself; it is the innocent-looking phrase in 'Joseph went to the house *to do his work*'—which, this second school of thought holds, is merely a euphemism for 'to satisfy his desires'" (*In Potiphar's House*, 95). Kaminsky: "Even the biblical text leaves one wondering whether Joseph, who is in charge of Potiphar's house (Gen 39:4), knew that no servants were in the house on the day Potiphar's wife accosted the scantily clad Joseph. Did Joseph, flattered by all this attention, enter the house with the thought of consummating the relationship, but at the last moment change his mind and flee?" (*Yet I Loved Jacob*, 61).

cupbearer to the side of Pharaoh in three days. Joseph senses an opportunity, saying: "Only remember me when it is well with you, and please do
for me the kindness to mention me to Pharaoh, and so get me out of this
house" (40:14). While this may seem a natural and harmless attempt to
restore himself, there is a deeper problem.

The Lord has always been with Joseph. The narrator points out the
presence of the Lord with Joseph and how the Lord prospers and blesses
all that he does. Joseph even attributes any ability to interpret as coming
from God. Why this sudden self-reliance? One moment total trust and reliance on the Lord, the next an attempt to orchestrate his own release from
prison. This sudden self-reliance is a new facet to Joseph's character that
has not been previously seen.

GENESIS 41–50: JOSEPH THE EGYPTIAN

The greatest difficulty and that which represents the most challenging
attack on the character of Joseph is his transformation into an Egyptian.
Joseph is defended against this charge as his advocates point to the inevi-
table and irresistible nature of the circumstances Joseph faced. Egypt and
its culture are forced on him, and he has no choice in the matter of being
adopted in, but a careful reading of the text may advocate otherwise.

The beginning of this transformation is read in 41:37, but it is Joseph's
own proposal in 41:33 that sets the wheels in motion. Joseph suggests to
Pharaoh that he select a discerning and wise man and set him over the land
of Egypt in order to make proper preparations for the upcoming famine.
Joseph is clearly pressing his advantage. He has just interpreted Pharaoh's
dreams, which all the wise and discerning men of Egypt failed to do. Now,
he suggests choosing a wise and discerning man. He is clearly trying to
influence Pharaoh to choose him, and, Pharaoh complies. "Can we find a
man like this, in whom is the Spirit of God?" (41:38). Joseph certainly understands what it would mean for him to be chosen for this fourteen-year
task. He is committing himself to life in Egypt as an Egyptian. Still, it is
the doing of the Lord God that Joseph be set in place to preserve and save
the people of Israel.

Immediately, Pharaoh dresses Joseph as an Egyptian, one of the high-
est rank (41:42), then he gives him the second chariot in which to ride
(41:43), and the people of Egypt acknowledge his authority (41:43–44). These

things are unavoidable, but now Pharaoh bestows on Joseph an Egyptian name (41:45; Zaphenath-paneah) and an Egyptian wife (41:45; Asenath). The name is, perhaps, also unavoidable, but with the giving of Asenath as his Egyptian wife the difficulties begin. Note the similarities to Judah. Both have a foreign wife, which is a problem if a Hebrew is to remain faithful. Joseph, however, has married the daughter of a pagan priest.[13] This brings his life and character into greater question.

This union between Joseph and Asenath results in two male children, and now the text clearly shows Joseph's new direction. He names his first son Manasseh: "God has made me forget all my hardship and my father's house" (41:51). This name points to Joseph's attitude. It appears that Joseph has made the decision to adopt Egypt as his new country as he forgets his father Jacob's house. The next son is named Ephraim: "For God has made me fruitful in the land of my affliction." Again, Joseph has settled on Egypt as his new homeland.

Now that Joseph has become the second-most powerful in all of Egypt, it is logical that he would endeavor to seek out and find his father.[14] Even if he is too involved in the collecting of grain to search in person, he could send others to learn of Jacob's health and whereabouts and to inform him of Joseph's safety and new position. Why does Joseph make no attempt? In his defense, he may not know the true circumstances of all that led him to be in Egypt. He also does not realize that Jacob thinks him dead. He may actually be hurt and angry that his father has made no attempt to search him out. Still, it is not fitting that Joseph would not look for his father and that he would turn to Egypt as his new and permanent dwelling place.

The next puzzling development is in Genesis 44, where the narrator introduces us to Joseph's cup of divination. Joseph's steward, under orders, places Joseph's silver cup in the mouth of Benjamin's sack of grain. Then Joseph sends his steward after the brothers in search of the "stolen" cup. At this point we hear from Joseph the words: "Say to them, 'Why have you repaid evil for good? Is it not from this (cup) that my lord drinks, and by this

---

13. Asenath the daughter of Potiphera, priest of On.

14. This deficiency is noted by Eusebius as he quotes third-century Greek Demetrius the Chronographer: "But though Joseph had good fortune for nine years, he did not send for his father because he was a shepherd as were his brothers too, and Egyptians consider it a disgrace to be a shepherd" (*Praeparatio Evangelica* 9.21.13).

that he practices divination?'" (44:4–5). When Benjamin is found with the
cup, all the brothers return to the household of Joseph, and he says to them:
"What deed is this that you have done? Do you not know that a man like me
can indeed practice divination?" (44:15). Joseph claims to be able to practice magical arts, which were considered anathema to a Hebrew, for they
were seen as the realm of evil and the work of false gods. These arts were,
however, a common practice among the upper class of Egyptian society.[15]

When Joseph, his brothers, and his father are finally reunited in Genesis
45, Joseph in his address toward his extended family always speaks of them
as separate from him. Genesis 45:7 is the first example: "And God sent me
before you to preserve for *you* a remnant on earth, and to keep alive for *you*
many survivors." Joseph speaks of his family and the preserved remnant
as separate from himself, as if he no longer considers himself a part. This
is observed in the setting up of a dwelling place for Israel in the land of
Goshen. "You shall dwell in the land of Goshen, and you shall be near me"
(45:10). Once again, Joseph is keeping himself separate from his Hebrew
family, choosing instead to dwell with the Egyptians. There is no indication in the text that Joseph ever dwells in the land of Goshen, even after
he has finished with his grain-distribution duties.

This transformation is not lost on Joseph's father. Jacob makes note of
the choice Joseph has made, but the one thing that clearly irritates him
is the name of Manasseh. The idea that Joseph would declare that he has
forgotten his father's house and its troubles by naming his son Manasseh
does not sit well. As a result, in Genesis 48, when Jacob blesses the two
sons of Joseph, he crosses his arms and places his right hand on the head
of Ephraim and his left hand on the head of Manasseh (48:14). This is the

---

15. In regards to this incident, von Rad writes: "We have here one of those not uncommon
cases where our narrator reports something in passing without commenting upon it and
without intending the reader to form any serious judgment. He is not to ask here whether
what is said in passing about Joseph was theologically permitted, pardonable, or not permitted. It is, of course, not implied that Joseph had completely forsaken the faith of his fathers,
though there is no doubt that Joseph had adopted more and more of the customs and habits
of the Egyptians" (*Genesis*, 387). Wenham writes: "It is dubious whether this remark by the
steward describes Joseph's practice; it is just a threatening comment to stress the gravity of
the offense and to explain why he is sure the brothers are guilty" (*Genesis 16–50*, 424). Sarna:
"It is not stated that Joseph actually believes in divination. He wants the brothers to think he
does. ... The aim of the exercise was to determine the future, to locate the source of trouble,
or to apportion blame or credits, as in 30:27. The legislation in Deuteronomy 18:10 outlawed
divination in Israel" (*Genesis*, 304).

opposite of what is expected, as Manasseh is the eldest, but when Joseph attempts to correct his father, Jacob is firm in stating that he knows what he is doing (48:17-20). "Thus he put Ephraim before Manasseh" (48:20).

The final notation in Joseph's transformation into an Egyptian takes place at his death. While Jacob is buried in Canaan in the cave of the Patriarchs, Joseph's remains are embalmed and remain in Egypt (50:26). However, Joseph makes his brothers swear that when God visits them they will carry his bones with them when they return to the promised land of Canaan (50:24-25). This may be Joseph's confession that, while he has lived as an Egyptian, he prefers to be buried as a Hebrew in the land promised to his ancestors. The narrator twice tells us that Joseph died at 110 years old (50:22, 26), considered to be the perfect age for an Egyptian.

GENESIS 42-44: TESTING, TESTING, TESTING

There are many who read these narratives and are uncomfortable with the hero, Joseph, because of how he treats his brothers. No one would argue with the idea that the brothers have acted with hatred and jealousy toward Joseph, causing him to endure terrible trials and tribulations. Nevertheless, some find Joseph's initial actions toward his brothers difficult as well.

It begins when the brothers are sent to Egypt by Jacob to buy grain (Gen 42:2). When the brothers, minus Benjamin, appear before Joseph, he treats them badly, accusing them of coming to uncover the nakedness of the land (42:7-9). He throws them in prison for three days (42:17-18), and when he brings them out, he has devised a way to test them. "Do this and you will live, I fear God" (42:18).

Joseph's testing has three main parts, with many smaller tests interspersed within. The first part is keeping Simeon in custody while the rest return home to Canaan to bring back Benjamin. To make this test more difficult, Joseph has the payment for their grain placed in the mouth of their sacks. Jacob is not a willing participant in this plan and refuses to allow Benjamin to return; however, when the grain runs out, they return, and Judah convinces his father to allow Benjamin to accompany them in the journey. When Joseph sees Benjamin, the first part of the test is passed (43:16-23).

Before the official beginning of part two, Joseph prepares a feast, and Benjamin is accorded the greatest favor, making him stand out above the other brothers (43:34). This allows Joseph to observe their reactions, for it was such things that had caused the brothers to hate him and harbor great jealousy. The second major portion of Joseph's testing begins in Genesis 44. The brothers load up their grain and prepare to return to Canaan, but Joseph, once again, has each man's money returned in his sack. To put this test into motion, Joseph's steward is instructed to place Joseph's silver cup into the mouth of Benjamin's sack (44:2). Once the brothers are on their way, Joseph sends his steward after them. "Why have you repaid evil for good? Is it not from this that my lord drinks?" (44:5). The brothers are so certain of their innocence that they vow that if the cup is found in any of their sacks, that man shall die (44:9). The trap is sprung as the cup is discovered in Benjamin's sack. The brothers refuse to leave Benjamin behind, and they all return to Joseph's house (44:14–16). In so doing they have passed phase two of the testing. However, Joseph is going to up the ante in the third phase.

Joseph refuses to hold all the brothers accountable for the actions of one. He tells them to leave Benjamin and return home (44:17). This is the third portion of his test. Will the brothers be satisfied to save themselves? Will they overlook the distress of both Benjamin and Jacob? This is what they did years ago; will they repeat their actions? It is Judah who steps forward and, taking Joseph aside, makes a plea for his brother, pointing to the emotional attachment between Benjamin and Jacob. Then, in a dramatic reversal, Judah offers himself up as a replacement for Benjamin (44:33). Judah has successfully negotiated the brothers' way through the third test, and Joseph decides to reveal his true identity (45:1–4).

The brothers have passed the tests of Joseph, but the trauma to which the brothers were subjected seems overdone. Perhaps Joseph is getting even for the way he has been treated, giving a taste of what he has suffered at their hands.

DYSFUNCTION AND DECEPTION: A FAMILY HERITAGE

Describing the family of Israel as dysfunctional may be an understatement. As has been mentioned, Jacob is the cause of many of his own problems. By playing favorites and using son against son, he has created a climate of hatred and jealousy that manifests itself against Joseph, but is likely to have been played out among the rest as well. Can this be traced back to Jacob and his legacy?

From his birth when he is named Jacob (supplanter, heel grabber, deceiver), Jacob has spent considerable effort living up to his name. He deceives Isaac and Esau out of the blessing; he has a strange relationship of mutual deception with his father-in-law, Laban; and he is constantly playing favorites with his parents, his wives, and his sons. This is Jacob's legacy, and what he sows he also reaps. Reuben deceives him by entering into a relationship with Bilhah; Simeon and Levi betray him in the matter with the men of Shechem, and the sons, minus Benjamin, deceive him with a bloody tunic, allowing him to think that Joseph has been killed. We also see this deception as Tamar deceives Judah because he has deceived her and as Joseph deceives his brothers.

There is a demonstrated lack of trust for a family dynamic. Jacob no longer trusts Joseph to do as he requests; rather, he makes him swear an oath to bury him in Canaan (Gen 47:30–31). The brothers in turn do not trust Joseph following the death of Jacob, and they deceive him concerning the last wishes of their father (50:15–17). Finally, Joseph does not trust his brothers to carry out his last wish to be buried in Canaan. He also makes the brothers swear an oath (50:25). There is no climate of trust in this family, and because these are foundational ancestors of the people of Israel, concern is evident among their descendants.

CONCLUSION

A careful reading of the Joseph narratives results in discoveries that may challenge one's comfort level. This has proven true historically among those who consider Joseph, and to a certain extent Judah, to be heroes of their faith. For the earlier Hebrews and the later Jewish communities, who desire to see all the sons of Jacob as heroic figures, these accounts can be awkward. It is challenging to hold one's heroes under a microscope. All the flaws are revealed in detail, and so there is a felt need to deal with these perceived problems and difficulties.

The way in which various faith communities choose to deal with these challenges can prove to be helpful in discerning the deeper meaning of the text. Changes made to the text signal perceived difficulties and should draw the attention of the interpreter. Even the most minute and minor change can be understood as an attempt to polish or enhance the stature of the character.

In some instances, the difficulties are significant enough to warrant the use of extrabiblical literature to inform the understanding. In the case of Joseph, there were a number of pseudepigraphal documents written for this purpose.[16] A great amount of narrative information is provided in these writings so that the reader may form a proper understanding and respect for the hero and not be distracted by perceived textual difficulties in the MT.

At first, this revisionist approach may disappoint or even offend the reader, but one should consider the advantages it provides. These attempts at revision point out nuances in the text that otherwise might be overlooked. These questions, raised by the MT, are frequently addressed by the LXX and targum versions. In some cases, they alert us to a question; in other cases, they answer our questions.

The examination of the Septuagintal text and Targum Onqelos in the upcoming chapters will demonstrate how some of these difficulties have been dealt with. It is interesting the lengths to which translators and editors are willing to go to polish and restore the image of Joseph. By noting these efforts, we gain insights into the meaning of the MT and come to a fuller understanding of its intended message.

---

16. For example, Joseph and Aseneth, which deals with the difficulty of Joseph's marriage to the daughter of a pagan priest. This is a serious problem and requires serious explanation.

5

The Death-and-Resurrection Motif in the Joseph Narratives

INTRODUCTION

There are certain narratives and characters in the Old Testament in which the death-and-resurrection motif manifests itself more powerfully. This is particularly the case in the Joseph narratives. I would argue that no other figure in the Old Testament canon provides as strong a case for the complexity of the Hebrew understanding of, and belief in, the idea of resurrection from the dead.[1] As we examine each of these manifestations in some detail, we will observe their intersection in the Joseph narratives, thus showing Joseph to be a powerful death-and-resurrection figure in the received text. As we read this text as a unified theological narrative it will help demonstrate the coherence and the sense of the Joseph narratives and its dying and rising character.

THE DEATH-AND-RESURRECTION MOTIF OF THE JOSEPH NARRATIVES

We should bear in mind Levenson's remarks about the expectations raised by the story of Joseph when he states:

---

1. Daniel also provides strong and frequent examples of the death-and-resurrection motif. Much has been said concerning the similarities of these OT figures. I have chosen Joseph because of his early place in the history of the Israelites. For critical overviews of scholarly discussion of this topic, see J. N. Bremmer, *The Rise and Fall of the Afterlife* (London: Routledge, 2002), 1–4; G. W. E. Nickelsburg, *Resurrection, Immortality and Eternal Life in Intertestamental Judaism and Early Christianity* (Cambridge: Harvard University Press, 1972), 31, 41–42; A. F. Segal, *Life after Death: A History of the Afterlife in Western Religion* (New York: Doubleday, 2004), 120–24, 142 45, 248 57; R. Rosenburg, *The Concept of Bibilcal Sheol within the Context of Ancient Near East Belief* (Cambridge: Harvard University Press, 2001), 161–92; K. Spronk, *Beatific Afterlife in Ancient Israel and in the Ancient Near East* (Kevelaer, Germany: Butzon and Bercker, 1986), 65–81. Other modern treatments include R. Martin-Achard, "Resurrection (OT)," in *The Anchor Bible Dictionary*, ed. D. N. Freedman (New York: Doubleday, 1992), 5:680–84; G. Stemberger, *Der Leib der Auferstehung*, Analecta Biblica 56 (Rome: Pontifical Biblical Institute, 1972).

There is, nevertheless, a lesson to be learned from this tale about the expectation of resurrection that will first appear much later. It is simply that long before the apocalyptic framework came into existence, the resurrection of the dead was thought possible—not according to nature, of course, but through the miraculous intervention of the living God.[2]

As we examine the Joseph story, we find corroboration of Levenson's words. No fewer than twelve manifestations of the motif of death and resurrection may be discerned in the fourteen chapters before us. The structure of these chapters provides for a certain dramatic ebb and flow that supports the motif. As we shall soon see, the Joseph narratives are quite dramatic, containing all the elements of a divine tragedy. This structure has resulted in the narratives being employed in the theater, on the stage, and, in our day, in the movies. The ebb and flow of this dramatic story is an ongoing downward/upward movement. Joseph, the members of his family, and even the Egyptians are brought low only to be raised up time and time again. As might be expected, this downward/upward movement lends itself quite nicely to the various manifestations of the death-and-resurrection motif. Jon Davies writes: "Going upward and going downward implies a cosmology, a spatial and a moral division of the universe. In Hebrew cosmology the earth is located underneath heaven and above Sheol, Hades or hell—the underworld."[3] This downward/upward movement is an important part of the structure of these narratives and dovetails with the submotifs to be discussed.[4]

The manifestations of this death-and-resurrection motif in the Joseph narratives are as follows:

---

2. Levenson, *Resurrection and Restoration*, 132.

3. J. Davies, *Death, Burial and Rebirth in the Religions of Antiquity* (London: Routledge, 1999), 88.

4. Levenson notes this downward/upward movement and its relationship to death and resurrection: "The son's descent into Egypt is a kind of death; his ascent to rulership, a kind of resurrection. Whereas the pit is a metaphor of Sheol in the case of Joseph's descent, in the case of his second, the metaphor is Egypt, or, to be more precise, slavery in Egypt. Each descent is a manifestation of his symbolic death, and with each, Joseph moves farther from the source of his vitality—his family and his native land" (*Death and Resurrection*, 152).

1. separation and reunion

2. three-day/three-stage separation and restoration

3. the barren womb and the opening of the womb

4. being cast into a pit/Sheol and being raised up/lifted up

5. going down to Egypt and up to Canaan/the promised land

6. slavery and freedom

7. thrown into prison and released from prison

8. famine and deliverance (drought and rain/dew)

9. seeds/planting and growth/fertility/fruitfulness

10. going down into the water/being drowned and being brought up out of the water/new life

11. exile and return from exile

12. stripped and clothed (garment motif)[5]

As we examine these submotifs, I will note how they intersect with and build on one another. Historically, this intersecting and building is essential in comprehending the Hebrew understanding of death and resurrection. It is interesting that the downward/upward movement of the death-and-resurrection motif is alluded to already in the Testament of Joseph:[6]

---

5. Another death-and-resurrection submotif in Scripture is sick/diseased and being healed. However, it is not easily found in the Joseph narratives.

6. J. H. Charlesworth dates the Testaments of the Twelve Patriarchs to around 250 BCE. However, he also notes the existence of Christian interpolations from the early second century CE, which most likely have affected this portion of the Testament of Joseph. See Charlesworth, *The Old Testament Pseudepigrapha* (New York: Doubleday, 1983-85), 1:777, 819; and R. H. Charles, *Apocrypha and Pseudepigrapha of the Old Testament* (Oxford: Clarendon, 1913), 2:282-95, especially 291, detailing possible Christian additions. M. de Jonge has steadfastly argued that the Testaments originated as a Christian work. See his *The Testaments of the Twelve Patriarchs: A Study of Their Text, Composition, and Origin* (Leiden: Brill, 1953), and the recapitulation of his thesis in "The Main Issues in the Study of the Testaments of the Twelve Patriarchs," in his *Jewish Eschatology, Early Christology, and the Testaments of the Twelve Patriarchs* (Leiden: Brill, 1991), 147-63. His view has not been generally accepted, most scholars arguing that the work as we have it began life as a Jewish enterprise modeled on testaments of great men: the

A copy of the testament of Joseph. When he was about to die, he called his sons and his brothers and said to them:

> "My brothers and my children.
> Listen to Joseph, the one loved of Israel.
> Give ear to the words of my mouth.
> In my life I have seen envy and death.
> But I have not gone astray: I continued in the truth of the Lord.
> These, my brothers, hated me but the Lord loved me.
> They wanted to kill me, but the God of my fathers preserved me.
> Into a cistern they lowered me; the Most High raised me up.
> They sold me into slavery; the Lord of all set me free.
> I was taken into captivity; the strength of his hand came to my aid.
> I was overtaken by hunger; the Lord himself fed me generously.
> I was alone, and God came to help me.
> I was in weakness, and the Lord showed his concern for me.
> I was in prison, and the Savior acted graciously in my behalf.
> I was in bonds, and he loosed me;
> falsely accused, and he testified in my behalf.
> Assaulted by bitter words of the Egyptians, and he rescued me.
> A slave, and he exalted me." (T.Jos. 1.1–7)

The downward/upward movements in the Joseph story were already pointed out as early as 250 BCE, and, even if we attribute these to a later Christian interpolation from the second century CE, the recognition of this movement by both Jewish and Christian faith communities lends support to a death-and-resurrection motif.

SEPARATION AND REUNION

Separation and reunion is a theme instantiated in key canonical narratives including the expulsion of Adam and Eve from the garden of Eden (Gen 3:1–24) and the story of the Tower of Babel (11:1–9), which dramatically represent the separation of God and humanity. A sense of the possibility of reunion

Qumran caves have yielded several examples of such testamentary literature. The relevant Qumran manuscripts, and other related evidence, are thoroughly examined by R. A. Kugler, *Testaments of the Twelve Patriarchs* (Sheffield: Sheffield Academic Press, 2001).

is provided by the Abraham narratives (12:1–3; 15:7–21; 17:4–8), which point forward to a blessed and prosperous future for Abraham's descendants.[7]

How do we observe this manifestation of the death-and-resurrection motif in the Joseph narratives?[8] It begins immediately as Joseph is separated from his father by the evil intentions of his brothers. Jacob even refers to his separation from Joseph as a death (37:34–35) and later worries about the same separation from his son Benjamin (42:38; 43:14). Joseph is separated from his father, his kinsman, and his homeland just as Abram was separated in Genesis 12:1–3, but just as Abraham's separation was intended to eventually bring about reunion, so also did Joseph's separation result in a later reunion as the Lord God used him as an instrument to save his people from famine.[9] Once again the family is reunited, albeit in a foreign land.[10] Yet, even in Egypt the Lord maintains the separation between the Hebrews and the Egyptians by establishing them in the land of Goshen (45:9–11; 46:34; 47:1, 4, 6). Thus, the distinct and separate nature of the people of God was preserved even in a foreign country, so that the ultimate reunion could take place.[11]

---

7. C. J. H. Wright uses the language of "particularity" instead of separation. The people of Israel are chosen and set apart. The purpose of this particularity is to fulfill the mission of God, which is the redemption (reunion) of his people Israel, and therefore the redemption of all people (Wright, *Mission of God*, 324–35). Kaminsky prefers the language of "election" and identifies three distinct groups; the elect (Israel), the antielect (groups doomed for destruction), and the nonelect (all other non-Israelites). Kaminsky explores the relationship between election and the themes of promise and covenant (*Yet I Loved Jacob*, 10–11).

8. Levenson: "It occurred to me that the loss and restoration of Joseph to his father constitutes an analogy in narrative to the several Israelite rituals that substitute for the literal sacrifice of the first-born son. In the Joseph Novella, as in those rituals, the father's choicest son receives his life anew, and the man who, one way or another, gave him up or should have done so, gets back the offspring who had been marked for death. Further reflection led to the conclusion that the analogy holds for other important sons in Genesis as well—Ishmael, Isaac, and Jacob—and for the man the Church believes to be the son of God" (*Death and Resurrection*, ix).

9. Wenham: "Christian exegetes have often seen Joseph as a type of Christ, the innocent man who through his sufferings brings reconciliation to his human brethren and life to the world. It is possible to go further and view him as a model for all believers, who like him must die to self, if they are to make peace with their neighbors" (*Genesis 16–50*, 360). By his comments Wenham in essence negates the prominence of the submotif by placing the theme of forgiving one's brothers on a higher plane than the reunion accomplished in Christ.

10. Westermann, while acknowledging the separation and reunion theme within the Joseph narratives, focuses more on the conflict and its resolution—conflict and forgiveness. He also claims the narrator wants to say something about the conflict between family and monarchy (*Genesis 37–50*, 45, 148–49).

11. We observe this once again when the people of Judah are in exile in Babylon, and yet allowed to be separate and maintain their distinct character as a people.

Again the Lord God has acted in an illogical manner in order to accomplish his purposes. Judging from the text of Genesis 37, the relationship between Joseph and his older brothers is tenuous, to say the least. Reconciliation seems highly unlikely, and yet, by using separation, the Lord does indeed accomplish this reconciliation and reunion as Joseph forgives his brothers when he confronts them in Egypt and as they seek his forgiveness (45:3–7; 50:15–17).

THREE-DAY/THREE-STAGE SEPARATION AND RESTORATION

The three-day/three-stage separation and restoration submotif of the death-and-resurrection motif is similar in nature but distinct in character from the basic separation-and-reunion submotif. While it shares the basic component of separation, it is much more distinct in detail as it employs either three days/years or three stages to illustrate the separation.[12] And while reunion and restoration are also similar, there remains a subtle nuance of difference.[13] Restoration indicates a return to or a giving again of that which once was, while reunion does not necessarily share this theme.[14]

The use of three days as a time period of separation is attested in the canon of Scripture in the account of Abraham's call to offer up his son Isaac. The journey from their home to the place of sacrifice was a three-day journey, and Abraham, by faith (Heb 11:17–19), believed that the Lord would provide and restore his son to him, and God stayed Abraham's hand

---

12. The Hebrew language also uses "three days/years" as an idiom indicating a short period of time. However, in the material examined in the Joseph story where we encounter the use of "three," the narrative strongly suggests a specific three-day/year time frame.

13. Levenson, in dealing with the subject of restoration, correctly notes the connection between the restoration of the people of Israel and the restoration that is associated with resurrection. Unlike others, Levenson associates the Israelites' expectations for resurrection with restoration. "I argue that the expectation of the resurrection of the dead was a weight-bearing beam in the edifice of rabbinic Judaism. It was central to two major and inseparable elements of rabbinic Judaism, the rabbis' vision of redemption and their understanding of Jewish peoplehood. Without the restoration of the people Israel, a flesh-and-blood people, God's promises to them remained unfulfilled, and the world remained unredeemed. Those who classify the Jewish expectation of resurrection under more universal and individualistic rubrics, such as 'life after death,' miss the promissory character of the expectation and its inextricable connection to a natural family, the Jews" (*Resurrection and the Restoration of Israel*, x).

14. In regard to relationships, the difference between reunion and restoration is often indiscernible, and the terms are used interchangeably.

and provided a ram for sacrifice. [15] Joshua, as he prepared to lead the people into the promised land of Canaan, waited three days before the priests were commanded to carry the ark of the covenant into the Jordan. The waters heaped up (Josh 3:13), and at the end of three days the people were standing in the promised land, restored to their covenantal heritage. The prophet Jonah, in an attempt to flee his God-given task, ended up in the belly of a great fish for three days and three nights before he was restored to dry ground as the fish regurgitated him on the shore (Jonah 1:17).

In the Joseph narratives the three-day separation and restoration is clearly illustrated in the dreams of the chief baker and the chief cupbearer and their fulfillment. The three branches in the chief cupbearer's dream and the three baskets of bread in the chief baker's dream each represent three days. In the case of the cupbearer, Joseph interprets that after three days Pharaoh will lift up his head and restore him to his office, but in the case of the baker, after three days Pharaoh will lift up his head from him! So it is that the third day is Pharaoh's birthday, and things transpire just as Joseph interpreted. Sarna writes:

> Joseph deciphers the dream by a scheme of equivalences. The rapidity of the action suggests imminent fulfillment. The recurrence of the number three indicates specifically three days, three branches, three stages of growth, three actions performed; and both "Pharaoh" and his "cup" are mentioned three times. It is quite likely that Joseph actually has knowledge of Pharaoh's impending birthday celebration, as Bekhor Shor and Ibn Ezra suggest. Moreover, he cannot help noting that in the dream the cupbearer is actually performing his duties in the presence of Pharaoh. [16]

We see in Genesis 41:1 that it was two whole years later—the text is very specific—that Joseph was mentioned on the occasion of Pharaoh's dreams. The conclusion is that Joseph spent three years in the prison before he was

---

15. Genesis 22: The Akedah, or binding of Isaac, is an important text for the faith communities of both Jews and Christians. It contains many references to the coming sacrificial system and the sacrifice of the only-begotten Son of God. After three days Abraham lifts up his eyes and sees Mount Moriah, later to become the Temple Mount.

16. Sarna, *Genesis*, 278.

restored to freedom. The three-day/three-stage separation-and-resto-ration submotif is also seen in Genesis 42 on the occasion of the brothers' first visit to Egypt when Joseph "put them all together in custody for three days. On the third day Joseph said to them, 'Do this and you will live, for I fear God'" (42:17-18). This three-day imprisonment reflected his own three years in prison. At that point Joseph sends his brothers back to Canaan for Benjamin while Simeon remains in custody.

The second manifestation in this submotif is the three-stage sepa-ration and restoration. This kind of separation becomes more of an important reality in the life of Israel and its religious culture than the three-day separation. The first important occurrence of this has already been alluded to in the discussion of Abram's separation from his home. The text clearly speaks of a threefold separation: "Now the LORD said to Abram, 'Go from your country and your kindred and your father's house to the land that I will show you'" (Gen 12:1). Your country, your kindred, and your father's house—three degrees or three stages of separation that are mirrored in the life of Joseph as he is taken from his country, his kin-dred, and his father's house to the land of Egypt.

Other examples of this become even more important to the Israelites as we look at Mount Sinai in Exodus 24. This is an unusual text. Within it we see another example of the three stages of separation. The people of Israel stay at the foot of the mountain while Moses, Aaron, Nadab, Abihu, and seventy elders go up and banquet with God. However, in verse 12, God instructs Moses to come further up, for as we have seen in verse 2, "Moses alone shall come near to the LORD, but the others shall not come near, and the people shall not come up with him." What purpose do these three stages of separation serve, and where do we find the restoration? The answer lies in the priesthood and the structure of the tabernacle and temple.[17]

When God establishes the priesthood from the tribe of Levi, there is a clear distinction between the priests and the rest of the Israelites.

---

17. J. Kleinig uses the language of holiness. The unholy cannot come into the presence of the holy. So, the separation is a result of being profane, or unholy. The various rituals associ-ated with OT worship center on the restoration of the unholy with the holy. This can also be observed in NT worship. See Kleinig, *The Glory and the Service: Worship in the Old Testament* (Fort Wayne, IN: Concordia, 2004), 32–47.

They have been set apart/separated in order to accomplish the tasks that lead to reunion and restoration.[18] Note the three degrees or stages: Israel, priests, and the high priest reveal this submotif, as does the floor plan of the tabernacle and temple with the court, the holy place, and the holy of holies. Each stage brings one closer to the presence of the Holy One and requires greater degrees of purification and atonement.[19] Even in the materials used to construct the tabernacle and temple we witness these three stages, each one bringing one closer to God. The metals of bronze, silver, and gold and the curtains dyed scarlet, purple, and blue show the stages of holiness by means of the costliness of the materials. The closer to the Holy One, the more expensive the materials used.[20] Later, when the people are established in the promised land and Solomon has completed construction of the temple, we see the three stages represented by the land of Israel, Jerusalem, and the temple. The closer one came to the Holy City and the shining jewel of its temple, the closer one came to the Holy One of Israel. This progression continued as one entered the temple itself, where the holy of holies was off limits to everyone except the high priest, and then only once a year on the Day of Atonement. Remember that it was the rituals that took place in the temple, and especially those carried out behind the veil of the holy of holies, that restored the Israelites in the eyes of God.

The Joseph narratives also provide examples of the three-stage separation and restoration. It was only after three separate journeys to Egypt from Canaan by Joseph's brothers that Joseph was finally restored to his father. Another example, although perhaps less convincing, is the eating arrangement before Joseph was revealed to his brothers (Gen 43:32). Joseph ate by himself, his staff and servants ate at another table, while Joseph's brothers dined together. This eating and drinking preceded the revelation of Joseph's identity and his restoration as their brother.

---

18. The entire sacrificial system is about reunion and restoration, and this is seen most clearly in the institution of the Day of Atonement in Lev 16.

19. M. Haran goes into great detail concerning grades of sanctity as one approaches the Holy One, as well as delving into discussion in relation to the materials used to construct tabernacle and temple. He even divides the prohibitions to this holy place into three: touch, sight, and approach (see Haran, *Temples and Temple Services*, 149–74).

20. P. P. Jenson goes into some detail focusing on the material and spatial aspects of the tabernacle/temple. He also notes the close alignment between the spatial and personal dimension (see Jenson, *Graded Holiness*, 89–114).

BARREN WOMB AND THE OPENING OF THE WOMB

The barren womb and the opening of the womb has long been considered a death-and-resurrection motif. The Jewish rabbis recognized this and often referred to the barren womb as a tomb and birth as leading forth from that tomb.[21] Certainly, for the Hebrew woman, being barren was seen as a curse from God. However, there is more to this theme. Levenson:

> If childlessness is the equivalent of death, what is the equivalent of resurrection here? The stories about Abraham and Job, and of many other figures, male and female, throughout the Hebrew Bible, provide the answer: birth is the reversal of death and thus to a large degree the functional equivalent of resurrection (or of afterlife in general) in later cultures, including our own.[22]

There are many barren wombs mentioned specifically in the biblical text. Sarah was barren in her old age (Gen 19:10-12); and in spite of the attempts on her own part and on Abraham's to make arrangements for an heir, she remained barren until God "opened her womb" and Isaac was born.[23] The womb of Rebekah, Isaac's wife, was also barren (25:21) before God blessed her with two sons, Esau and Jacob. Following this patriarchal tradition, the womb of Jacob's second wife, Rachel, was also barren. Her

---

21. I am especially referencing Targum Neofiti on Gen 30 and the description of the "four keys": "Four keys there are which are given into the hand of the Lord, the master of all worlds, and he does not hand over them either to angel or to Seraph: the key of rain and the key of provision and the key of sepulchers and the key of barrenness. The key of rain, for thus does the Scripture explain and say: 'The Lord will open for you the good treasure from the heavens.' The key of provision, for thus does the Scripture explain and say: 'You open your hand and satisfy all living things in whom there is good pleasure.' The key of the sepulchers, for thus does the Scripture explain and say: 'Behold, I will open your graves and will lead you from your graves, my people.' The key of barrenness, for thus does the Scripture explain and say: 'The Lord in his good mercies remembered Rachel and the Lord heard the voice of the prayer of Rachel and said in his Memra to give her sons.'" See M. McNamara, MSC, trans., *The Aramaic Bible*, vol. 1A, *Targum Neofiti 1: Genesis* (Collegeville, MN: Liturgical Press, 1992), 148.

22. Levenson, *Resurrection and Restoration*, 115-16. Levenson also writes, "Both the birth of a child to an infertile couple and the resurrection of a dead person testify to the triumph of the wonder-working God (and the validity of his wonder-working prophet, the 'man of God') over the cruel course of nature" (125).

23. First, Abraham thought Eliezer of Damascus, his chief servant, would be his heir (Gen 15:2-3), then Sarah gave her maidservant, Hagar, to Abraham (16:1-2), and Ishmael was born. Neither was the promised son. This son would come from the loins of Abraham and the womb of Sarah (17:19; see 21:1-5).

plea to Jacob in Genesis 30:1 helps illustrate what a devastating situation this was for a Hebrew woman: "Give me children, or I shall die!" We could also translate this as: "Give me children, or I am dead!" Such was the trauma associated with the barren womb. In 30:22–24 we read: "Then God remembered Rachel, and God listened to her and opened her womb. She conceived and bore a son and said, 'God has taken away my reproach.' And she called his name Joseph, saying, 'May the LORD add to me another son!'" As we further explore this manifestation of the death-and-resurrection motif, Joseph's birth from a barren womb will prove to be significant.[24]

The first barren womb that does not fit our general understanding is that of Tamar.[25] Both of her husbands, Judah's sons, have died before a child could be conceived, and Judah is not interested in providing his last son to her. Therefore, her womb is barren until her deception of Judah changes the matter (Gen 38).[26]

Rather different concerns are apparent in the case of Samson's mother, the wife of Manoah.[27] The account that follows the angel of the Lord visiting to announce a forthcoming birth has many correlations to the three visitors of Abraham and Sarah: this theme is taken up by New Testament writers in the account of the angel's visit to Zechariah and Elizabeth, announcing the birth of John the Baptizer—another example of a barren womb opened (Luke 1:7, 24, 57). Ruth, too, was childless: her husband had died, and she had no brothers-in-law living to fulfill the levirate law; she was left barren with few if any prospects. However, Naomi sent her to glean in a relative's field, and she met Boaz, and eventually they were married, her womb was opened, and Obed was born (Ruth 4:13–17). Hannah's barren womb was also

---

24. See C. M. Kaminski, *From Noah to Israel: Realization of the Primaeval Blessing after the Flood* (New York: T&T Clark, 2004), 1, noting the importance of the primeval blessing "be fruitful and multiply" (Gen 1:28).

25. C. D. Bergmann, *Childbirth as a Metaphor for Crisis* (New York: de Gruyter, 2008), 63, recognizes Tamar as an example of a barren womb. However, she explores a different avenue in her discussion of barrenness and giving birth. In this exploration, she focuses on the possibility of tragedy and death rather than joyful expectation (6). While these metaphors do exist, I would argue that the motif of giving birth/new beginning/new life is not only more prevalent, but it holds overwhelming force against the other.

26. It is also important that both main characters in the Joseph narratives, Joseph and Judah, are involved in the barren-womb submotif.

27. This account is written in Judg 13. It is very detailed and as interesting as the life of Samson itself. The mother of Samson remains unnamed by Scripture.

opened when she gave birth to Samuel (1 Sam 1:5–20); and we also recall the case of Mikal, Saul's daughter and first wife of King David (2 Sam 6:16–23).

On close examination, all the barren wombs mentioned are somehow connected to the covenantal promise and the Davidic line.[28] In the cases of Sarah, Rebekah, Tamar, Ruth, and Mary, if their wombs were not opened, the Davidic line would have been terminated. Rachel, Manoah's wife, and Hannah produced children who were essential for preserving and supporting the people of Israel.[29] We see Joseph's role as a salvific figure in the history of Israel as he provides the food that preserves his family and the subsequent nation of Israel. This is the role that is spoken of by the early church fathers, particularly because of their reliance on the LXX texts where the salvific role of Joseph is subtly enhanced.[30]

BEING CAST DOWN INTO A PIT/SHEOL AND
BEING RAISED UP/LIFTED UP

In this manifestation of the death-and-resurrection motif we see the downward/upward movement first employed. This is an important part of the structure of the Joseph narratives and contributes to the dramatic nature of

---

28. Kaminski, in referencing the proliferation of barren wombs among the patriarchs, writes: "The patriarchal narratives thus underscore that God miraculously enables the patriarchs to multiply. ... It is evident that an important motif that runs through the patriarchal narratives is that the patriarchs increase amidst humanly impossible circumstances. ... These threatening circumstances underscore that the increase of the patriarchs will be realized only with divine intervention" (*From Noah to Israel*, 102–3). Kaminsky asks the question: "Why is the elect child frequently born to a woman who has trouble bearing children?" His answer: "The motif of the child born to a barren woman is one marker used to indicate that the child who is eventually born to such a mother both comes from and belongs to God. This idea is explicitly stated in the birth stories of Samuel (1 Sam 1) and Samson (Judg 13:2–5), and it seems operative in the narratives surrounding Isaac, Jacob, and Joseph. Frequently, the barrenness is ended by a direct prayer to God, as in the cases of Rebekah (Gen 25:21), Hannah (1 Sam 1:10–18), and Sarah in Gen 21:1–2, where Isaac's birth follows directly after Abraham's intercessory prayer for the women in Abimelech's household (who had been temporarily barren) (Gen 20:17–18). At other times the barrenness ends by means of a direct announcement from God or an angelic being, as in the case of Samson (Judg 13:3), the P and J accounts announcing Isaac's birth (Gen 17:15–19 and 18:9–15), and the birth narratives surrounding John the Baptist and Jesus (Luke 1)" (*Yet I Loved Jacob*, 35).

29. The birth of Samson has been considered a fulfillment of the blessing given to Dan in Gen 49:16–17, as Samson is a judge-deliverer from the tribe of Dan.

30. J. W. Wevers, *Notes on the Greek Text of Genesis* (Atlanta: Scholars Press, 1993), 833. See also chap. 6.

the story.[31] It is also significant that this submotif finds its beginning in the first chapter of these narratives. In addition, Genesis 37 is the first occurrence of the Hebrew word "Sheol" (שְׁאֹל) in the MT as Jacob, on receiving the bloody garment of Joseph, assumes the worst, and when his sons and daughters attempt to comfort him, he replies: "No, I shall go down to Sheol to my son, mourning" (37:35). As a result of this first occurrence, this is also the beginning of the "pit" (בֹּר) and "Sheol" correlation, which proves to be very important in the Psalms (Pss 30:1–3; 88:3–6) and the Latter Prophets (Isa 14:15; 28:14–18; 38:17–18; Ezek 31:15–17; 32:20–29).

Being cast into a pit, or going down to Sheol, is not a positive movement. It has a consistent negative context throughout Scripture and is clearly used euphemistically to refer to eternal death in the bowels of hell. Some have suggested that this negative connotation developed at a later date as the Hebrews' concept of the afterlife developed.[32] While it is true that the equating of Sheol with eternal death did take on a greater negativity in the course of time, there was never a time when it was viewed in a positive way.[33] In this first occurrence, Jacob is not considering Sheol to be a positive or even a neutral place. It is the place one goes in sorrow and mourning, with no hope and no joy, as he again states in Genesis 42:38 what will become of him if Benjamin is lost to him as was Joseph: "You would bring

31. Levenson points to the multiple descents of Joseph as manifestations of his symbolic death (see *Death and Resurrection*, 152). In regard to the pit he writes: "The symbolic death that Joseph undergoes takes the form of a threefold downward movement. The movement begins with his descent into the pit into which his brothers cast him at Reuben's behest (Gen 37:18–24). The text goes out of its way to note that 'the pit was empty; there was no water in it' (v 24), a sure sign that the boy would not long survive. In truth, the pit is a symbol of the grave, and the same word can denote both" (150).

32. Rosenburg, *Concept of Biblical Sheol*, 161–92; Segal, *Life after Death*, 136; Spronk, *Beatific Afterlife in Ancient Israel*, 65–81; N. J. Tromp, MSC, *Primitive Conceptions of Death and the Nether-World in the Old Testament* (Rome: Pontifical Biblical Institute, 1969).

33. P. S. Johnston: "Sheol cannot be identified simply as the Hebrew term for the underworld which awaits all. It is almost exclusively reserved for those under divine judgment, whether the wicked, the afflicted righteous, or all sinners. It seldom occurs of all humanity, and only in contexts which portray human sinfulness and life's absurdity. Thus Sheol is not used indiscriminately to describe human destiny at death." See Johnston, *Shades of Sheol: Death and Afterlife in the Old Testament* (Downers Grove, IL: InterVarsity Press, 2002), 83. Conversely, Segal writes, "Indeed, the Septuagint routinely translates the Hebrew 'Sheol' with the Greek, 'Hades.' And, like the Greek Hades, it was neither a place of reward nor of punishment inherently, merely the final destination where the dead go. It is dark and disordered (Job 10:20–21), a land of silence (Pss 94:17; 113:17), sometimes a grim city with gates (Job 38:17; Isa 38:10), and far from the presence of God, exactly as in Mesopotamian and Canaanite myth" (*Life after Death*, 136).

my gray hairs with sorrow to Sheol." This is seen in contrast to Jacob's words later in the narratives as he prepares to die and instructs Joseph: "Do not bury me in Egypt, but let me lie with my fathers" (47:29–30). Again, he instructs all his sons: "I am about to be gathered to my people; bury me with my fathers in the cave that is in the field of Ephron the Hittite" (49:29). Finally, as his death is recorded: "When Jacob finished commanding his sons, he drew up his feet into his bed and breathed his last and was gathered to his people" (49:33). Being gathered to one's people, or sleeping with one's ancestors, was considered the blessing of death, especially in one's old age.[34] Going down to Sheol does not carry the same idea of blessing or any positive connotation in the Hebrew Scriptures.[35]

As the submotif of being cast into a pit/Sheol and being raised up/lifted up begins in Genesis 37, we see the familiar account of Joseph's brothers, in their jealousy and anger, throwing Joseph into a pit.[36] While their subsequent debating and arguing changes their plan more than once, eventually they decide to sell Joseph to slave traders who will sell him in Egypt. Regardless of who is ultimately responsible for it, the text states, "And they drew Joseph up and lifted him up out of the pit" (37:28).[37] This begins the submotif. Note the doubling in this verse; Joseph is drawn up and lifted up out of the pit. This doubling continues as a common occurrence in the narratives.[38]

---

34. Johnston, in noting the selective use of Sheol in the Joseph narratives, writes: "Jacob twice envisages sorrowful descent there, (Sheol) on hearing of Joseph's death and on fearing Benjamin's harm. But, many years later, after his family has been happily reunited, Jacob's death is mentioned repeatedly and in different ways, but Sheol is conspicuously absent" (*Shades of Sheol*, 82). He also points out that this distinction in Sheol's usage is largely unnoticed by commentators (82). Again, Segal contradicts: "But nowhere in Hebrew society is the abode of the dead regarded as a place of special punishment. The notion of a fiery hell or place of punishment is a much later concept, likely due to Persian influence" (*Life after Death*, 136).

35. For a concise, readable explanation of Sheol in the OT, see R. Lessing's *Jonah*, Concordia Commentary Series (St. Louis: Concordia, 2007), 249–55. Of particular importance for our discussion is Lessing's assertion that "Yahweh saves believers from Sheol" and that this deliverance is a "resurrection" (252–55).

36. Fung: "The pit prefigures a series of alternatives in the affliction which Joseph suffers under the hand of others: grave/refuge at Reuben's hand, death/slavery at Judah's hand, death/imprisonment at Potiphar's hand. Each pair is imposed on Joseph by others. There are alternatives for him but he has no choice" (*Victim and Victimizer*, 29). See also Johnston for "pit" as a synonym of Sheol (*Shades of Sheol*, 83–85).

37. See discussion in chap. 3.

38. See chap. 3, where this is discussed throughout the examination of the MT.

Moving on from Joseph, we see the same language used in connection with death and life in 1 Samuel 2:6. Hannah, whose womb was opened with the birth of Samuel, has dedicated him to the Lord and his service and is now singing a song of praise. "The LORD kills and brings to life; He brings down to Sheol and raises up." This common structure of parallelism in Hebrew poetry equates Sheol with death, and life with being raised up. The prophet Jeremiah is also cast into a cistern and raised up (Jer 38), but it is Daniel's experience that is most interesting. Daniel is thrown into a pit of hungry lions for refusing to follow the national edict to worship no other god but King Darius (Dan 6). This was a scheme devised by his adversaries at court to trap him and remove him from competition. He is trapped, and the punishment for disobeying the edict is to be thrown into a pit of ravenous lions. Daniel is cast into the pit, or den, of lions, and a stone is rolled across the mouth and sealed. The following morning Daniel is still alive; no harm has befallen him. Daniel is taken up out of the pit, his adversaries take his place with the lions, and all perish.

The Psalms make continual use of this motif as they describe the curse of death apart from the Lord and the blessing of life as one walks with the Lord. The pit, Sheol, death, the cords of death, destruction, the snares of death, and so on are all equated, just as lifted up, raised up, delivered, saved from enemies, life restored, and so on are equated with life and resurrection (Pss 18:1–6; 28:1; 35:7–8; 40:2; 49:11–15; 55:15; 69:15; 86:13; 89:48; 103:4; 143:7; etc.). An excellent example of this submotif is found in Psalm 30:1–3:

I will raise You up, O LORD, for you have drawn me up and have not let my foes rejoice over me. O LORD my God, I cried to You for help, and You have healed me. O LORD, You have brought up my soul from Sheol; You restored me to life from among those who go down into the pit.

While this psalm is attributed to David, it would not be difficult to imagine these words on the lips of Joseph as he was lifted up from his pit. The entire psalm could be his hymn of praise. On the other hand, Psalm 88, a psalm of lament, illustrates clearly the despair of being separated from God, using the pit/Sheol language.

For my soul is full of troubles and my life draws near to Sheol. I am
counted among those who go down to the pit; I am a man who has
no strength, like one set loose among the dead, like the slain that
lie in the grave, like those whom You remember no more, for they
are cut off from Your hand. You put me in the depths of the pit, in
the regions, dark and deep. (Ps 88:3–6)

In Psalm 116:3–4 the theme of death and deliverance is also seen: "The
snares of death encompassed me; the pangs of Sheol laid hold on me; I
suffered distress and anguish. Then I called on the name of the Lord: O
Lord, I pray, deliver my soul!"

The matter of going down to Sheol is deeply embedded in the Joseph
narratives: equally prominent is the language of going down to Egypt. This
apparent straightforward expression carries with it strong symbolic and
metaphorical connotations.

GOING DOWN TO EGYPT AND UP TO CANAAN/THE PROMISED LAND

The submotif of going down to Egypt and up to Canaan/the promised land
is not a simple geographical notation indicating north and south positions
on a map; nor is it a geological comment concerning the highlands and the
lowlands.[39] This particular manifestation of the death-and-resurrection
motif begins early in the patriarchal narratives of Genesis with Abram
in Genesis 12–13. From this point on in Genesis, the reference is always
a downward movement to Egypt and an upward movement to Canaan.[40]
In 12:10, due to a famine, Abram went down to Egypt (וירד אברם מצרימה),
with the verb, ירד, meaning "to go down." When the famine was over (13:1),
Abraham went up from Egypt (ויעל אברם ממצרים), the verb עלה meaning
"to go up." Once this pattern is established early in Abram's life, we see it

---

39. Sarna disagrees, concluding that the language of going down and going up is standard
for describing the journey from hilly Canaan to low-lying Egypt (*Genesis*, 93).

40. Alter alludes to this downward/upward movement, noting Jacob's reaction to the
bloody tunic and his refusal to be consoled: "'"No, I will go down to my son in the underworld
mourning," thus did his father bewail him' (Gen. 37:34–35). In two brief verses half a dozen
different activities of mourning are recorded, including the refusal to be consoled and direct
speech in which the father expresses the wish to mourn until he joins his son in death. (Later,
ironically, he will 'go down' to his son not to Sheol, the underworld, but to Egypt)" (*Art of
Biblical Narrative*, 4).

repeated again and again. The patriarch Isaac is never recorded as going down to Egypt, but at the time of another famine God clearly told him: "Do not go down to Egypt" (26:2).

This movement is established in the Joseph narratives when the older brothers of Joseph look up and see a caravan of Ishmaelites going down to Egypt. The result is Joseph's descent into the land of Egypt.[41] This is used repeatedly throughout the narratives because of the three trips of Joseph's brothers from Canaan to Egypt. Also, in God's only speaking role in these narratives, he reiterates this theme. Jacob has stopped at Beersheba on his way to be reunited with Joseph, and there God speaks to him in a vision, saying: "I am God, the God of your father. Do not be afraid to go down to Egypt, for there I will make you into a great nation. I myself will go down with you to Egypt and I will also bring you up again, and Joseph's hand shall close your eyes" (46:3-4). When Jacob dies in Egypt, Joseph carries out the promise to bury Jacob in Canaan. The language is repetitive in the extreme as Joseph approaches Pharaoh: "'Now therefore, let me please go up and bury my father, then I will return.' And Pharaoh answered: 'Go up, and bury your father, as he made you swear.' So Joseph went up to bury his father. With him, went up all the servants of Pharaoh ... and there went up with him" (50:5-9). Finally, Joseph gathers his brothers as he is about to die, and he tells them: "'I am about to die, but God will visit you and bring you up out of this land to the land He swore to Abraham, to Isaac and to Jacob.' Then Joseph made the sons of Israel swear, saying: 'God will surely visit you, and you shall carry up my bones from here'" (50:24-25).

In Exodus 3, when the Lord calls Moses and tasks him with leading his people out of Egypt, he tells Moses: "And I have come down to deliver them out of the hand of the Egyptians and to bring them up out of that land to a good and broad land, a land flowing with milk and honey" (Exod 3:8).

---

41. Coats clearly understands the descent/ascent aspect of the journey from Canaan to Egypt and the reverse, from Egypt to Canaan. "First Joseph, then Benjamin, finally Jacob descend from Canaan to Egypt. They leave the land. But they shall return. The descent is, in a manner, descent into Sheol. But they shall return. From death to life. From Egypt to Canaan" (*From Canaan to Egypt*, 92). Levenson writes: "The son's descent into Egypt is a kind of death; his ascent to rulership, a kind of resurrection. Whereas the pit is a metaphor of Sheol in the case of Joseph's first descent, in the case of his second, the metaphor is Egypt, or, to be more precise, slavery in Egypt. Each descent is a manifestation of his symbolic death, and with each, Joseph moves farther from the source of his vitality—his family and his native land" (*Death and Resurrection*, 152).

Throughout the Old Testament Scriptures, Egypt is referred to in a negative way. King after king is warned not to turn to Egypt for help against other nations (Isa 19; 20:2–6; Jer 2; 43–44; Hos 7:11; 12:2; Ezek 29–32). The prophet Ezekiel calls Egypt a broken reed of a staff that pierces the hand (Ezek 29:6–8). Egypt is spoken of as the worst of the foreign nations. Perhaps this is due to the multiplicity of gods worshiped or the highly developed cult of the dead; whatever the reason, nothing good can come from making an alliance with this nation, and a journey there is a trip down into the depths of the pit.

Canaan, on the other hand, is the promised land as spoken of in the Abrahamic covenant.[42] This promised land also becomes a metaphor for the courts of heaven, so it makes sense in light of the Hebrew cosmology that one should go up to the promised land. Going up to the promised land of Canaan is only the first step of this upward movement. One also goes up to Jerusalem and then up to the temple, and finally up to heaven itself—the ultimate promised land. The idea is a step-by-step ascension to the dwelling of God.

SLAVERY AND FREEDOM

Slavery and freedom is the next manifestation of the death-and-resurrection motif that demonstrates a downward/upward movement. When one becomes a slave, whether by selling oneself to pay a debt or being captured and sold into slavery, it is not an upward move.[43] For Joseph this downward movement is pronounced. Once the favored son of a wealthy man, now he has been stripped, thrown into a pit, and sold into slavery in a foreign land, a definite downward trend. Genesis 39 begins with Joseph

---

42. W. D. Davies discusses the link of the promised land of Canaan to the covenant established with the Israelite people. To be separated from the land was to be removed from the covenant, which could result in a removal from the presence of God. "Of all the promises made to the patriarchs, it was that of The Land that was most prominent and decisive. It is the linking together of the promise to the patriarchs with the fulfillment of it in the settlement that gives the Hexateuch its distinctive theological character" (*Territorial Dimension*, 13).

43. J. Byron makes an interesting comment concerning slavery and Israel: "Slavery in one form or another was regarded as unavoidable. Israel was never given a choice between slavery and freedom, but between to whom they would be enslaved, whether to God or someone else. Israel did not possess the right of self-determination. The only option was slavery." See Byron, *Slavery Metaphors in Early Judaism and Pauline Christianity* (Tübingen: Mohr Siebeck, 2003), 59. While this is true, as far as it goes, Byron does not do enough to show the distinction between the various kinds of slavery and slavery to God.

being purchased for a slave in the house of Potiphar, but immediately the upward movement begins, as the text notes five times in five verses (39:2–6) that the Lord is with Joseph, and it is the Lord who ensures his success in all that he does.[44] Potiphar recognizes this, and he raises Joseph up to be in charge of his entire household. Joseph is second in command and enjoys freedom even as he serves at his master's will.[45]

Later in the Joseph narratives, when Joseph is second in command of all Egypt, the people come to him for food, but they have nothing left to pay. They have spent their possessions and their land, all that remains are their lives. So, Joseph purchases them as slaves for Pharaoh that they might eat and live. This is an ironic turn of events as Joseph enslaves the country that once enslaved him, but the irony does not end here, for the time will come when the tables turn once again and a pharaoh will rise up who does not know Joseph, and he will enslave the people of Israel (Exod 1:8–14). Whether Joseph is prophesying concerning this enslavement when he is on his deathbed is difficult to say, but he does speak of the day when God will surely visit the Hebrew people and bring them up out of the land of Egypt to the land he swore to give to Abraham, Isaac, and Jacob (Gen 50:24). The Lord will remember and visit and set his people free.

The slavery of the Hebrews in Egypt sets up the greatest deliverance in Old Testament history. The exodus will be proof and sign of the Lord's favor as he delivers them from slavery in Egypt and sets them free to be his people. The Psalms proclaim this mighty act (Pss 66:5–6; 74:13–14; 77:13–20;

---

44. Fung comments on the dual nature of Joseph's pit as a place of refuge and death; as a slave, he also encounters in Potiphar's house a "pit" and a place where he escapes fratricide. "But the temporary loss of freedom in the pit becomes permanent slavery in Potiphar's house" (*Victim and Victimizer*, 28). Kugel notes the rise of Joseph's fortune, even as a slave, but his main focus is on Potiphar's wife and her obsession with the slave Joseph (*In Potiphar's House*, 28–60).

45. F. Steiner does not note the death-and-resurrection aspect of slavery and freedom. Rather, he focuses on the separation and divorce from kinship bonds that result accordingly. "There seems to be only one answer: that Joseph, because of his sale into slavery, is legally no longer Jacob's son. This selling is a renunciation of family solidarity with and responsibility for Joseph, and although the sale took place without the father's knowledge, it must affect the father as it does all other kinsmen. ... It is not within the power of Joseph's former kinship group to take him back. He has become a freeman in Egypt, but this does not make him a member of his family again. On the contrary, having been freed in Egypt he then became attached to the court of the king, and in that capacity he is part of the Egyptian social structure." See Steiner, "Enslavement and the Early Hebrew Lineage System: An Explanation of Genesis 47:29–31; 48:1–16," in *Anthropological Approaches to the Old Testament*, ed. B. Lang, Issues in Religion and Theology 8 (Philadelphia: Fortress, 1985), 22–23.

78:12–55; 105:26–44; 106:7–33; 114; 135:8–9; 136:10–22), the prophets point to this event to remind the Israelites of their relationship to the Lord (Isa 19:19–21; 63:12; Jer 46:25–28; 34:8–17; Ezek 20:4–20), and many of the commands and statutes concerning slaves and foreigners in the midst of the Israelite people center on being good and just with these peoples because the Israelites were once slaves in a foreign land as well (Deut 15:12–15; Lev 25:38–55).

THROWN IN PRISON AND RELEASED FROM PRISON

This submotif of the death-and-resurrection motif must necessarily begin in the Joseph narratives because it is here that we find the first mention of prison in the Old Testament. This is not surprising, since we have been dealing with a nomadic people who would have no use for a prison. It would have confined them as much as their prisoners. However, the Joseph narratives predominantly take place in a sedentary society, and prisons were in use.

When we spoke of Joseph in the slavery-and-freedom submotif, we mentioned that he has been raised to second in command in the house of Potiphar, but this is not destined to last. Joseph is not only a good steward of his master's house, but he is also handsome in form and appearance, and this proves to be his undoing. He catches the eye of his master's wife, and his newfound freedom is soon in jeopardy. Even though Joseph runs from her, she uses his garment as evidence against him—false evidence that deceives her husband—and Potiphar, in anger, puts Joseph in prison, the place where the king's prisoners are confined (Gen 39:6–20).

Joseph has suffered a downward move and finds himself in the worst of straits yet experienced in his life.[46] However, immediately the text points to the Lord's presence with Joseph; he prospers all that Joseph does. Again, Joseph rises to second in command, serving the wishes of the keeper of the prison (39:21–21). Nevertheless, being second in command of the prisoners

---

46. Nickelsburg, using Joseph and his condemnation to prison as a death and his release as an exaltation illustrated by Wisdom of Solomon 1–6, writes: "Although the plot succeeds and the wise man 'seems to die,' God protects his servant; and after death the righteous man's enemies confront him in the heavenly courtroom, where he is exalted among the ranks of the angelic courtiers. There the ungodly are forced to vindicate his former claims and behavior, and the story ends as they anticipate their own condemnation and destruction" (*Resurrection, Immortality*, 67).

leaves him still a prisoner, and though he enjoys some freedoms and nice-
ties that many of the other prisoners do not: a prisoner is a prisoner. Joseph
has moved upward, but not by much; but then the opportunity to interpret
dreams presents itself. Two of the prisoners were incarcerated at the whim
of Pharaoh. Whatever their offenses, they have landed in prison, and one
night each has a dream. Joseph interprets these dreams, which have their
own downward/upward movement.[47] Upon delivering a favorable interpretation to the chief cupbearer, Joseph pleads his innocence and entreats the
chief cupbearer to mention him to Pharaoh.[48] His interpretation for the chief
baker is not favorable, so entreating him would serve no purpose.[49] This sets
up Joseph's eventual release from the prison, although it is a "whole two years"
after the chief cupbearer is restored (41:1).

After Joseph has been in prison for approximately three years, Pharaoh has
a pair of dreams that confuse everyone, and at this time the chief cupbearer
remembers his promise to Joseph. Note that when Joseph is released from
prison the text says: "They quickly brought him out of the pit." Undoubtedly,
the prison proper was below ground, but the use of "pit" for prison helps the
reader to focus on the upward movement that release from prison provides.[50]

Later, Joseph accuses his older brothers of being spies and imprisons
them for three days. The duration of time is mentioned twice in these two
verses (42:17–18). When he sends the brothers back to Canaan, he keeps

---

47. Both the chief cupbearer and the chief baker, who have been sent down from their
important positions in the house of Pharaoh into the prison, are "lifted up" in three days. The
chief cupbearer is lifted up, and his position is restored; the chief baker, on the other hand,
has his head lifted up and removed!

48. This is the first time that Joseph has taken matters into his own hands in regards to
his fate. Many rabbinic commentators view this as the reason Joseph remains in the prison
another two entire years. Note especially Tg. Ps.-J. 40:14: "Joseph abandoned his trust in
heaven and put his trust in a human being, and he said to the chief cup-bearer, 'But remember
me ...'; v. 23: "Because Joseph had abandoned the favor that is above and had trusted in the
chief cup-bearer, in the flesh that passes." See M. Maher, MSC, trans., The Aramaic Bible, vol.
1B, Targum Pseudo-Jonathan: Genesis (Collegeville, MN: Liturgical Press, 1992), 134. Targum
Neofiti has a longer version; see McNamara, Targum Neofiti: Genesis, 184.

49. The dreams of the chief cupbearer and chief baker have a strong death-and-resurrection motif running through them. However, it is only when they are translated as one
dream combined that the full texture and meaning is observed.

50. After his interpretation of Pharaoh's dreams, Joseph rises to second in command
once again. This provides an interesting pattern in these narratives. Joseph was second in
his father's house as favored son, second in Potiphar's house, second in the prison, and now
second in command of all Egypt. Rabbinic and targumic sources note that this reminds Joseph,
and us, that God is always above us.

Simeon in custody until they return with Benjamin. Simeon is released from prison when the brothers return with the youngest brother.[51]

Prisoners in a pit and their release is a common theme among the prophets (Isa 24:22; 42:7; Zech 9:11–12), and Psalm 146:7–8 states: "The LORD sets the prisoners free; the LORD opens the eyes of the blind. The LORD lifts up those who are bowed down, the LORD loves the righteous." The idea that the Lord sets the prisoners free and releases them from bondage is picked up by Isaiah 61:1: "The Spirit of the LORD God is upon me, because the LORD has anointed me to bring good news to the poor, He has sent me to bind up the brokenhearted, to proclaim liberty to the captives and the opening of the prison to those who are bound." The Christian understanding of this important theme is clearly exemplified in Luke 4:16–21, where it occupies a key position almost at the beginning of the Gospel. The theme runs throughout the Old and New Testament canon, with a prominent role in the Joseph narratives.

FAMINE AND DELIVERANCE (DROUGHT AND RAIN/DEW)

This manifestation of the death-and-resurrection motif is common to the Scriptures, both Old and New Testaments. As God created the world and placed humanity in it, he provided for their every need. This provision began in the form of a garden that needed neither planting nor tending; rather, it fed and nourished humanity by God's accord and good favor. With the entrance of sin came the exit from the garden of Eden along with the cursing of the ground humanity was destined to toil over.

So enters into the biblical text another submotif for death—famine. It is not long before we read of the first famine.[52] In Genesis 12:10, Abram

---

51. Fung, while noting the significance of "pit and prison" and Joseph's release from each, focuses on the "victim who becomes the victimizer" character of Joseph, in relation to his brothers, but especially in regard to the people of Egypt. "Joseph, on the one hand, is a great savior and, on the other, is also a great enslaver. Salvation and enslavement at the same time on such a scale of magnitude are remarkable. ... Joseph as a prisoner has had a painful experience of slavery that he never really forgets or recovers from and this may be the reason why he cannot prevent himself from spreading it to others" (*Victim and Victimizer*, 201).

52. Sarna makes this interesting observation: "In reality, true famine due to natural causes, as distinct from the threat of famine, is not so common in the Bible. The fact, therefore that each of the patriarchs experiences famine in the land (26:1, 42:1, 43:1) has special significance. In the Book of Genesis, the promised land is not 'flowing with milk and honey,' and the divine promises are not intended to bring quiet and repose to their recipients. The realities of nature and of the human landscape are harsh. Living in the land is difficult,

finds himself in the midst of a famine and journeys down to Egypt to escape
death. Isaac also faces famine (26:1–2) but is instructed not to go down
to Egypt; instead he travels to Philistia and Abimilech. In keeping with
the patriarchal pattern, Jacob and Joseph also face famine. Jacob journeys
to Egypt (46:1–4) to be saved by his lost son from famine's grasp. When
the land does not produce, famine ensues, and the people die.[53] Generally,
famine is a result of drought. When the life-giving rains do not fall, the
land dies.[54] In the Joseph narratives this is how the Egyptian people view
the circumstances of the famine. In 47:18–19 the people plead with Joseph
for food even though their money and possessions have already been spent:
"There is nothing left in the sight of my lord but our bodies and our land.
Why should we die before your eyes, both we and our land?"[55] Joseph buys
the land and the people for Pharaoh and imposes a 20 percent tax on all that
the land produces (47:24), and the people gladly agree and by their words
complete the death-and-resurrection motif of famine and deliverance.[56]
"And they said, 'You have saved our lives; may it please my lord, we will be
servants to Pharaoh'" (47:25). Joseph is the deliverer, the savior from the

---

sometimes precarious. All this continually impinged upon the religious consciousness of
Israel. It generated a heightened sense of dependence upon God's protection and a more
intense awareness of His mysterious workings" (*Genesis*, 93).

53. R. Knierim: "The human condition as life from the ground brings the relationship
between ground and food into sharp focus. Food is not only the material by which humans
live from the ground; it is also a part of the very substance of human life as earthly life. In
addition, that which makes the sustenance of human life possible is the life of the ground
itself. The ground is blessed." See Knierim, *The Task of Old Testament Theology*, 237.

54. Sarna: "Although famine might sometimes result from plagues of insects, as indicated
in Deuteronomy 28:38 and Joel 1–2, or from enemy action, as described in 2 Kings 6:25 and
25:3, its primary cause in Canaan would have been prolonged failure of the seasonal rains"
(*Genesis*, 93).

55. Longacre notes the descent of the Egyptian people into serfdom as a result of the
famine, while the Hebrews and the priests rise to prominence. "Successively the Egyptians
lose their money, their livestock, their lands, and their liberty in exchange for bread. Egypt
is reduced to serfdom by the end of the famine. Only the priests of Egypt—and Jacob's little
clan—are exempt from these pressures. Israel dwelt in Egypt and prospered as royal pension-
ers (as did also the priest to whom Joseph was personally related by marriage). In contrast to
the Egyptians, who were reduced to serfdom, the descendants of Israel 'gained possessions,
and were fruitful and multiplied exceedingly'" (*Joseph*, 50).

56. Westermann goes into some detail concerning the three stages of the famine and
the enslavement of the people of Egypt. When they receive the "seed," they consider it their
salvation even though their slavery continues. The incongruity of this troubles Westermann,
and he purposes two sources poorly woven together (*Genesis 37–50*, 172–77).

famine in the eyes of the Egyptians, but he has also been used by God to save his own people, Israel, from a similar fate.[57]

An excellent example of this submotif is seen in 1 Kings 17 and the story of Elijah and his confrontation with Ahab and his wicked queen, Jezebel. Elijah declares to Ahab: "As the LORD the God of Israel lives, before whom I stand, there shall be neither dew nor rain these years except by my word" (1 Kgs 17:1). And there is no rain or dew for three years. For three years there is death in the land as the famine is severe (1 Kgs 18:2). After Elijah's great victory over the prophets of Baal and Asherah, the Lord sends rain on the land again (1 Kgs 18:34–36).

Due to the importance of rain and dew in the land, as the way by which the land produced and famine was avoided, the blessing of rain and dew is frequently mentioned throughout Scripture.[58] Without the rain in the rainy season, there were no crops, and without the dew in the dry season, the crops withered and died. Therefore the language of rain, dew, and watering is used as a way to speak of the provenance of the Lord (Pss 147:8; 104:10–16; 107:33–38; Isa 55:10–11; 58:11; Jer 31:12), and the same language is used when blessings are bestowed on one's children.[59]

We see this in the blessing that Isaac bestows on Jacob in Genesis 27:28. "May God give you of the dew of heaven and of the fatness of the earth and plenty of grain and wine." Esau's blessing seems more of a curse: "Behold, away from the fatness of the earth shall your dwelling be, and away from the dew of heaven on high" (27:39). The blessing of Joseph by Jacob in 49:22–26 also contains blessings involving the bounties of the everlasting hills (49:26), which Moses reiterates in Deuteronomy 33:13–16.[60]

---

57. The LXX focuses on this salvific character of Joseph. Later, the early church used this focus to see in Joseph a figure typifying Christ, the Savior.

58. R. Syrén notes with great detail the prominence of the language of dew in the blessings of Gen 49 and Deut 33 and its relation to prosperity and fertility. See Syrén, *The Blessings in the Targums: A Study on the Targumic Interpretations of Genesis 49 and Deuteronomy 33* (Abo, Sweden: Abo Akademi, 1986).

59. "'The miracle of rainfall must be mentioned in the benediction about resurrection.' What is the reason? Rabbi Joseph said: Since it is on the same level as the resurrection from the dead, they inserted it into the benediction about the resurrection of the dead" (b. Ber. 33a). Also significant is the Exodus account of the giving of the manna. It comes in the morning with the dew (Exod 16:13–14).

60. See chap. 7.

Such a strong manifestation of the death-and-resurrection motif carries through into the New Testament and intersects with the life of Christ.
The most significant occurrences are seen in the large feedings, where Jesus
feeds five thousand and then again four thousand, not including women
and children (Matt 14:13–21; 15:32–39 // Mark 6:30–44; 8:1–10 // John 6:1–15).
Christ takes people from hunger (famine) and feeds them (deliverance).

The divine presence and provenance of the Lord is frequently seen in
relationship to feeding, eating, and even feasting. In Exodus 24, Moses,
Aaron, Nadab, Abihu, and seventy elders of Israel eat with God; in
Isaiah 25 the Lord prepares a rich feast for all who come to his holy mountain—both texts foreshadow an eschatological fulfillment.[61]

SEEDS/PLANTING AND GROWTH/FERTILITY/FRUITFULNESS

Like the previous submotif, the submotif of seeds/planting and growth/
fertility/fruitfulness is land based. It is the rain and dew from heaven that
gives life.[62] It causes the seed to sprout and restores fruitfulness to the land.[63]
The significant difference is that the seed and planting are not seen as life,
but rather as death. The seed and the planting of the seed into the ground
are viewed as a burial, with the hope that life will sprout forth in a birth
or resurrection. This kind of language is used in two of the distinct resurrection texts in the Old Testament Scriptures. Isaiah 26:19 reads: "Your
dead shall live; their bodies shall rise. You, who dwell in the dust, awake
and sing for joy! For your dew is a dew of light, and the earth will give

---

61. Revelation 19 expresses the Christian understanding of such a fulfillment with the
marriage feast of the Lamb.

62. Bergmann rightly notes the connection between conception and the sowing of seed
as well. "The Hebrew Bible often portrays conception as a sowing of seeds. It is debated
whether the woman was seen as active participant in the creation of a new human being,
and it appears that the Hebrew Bible itself does not provide an answer to this question. Num.
5:28, for example, portrays the woman as fertile ground that 'is being sown with seed,' while
Lev. 12:2 calls the woman the one who brings forth the seed" (*Childbirth as a Metaphor*, 61).

63. Y. H. Chung considers the sexual activity centered on the fertility cult of Baal to be
overemphasized, a possible addition to or redaction of the text by those who represented
the official keepers of religious practice in Israel. However, the connection of fertility and
seed and the Canaanite worship of Baal and Asherah cannot be thus dismissed. Once again,
the understanding of seed and fertility, death and life, is seen in the practices of the pagan
cultures surrounding the Hebrew people with the presence of temple prostitutes, both male
and female. In fact, it is likely that Tamar in Gen 38 has exchanged her garments of widowhood
for those of a temple prostitute in order to entice Judah. See Chung, *The Sin of the Calf: The Rise
of the Bible's Negative Attitude toward the Golden Calf* (New York: T&T Clark, 2010), 1–20, 142–48.

birth to the dead." Daniel 12 speaks of sleeping in the dust until the people are awakened, some to everlasting life and some to everlasting contempt (12:2). While seeds and planting are not mentioned in these texts, this is the imagery the people of Israel considered as they planted seeds into the dust of the earth.[64] In line with this Old Testament symbolism, the apostle Paul writes: "So it is with the resurrection of the dead. What is sown is perishable; what is raised is imperishable" (1 Cor 15:42). Thus, he explores the implications of death and resurrection inherent in the language familiar from the Hebrew Bible.

In the Joseph narratives the people of Egypt entreat Joseph not just for food, but also for seed. The food nourishes and sustains the body, but the seed brings life back to the desolate land. In each case, salvation occurs. "Buy us and our land for food, and we with our land will be servants to Pharaoh. And give us seed that we may live and not die and that the land may not be desolate" (Gen 47:19). The people realize the death of the land will also be the death of them. Planting seed will eventually bring life to the land and to them.[65]

GOING DOWN INTO THE WATER/BEING DROWNED AND BEING BROUGHT UP OUT OF THE WATER/NEW LIFE

A submotif that is strongly implied, but not explicitly described, in the Joseph narratives is going down into the water and new life. It may be discerned in Joseph's words at Genesis 50:25, as he instructs his brothers that God will surely visit them, and when he does bring them up out of Egypt, they must remember to bring his bones with them. God remembers, visits his people, and delivers them from the land of Egypt by means of the prophet Moses, and, as promised: "Moses took the bones of Joseph with him, for Joseph had made the sons of Israel solemnly swear, saying, 'God

---

64. There is also the imagery of the seed planted in the womb, first encountered in Gen 3:15.

65. Greidanus notes the connection of the barren womb and the lack of seed—both motifs of death. "Genesis will follow the development of these two kinds of seed, tracing especially the line of the seed of the woman, whose continued existence often appears in doubt: Abel is killed (4:8); Sarai is barren (11:30); Rebekah is barren (25:21); Rachel is barren (29:31); Jacob and his family are about to starve in Canaan (42:2). But in his grace, God continually intervenes so that the seed of the woman can advance from Adam and Eve to Seth, to Noah, to Abram, to Isaac, to Jacob, and, by the end of Genesis, to the beginning of numerous seed—the full number of 70 (10x7) people (Gen 46:27; Exod 1:5)" (*Preaching Christ from Genesis*, 20).

will surely visit you, and you shall carry up my bones with you from here'"
(Exod 13:19). The result is that the bones of Joseph are carried throughout
the exodus journey, and therefore, Joseph's bones go down into the Red Sea
and back up, and his bones cross the River Jordan into the promised land of
Canaan.[66] Joseph also experiences this manifestation of the death-and-resurrection motif, albeit posthumously. His bones are then buried in the
promised land (Josh 24:32).

EXILE AND RETURN FROM EXILE

The submotif of exile and return from exile is quite common. Whether this
involves a self-imposed exile because of famine, fleeing from some perceived threat, or an exile that is the result of a foreign power conquering
and carrying away, the exile is always a parting from the land of Canaan.
One does not read of an exile from any other place in Scripture. Abraham
is never spoken of as being in exile from Ur of the Chaldees, nor is Moses
referred to as in exile from Egypt in his forty years in Midian. Scripture
sees exile as a separation from one place, the promised land.[67]

The first exile noted in Scripture is self-imposed as Abraham escapes
famine by going down to Egypt (Gen 12:10), and then Isaac, who leaves
Canaan because of famine but at the Lord's command stays in close proximity by traveling only to Philistia (26:1–6). The next exile in the patriarchal
era takes place as Jacob flees Esau by going to Haran to stay with Laban,
his uncle (28:5). This exile is also self-imposed but in his best interest, as
his brother was breathing threats of murder because of the stolen blessing. Each of these exiles comes to an end when the threat passes, and the
patriarchs return to Canaan, the land promised in the covenant.

It is Joseph's exile to Egypt at the hands of his brothers that records the
first unplanned and unwanted exile from Canaan. Because of his brothers'

---

66. For more on Joseph's traveling bones, see chap. 10.

67. Davies focuses on the role of those who remain in exile/diaspora, most of whom chose
not to return to Israel. "The loss of Temple and The Land, the centres of Judaism, could be sus-
tained only because there were organized Jewish communities scattered elsewhere. Disaster
at the centre did not spell the end of Judaism but could be, and was, offset and cushioned by
its existence elsewhere" (*Territorial Dimension of Judaism*, 94–95). D. L. Smith-Christopher,
while titling his work *A Biblical Theology of Exile*, never seems to quite engage the theological
understanding and dimensions of exile in the Scriptures, choosing rather to concentrate on
the historical and social realities, which can effect theology but not necessarily define it. See
Smith-Christopher, *A Biblical Theology of Exile* (Minneapolis: Fortress, 2002).

plotting, Joseph is exiled as a slave in a foreign land. Later, due to another famine, he is joined by Jacob and all the family members—a planned exile, but one that lasts longer than they expected.[68] Before this exile ends, the Israelites no longer have the freedom to simply return to Canaan. They are no longer guests, but slaves in a foreign land (Exod 1:8–14). This sets up the greatest return from exile in Scripture. No other return is as dramatic as the exodus, and so the exodus event becomes the defining moment of this submotif.[69] To be separated from Canaan is to be lost in the depths, and with the advent of the Holy City of Jerusalem and the sacred temple, this reality only heightens. Canaan is the promised land—the Holy Land where the Lord dwells with his people. It is the only place where sacrificial worship is allowed, the only place where the Day of Atonement may be observed. Separation by exile for any reason is a traumatic event, but to return to the Holy Land with its Holy City and the holy temple was a return to life itself, a going up to the sacred presence of the Holy One.[70] Therefore, the exodus and the return to Canaan cement this reality as the land is possessed, Jerusalem is occupied, and the temple is built. Levenson writes:

> The exodus has become the prototype of ultimate redemption, and historical liberation has become a partial, proleptic experience of eschatological liberation, a token, perhaps *the* token, of things to

---

68. It is sometimes alleged that the Joseph narrative as a whole was written under the influence of the Babylonian exile. Those who insist on this overlook two key items: (1) Joseph describes himself not as being in exile, but as having been "stolen or kidnapped" from his people (Gen 40:15); (2) Jacob and his sons are invited to Egypt, not compelled to go there by force of arms.

69. Knierim notes that the exodus and this return from exile has a distinct downward/upward motif. He points out the structure of Exod 19–39 and its ascent-descent pattern as an important part. "Six times Moses goes up to the mountain and six times he comes down into the camp. Whenever he is on the mountain he receives an instruction from Yahweh, and whenever he is in the camp he conveys it to the people. While the response of the people to Moses is mentioned repeatedly, it is returned by Moses to Yahweh only once, in 19:8b. The ascent-descent pattern must be considered as the basic structural signal for the organization of Exodus 19–39" (*Task of Old Testament Theology*, 361).

70. P. Ackroyd speaks of the return from exile as restoration: "The restoration, the returning of the exiles and the redeeming of Zion, are proclaimed by Trito-Isaiah in terms often strongly reminiscent of Deutero-Isaiah. In particular there will be a new land, restored to life because brought back into relationship with God (ch. 62), with a new people set in new heavens and earth in which life will no longer be curtailed and vain, but there will be security and the complete reordering of the natural world (ch. 65)." See Ackroyd, *Exile and Restoration* (Philadelphia: Westminster, 1968), 228–29.

come. The full activation of God's potential in the foundational past has been transformed into a sign of the still greater activation of his potential in the future consummation—a consummation that moves the Jews not merely from slavery to freedom but quite literally from death to life as well. Beneath this last transformation lies a conviction that so long as human beings are subject to death, they are not altogether free: resurrection is the ultimate and final liberation.[71]

Even Joseph finally returns from his exile in Egypt as his bones are remembered (Exod 13:19) and carried back to the promised land and buried in a plot of ground near Shechem (Josh 24:32).

Once the land of Canaan is established as Israel and the people of God are fully rooted in place, after the conquering of the land by Joshua and the expansion of borders by David and the building of the temple by Solomon, leaving this land becomes even more traumatic.[72] This is what the Lord God threatens if the people are not faithful—exile (Isa 5:13; 39; Jer 4; Ezek 12). As the kingdom is divided after Solomon (1 Kgs 12), exile is the promised punishment for unfaithfulness for both Judah and Israel.

Eventually, the Northern Kingdom of Israel is conquered and carried into exile by the Assyrians (2 Kgs 17), never to return. Later, the Southern Kingdom of Judah meets the same fate at the hands of the Babylonians (2 Kgs 25), but with an important difference—they return. This is the second-most significant exile and return from exile manifested in the Old Testament. Israel's time of exile in Babylon, while short in comparison

---

71. Levenson, *Resurrection and Restoration*, 27–28.

72. Levenson notes another individual return in the book of Ruth. "Similarly, in the book of Ruth, one of the great masterpieces of biblical narrative artistry, a tale that begins with famine, expatriation, and death (Ruth 1:1–5) is transformed into one of abundance, return home and integration of the alien, and, most of all, birth (2:14–19; 4:7–15)" (*Resurrection and Restoration*, 116). In reference to Ezekiel and the dry bones of Ezekiel 37 he writes: "The vision of the dry bones resurrected is, by way of contrast, one of the prophet's oracles of restoration and thus appropriately speaks of the people Israel's future obedience to the God who has revived them and restored them to their own land (Ezek 37:13–14). To ask whether he restores them from hopelessness, slavery, exile, estrangement from God and his righteous will, or, rather, from death is excessively academic and misses the way Israel conceives these things. Most seriously, it misses the deep inner connection between the substance of the symbol (resurrection from death) and its decoded message (a return to the land, to the knowledge of God, and to obedience to him)" (162).

to the Hebrews in Egypt, is a difficult time. The inward groaning and gut-wrenching emotion is clearly heard in the words of Psalm 137 as the Jews lament their conditions. "By the waters of Babylon, there we sat down and wept, when we remembered Zion" (Ps 137:1). The exile is a death to the Israelites; the city of Jerusalem and its temple are no more, and they are away from the promised land. When Cyrus the Great of Persia arises and conquers the Babylonians, the hopes of God's people are restored. Isaiah, the prophet, foretold this, calling Cyrus the Lord's anointed (Isa 45:1). Now the people of Judah can return to rebuild and restore. Now they can return from exile to new life.

STRIPPED AND CLOTHED

The death-and-resurrection motif of Scripture is interwoven and intertwined with the garment motif in many ways. The submotif of stripped and clothed is one of the clearest interconnections. We previously examined the garment motif in part 1 by way of example.[73] However, the aspect of stripped and clothed distinguishes itself in important ways.

When Adam and Eve disobeyed the command not to eat of the fruit of the tree of the knowledge of good and evil, the text reports that their eyes were opened, and they knew that they were naked (Gen 3:7). Whether it was strictly their nakedness or the shame of their actions this newfound knowledge revealed, their reaction was to cover up. Adam and Eve sewed fig leaves together, making loincloths, which apparently did not ease their guilt, for they hid from God as he was walking in the garden (3:10). The Lord God apparently did not consider these garments adequate either, for after the pronouncement of what their disobedience had accomplished, the Lord God stripped away the garments of fig leaves and clothed them with garments of skin (3:21).[74]

---

73. See chap. 3.

74. Levenson points out the recurring theme of goats and goat (animal) skins connected with this motif. "Here it bears mention again that it was through two goats of the flock that Jacob had deceived his own father, Isaac. Rebekah, it will be recalled, used the goats for a tasty dish that the blind old man mistook for Esau's venison, and she clothed her smooth-skinned son in the hides of the same animals in order to perpetrate the same momentous act of impersonation (Gen. 27:5–17). It is as though some strange karmic force keeps this act of deception in continual ricochet, dooming the chosen family to re-experience it in succeeding generations and even within the same generation" (*Death and Resurrection*, 159).

Moving to the Joseph narratives, this submotif manifests itself in Joseph's special tunic given by his father, Jacob.[75] The beautiful garment shows Joseph's status in the eyes of his father, and such a statement is more than his brothers can tolerate.[76] So they strip him of this robe and throw him into the pit (37:23–24). Joseph is lifted up from the pit and is taken down to Egypt to a life of slavery, and though he rises to second in command of Potiphar's household, he is stripped again by Potiphar's wife and ends up down in the pit of prison. He becomes second to the keeper of the prison, but Joseph does not realize the culmination of this submotif until he has been appointed as second in command of all Egypt. At the declaration of his vaulted position, Pharaoh "took his signet ring from his hand and put it on Joseph's hand, and clothed him in garments of fine linen and put a gold chain about his neck" (41:42). While there have been many peaks and valleys in this stripped-and-clothed submotif of both the death-and-resurrection motif and garment motif, Joseph has finally been clothed in worthy garments.

Leviticus 16 is another example of stripped and clothed as the high priest is prepared for the Day of Atonement. In this case, Aaron, the high priest, enters into the tabernacle, where he must strip off his high-priestly garments (Lev 16:4), bathe, and put on the special, holy linen garments that must be worn when he enters the most holy place. The whole process is reversed when the high priest prepares to leave the tabernacle (16:23–24). The linen priestly garments are not to leave the sanctuary, for they are holy

---

75. Alter connects the act of deceit to the garment and notes the irony of Judah being taken in just as he had taken in his own father. "Now he (Judah) becomes their surrogate in being subject to a bizarre but peculiarly fitting principle of retaliation, taken in by a piece of attire, as his father was, learning through his own obstreperous flesh that the divinely appointed process of election cannot be thwarted by human will or social convention. In the most artful of contrivances, the narrator shows exposed through the symbols of his legal self, given in pledge for a kid (*gedi 'izim*), as before Jacob had been tricked by the garment emblematic of his love for Joseph which had been dipped in the blood of a goat" (*Art of Biblical Narrative*, 10).

76. Anderson sees the stripping of Joseph and the acts that accompany this act as the establishing of enmity between Joseph and his brothers, thus setting the tone of Ps 30: "The account of the angry act of stripping Joseph of his sign of favor is accompanied by two important details. First is the notice that the pit was empty and without water, a sure indicator that murder was the initial intention. Second is the surprising revelation that they promptly sat down to eat. This seemingly inconsequential detail sets the actions of these brothers against a much wider canvas. For in the Psalter, to eat and drink in the presence of the demise of another is to put oneself in the role of the 'enemy'" ("Joseph and the Passion of Our Lord," 209).

by virtue of being in the presence of the Holy One in the most holy place. So, the high priest is stripped of his robes and clothed in the holy garments used in the rite that atones for the sin of the people of God.

Another example concerning Aaron and the office of high priest occurs at the death of Aaron (Num 20:22–29). The Lord has determined that it is time for Aaron to be gathered to his people, and so he instructs Moses to take him and his son Eleazar to the top of Mount Hor. There on the mountain, Moses strips Aaron of his garments and places them on Eleazar, his son, and then Aaron dies on the mountain (20:28). The stripping off of the high-priestly garments is associated with death.

The last example we will examine in the Old Testament is in the book of Isaiah, although it is not in sequence. In Isaiah 64:6 it reads: "We have all become like one who is unclean, and all our righteous deeds are like filthy rags (menstrual rags)." This is the nature of humanity in its fallen condition. So polluted is humankind in its sin that even its righteous deeds are filthy/unclean garments. It is helpful to connect this passage back to Genesis and humankind's poor attempt to clothe itself with fig leaves (Gen 3:10). However, as we look to Isaiah 61:3, where the year of the Lord's favor is being foretold, we read: "To grant to those who mourn in Zion—to give them a beautiful headdress instead of ashes, the oil of gladness instead of mourning, the garment of praise instead of a faint spirit." It is the Lord who is clothing his bride, the people of Israel. Though the righteous deeds of humanity are as filthy/unclean rags and lead to nothing but death, the Lord provides by removing these rags that cause mourning and sorrow and clothes his people with garments of praise, garments of salvation, and robes of righteousness (Isa 61:10).

CONCLUSION

As one reads the Scriptures in a narrative fashion and approaches the text as a unified theological narrative, the various motifs winding their way through the writings become apparent. The way in which these motifs are incorporated into every portion of the canon demands attention. Such consistent patterns, and a continual adherence to common motifs, cannot be happenstance. Approaching the Scriptures as a unified theological narrative helps one to appreciate the integrity of the text, while, at the same time, combating an overemphasis on the diversity of the text.

In a careful reading of the text, one can observe and examine several motifs that are prevalent in the writings and, taken together, are intertwined and inseparable. Each one of these motifs and submotifs proves to be an integral thread in the tapestry of the Scriptures. Taken together they provide a consistent, tightly woven fabric and convey a common theological narrative. It is instructive to note the locations where they intersect.

There are characters and scenes that are central, intersecting locations of the various motifs. The Joseph narratives are one such place. In regard to the death-and-resurrection motif, there is no other character and no other narrative in the Old Testament that brings together so many of the themes of this motif.[77] None of the explicit resurrection texts of the Old Testament Scriptures are found in the Joseph narratives. However, this does not weaken the claim of the Joseph narratives to play a crucial part in the death-and-resurrection motif. This chapter has provided evidence for no fewer than twelve different submotifs, and the presence of such a large number of these items in one relatively small section of the canon is striking and demands careful attention. We shall need as ask how the Israelites understood these narratives; how they might have read them in conjunction with canonical material represented in the Prophets and Writings, which seem more strongly to imply ideas of death and resurrection; and why Joseph came to such prominence in literature of the Second Temple period. These are questions that will be addressed in subsequent chapters. In the interim, reading the Joseph narratives with the rest of the Old Testament as a unified theological narrative shows a multiplicity of death-and-resurrection submotifs that cannot be ignored. For whatever reason or purpose, Joseph was chosen to portray the early Hebrew understanding of the afterlife in this way. While the New Testament also contains and continues this motif, it is not the origin of the theme of death and resurrection. It was Genesis, and especially Joseph and his life, that provided the foundation on which the rest of the Scriptures build and were used to elucidate this theological teaching.

---

77. There are those who would argue that Daniel is even more of a death-and-resurrection figure, although I would respectfully suggest that due to the earlier place in history of Joseph, it is likely that Daniel and his narrative are intended to reflect Joseph.

Part III

—

Other Texts of Genesis 37–50

6

The Septuagint in Comparison to the Masoretic Text

INTRODUCTION

The MT has been passed down through the work of certain Jewish scribal families dedicated to the preservation of the Hebrew text for the Jewish community. The methods employed in this effort were both intense and strict as scribes adhered to the text with great precision.[1] As useful as this process was for the sake of the accurate transmission of the Hebrew text, these efforts began late on the historical time line.[2] Due to this, it is important to refer to and to compare the oldest texts available with the MT in order to come to a fuller understanding and to make an effort to reconstruct the *Vorlage*.

The oldest extant text available is the Septuagint (LXX).[3] This Greek text, translated circa 270 BCE in Alexandria, Egypt, provides an important window into the Hebrew text. It is certainly the oldest interpretation of the Hebrew known to us and therefore demands attention. Its Hebrew

---

1. E. Wurthwein. *The Text of the Old Testament: An Introduction to Kittel-Kahle's Hebraica* (Oxford: Basil Blackwell, 1957), 9–16. For scribal practices in the biblical and postbiblical periods, see A. J. Saldarini, *Pharisees, Scribes and Sadducees in Palestinian Society: A Sociological Approach*, 2nd ed. (Grand Rapids: Eerdmans, 2001); W. M. Schniedewind, *How the Bible Became a Book: The Textualisation of Ancient Israel* (Cambridge: Cambridge University Press, 2004); D. M. Carr, *Writing on the Tablet of the Heart: Origins of Scripture and Literature* (New York: Oxford University Press, 2005); K. van der Toorn, *Scribal Culture and the Making of the Hebrew Bible* (Cambridge: Harvard University Press, 2007).

2. See Wurthwein, *Text of the Old Testament*, 12–14.

3. The Samaritan Pentateuch provides another ancient text, which, despite theological modifications, remains a valuable resource. I have chosen not to specifically deal with the Samaritan Pentateuch because of its similarities with the MT, and, where its readings differ from the Hebrew, they quite often correspond to readings found also in LXX and the targum. The Samaritan community held Joseph in high regard, but my thesis is specifically concerned with the Jewish portrayal of Joseph. For more information on the Samaritans and the Samaritan Pentateuch see J. Bowman, *The Samaritan Problem* (Pittsburgh: Pickwick, 1975); J. MacDonald, *The Theology of the Samaritans* (London: SCM, 1964); G. Knoppers. *Jews and Samaritans: The Origins and History of Their Early Relations* (Oxford: Oxford University Press, 2013), 178–261.

Vorlage predates the MT by several centuries, and knowledge of that *Vorlage* allows us to glimpse a picture of the Hebrew, which differs, sometimes significantly, from our present MT. However, the LXX translators had certain objectives as they translated, and it is their interpretation of the Hebrew available to them that will be important for our purposes. The LXX only exists in complete form in critical editions compiled by and agreed on by modern textual criticism. The critical edition of the LXX used in this study is Alfred Rahlfs's *Septuaginta*.[4]

In approaching the LXX of the Joseph narratives there are two goals. First, to gain insight into the Hebrew text available to the Jews of third-century BCE Alexandria; second, to reconstruct the third-century BCE Alexandrian Jewish attitude concerning Joseph. It is important not to read too much into the minor variants between texts, and, at the same time, remember that the attitude of third-century BCE Alexandrian Jews toward Joseph and these narratives may not exactly reflect the attitudes of the Hebrew community for whom these narratives were originally produced.

THE TEXT: THE SEPTUAGINT IN COMPARISON
TO THE MASORETIC TEXT OF GENESIS 37–50

Rather than follow a word-by-word analysis of the LXX in comparison to the MT, an approach accomplished admirably by John Wevers and, to a lesser extent, Marguerite Harl, is an examination of the LXX for trends and themes reflected in its translation and rendering of the Hebrew text available at that time, especially in regard to the character and image of Joseph.[5] Attention will also be given to how the LXX deals with the various motifs and the downward/upward movement as discussed in chapter 3 and expounded on in chapter 5. The examination is divided into the following categories:

---

4. A. Rahlfs, ed., *Septuaginta* (Stuttgart: Deutsche Bibelgesellschaft, 1935). Other works that have critically informed my research include J. Dines, *The Septuagint*, Understanding the Bible and Its World (London: T&T Clark, 2004); M. Harl, *La Genèse: La Bible D'Alexandrie* (Paris: Éditions du Cerf, 1994); S. Jellicoe, *The Septuagint and Modern Study* (Winona Lake, IN: Eisenbrauns, 1989); O. Munnich, *Le texte du Pentateuque grec et son histoire* (Paris: Éditions du Cerf, 2001); E. Schürer, *A History of the Jewish People in the Time of Jesus Christ*, rev. and ed. G. Vermes, F. Millar, and M. Goodman, 5 vols. (Edinburgh: T&T Clark, 1987); Wevers, *Notes on the Greek Text*.

5. Wevers, *Notes on the Greek Text*; Harl, *La Genèse*.

1. The attitude and approach to the text by the translators

2. Translation trends and their effect on the text

3. Cultural reflections of third-century BCE Jewish Alexandria

4. Joseph's image supplemented

5. Joseph's image tarnished

In dealing with each of these categories, I will attempt to demonstrate how these approaches and trends have contributed to a better understanding of the Joseph narratives, or how they have detracted from a clear understanding.

THE ATTITUDE AND APPROACH TO THE TEXT

It is not my intention to investigate the LXX's translation technique, nor am I trying to delve into the minds of the translators.[6] Both have been attempted, but the danger of this becoming a subjective process on the modern scholar's part cannot be ignored. What I am doing is taking the text of the LXX, as agreed on by modern textual criticism, and looking at it as a finished work of literature in its own right. The original readers regarded this work as Scripture, and I am concerned with demonstrating for the modern reader the particular emphasis and nuance of the Joseph narratives provided by this Greek Bible. Jan Joosten writes:

The translators of the Pentateuch did not come to their task with ready-made recipes. Although they were rather proficient in

---

6. K. De Troyer notes the struggle and the challenge: "In Septuagint studies there is a fine balance between two activities that Septuagint scholars constantly do. On the one hand, we try to establish the Old Greek text as it left the hands of the first translators who were rendering the Hebrew text into Greek. On the other hand, we study the recensions, especially the early ones, namely the so-called proto-Lucian, kaige, Symmachus, and Aquila, etc., in order to find out how the Old Greek was corrected towards a later Hebrew text. ... But it is precisely what goes beyond the standard rendering that is also a subject of discussion. Is the element in a text that cannot be explained as the result of Translation Technique an interpretive variant or does it reflect a *Vorlage* different from the MT?" See De Troyer, "The Hebrew Text behind the Greek Text of the Pentateuch," in *XIV Congress of the International Organization for Septuagint and Cognate Studies, Helsinki, 2010*, ed. M. K. H. Peters (Atlanta: Society of Biblical Literature, 2012), 15–16.

Hebrew, and had at least some knowledge of traditional exegesis, they had not been trained as translators—let alone as translators of Scripture. They learned their trade "on the job," dealing with particular problems as they arose in their successive rendering of the Hebrew text. Recurrent problems were solved not by following one consistent course but by applying a mix of strategies, now privileging the form, now the perceived content of the source text.[7]

Those who translated into Greek the Hebrew text available to them in the third century BCE evidently had a high view of the Hebrew manuscripts.[8] They did not all work in quite the same way. Some approached their task translating the Hebrew word-for-word, according to the letter. Others sought to provide more readable versions for the people of that day by translating a more readable Greek version.[9] These differing approaches are not dissimilar to the various translations and versions of Scripture we have today. The LXX in these fourteen chapters of Genesis generally adopts a more fluid approach to the narrative.

The MT commonly repeats phrases and doubles words to provide emphasis and to build the level of emotion within the story. This is also true with the doubling of dreams, blessings, and so on. The LXX often omits these doubling phrases to provide a more fluid narrative in the Greek language. In Genesis 37:5 the MT, ויוספו עוד שנא אתו, "and Joseph they hated him more," is left out, deemed an ill fit.[10] In 37:9, the two accounts of Joseph's dreams, first to his brothers and then to his father, are combined into one; και διηγησατο αυτο τω πατρι αυτου και τοις αδελφοις αυτου, "and he described in detail to his father and to his brothers." In the case of 39:5 the MT repeats the phrase כל-אשר יש-לו, "all that there was to him," but the LXX translates επι παντα, οσα ην αυτω, "upon all, as much as there was to him," and then εν πασιν τοις υπαρχουσιν αυτο, "in everything belonging to him,"

7. J. Joosten, "Translating the Untranslatable: Septuagint Renderings of Hebrew Idioms," in *"Translation Is Required": The Septuagint in Retrospect and Prospect*, ed. R. Heibert (Leiden: Brill, 2010), 69.

8. "It is equally possible, however, and on balance much more likely, that the Septuagint translators did regard their source text as divinely inspired, and that they knew what they were doing—or at least thought they did" (Joosten, "Translating the Untranslatable," 60).

9. Harl, *La Genèse*, 74–99.

10. Wevers, *Notes on the Greek Text*, 615.

for no apparent reason other than to avoid monotony. While these translation choices may provide a smooth Greek rendering, they also miss the character of the Hebrew. This is true in the failure to preserve examples of doubling and thereby the original intent of the narrator. An example of this is the dream accounts. The Hebrew uses the clause "He dreamed a dream" (ויחלם חלום), but the LXX chooses to translate singly,[11] as it does with much of the other doubling in the Joseph narratives (37:14, 23; 38:29; 39:4, 5, 16; 41:5; 43:2, 6, 16, 20; 44:1, 25; 46:29; 49:8, 16).

In 39:10 we encounter the first use of the idiom ויהי כ־, "and it was that," which is used six times in this chapter (39:10–11, 13, 15, 18–19). The LXX renders these in five different ways. Another example of an attempt to improve the narrative is the omission of a large portion of the text of 43:24. The LXX omits ויבא האיש את–האנשים ביתה יוסף, and yet chooses to translate it word-for-word in verse 17b.[12]

The LXX rendering of the MT הנה also shows the freedom assumed by the translator. At times the הנה is ignored altogether (37:7; 40:6; 42:28). At other times it is not recognized and therefore mistranslated (39:8; 44:8, which translates it as an Aramaic word). In the seven verses of 41:1–7 it is rendered in four different ways.

The LXX translators avoid a slavish rendering of the Hebrew (38:25; 39:20; 41:1; 42:25; 43:22; 49:30; 50:19). In this effort there are additions made to the Hebrew text so the more difficult passages are understood properly— at least from the perspective of the LXX translators (37:30, 31; 38:12, 14, 26, 29; 39:14, 17; 40:13, 17; 41:20, 26, 36; 42:27; 43:5; 44:4; 47:5–6, 14, 19; 48:1, 21; 50:12). In 38:15 the LXX adds και ουκ επεγνω αυτην ("for he did not know her"), to make certain the readers/hearers understand that Judah did not recognize Tamar before he "went in to her."[13] In 38:29 where the MT reads מה–פרצת עליך פרץ, "What a breach you have breached for yourself," the LXX attempts an interpretation rather than a translation,[14] rendering the words as "Why has a hedge been cut through because of you?" (38:29).

---

11. Dream doubling: 37:5, 6, 9 (2×), 10; 40:5, 8; 41:11 (2×), 15.

12. Other examples of large sections of text being deleted: 41:12, 45, 56; 43:7; 46:31; 47:24; 48:14; 50:5, 13, 18.

13. This is also an example of the moral character and ethical image of Judah being built up.

14. Wevers, Notes on the Greek Text, 648.

The LXX also misses the connection of פרץ, "to breach," with פרץ, "Perez."[15]
Another example is noted in 46:20, where the LXX has included the sons
and grandsons of Manasseh and Ephraim in the list of those who came to
Egypt, while the MT has not.[16] Also, in 47:5 the LXX has added Ηλθον
δε εις Αιγυπτον προς Ιωσηφ Ιακωβ και οι υιοι αυτου, και ηκουσεν Φαραω
βασιλευς Αιγυπτου, "for Jacob and his sons came into Egypt before Joseph, and they
listened to Pharaoh, King of Egypt," in order to make a smooth reading
with clean transitions to deal with the inconsistent numbers of the MT.

TRANSLATION TRENDS AND THEIR EFFECT ON THE TEXT

As the LXX translators trended toward a more fluid, readable, and hearable
Greek version of the text, changes were implemented to provide a clean
narrative style for the Greek-speaking community. The product desired
was a text that was both used and useful. In order to reach this goal the
translators made use of Greek words and phrases that alter the Hebrew
(Gen 39:5; 41:1, 12, 18; 43:15, 22; 44:12, 13, 32; 47:5–6; 48:21; 50:13–14, 18), and
a preference was shown for phrases previously used in the narrative even
when the Hebrew differs (39:14: 41:19, 20, 26; 42:19; 44:29, 31).

Another trend is the LXX's use of the imperfect verb. Many Hebrew
particles and verb forms have been translated with the Greek imperfect,
quite often to convey the idea of continuous, ongoing action. In most cases,
this proves to be both useful and effective, especially in working with a
narrative text (37:18, 25, 28; 38:9, 27; 39:10, 21; 41:2, 3, 5; 42:23; 47:12).

The translators, in other cases, have taken it on themselves to make
corrections to perceived errors in the Hebrew text (42:33; 43:18). Some of
these "errors" may well have been the result of scribal/copyist mistakes,
although we do encounter cases where such readings coincide with the
Hebrew text known to us from the Samaritan Pentateuch.[17] Occasionally,
the LXX translators have recourse to Aramaic to assist them. In 37:27 the
translator assumes the lack of a ו is a haplography, as the preceding word
is אחינו, and thus adds a και to the translation. In 39:10 the MT and LXX
show great variance. According to Wevers, the Hebrew text is corrupt,

---

15. Harl, *La Genèse*, 267.

16. This may be an attempt on the part of the translators to make the numbers coincide.
In the Hebrew the numbers are justified if one adds Jacob, Joseph, Manasseh, and Ephraim.

17. See chap. 6.

and the LXX attempts to make better sense of the Hebrew by ignoring the final two words, להיות עמה, "to be with her."[18] In his Hexapla, Origen tends to correct the LXX in these cases by providing a Greek alternative for the difficult Hebrew word or phrase, or by adding a word that has been omitted by the LXX. Many examples exist, among them 39:9, 12, 16, 19; 40:11.

The LXX translators accomplished their goal and provided a more "readable" text. Employing Greek vocabulary and idioms their readers would have found familiar, they smooth out the narrative by avoiding repetition and unnecessary Hebraisms that would have passed on little information and meaning to the Greek-speaking Jew of third-century BCE Alexandria. However, many of these changes miss the point of the text. While the basic meaning is conferred, the more subtle meaning may be missed.

When the translators do not treat the textual doubling in the Hebrew text, they ignore the narrator's purpose for the frequent doubling, and several important aspects of the text are overlooked. By way of example, the doubling is used to clearly and emphatically draw the line between downward/upward movements. When Joseph is cast into the pit in Genesis 37, he is then "raised and lifted up" (Gen 37:28). The narrator uses doubling to strongly divide the downward from the upward.

Another example of changes within the LXX missing the mark of the Hebrew text is observed in Genesis 38. The LXX changes the gender and number of pronouns with little justification. In verse 3 the MT says that Judah named his firstborn son Er. In verse 5 the MT speaks of the location

---

18. Wevers, *Notes on the Greek Text*, 655n13. Other examples of the translators correcting the Hebrew text: 38:5; 42:25, 33; 46:27. Aquila and Symmachus often provide alternative translations that seek to follow the Hebrew text: 39:20; 40:10; 41:43; 42:15, 30; 43:17, 23; 44:1, 18; 45:16; 47:31; 49:3, 12; 50:3, 19. A. Salvesen notes: "It seems very likely the 'Theodotion's' work is associated with a pre-Christian movement of revision that sought to 'improve' the older LXX by conforming it more closely to the Hebrew text of that time. The principles of this movement culminated in Aq.'s revision. Aquila's version has an etymologizing style that is very consistent, and reflects the increasing importance of the details of the Hebrew text for exegesis. Symmachus' translation may have been a reaction in the other direction, because he is interested in fidelity to the Hebrew without the compromises of Greek style that Aq.'s approach entailed. ... So the readings of the Three witness to the development of MT and to possible variants of their period." See Salvesen, "The Role of Aquila, Symmachus and Theodotion in Modern Commentaries on the Hebrew Bible," in *Let Us Go Up to Zion: Essays in Honour of H. G. M. Williamson on the Occasion of His Sixty-Fifth Birthday*, ed. I. Provan and M. Boda (Leiden: Brill, 2012), 98.

of Judah at the time his wife gave birth, and in verse 6 the MT tells us that
Judah chose a wife for Er (Tamar). The LXX changes the first two of these
to represent Judah's wife. This is unfortunate because it misses the text's
inherent message that the main character in this chapter is Judah.[19]

The translator is faced with an arduous task. For the LXX translators,
the task was more difficult, as Hebrew is an Eastern language and Greek
is Western one. Joosten writes:

> When one translates a piece of discourse, one changes it. On a
> purely linguistic level, the words and the grammar of one language
> are never precisely equivalent to those of another language: mean-
> ing cannot be expressed in exactly the same way in two different
> languages. And on a more general communicative level, the trans-
> position of a text from one language into another cuts it off from its
> original situational context and puts it into an entirely new situa-
> tion. Since meaning is essentially determined by pragmatic context,
> this cutting-off is bound to affect the text profoundly.[20]

In addition, the Hebrew text of the Joseph narratives contains a significant number of *hapax legomena* and loanwords that challenge the translators and result in many *hapax legomena* in the LXX text.[21]

---

19. Genesis 37 introduces Joseph, while 38 focuses on Judah. From this point forward the
narrative centers on these two brothers.

20. Joosten, "Translating the Untranslatable," 59.

21. *Hapax legomena* in the Hebrew: 40:16, חֹרִי; 41:34, וְחִמֵּשׁ; 43:11, זִמְרָת; בָּטְנִים; 45:17, טַעֲנוּ;
47:13, וַתֵּלַהּ; 47:26, לְחֹמֶשׁ; 48:16, וַיְדַגּוּ; 49:4, פַּחַז; 49:5, מְכֵרֹתֵיהֶם; 49:11, וְלַשֹּׂרֵקָה; סוּתֹה; 49:12, חַכְלִילִי; 49:17,
שְׁפִיפֹן; 50:3, הַחֲנֻטִים. *Hapax legomena* in the Greek: 37:26, χρησιμον (pent.); 38:28, προεξηνεγκεν;
39:9, υπεξηρηται; 40:4, αρχιδεσμωτης; 40:8, διασαφησις; 41:7, ανεμφθοροι; 41:56, οιτοβολωνας;
42:1, ραθυμειτε; 42:23, ερμηνευτης; 43:7, επερωτησιν; 44:28, θηριοβρωτος γεγονεν (as a compound); 45:1, ανεγνωριζετο; 45:7, καταλειψιν; 45:16, θεραπεια; 48:10, εβαρυωπησαν; 49:12,
χαροποι; 49:17, εγκαθημενος; 50:2, ενταφιασταις ενταφιασαι (as a compound).

CULTURAL REFLECTIONS OF THIRD-CENTURY BCE JEWISH ALEXANDRIA

Alexandria, Egypt, in the third century BCE had a large and active Jewish community.[22] It is assumed that the LXX translators came from this community. Their world and culture had a double effect on the translated text and the product produced. First, the translator (exegete) was affected (encountered) by the open text of Scripture. Second, he was encountered by his world, his culture.[23] Therefore, the translation produced, while attempting fidelity to the original, will by necessity also reflect the culture to which he belonged. The LXX of Genesis 37–50 gives several insights into this culture.

In 37:28, for the sale of Joseph to the Ishmaelites for the price of twenty shekels of silver (MT: כסף), the LXX renders this as twenty shekels of gold (χρυσων). As J. A. L. Lee has pointed out, the average price for a slave was much higher than twenty shekels of silver in third-century BCE Alexandria. Gold was equal to twenty equivalent weights of silver.[24] Continuing with the culture reflected in the currency of the day, 43:23 shows the Hebrew כספכם בא אלי, "Your money came to me," translated with αργυριον υμων ευδοκιμουν απεχω. The translator has added that the money is genuine. In other words, the money is not counterfeit. This reflects the third century BCE, when money was in coins and could be counterfeited, whereas at the time of the Joseph narratives money (silver) was generally measured by weight (also 45:22).[25]

In 37:33 the LXX reads θηριον πονηρον κατεφαγεν αυτον, θηριον ηρπασεν τον Ιωσηφ, "An evil beast has devoured him, a beast has carried off Joseph." This is toned down from the MT, where the second phrase reads טרף טרף, "torn to pieces." For Greek-speaking Jews, this may have been done as an issue of human dignity. The Hebrew טרף usually signifies meat of an animal improperly or violently killed, thus making it unfit for Jewish consumption and unclean for sacrifice. It would have been offensive for later Jews to think of Joseph in such a way.[26]

---

22. Fraser, *Ptolemaic Alexandria*, 1:54–60.

23. Maren Niehoff, *The Figure of Joseph in Post-biblical Jewish Literature* (Leiden: Brill, 1992), 1.

24. J. A. L. Lee, *A Lexical Study of the Septuagint Version of the Pentateuch* (1983), 63–65.

25. Wevers, *Notes on the Greek Text*, 733–34.

26. See also Grossfeld, *Targum Onqelos to Genesis*, 129n10.

Genesis 37:36 of the LXX uses σπαδοντι to render the MT סריס. The root of the Greek word literally translates as "eunuch" and is found only twice in the LXX (Isa 39:7). The Hebrew סריס translates as "a court official of high rank."[27] The term for "eunuch" did not develop until much later in Hebrew tradition. We also find examples in the LXX of Egyptian-Greek words such as αρχιδεσμοφυλακος in Genesis 39:21 and a word with probable Persian origin in 44:2, κονδυ. In 41:34 we read, ποιησατω φαραω και καταστησατω τοπαρξας, "let him create a position and appoint toparchs." The LXX presupposes that the divisions that existed in Ptolemaic times in Egypt (toparchs) were established in Egypt by Joseph. There is no historical evidence to support this. Another possible example, as pointed out by Wevers, is the translator's decision to alter the Hebrew in 45:8, בכל–ארץ מצרים, "in all the land of Egypt," to πασης γης Αιγυπτου, "of all the land of Egypt."[28] Wevers notes that to an Alexandrian "a ruler in" might represent a "nomarch," and so the translator avoids this impression by using the genitive—Joseph was not a nomarch (or toparch); his authority extended over the entire country.[29]

In 47:19 the Hebrew reads: "Why should we die before you, even we and our land?" But the LXX reads: "So lest we should die and the land be desolated." The Hebrews were intimately tied to the land, as evidenced by the covenantal promise to Abraham, Isaac, and Jacob. As a result, famine meant more than death for the inhabitants; it meant death for the land as well. In third-century BCE Alexandria the Jews were no longer as focused on the promised land of Canaan. Due to their circumstances and location, their emphasis was on other aspects of the covenant (46:4; 48:4; 49:1, 10, 11, 24; 50:24, 25).

Another example that should be noted is the translators' use of Αιγυπτιοις, "Egyptians," to render the Hebrew מצרים, "Egypt." The Jews of Alexandria were obviously residents of Egypt, most by choice; therefore the translators distinguish between the land of Egypt and the Egyptians themselves. This is a consistent pattern employed in these narratives (46:34; 50:3; etc.).

---

27. Harl, *La Genèse*, 263.

28. Wevers, *Notes on the Greek Text*, 760.

29. See also 45:21, where the LXX refers to Pharaoh as "king."

The language of Septuagintal Greek provides some insight into the Alexandrian culture. It varies in many ways from Classical/Attic Greek and also from the later Koine Greek. Examples include the use of εις rather than εν in a locative sense; the use of ουθεν in place of the older ουδεν; various other Hellenistic words and usage, such as in 37:3 the use of ηγαπα (αγαπαω) for אהב as opposed to φιλεω; the use of the Hellenistic future αφελει (αφειλον) in 40:19; and the technical term οι ενταφιασται for "the embalmers" in 50:2.[30]

How did this translation affect Joseph's image among Greek-speaking Jews? All of the character issues and image problems suffered by Joseph in the Hebrew could not help but be noted by the LXX translators.[31] How did they deal with these difficulties as they attempted to paint a positive picture of Joseph, not only for the Jewish population, but also for the Greeks and Egyptians among whom they dwelled?

JOSEPH'S IMAGE SUPPLEMENTED

Joseph became an important figure in Second Temple Judaism. Following the Joseph narratives in Genesis, he suffered from neglect. However, Second Temple Judaism elevated him back into a position of prominence. He is spoken of frequently in postbiblical Jewish literature by Philo, Josephus, Ben Sira, the targums, and many pseudepigraphal writings.[32] This being said, not all the writings or writers have the same view toward Joseph. The LXX of the Joseph narratives shows examples of supplementing Joseph's image, but hidden away within the revisions and recensions are also examples of tarnishing that same image. As Maren Niehoff notes:

> Biblical characters are presented in a different way than the modern reader used to novels would expect. In fact, few direct descriptions of personality, individual looks or detailed expositions of inner life are to be found. On the other hand, indirect means of

---

30. Note also the attempt by the LXX translators to identify various geographical places and names: 45:10; 46:29, 34; 48:7.

31. See chap. 4.

32. Testaments of the Twelve Patriarchs, Joseph and Aseneth, Enoch, Jubilees, etc. See Niehoff, *Figure of Joseph*.

characterization are used with great sophistication; and usually every detail of the text is intended to contribute to the portrait.[33]

The first example of Joseph's image being enhanced is found at the beginning of the narratives in 37:2. Joseph was an assistant/apprentice shepherd with the sons of Bilhah and Zilpah—the MT reads, ויבא יוסף את– דבתם רעה אל–אביהם, "and Joseph brought back a bad report of them to their father." The LXX and Aquila follow the intent of the MT, although Aquila more literally. Symmachus, however, treats it differently. By using the imperfect εφερεν with διαβολην κατ αυτων πονηραν, he implies that Joseph continually brought back evil slander against them. Theodotion, on the other hand, translates using the plural κατηνεγκαν, which indicates that the brothers brought back evil reports on Joseph, an obvious attempt to build Joseph's character.[34]

We have dealt with the טרף טרף of 37:33 in the preceding section. However, in 37:15 there is a subtle example that bears examination. Joseph has been sent out to his brothers to check up on them and the flocks, but he is unable to locate them because they have relocated to Dothan. The MT speaks of Joseph "wandering in the field," but the LXX chose to render the Hebrew with πλανωμενον, which emphasizes Joseph wandering about, hopelessly lost. This translation intends to make us feel sorry for Joseph, or to picture him as helpless and foolish.

In 39:23, when Joseph is placed in charge of the prisoners, the LXX para-phrases the MT, making the account more favorable to Joseph, with the addition of δι αυτον, "because of him." Then, in 43:28, the LXX adds και ειπεν Ευλογητος ο ανθρωπος εκεινος τω θεω, which has no equivalent in the Hebrew text.[35] The Greek leads us to understand that Joseph invokes a blessing on his absent father. Considering Joseph's lack of drive to search out his father and the "forgetting of his father's house," as noted in the

---

33. Niehoff, Figure of Joseph, 27.

34. Niehoff: "The first piece of individual characterization thus reflects negatively on Joseph. The brothers are presumably unaware of what he has done. But the reader's image of Joseph is shaped by it and he consequently anticipates complications in the family relations" (Figure of Joseph, 28).

35. Possibly patterned after the Samaritan Pentateuch: ויאמר ברוך האיש ההוא לאלהים.

name of his firstborn, Manasseh, it appears the translator intends to build Joseph's stature.

Looking at 49:22–26, where Jacob imparts his blessing on Joseph, the translator changes the Hebrew to bestow a blessing that in effect lays out the history of Joseph and indicates that it is from Joseph that the one who strengthens Israel will come. This translation had important implications later in Second Temple times. The Jews of Qumran and others in the Second Temple era took this to indicate a great leader, even a second messianic figure.[36]

Genesis 41:51 is an obvious case of protecting or enhancing the image of Joseph. At the birth of his firstborn son, Joseph names him מנשה (*piel* participle; "one who makes to forget"). The כי clause is his rationale for this name: "because God has made me forget all my hardship and all my father's house." The LXX οτι clause agrees with the first phrase but not the second; παντων των πονων μου και παντων των του πατρος μου, "all my troubles and all matters connected with my father." Wevers explains:

> Joseph has not forgotten his father's house; such an ungrateful and thoughtless son would hardly fit the character of Joseph as Gen pictured him, and so an intentional ambiguous translation which removes "house" and substitutes των "the (things, matters connected with)." Its vagueness can include possessions, peoples, memories, etc.[37]

JOSEPH'S IMAGE TARNISHED

There are aspects of Joseph's character and his actions that can and have called into question his place as a father/patriarch of the Jewish people. The Aramaic targums and midrashic traditions have struggled with several of these issues.[38] These issues include Joseph's role as "bad report bringer/spy" and his apparent insensitivity concerning his brothers' animosity toward

---

36. Note Testaments of the Twelve Patriarchs.
37. Wevers, *Notes on the Greek Text*, 700.
38. Targum Onqelos, Targum Pseudo-Jonathan, Targum Neofiti.

him, which appear early on in these narratives.[39] The Jewish community also struggled with Joseph's marriage to an unbeliever, a daughter of a pagan priest, and wondered why he chose to "forget" his father's house rather than use his newly bestowed power to seek him out. These examples, which give evidence of Joseph's transformation into an Egyptian, caused concern.[40] They have caused some struggle to understand how Joseph can be an example of religious piety and faithfulness, yet they still allow that he was a good statesman.[41] These conflicting and often confusing views can occasionally be glimpsed in the LXX, although it is more difficult to perceive because it represents the minority view.

In Genesis 49, the blessings of Jacob, the translator has toned down Jacob's invocations on Joseph's brothers. Then, in 50:16, the LXX reads that Jacob made his sons swear that they would ask Joseph's forgiveness for past wrongs, while the MT indicates this was another scheme to keep Joseph from enacting vengeance on them for their past actions. The LXX also says that the brothers came in person with this message, while the MT states that the message was sent ahead of them. These examples from Genesis 49 and 50, although not directly related to Joseph's character, show where the translators have built up and improved the image of the brothers, which suffered earlier in these narratives. It appears that when the image of the brothers is improved, it is at the expense of Joseph.[42]

CONCLUSION

In studying the LXX rendering of these Joseph narratives, a certain style and form appears. The translator appears to be writing for his hearers, not so much his readers. While the Hebrew text was already in a narrative and somewhat dramatic form, the LXX adds, deletes, and reorders phrases for

---

39. The beginning verses of Gen 37.

40. See discussion in chap. 4.

41. Philo, *On the Life of Joseph* 1, the political man.

42. In a careful examination of the LXX, a certain trend develops. The translators of the LXX, along with Aquila, seem to adopt a more balanced approach toward Joseph, although both Symmachus and Theodotion tend to enhance Joseph's image when they felt it necessary. Symmachus tends to agree with Aquila except when it comes to Joseph, being more negative and less forgiving in his treatment (37:2; 39:2). Theodotion, when available, is always more positive toward Joseph and his actions—note 37:2 especially.

a better, more dramatic flow, and thereby produces a better narrative for hearing. The translators' frequent use of dramatic license accents the text and captures the attention of the audience (Gen 39:12, 17, 20; 44:30; 47:15; 49:1; 50:20). Nevertheless, the LXX does not significantly alter the flow of the Hebrew narrative. M. Harl points out that the Greek faithfully reproduces the narrative style of Hebrew Genesis, giving simple sentences coordinated with "and." This style is known as parataxis and is more or less unknown in Classical Greek prose style.[43]

It was never the intention of the translators to provide a rendering that literally (slavishly?) reproduced the Hebrew text. Their intention was to produce a translation that was heard well as it was read aloud. They produced a fluid, more dramatic text that was less objectionable to their audience than the original (37:33; 49; 50:16). We have made the mistake of assuming the intent of the translators was a more precise rendering of the Hebrew text, and thereby we have assumed a parent text different from the MT. That the LXX does not alter the MT in ways other than described suggests that overall it maintains the stance of the MT toward the important motifs and themes that are found there.

How this translation was used in third-century BCE Alexandria is mainly conjecture, but when we take into account the context of the city in that era, the dramatic character of this narrative makes better sense. Alexandria prided itself as a center of Greek culture and learning and as a patron of the arts.[44] Not only did it possess the great library, but it also boasted of great amphitheaters and a culture of poetry, epics, and drama greater than Athens itself.[45] Perhaps it was this environment that lead the translators to adopt the approach taken toward the Hebrew text. This context may also provide hints as to how this work was presented and perceived.[46]

---

43. Harl, *La Genèse*, 71–74.

44. D. J. Moo, *Major Cities of the Biblical World: Alexandria* (Nashville: Thomas Nelson, 1985), 3.

45. Athens remained the center for dramatic comedy, but in the arena of tragedy, Alexandria was its rival. Read also Fraser, *Ptolemaic Alexandria*, 618–73.

46. Letter of Aristeas 312–316, where the author of the letter addresses the issue of tragic poets who sought to adapt some of the biblical stories into their plays.

Where the LXX does differ from the MT, two things stand out. First, the Jews of Alexandria were looking for ways to prove their worth and cement their place in this Greek city. The despised, persecuted, ostensibly clueless Joseph not only rises to be Pharaoh's second in command, but he also saves the lives of countless people by his wisdom. He provides food not otherwise available. While this may not represent death and resurrection in the same sense that the MT and Targum Onqelos set forth that theme, perhaps the Greek translators are directing our attention to it from a different perspective. Joseph would have provided them with the opportunity to point to a Hebrew rising to a high government position and flawlessly carrying out an important task that saved the Egyptians. With the presence of wisdom already explicitly included at the Hebrew level of the narratives, the perceptive reader might be led to consider Wisdom in Proverbs and her association with food and drink. As third-century BCE Alexandrian Jews sought to involve themselves in the affairs of the city, they could refer to Joseph as a precedent. Did the LXX version of Joseph prompt and encourage Jews to walk with confidence in their host society? A Jew had once saved Egypt. Perhaps the presence of Jews provided security for the land.

Second is the updating of the narrative to fit the Greek-Egyptian setting of third–century BCE Alexandria Egypt. We know that Egyptian culture was continually preoccupied by death and what came after it. The LXX translators would certainly have been aware of this and may have addressed aspects of it to accommodate their translation to the world around them.

In the MT we have observed a strong downward/upward movement, which supports the death-and-resurrection motif and recommends Joseph as a dying and rising character for the Hebrew people. Joseph came from a barren womb and rose to favorite son. He was cast into the pit and raised back out; sold into slavery but became second head of the household; thrown into prison but put in charge of the prisoners; and, finally, rose to second in command of all Egypt. Joseph rescued the people and the land from famine and death, and rescued and saved his own family, bringing them to the land of Goshen. Finally, it is recorded that his bones were carried by the people of Israel out of Egypt and up to the promised land of Canaan. The LXX has maintained this motif, although not as strongly. Joseph is still a death-and-resurrection figure. However, the translators tend to focus more on his salvific role, indicating the possible advent of a second messianic figure that will arise from his house in the blessings of Genesis 49.[47]

Why does the LXX focus on the salvific nature of this story? Why not death and resurrection, or death and life? Why not take the direction that Targum Onqelos does and center on the moral and ethical character of Joseph? The LXX translators have intentionally chosen the salvific direction, and considering their position in Alexandria at the time and the desire to be more deeply entrenched in the culture, it may have proven to be counterproductive to focus negatively on Egypt as a country. More could be gained by emphasizing Joseph's role in saving the country and enriching the ruling class. Joseph's role in enslaving the Egyptian people would not have been viewed in a negative way due to their low estate in comparison to the Greeks, but anything casting dispersions on the country itself would have proved detrimental to the cause. Choosing not to focus on the ethical and moral character of Joseph could have avoided a negative reaction by the Greek ruling class, not known for its moral and ethical ethos.

As is often the case with Joseph, ancient exegetes chose to use him in a way that best suited the purposes of their current situation.[48] Nevertheless, the LXX sees Joseph as a figure who reminds the third-century BCE Alexandrian Jews that they remain God's chosen people, and while the return to the promised land, now Israel, may not have been as crucial to their identity as previous generations, the implications of that journey and the restoration of the people would still include a resurrection to new life in the presence of the Holy One of Israel.

---

47. The rabbinic sources that refer to this figure are collected by P. Alexander, trans., *The Aramaic Bible*, vol. 17A, *Targum of Canticles Translated, with a Critical Introduction, Apparatus, and Notes* (Collegeville, MN: Liturgical Press, 2003), 135. This messiah features principally in the Babylonian Talmud (e.g., Sukkah 52a; Sotah 14a) and later texts, and is known to Targum Pseudo-Jonathan of Exod 40:11.

48. Thus Philo can represent Joseph as a political figure: see, for example, his *Legum Allegoria* 3.179; *De Migratione* 158–162; *De Somniis* 1.220–221. Josephus, by contrast, tends to relate the patriarch to incidents in his own life (see Niehoff, *Figure of Joseph*, 84–110), remarking in passing in *Jewish War* 3.352 that he was a skilled interpreter of dreams. The reader here is no doubt expected to pick up the implicit reference to the biblical Joseph. The targumim emphasize Joseph's moral integrity: this is perhaps best exemplified in the long *haggadah* recorded by Targum Neofiti of Gen 49:22.

7

A Comparison of Targum Onqelos with the Masoretic Text

During the Babylonian captivity, two important developments occurred that affected the internal fabric of the Jewish people. The first was almost certainly the development of the synagogue, a place for the reading and study of the Torah.[1] Without the temple such a place became essential. Even with the advent of the new temple, the synagogue continued to exist and does to this day. The second development was the adoption of the Aramaic language. This was the language of the Jews' captivity, and they brought it back from exile when they returned to Jerusalem. As time went on, Jews became more dependent on the Aramaic tongue. By the first century CE it was the language most commonly spoken on the streets of Jerusalem. This transition to Aramaic led to the necessity for an Aramaic translation of the Torah available for reading in the synagogues, teaching in the study houses, and private study, especially in the regions of Palestine and Babylonia. The Septuagint, the Greek translation, was already being used in Alexandria and surrounding areas.

The Aramaic translations of the Hebrew text are referred to as targums. Rabbinic tradition traces the use of the targum to the reading of the book of the law of Moses by Ezra the scribe in Nehemiah 8:8: "And they read from the book, from the law of God, clearly, and they gave the sense, so that the people understood the reading."[2] The oldest extant targum of the entire Pentateuch is attributed to Onqelos.[3] While there is much debate on the subject, it is generally thought that Targum Onqelos first appeared as a "Palestinian Proto-Onqelos" between 100 and 130 CE, with later redactions

---

1. L. I. Levine, *The Ancient Synagogue: The First Thousand Years* (New Haven: Yale University Press, 2000), 19–41.

2. H. Sysling, *Tehiyyat Ha-Metim: The Resurrection of the Dead in the Palestinian Targums of the Pentateuch and Parallel Traditions in Classical Rabbinic Literature* (Tübingen: Mohr Siebeck, 1996), 11.

3. Fragments of targums have been found at Qumran: 11QTgJob; 4QTgLev. See Sysling, *Tehiyyat Ha-Metim*, 31–33.

reflecting a Babylonian character.[4] The final redaction took place in the third century CE. Onqelos was regarded by some rabbinic authorities as both a proselyte and nephew of the emperor, either Titus or Hadrian.[5] The rabbinic sources on this matter, however, are notoriously complicated.[6]

The use of targums in the study of the MT varies in relation to the targums themselves. Targum Onqelos, because of its antiquity and a general adherence to the original Hebrew text, provides important insights into the original text and also into the Jewish rabbinic understanding of the text in the first-century CE Roman era. For these reasons, this study has chosen Onqelos for comparison with the MT of Genesis 37–50. As one compares Targum Onqelos with the MT, there is opportunity to observe early rabbinic attitudes toward various characters. Of particular interest in this study is the rabbinic attitude toward Joseph.

A COMPARISON OF TARGUM ONQELOS WITH THE MASORETIC TEXT OF GENESIS 37–50

It is not necessary to engage in a word-by-word analysis of Targum Onqelos in comparison to the MT to observe the early rabbinic attitudes and approaches in the Joseph narratives.[7] I have divided the examination into the following categories:

1. Targum Onqelos as interpretation: A commentary to explain the text

2. The piety of Targum Onqelos: A reflection of talmudic and rabbinic tradition

3. Cultural reflections of the Roman era

4. Images improved

---

4. Sysling, *Tehiyyat Ha-Metim*, 24–29.

5 Grossfeld, *Targum Onqelos to Genesis*, 31–32.

6. See, most recently, the detailed discussion in W. Smelik, *Rabbis, Language, and Translation in Late Antiquity* (Cambridge: Cambridge University Press, 2013), 449–76.

7. Resources used include Alexander Sperber's edition of *The Bible in Aramaic*, vol. 1, *The Pentateuch according to Targum Onkelos* (Leiden: Brill, 1959); Grossfeld, *Targum Onqelos to Genesis*.

While there are also numerous additions, deletions, and emendations that are not included in the above classifications, those additions, translations, and explanations that do fit the categories will provide a clearer understanding of the rabbinic mind.

TARGUM ONQELOS AS INTERPRETATION: A COMMENTARY TO EXPLAIN THE TEXT

The largest category for comparison is Targum Onqelos as interpretation of the MT. Examples of Targum Onqelos providing explanation and making brief commentary are plentiful in these fourteen chapters.[8] These are not to be understood as moves that attempt to change the meaning of the text, but rather as opportunities to provide a clearer understanding of the intended meaning. Targum Onqelos takes a conservative approach in this arena as compared to other targums such as Pseudo-Jonathan and Neofiti.

There are three basic ways in which Targum Onqelos serves as interpreter of the Hebrew text. The majority of his work as interpreter comes in the form of explanation and frequently is quite helpful in deciphering difficult portions of the Hebrew text.

In 37:3, where the MT reads זקנים, "son of his old age," Targum Onqelos translates חכים, "a wise one (son)." One may think that Targum Onqelos corrects the text due to its apparent contradiction in 44:20, where Benjamin is given a similar title, "child of his old age." However, Targum Onqelos is more likely pointing to the rabbinic understanding that זקנים implies wisdom. Old age brings wisdom, so Joseph is a "son of his wisdom."[9] Another possibility is that Jacob's favor toward Joseph is based on Joseph's wisdom.[10] Continuing in 37:25-28, we encounter the perplexing story of Joseph's sale into slavery; but who sold who to whom? Targum Onqelos indicates that while the brothers were contemplating selling Joseph, Midianites came on Joseph in the pit and sold him to a caravan

8. Sysling, *Tehiyyat Ha-Metim*, 3–5.

9. Weiss, *Sifra debe Rab*, Sifra Qod. 3.7, p. 91a; Theodor, Genesis Rabba acc. to *Bereshith Rabba*, 84:8, p. 1010; b. Qid. 32b.

10. S. D. Luzzato, *Ohev Ger*, op. cit., p. 9.

of Arabs, who brought Joseph to Egypt.[11] This explains the confusing circumstances that are less clear in the MT.[12]

Moving to 38:9, Targum Onqelos uses words that explain the levirate marriage custom of Deuteronomy 25:6. In 38:14 scholars have long
struggled to identify the location of Tamar's trickery. The Hebrew עינים is
unclear. The LXX has "at the gates of Ainan," but Targum Onqelos explains
by use of the word "crossroads/entrance," "at the crossroads/entrance of
Eynayim." Again in 41:9, Targum Onqelos considers the Hebrew word חטאי
imprecise because it indicates an offense between God and human and
the offense committed is between human and human. Instead of using חוב
(Exod 10:17; Lev 24:15; Num 5:6; Deut 15:9) "sin/offenses" (between God and
human), he chooses סרח (Gen 40:1; Num 12:11), "offense" (between human
and human), which helps to clearly defines the circumstances of the text.

Genesis 48:14 provides example of the translator struggling with the
Hebrew. Targum Onqelos explains the rare Hebrew word שכל, "crossing"
(?), with "he shrewdly directed." The same situation occurs in 38:29, where
the MT reads: "What a breach you have breached for yourself,"מה–פרצת
עליך. Targum Onqelos translates מא תקוף סגי עלך למתקף, "What great power
is upon you to have such strength."[13] While Targum Onqelos misses the
alliteration associated with Perez's name, he alludes to the great power to
be displayed by the Messiah, who will be a descendent of Perez.[14] Certainly
the greatest examples of this occur in Genesis 49. Genesis 49 constitutes
the blessings of the twelve sons of Jacob, but because of the poetic nature
of the Hebrew, its use of multiple *hapax legomena*, and the peculiar ways
and words in which the blessings are delivered, this is one of the more
difficult sections in the MT. Whether Onqelos is correct in all his explanations and interpretations or not, he does provide us with an older understanding, which can prove helpful. We will revisit 49:22–26, the blessing
of Joseph, later. Many other examples of this nature are present but will
not be considered at this time (37:2; 40:10; 41:40, 43–44, 47, 52, 56–57; 42:4;
43:16, 30; 44:8; 45:12, 18, 21, 22; 47:19, 24, 27; 48:9, 12, 16).

---

11. Horowitz, Rabin, *Mechilta D'Rabbi Ismael*, 13:19, p. 235; Theodor, Genesis Rabba acc. to *Bereshith Rabba* 84:17, p. 1021; Targum Neofiti has "Saracens."

12. See also chap. 3.

13. Also Targum Pseudo-Jonathan and Targum Neofiti.

14. Theodor, Genesis Rabba acc. to *Bereshith Rabba*, 84:14, p. 1049.

A second way in which Targum Onqelos provides commentary is by translating the Hebrew idioms and figures of speech, explaining their usage with
his rendering.[15] This could be considered a subset of the previous discussion,
but it occurs with such frequency it bears specific mention. In Genesis 42:9
the MT speaks of the "nakedness" of the land, but Targum Onqelos explains
with "the vulnerable part of." Again in verse 16, the MT reads "Whether there
is truth in you," and Targum Onqelos renders "Whether you speak the truth."
A final example from Genesis 45:26: MT reads "and his heart went numb," and
Targum Onqelos uses והוו מליא פיגן על לבה, "but the words were faint upon his
heart" (also Gen 42:28; 43:18, 30; 44:18; 45:9, 11, 26; 48:15; 50:13, 23).

One final way Targum Onqelos seeks to bring clarity to the Hebrew text
is by providing an intensification of emotion and tone. Due to the danger of
adding something to the text not intended, Targum Onqelos seldom resorts
to this, although other targums are less hesitant. Two noteworthy examples: in Genesis 45:28 Targum Onqelos renders "Great is my joy," while the
MT records "It is enough." This is Jacob's response in learning that his son
Joseph is still alive. It is easy to understand why Targum Onqelos choose as
he did. Also, in 48:11 the MT uses פללתי, "expected," which Targum Onqelos
renders with סברית, "hoped."

THE PIETY OF TARGUM ONQELOS: A REFLECTION
OF TALMUDIC AND RABBINIC TRADITION

There are several ways Targum Onqelos reflects the rabbinic piety of his
day. Some of this is in the structure of the text as the targum seeks to keep
the "proper" distance between God and humanity. One important and distinctive example is the use of Memra. Where the Hebrew has "the voice of
God," Targum Onqelos has "the voice of the Memra of God." The Memra
provides an insulating element between God and humanity, seeking to avoid
any implication of direct interaction between God and humanity that would

---

15. Joosten explains the challenge of idioms: "The Hebrew Bible is full of idiomatic expressions. For some reason, most of them consist of a verb and a noun referring to a part of the
body. Many of them, such as the expression 'to life up one's eyes,' are easily understood,
though some, such as 'to recognize someone's face,' are more difficult, and a few, like 'to
speak to someone's heart,' are entirely opaque. But the difficulty for translators is not one of
understanding only. Rather, the problem arises from the discrepancy between form and meaning. If one follows the words, one may miss the meaning completely; and if one aims at the
meaning, one may take all the savor from the text" ("Translating the Untranslatable," 61–62).

depreciate God's status.[16] Examples of this in the Joseph narratives abound (Gen 38:7, 10; 39:2, 21; 41:38; 43:29); however, "Memra" is also a word used to connote God's power or presence (40:8; 48:21) and seems to have little reference to communication.[17] C. T. R. Hayward has also provided discussion on Memra as substitute for the tetragrammaton. This certainly could be the case in Targum Onqelos 40:8 and 48:21.[18] Memra as acting in support or help of Joseph, and being present for his assistance, is seen in 39:2, 3, 21, 23; 48:21. This use ties Joseph into the earlier patriarchal narrative, where Targum Onqelos says that Memra of the Lord was for the help and support of Abraham, Isaac, and Jacob. However, Targum Onqelos also uses this to point us forward to Genesis 49:24–25, where it reappears in the context of Joseph's blessing.

Another example of this piety is the avoidance of anthropomorphisms. Often this is accomplished by transposing the active voice into the passive, as seen in 44:16. The MT reads "God has discovered the guilt of your servants," but Targum Onqelos renders "the guilt of your servants has been established by the LORD." In 48:3 the MT records נראה–אלי, "appeared to me," but Targum Onqelos has אתגלי לי, "was revealed." Again in 50:20 the MT reads "God intended it," but Targum Onqelos changes this into the passive with the addition of קדם in circumlocution to read "from before the LORD it was intended."[19]

The targum also avoids any mention of idols or idolatry that would give the false impression that they possess any power or accomplish any good.[20] An example, revisited later, is found in 44:5, 15, where the MT records Joseph speaking of his cup of divination with which he "divines," but Targum Onqelos renders it "tests."

A close comparison of the two texts reveals other examples of rabbinic piety in the Aramaic. In 39:9 the MT records Onan's wicked act as "waste the seed upon the ground," but Targum Onqelos renders this as "he corrupted

16. Grossfeld, *Targum Onqelos to Genesis*, 19.

17. Grossfeld, *Targum Onqelos to Genesis*, 19.

18. C. T. R. Hayward, *Divine Name and Presence: The Memra* (Lanham, MD: Rowman & Littlefield, 1981), 147–58.

19. See also 49:24 (2×). For more on this see Grossfeld, *Targum Onqelos to Genesis*, 25–26; Sysling, *Tehiyyat Ha-Metim*, 5–7.

20. Grossfeld, *Targum Onqelos to Genesis*, 20.

his way upon the ground." In rabbinic tradition sexual intercourse is called "way" and is related to Genesis 6:12; "Every creature corrupted its way on earth." In 38:18, Targum Onqelos avoids the use of "cord" in its translation, choosing to replace it with "staff." This appears strange, as Targum Onqelos usually uses חוט as a literal translation for "cord." However, according to midrash, "cord" is an allusion to the Sanhedrin, most of whom were from the tribe of Judah. Due to the circumstances in which the cord is being used, Targum Onqelos, out of piety and political correctness, substitutes "staff" to avoid offense. Again in 44:9 the Hebrew "Let him die," which infers curse by divine intervention, is changed by Targum Onqelos so that it reads "Let him be put to death,"[21] which indicates a punishment by humankind.

The next example is 46:30 (see also 41:16; 50:19). The MT reads אמותה הפעם אחרי ראותי את–פניך כי עודך חי, "now let me die, since I have seen your face for I know you live." This runs counter to rabbinic tradition, which considers such talk as giving opportunity to Satan. Targum Onqelos records אילו אנא מאית זמנא הדא מנחם אנא בתר דחזיתנון לאפך ארי עד כען קי ים את, "if I were to die now I would be comforted after I have seen it, your face, that you are still alive."

In closing we reference Genesis 49. Again, these blessings are of a very difficult nature and remain a challenge. While Targum Onqelos is of great help, it is also true that he imports a great deal of midrash material incorporating rabbinic understanding. Two cases for example: In verse 10 and the other verses involved in the blessing of Judah, we see a strong messianic flavor, even the importing of the word itself in verse 10. This is the same understanding reflected in the Talmud and midrash. Although the MT does have a messianic tone, Targum Onqelos nuances and intensifies. In the second example from verse 16, we again see rabbinic tradition guiding the Aramaic of the verse in the blessing of Dan. While the MT reads "Dan shall judge his people as one of the tribes of Israel," Targum Onqelos, in accordance with rabbinical understanding, structures the language so that the reader will see this as a reference to the judge Samson, who comes from the tribe of Dan.

---

21. Also Targum Neofiti and to a lesser extent Targum Pseudo-Jonathan.

CULTURAL REFLECTIONS OF THE ROMAN ERA

Targum Onqelos, in providing an Aramaic version of the Torah, also provides a window into of the customs of its day. It is not uncommon to find
examples of cultural relevance that do not fit into the same time frame
as the Joseph narratives, but they do help the readers/hearers better
understand and relate to the message that is being conveyed. One example previously mentioned is the reference to "Arabs" in 37:25. While this
would not have been appropriate to the first hearers of these narratives,
it certainly would have conveyed meaning to those at the time of Targum
Onqelos.

Looking at 37:25 and 43:33, we see the seating and eating habits of
the Roman era reflected. The MT of 37:25 says "they sat down to eat," but
Targum Onqelos writes "they reclined to eat bread." Genesis 43:33 in
Hebrew translates "and they sat," while Targum Onqelos renders "and
they were seated round about."

Genesis 41:34–35 paints a picture of the governing powers in talmudic and Roman times (perhaps also 37:8, 36; 39:1). The MT speaks of "officials" or "overseers," but Targum Onqelos is more specific in its translation:
"trustworthy officials." This reflects talmudic times, when the governing
authorities were notoriously corrupt in the administration of their duties
in the Roman Empire.

Finally, in 45:6 we note a possible reference to the agricultural practices
of that time. Targum Onqelos speaks of "sowing," but the MT actually reads
"plowing." The practice changed at various intervals throughout history.
Some cultures plow and then sow; others sow and then plow the seed under.

Before we conclude this section, we note that Genesis 49 not only
reflects the rabbinic teachings and customs of its day, but it also relies
heavily on the now-known history of the people of Israel in order to bring
clarity. Apart from the historical knowledge, the meaning of many of these
verses remains obscure (see also in this section 41:32; 48:15).

IMAGES IMPROVED

The targums carefully enhanced the image of their ancestors as they translated the Hebrew text. Throughout the fourteen chapters of the Joseph narratives, every opportunity is taken to polish and enhance these heroes of
the Jewish faith. First, it is important to show examples of Targum Onqelos

enhancing the image of the Hebrew people as a whole by enhancing the image of the group of brothers who sat in opposition to Joseph.

In 37:18 the MT reads ויתנכלו, "they conspired," but Targum Onqelos tones this down because "conspire" casts the brothers in an unfavorable light. Targum Onqelos renders "they conspired" with וחשיבו, "they thought."[22] Other examples include 42:19, 33, where the MT states "grain ration for your starving households," but Targum Onqelos renders "the grain that is lacking in your houses" (יט עיבורא דחסיר בבתיכון). This is in keeping with rabbinic teachings that Jacob's house was not out of food yet. This would have called into question Jacob's status with the Lord who provides.[23] Genesis 43:32, as the MT explains why the Egyptians ate separately from the Hebrews, writes "for it is an abomination." Targum Onqelos explains this in a way that is more favorable to the Hebrews and less so toward the Egyptians: "For Hebrews eat the cattle which the Egyptians worship."[24] In 48:4 Targum Onqelos focuses the blessing specifically on the twelve tribes when the MT may have intended a broader focus (MT: "peoples"; Targum Onqelos: "an assembly of tribes"). Finally in Genesis 49 and the blessings of Jacob, each of the blessings is enhanced, even those of Reuben, Simeon, and Levi.

Targum Onqelos also has one specific passage in which the image of Jacob is the focus. In 50:5 the MT records Joseph speaking to Pharaoh as he seeks permission to bury Jacob in Canaan. Joseph quotes Jacob in reference to his burial place: "my tomb that I dug (hewed out) for myself." The Midrash Tanhuma explains the concern by asking: "Was Jacob a grave-digger?"[25] Thus, Targum Onqelos uses דאתקנית, "prepared" or "I have acquired/bought."

Judah is also the recipient of an enhanced image in these narratives. Beginning in Genesis 37, we see how Targum Onqelos separates Judah out as the leader of the brothers early on. Genesis 37:27 in the MT reflects that the brothers "listened" to Judah, but Targum Onqelos writes that they "obeyed" him. This is a stronger response, generally reserved for one in a

22. Also Targum Neofiti and the Syriac; Targum Pseudo-Jonathan has "to counsel."
23. Also followed by the LXX, Peshitta, and the Vulgate.
24. Also Targum Pseudo-Jonathan.
25. Midrash Tanhuma *Wayechi* 6.

position of leadership. Then, in 38:26, we discover an even more interesting example. When Judah is confronted by his sin with Tamar and the
results of that liaison, according to the MT he says: "She is more righteous
from me." Targum Onqelos found the idea that Tamar was more right/
righteous than Judah objectionable. So, Targum Onqelos renders this as
"by me she is pregnant."[26]

Finally, we come to Joseph. No other character receives a makeover
as significant as Joseph. The Septuagint and the targums both attempt
to polish Joseph's image, some going to great lengths that he might serve
their purposes. The LXX, largely adopted by the early church fathers, has
laid the foundation for much of modern Christian thought, while the targums often reflect talmudic and rabbinic teachings and traditions, thus
providing the base for much of today's Jewish thought. How the LXX and
the targums have understood Joseph tends to be the way we interpret
Joseph today.

A careful reading of the Hebrew text reveals any number of concerns
and problems attached to Joseph's character that the LXX, the targums,
and other interpreters seek to address. A list of these includes:

1. Joseph was born to the "wrong" mother

2. Joseph served as a spy for his father

3. Joseph was foolish and arrogant in his early dealings and rela-
    tionships with his brothers

4. Joseph was thought to have been torn to pieces by a wild
    beast—rendering him unclean

5. Joseph went back into Potiphar's house when no other men
    were present when only Potiphar's wife was there

6. Joseph married the daughter of a pagan priest

7. Joseph married a non-Hebrew

8. Joseph became an Egyptian

---

26. Also Targum Neofiti and Targum Pseudo-Jonathan. Note the reference to this confession in 49:8: "Judah, you confessed and were not embarrassed."

9. Joseph is never referenced as worshiping the Lord or reading the Torah

10. Joseph named his oldest son Manasseh

11. Joseph made no effort to search out his father after he had been elevated to second in command of all Egypt

12. Joseph practiced or claimed to practice divination

13. Joseph tested his brothers

14. Joseph took advantage of the Egyptian people in the midst of the famine

Even more could be said concerning Joseph's attitudes and actions in other situations. These examples, however, provide a good basis for our discussion.[27]

Targum Onqelos attempts to deal with all but four of the above issues. In each case, the change from the reading of the MT made by Targum Onqelos is an attempt to polish the image of Joseph, making him more palatable to rabbinic tastes. Example 1: Joseph being born from the "wrong" mother. According to the MT and Jewish understanding, Leah was God's chosen wife for Jacob. While this involved trickery on the part of Laban (Gen 29), God's choice is evident by the events that followed. Leah was the most fruitful, and it was one of her sons, Judah, who was the chief tribe and blessed with the messianic line (49:8–12). It was also Leah, not Rachel, who was buried in the family tomb along with the other patriarchs and their wives (49:29–31). While Targum Onqelos chooses to ignore this issue, other targums, most notably Targum Pseudo-Jonathan, attempt to address it.[28]

The second example refers to Joseph serving as a spy for his father to bring back reports about his brothers (37:2). Targum Onqelos makes a subtle change: "Joseph brought their bad character to the attention of their father." The perceived fault of Joseph is shifted onto the brothers. In addition, in example 3—Joseph being foolish and arrogant in his early

---

27. See also chap. 4.

28. Targum Pseudo-Jonathan makes reference to a "switching of fetuses" in the wombs of Leah and Rachel. Joseph therefore belonged to Leah, and Dinah belonged to Rachel.

dealings and relations with his brothers—Targum Onqelos appears to deal with this by changing the MT of 37:3, "son of his old age," to "wise one (son)." Joseph is not shown being young and foolish, but rather wise for his seventeen years.[29]

In 37:33 we read of Jacob's reaction to the bloody tunic belonging to Joseph. The MT reads טרף טרף, "torn to pieces." This is a problem because not only was being torn to pieces by a wild animal an issue of human dignity, but also no animal that was torn by wild beasts was fit for sacrifice. It was rendered unclean (example 4). In view of this, Targum Onqelos simply changes this to "killed."[30]

Example 5 is one that continues to bother many people of faith. Joseph had been encouraged by Potiphar's wife time and time again to lie with her. He had been steadfast in his refusal, but then, in 39:11, Joseph returned to Potiphar's house when the rest of the men were absent. It seems obvious this is a mistake that Joseph would not make. He knew the situation of the household and about the other men being absent, for he was in charge of everything. Targum Onqelos, in accordance with rabbinic tradition, changes the MT, "to do his work," to read "to examine his accounts."[31] First, it makes clear what "work" Joseph came to accomplish, and second, it gives the impression this might have been a quick visit to examine his accounts and leave before Potiphar's wife was aware of his presence. Later, in 39:23, Targum Onqelos uses the word "blameless/without fault" in regard to Joseph's character, while the MT reads "paid no attention to anything." Nevertheless, it does not completely alleviate doubt concerning Joseph's wisdom or his intentions.[32]

Moving to examples 6 (Joseph's marriage to the daughter of a pagan priest) and 7 (Joseph married a non-Hebrew; 41:45, 50; 46:20): Again, this has proven difficult because of the various commands within the Torah that forbid this kind of union. The first issue has to do with the pagan priest,

---

29. Note earlier discussion in this chapter.

30. Also Targum Neofiti and Targum Pseudo-Jonathan.

31. Also Targum Neofiti and Targum Pseudo-Jonathan. See Gen Rab 87:7, p. 1071f; Sot. 36b vol 11 and y. Hor. 11:5 vol. 17, p. 46d; Cant Rab 1:1; Tanh. (A) *Wayyesheb* 9, PR *Wattishlam kol Ha-Mel'akah* 6, p. 23a, as noted by Grossfeld, *Targum Onqelos to Genesis*, 133. For detailed discussion of these and other rabbinic sources, see Niehoff, *Figure of Joseph*, 34–35, 79, 131–34.

32. Kugel, *In Potiphar's House*, 95.

Potiphera. Not only is he an Egyptian, but he is the priest of a pagan god. Targum Onqelos deals with this simply by changing all MT references of "priest" to "chief."[33] This is also in line with the rabbinic tradition that only Aaron and his descendants could be "priests" (B. Bat. 109b; b. Sanh. 82a, b; Num Rab 20:24). This leaves us with the second issue (example 7). Not only is Joseph's wife, Asenath, an Egyptian, but she is an unbeliever, the daughter of a pagan priest. Even with the "priest" concern alleviated by the targums and rabbinic teaching, there is still the problem of Joseph marrying outside the faith of Abraham, Isaac, and Jacob. Targum Onqelos does not deal with this concern, perhaps because of various pseudepigraphal writings that go to great lengths to address the problem.[34]

Examples 8 and 9 can also be dealt with simultaneously. These examples deal with the concern that Joseph became an Egyptian and that no reference is made of Joseph worshiping God or reading the Torah. In the MT it appears that Joseph has adopted his new home and life situation completely, although he does make reference to the power of God and his guiding presence. Targum Onqelos recognizes these problems and addresses both by adding to Joseph's blessing the phrase "because he observed the law secretly and placed his trust in the divine power" (Gen 49:24). However, we also see this addressed in 41:16 in Joseph's reply to Pharaoh on the occasion of his translation of dreams; he says: "Not through my wisdom, but from the LORD shall Pharaoh's welfare be restored." Then, notably, Targum Onqelos introduces the divine name in 43:29, when Joseph greets Benjamin.

The next two examples—10 (Joseph named his eldest son Manasseh) and 11 (Joseph made no effort to find his father after he had been elevated to second in command of all Egypt)—are both ignored by Targum Onqelos. This is surprising because to "forget all my troubles and all my father's house"—the meaning of Manasseh—is certainly an unacceptable attitude. This appears to carry over into his lack of desire to go and search out his father. Many excuses have been made for Joseph's attitude, but none deal with the problem. It seems peculiar that Targum Onqelos has chosen not

---

33. Also Targum Neofiti and Targum Pseudo-Jonathan.
34. See especially Joseph and Aseneth.

to comment on the MT in these matters.[35] However, in Genesis 45:12, Joseph speaks to Benjamin in the latter's own language, and this must be Hebrew. As far as Targum Onqelos is concerned, Joseph has not really forgotten his past. Those reading/hearing this targum in the Roman period could escape the implications of this issue. By that time, Hebrew was the language of the sages and was well on its way to becoming the "holy language." Targum Onqelos has dealt with the issue at hand, albeit in an implicit manner.

The twelfth example seems strange indeed. In 44:5 the MT reads "he practices divination," the words of Joseph's steward as he addresses Joseph's brothers. This may not have proven problematic, but in 44:15 Joseph himself says: "Do you not know that a man like me can indeed practice divination?" Any reference to divination, sorcery, or other magical arts being conducted by a hero of the faith and a father of the Jewish nation is cause for serious concern. In response, Targum Onqelos changes "practices divination" to "tests" and tones down the Hebrew.

Example 13—Joseph and his testing of his brothers—concerns Joseph's attitude toward his brothers. While it is true that Joseph could have avenged their earlier treatment of him, his attitude toward them, especially in this first encounter since his sale into slavery and exile in 42:7, seems less than brotherly. The MT writes "and he acted like a stranger toward them," but Targum Onqelos tones down this language and writes "and he considered what he should say to them."[36] This change portrays Joseph as one who is not certain how to act in this situation and not as one who has devised a plan.

The final example, 14, is that Joseph took advantage of the Egyptian people in the midst of the famine. Given the history of the Egyptians and Jews, of which Targum Onqelos was aware, it is no surprise that this is not addressed in any way by his translation.

Although these examples do not encompass all the concerns that a careful reading of the MT uncovers in regards to the character and image of Joseph, they do illustrate an interesting pattern in Targum Onqelos of

---

35. Note the discussion from chap. 6 concerning the way in which the LXX deals with this issue.

36. It is interesting to note that Targum Pseudo-Jonathan translates the Hebrew literally, while Targum Neofiti renders "and he showed himself hostile toward them."

enhancing and polishing the image of the main character of the Joseph narratives.

THE SEPTUAGINT AND TARGUM ONQELOS IN COMPARISON

Comparing the Septuagint (LXX) and Targum Onqelos and their respective translations of the MT shows many differences; however, neither version significantly alters the flow of the Hebrew narrative. In the previous chapter the Greek use of parataxis, not generally found in classical Greek, was noted. In all of the Aramaic versions, rather than inserting paraphrase or midrashic material, the targums translate/transliterate the Hebrew to keep close to the order and wording of the original Hebrew narrative.[37]

The LXX intended to provide a fluid and readable/hearable text for third-century BCE Alexandrian Jews. This intention has textual consequences. In regards to the Joseph narratives, the LXX misses many of the distinguishing features of the MT. It tends to ignore much of the doubling for which the narratives are known, and it is weak in its translation of various Hebrew idioms. Where we have available text from Aquila's Greek work, we discover a more literal adherence to the MT that maintains the majority of the MT's distinctive features.[38] Targum Onqelos remains truer to the MT, maintaining the majority of the doubling and translating the Hebrew idioms more correctly. The only area where this does not hold is in the blessings of Genesis 49.

Both the LXX and Targum Onqelos contain cultural references true to their own era. There appears to be, however, a subtle exegetical movement in both translations. This movement is distinct with each and may be related to its cultural context. In the LXX we see a tendency to build on the dramatic portions of the text. Emotional narrative is enhanced, and situations appear to be intensified. This is perhaps a response to the culture of Alexandria, Egypt, of that era. Alexandria wanted to be known as a patron of the arts, especially the theater, as it vied for attention with Athens.[39] In providing a Greek translation for this audience, it would be natural to intensify many of the dramatic scenes in the Joseph narratives. Targum

---

37. P. Flesher and B. Chilton, *The Targums: A Critical Introduction* (Waco, TX: Baylor University Press, 2011), 39–54.

38. Parts of Aquila's text appear in Origen's Hexapla.

39. See chap. 6.

Onqelos, in contrast, trends toward the opposite. Emotional and dramatic portions of the narratives appear to be toned down. This may be related to the desire to show Joseph and his brothers, along with Jacob, in a light that would not shine so harshly on the dysfunctional nature of their family.

Both texts display.an effort to enhance the image of Joseph. How they polish his image may reveal the agenda with which each approached the text. The LXX is interested in presenting Joseph as a salvific character, not only for the Jews of that day and place, but also for the rest of the Alexandrian community. This may go hand in hand with the dramatic approach. The LXX clearly gives the role of forgiver/savior to Joseph. With the issue of the great famine and Joseph's role in saving the people of Israel and many other nations, this emphasis is not surprising, and a Hebrew savior of the nation of Egypt could only enhance the role of the Jews in the city of Alexandria and surrounding areas.

Targum Onqelos also takes great care in polishing Joseph's image. The general direction of Targum Onqelos's image enhancement is different from the LXX. Targum Onqelos appears more interested in presenting Joseph as an ethical and moral example for the people. This is in keeping with the culture of talmudic and rabbinic tradition. In most cases, where there are perceived issues with Joseph's character, Targum Onqelos responds with efforts to enhance his moral and ethical image.

The best way to point out these distinct moves is to examine the text of 49:22–26. Both the LXX and Targum Onqelos modify the verses of Jacob's blessing of Joseph significantly and in different ways. Beginning with the LXX, the translator changes the Hebrew and renders a blessing that in effect lays out the history of Joseph and indicates that it is from Joseph that "the one who strengthens Israel will come." This appears to be a reference to some great leader, possibly a second messianic figure.[40]

Looking at Targum Onqelos and 49:22–26, we find a very telling phrase in verse 24: "And his prophecy was fulfilled in them, because he observed the law secretly and placed his trust in the divine power." The blessings that follow appear to be a result of Joseph observing the law (Torah) and

---

40. A second messianic figure, a "messiah of Joseph," or a "messiah of Ephraim," is mentioned in later rabbinic texts such as b. Sukkah 52a; Tg. Ps.-J. Exod 40:11, and Tg. Song 4:5; 7:11. See Alexander, *Targum of Canticles*, 135. It is possible that the idea of such a messiah was known in the days when Targum Onqelos was taking shape.

placing his trust in God (the divine power). Joseph is portrayed as a moral and ethical figure, a good example of what happens when you read the Torah and follow the Lord. That Joseph was chosen for this role is interesting. However, as one considers the ethical lessons implied in the targumic verses concerning Reuben and Joseph in Genesis 49, it is not surprising. In verses 3–4 Reuben is referred to as succumbing to temptation and sinning with Bilhah (Gen 35:22). The MT narrative implies that Reuben's character was not strong enough to resist temptations. Joseph was met with temptations of a similar nature, but he resisted and remained steadfast by holding true to his father's belief and teachings (Tg. Ps.-J. Gen 49:24). So, Joseph becomes the ethical and moral model for others to imitate.[41]

JOSEPH'S BLESSING IN GENESIS 49:22–26

A careful examination of Jacob's blessing of Joseph in 49:22–26 in Targum Onqelos reveals two main foci. The first is a theme of life interwoven through the blessing, and the second involves the covenant and the blessing associated with the patriarchs. These two realities are not unrelated, and together they help explain the closing verses of the Joseph narratives.[42]

Targum Onqelos's opening statement in verse 22 establishes the theme of life in these blessings: "Joseph is my son who shall be numerous."[43] This is the only place where Targum Onqelos translates פרת of the Hebrew with סגי, and at first glance this may seem unusual, until we note that Targum Onqelos is making the connection to 48:16, 19, where the translator chooses to use סגי in the sense of "multiply" and therefore ties this multiplication to both Ephraim and Manasseh, rather than just Ephraim, as the MT's פרת works with the meaning of Ephraim (Gen 41:52), "to be fruitful." Regardless, "to be numerous, to multiply, to be fruitful" are all references to life and its continuance and multiplication.

---

41. See, for example, T.Jos. 11.1–6; 18.1–4; and compare Syrén, *Blessings in the Targums*, 126–27.

42. Brueggemann makes cautious connection of this blessing with the blessings of creation in Gen 1–2 (*Genesis*, 366–67). See also T. Fretheim, "The Reclamation of Creation: Redemption and Law in Exodus," *Interpretation: A Journal of Bible and Theology* 45, no. 4 (October 1991): 354–79.

43. MT: "Joseph is a fruitful bough."

Verse 22 continues: "My son who shall be blessed like a vine that is planted."[44] This vine imagery is common in the Old Testament and is generally associated with fruitfulness. Targum Onqelos does not follow the MT precisely, intending to avoid repetition without addition of meaning.[45] Psalm 128:3, "Your wife shall be like a fruitful vine within your house," supports the "life" theme; however, Targum Onqelos is focused on a larger reality. Psalm 80 begins with, "Give ear O Shepherd of Israel, you who lead Joseph like a flock," and continues in verse 9 (MT) with, "You brought a vine out of Egypt; you drove out nations and planted it." Also note the prophetic statement of Isaiah 5:7: "For the vineyard of the LORD of hosts is the house of Israel, and the men of Judah are his pleasant planting" (see also Jer 2:21). Targum Onqelos appears to be using this understanding of vine, especially in light of Psalm 80. In these verses, the vine is associated with Israel, in particular with faithful Israel. Targum Onqelos also adds a vine "that is planted," which has no equivalent in the MT. A tree, a vine, or a seed is dead unless it is planted and given occasion to grow. Looking back to Genesis 47:19–26, the people of Egypt approach Joseph, first to sell themselves and then their land for food, saying: "Why should we die before your eyes, both we and our land?" and then adding: "And give us seed that we may live and not die, and that the land may not be desolate." Then (47:23) Joseph replies: "Now here is seed for you, and you shall sow the land," and the people respond (47:25) with the words: "You have saved our lives." Apart from seed that is planted, the land and the people will be dead. Whenever seeds or vines are planted, there is anticipation of life. Seeds and plantings resurrect the soil. This is common imagery found in many ancient cultures with their fertility cults. We also see this imagery at use in the New Testament (John 12:24; 1 Cor 15:36–49). This life theme is continued as this vine is planted "near a spring of water," indicating that its health and fruitfulness are dependent on this "spring of water." Targum Onqelos may be thinking of Psalm 1:1–3:

Blessed is the man who walks not in the counsel of the wicked,
nor stands in the way of sinners, nor sits in the seat of scoffers;

---

44. MT: "a fruitful bough by a stream."
45. Grossfeld, *Targum Onqelos to Genesis*, 170.

but his delight is in the instruction of the LORD, and on his law he meditates day and night. He is like a tree planted by streams of living water that yields its fruit in its season and its leaf does not wither. In all that he does, he prospers.

Jeremiah 17:8 also describes the righteous man: "He is like a tree planted by water, that sends out its roots by the stream ... for it does not cease to bear fruit" (see also Isa 60:12). In these references we note that the tree planted by streams of water is associated with a righteous man, or with righteous Israel. They are righteous because they delight in the Lord's instruction and meditate on his law/Torah. The Torah is associated with the stream of water that brings about fruitfulness and life. Targum Onqelos ties this in with Genesis 49:24 as he makes reference to Joseph's dreams and their fulfillment because of the "stream" by which he is planted. "And his prophecy was fulfilled in them, because he observed the law secretly and placed his trust in the divine power." Pharaoh, in Targum Onqelos of Genesis 41:39, describes Joseph as a man "in whom is the spirit of prophecy from before the LORD." This is taken up here by Jacob, where it is directly associated with Joseph's observance of the Torah in secret, which is the ultimate reason he "got possession of a kingdom." Targum Onqelos goes on to say: "Therefore, gold was cast on his arms; he took possession of a kingdom and became mighty." It appears that Targum Onqelos is referencing the fulfillment of Joseph's dreams, and, in a sense, justifying his attitude toward his brothers. Apparently, Onqelos is also concerned with the proper interpretation of Joseph's dreams. An important correlation is found in 41:43, where Targum Onqelos translates the difficult word אברך (MT perhaps "bend the knee") with "father of the king." Joseph rules over his brothers and many others, as his dreams indicate.

Following this we read in Genesis 49:24: "This happened from before El, the Mighty One of Jacob, by Whose Memra he sustains fathers and children, the seed of Israel." We see how Joseph, in his faithfulness and his fruitfulness, was used by the Mighty One of Jacob to preserve life for the "fathers and children, the seed of Israel." Targum Onqelos refers back to 47:12 and points forward to 50:20. Both verses refer to Joseph's role as provider of food for his father's household (47:12) and how God governed him in this role (50:20). Genesis 50:20 is very life specific, and is tied to verse 23 and the adversarial role played by Joseph's brothers: "Now, as for you, although you plotted evil against me, from before the LORD it was intended for good so that it may come about that many people should be kept alive, as it is this day."

Finally, we look at verse 25: "And he shall bless you with blessings that descend from the dew of heaven above." Targum Onqelos has translated the MT to closely reflect Isaac's blessing of Jacob in Genesis 27:28 and has avoided any inference of "rain."[46] Perhaps he was concerned with any reference that might suggest that Baal was the source of blessing. Yet, in other targums the imagery of rain being life giving is maintained.[47] The connection to the Genesis 27 blessing of Jacob appears to be another reference to fruitfulness and life. "See, the smell of my son is as the smell of the field that the LORD has blessed! May God give you the dew of heaven and of the fatness of the earth and plenty of grain and wine. Let peoples serve you and nations bow down to you. Be lord over your brothers, and may your mother's sons bow down to you" (Gen 27:27–28).

In Isaiah 26:19, life-giving dew is associated with resurrection: "Your dead shall live; their bodies shall rise. You, who dwell in the dust, awake and sing for joy! For your dew is a dew of light, and the earth will give birth to the dead."[48] Genesis 49:25 continues: "blessings that flow out of the depths of the earth below." Genesis 27:28 uses the term "fatness," which Targum Onqelos translates with "best" in other cases. Targum Onqelos continues the "stream," perhaps "spring," reference with his use of "flow" as he attempts to deal with the poetry of the MT.[49] The last third of the verse reads "blessings of your father and your mother." The MT reads "blessings of breasts and womb," but Targum Onqelos takes the שדים of the Hebrew (breasts) to be שׁדי (to shoot).[50] His thought is that

---

46. Also in midrashim: Midrash Aggadah on Genesis (p. 114); Midrash Leqah Tob on Genesis (p. 240). MT: "who will bless you with the blessings of heaven above." Buber, *Midrash Leqah Tob*, ed. S. Buber.

47. Read the "four keys" of Targum Neofiti as discussed by Sysling, *Tehiyyat Ha-Metim*, 137–49.

48. For more on this see Sysling, *Tehiyyat Ha-Metim*, 160.

49. MT: "blessing of the deep that crouches beneath."

50. See Grossfeld's discussion of this matter and his cataloging of other midrashic references (*Targum Onqelos to Genesis*, 172).

"to shoot" references ejaculation because in order to have procreation you need both a father and a mother.[51] This verse in Targum Onqelos is about fertility and life—life of the earth, as represented by productive fields, and the life of humanity, as seen in the reference to father and mother. These references to life in 49:22–26 establish a focus that is lacking in the other blessings of Genesis 49, which center on Joseph's brothers. Referencing life is a major component in all the patriarchal blessings and in the covenant.

This brings us to the second focus of the blessing—covenant and patriarchal blessings. Targum Onqelos makes strong allusions to the patriarchs and the covenantal blessings in Joseph's blessing. While the MT also alludes to these, Targum Onqelos helps to clarify. Verse 22 makes immediate reference to the covenant with the phrase "who shall be numerous/who shall multiply." One of the foremost promises of the patriarchal covenant, beginning with Abraham, is descendants as numerous as the stars of heaven (Gen 15:5; 22:17), the dust of the ground (13:16), or the sand on the seashore (22:17). In Genesis 17:6 Abraham is promised by the Lord: "I will make you exceedingly fruitful, and I will make you into nations, and kings shall come from you." Jacob refers to God Almighty blessing him in like manner in 48:4. "Behold, I will make you fruitful and multiply you, and I will make of you a company of peoples and will give this land to your offspring after you for an everlasting possession." None of the brothers, apart from Joseph, have this language in their blessings. The final portion of verse 22 reads: "Two tribes shall emerge from his sons; they shall receive an inherited portion." The MT is difficult here and is generally interpreted as "his branches run over the wall" or "his wild colts beside the wall." Targum Onqelos renders the entire phrase as a reference to two tribes coming from Joseph, Ephraim and Manasseh. This is in accordance with 1 Chronicles 5:1–2:

> The sons of Reuben the firstborn of Israel (for he was the firstborn, but because he defiled his father's couch, his birthright was given to the sons of Joseph, the son of Israel, so that he could not be enrolled

---

51. It is interesting to note this phrase used in Luke 11:27: "Blessed be the womb that bore you, and the breasts at which you nursed." This is in reference to Jesus. Some scholars have concluded that it was a common saying of the day. See Syrén, *Blessings in the Targums*, 151.

as the oldest son; though Judah became strong among his brothers and a chief came from him, yet the birthright belonged to Joseph).

This sheds light on Genesis 48:5. As Jacob takes possession of Ephraim and Manasseh, he says: "And now your two sons, who were born to you in the land of Egypt before I came to you in Egypt, are mine; Ephraim and Manasseh shall be mine, as Reuben and Simeon are." The priesthood goes to Levi, the line of kings and messianic promise go to Judah, but the "inherited portion," the birthright of the double portion, belongs to Joseph.

In Genesis 49:24, at the conclusion, there is a gloss, which reads "the seed of Israel," which is intended to reiterate the "fathers and children" that precede.[52] From the reference of "seed" in Genesis 3:15, the זרע, (זרעא; Aramaic) has been part of covenantal language (13:15; 15:5; 17:7, 8; 22:17; 24:7; 26:3–4) for the Hebrews. Sometimes translated as "offspring," it generally refers to the children of Israel, although it also can be a reference to the Seed, the promised Messiah.

Genesis 49:25 reads: "He shall bless you with blessings that descend from the dew of heaven above, blessings that flow out of the depths of the earth below." Again, this is a reference to Genesis 27:28, the blessing that Isaac bestowed on Jacob. The MT alludes to this as well, but Targum Onqelos makes certain that we do not miss the reference. Here Joseph receives a blessing from Jacob that Jacob's father gave to him—from patriarch to patriarch to Joseph. If what is taking place is not yet obvious, Jacob makes it more clear in 49:26. Targum Onqelos renders: "Your father's blessing shall be added to the blessings with which my ancestors blessed me."[53] Joseph is to be heir of the combined blessings of the patriarchs. He has not only received the double portion of the birthright, but he has also received the blessing in all its fullness, just as Jacob received both birthright and blessing from Isaac (25:29–34; 27:1–29). It appears that Targum Onqelos thought this blessing was meant to be passed on to Joseph, just as was the birthright. Upon close inspection of the language of Jacob's blessing in 27:27–28, it seems to fit Joseph better than Jacob. Not only do we see Targum Onqelos echo the language of "dew of heaven" and the other life/fertility aspects of

52. Grossfeld, *Targum Onqelos to Genesis*, 171.
53. MT: "The blessings of your father are mighty beyond the blessing of my parents."

27:27–28 in 49:22–26, but we also note the words "Let the peoples serve you
and nations bow down to you," and "Be lord over your brothers, and may
your mother's sons bow down to you." Nowhere is it recorded that nations
bowed down to Jacob as they bowed down to Joseph, seeking food during
the famine. Jacob had one brother, Esau, but it was Joseph's brothers who
bowed before him, and as Targum Onqelos renders in 49:26, Joseph was
distinguished above his brothers as the second in command of Egypt, and
he did serve as lord over them.

It is also appropriate to mention Deuteronomy 33 and the blessings
of Moses on the tribes of Israel. Special attention needs be paid to verses
13–17, the Joseph blessing, and verse 28, the Jacob blessing. Once more we
see that the blessings of Joseph and Jacob seem to be related, just as Genesis
49:22–26 and 27:27–28, and once again the imagery of "dew from heaven" is
used. We read in Deuteronomy 33:13: "Blessed by the LORD be his land with
the gifts from the dew of heaven," and 33:28: "in a land of grain and wine
whose heavens drop down dew." Again, this is a reference to the blessing
of life that comes from heaven, and perhaps a resurrection reference in
light of Isaiah 26:19.

Continuing on with Deuteronomy 33:13, we note the same language
in the MT text of 49:25: "and of the deep that crouches beneath." Targum
Onqelos renders each in a similar manner with "that flow out of the depths
of the earth below" (דנגדין ממעמקי ארעא מלרע).

Deuteronomy 33:14 carries on with the life focus by referencing the
fruits of the bountiful crops, and the MT carries this through into verse
15: "with the finest produce of the ancient mountains and the abundance
of the everlasting hills." Frequently, the targums and rabbinic writings
take "mountains and hills" as referencing the patriarchs and matriarchs
of Israel.[54] While Targum Onqelos follows this through in Genesis 49:26, he
does not choose to do so in Deuteronomy 33:15.[55] The thought expressed by
this allusion of mountains and hills to fathers and mothers is that "The PTs
to Dt. 33:15 point to the merits of the fathers as bringing profit to Joseph;
the fertility of his land derives from the blessings and merits of his parents and grandparents: 'It/viz. the land of Joseph/produces good fruits

54. For example: Tg. Ps.-J. Exod 17:9 and Palestinian Targums in Numbers 23:9; Ber. 98:20
(1271); Shem 15:26 (22a-b); Roš. Haš. 11a; Midrash Aggadah (858); Midrash Leqah Tob (240).

55. For more on this discussion see Syrén, *Blessings in the Targums*, 58ff, 135–36.

by the merits of our fathers ... and by the merits of the mothers ...' (N)."[56]
While Targum Onqelos does not deal with Deuteronomy 33:15 in this way,
we see how he has taken this approach with Genesis 49:26. The MT reads:
"the blessings of your father are mighty beyond the blessing of my parents,
up to the bounty of the everlasting hills." Targum Onqelos renders: "Your
father's blessings shall be added to the blessings with which my ancestors
blessed me, for which the great ones of the world had longed." The "great
ones" is likely a reference to the patriarchs and matriarchs.

In Targum Onqelos Deuteronomy 33:15 and Genesis 49:26, we see the
same phrase used in reference to Joseph, כל אלין לרישא דיוסף גברא פרישא
דאחוהי, "All of these shall be upon the head of Joseph, a man distinguished
among his brothers."

Finally, in Deuteronomy 33:17: "the first born bull" is likely referring to
the "inherited portion" of Genesis 49:22. Mentioned previously, the inheritance of the firstborn was given to Joseph—a double portion. The two tribes
(Gen 49:22) are his sons, Ephraim and Manasseh (Deut 33:17).

These two blessings show significant resemblance, with each helping
to define the other. Both support the idea of Joseph receiving the birthright and the blessing, and once again, Jacob's blessing and the blessing of
Joseph bear similarities.

In the last verses of Genesis 50 (50:24-26), the end of the Joseph narratives, we read:

> Then Joseph said to his brothers, "I am about to die, but God will
> surely remember/visit you and bring you up out of this land to the
> land that He promised on oath to Abraham, to Isaac and to Jacob."
> Then Joseph made the sons of Israel swear (on oath) saying, "God
> will surely remember/visit you, and you shall bring my bones from
> here." Then Joseph died, a son of a hundred and ten years, and they
> embalmed him and he was placed in a coffin in Egypt.

In the MT the word for "to remember/visit," פקד, is somewhat ambiguous, leaving itself open to various translations. Targum Onqelos uses a
word, דכר, that specifies the translation as "remember." He also uses this

---

56. Syrén, *Blessings in the Targums*, 125.

word to translate זכר of Exodus 2:24 and 3:15. The reason for this consistency on the part of Targum Onqelos may be that he sees all of these as being remembrances based on the covenant God established with the people of Israel. The exodus examples are specific in this regard, and because of the positioning of the Genesis 50 remembrances, they too are connected with the covenant.

Joseph understood the meaning and importance of his blessing. As he gathers his brothers to him as he nears the hour of his death, he invokes the covenant to them. He tells them he is about to die, but God will remember them and bring them out of this land to the land he swore as a possession to Abraham, Isaac, and Jacob. There is little doubt that he speaks of God "remembering" his people and thereby remembering his covenant. A portion of the covenant has always been the possession of the land of Canaan, so he makes a peculiar command. He makes his brothers swear an oath, perhaps on the covenant, that they will bring up his bones from Egypt to Canaan. In Targum Onqelos, the language "to swear an oath" is always used in relation to the covenant. This covenantal language seen here in 50:24, 25 is also noted in 50:5; 47:31 and in Exodus 2:24, as God remembers the covenant that he swore on oath with the people of Israel.[57]

Joseph's request to have his bones transported seems unusual at best, perhaps the result of the feeble, eccentric mind of an old man. Joseph is not asking for immediate interment in the land of Canaan; he is asking to go to Canaan when the Lord leads them up to possess the land. However, in light of Genesis 49:22–26, this may not be an odd request. Joseph is the last individual to receive the patriarchal blessing and covenant. This identifies him as the last patriarch, and every patriarch has been promised by the Lord that they will dwell or return to dwell in the promised land of Canaan. In the case of Jacob it was after his death, but so it was promised (46:4). Abraham died and was buried in Canaan (25:9), Isaac died and was buried in Canaan (35:29), Jacob died in Egypt and was returned and buried in Canaan (50:13–14), and now Joseph will die, and his bones will be transported to Canaan to be buried (Josh 24:32). This is not the only theme that identifies Joseph as a patriarch. All of the patriarchs sojourned because of famine:

---

57. On the terminology of the covenant and its representation in the Pentateuchal Targumim as an oath, see Hayward, *Divine Name*, 71–86.

Abraham sojourned to Egypt during famine (Gen 12:10), Isaac sojourned during famine but was instructed not to go to Egypt (26:1), Jacob sojourned to Egypt during famine (46:2–4), and Joseph sojourned to Egypt in order to preserve God's people in time of famine (50:20). Apart from Abraham, all the patriarchs were born from women who had been barren. Sarah was barren before she was able to give birth to Isaac in her old age (17:17–19), Rebekah was barren but was blessed with twins, Jacob and Esau (25:21), and Rachel was barren for quite some time before Joseph was born (30:22–24).

Since Joseph is established as one of the patriarchs in Genesis 49:22–26, it is assumed that he should return to dwell in the land promised by oath to his fathers. Two issues remain. First, why was Joseph's embalmed body not buried in Canaan immediately, as was that of his father, Jacob? Joseph's request does not appear to ask for this. Not only did Joseph's bones remain in Egypt with the Israelite people until the exodus, but the Israelites did not bury him in Canaan until they possessed the land. Because Joseph is the last patriarch, he also signals the end of the patriarchal era. However, the tribal era, which follows the patriarchal, does not really have its beginning until the land of Canaan is possessed and divided among the various tribes. It was when this had been accomplished that Joseph's bones were finally interred in Canaan, at Shechem, with the words of the covenant spoken to remind the Israelites of who they were (Josh 24:2–4).

The last issue is that Joseph is not buried in the cave of Machpelah with the other patriarchs and matriarchs (Gen 49:29–32). Perhaps Joseph assumed this is where the Israelites would bury him, but it did not happen, as he was buried at Shechem on the plot of ground his father Jacob gave to him (48:22).

"DEW" AND "BONES"

Targum Onqelos chooses to add the phrase "blessings that descend from the dew of heaven above" to the Hebrew of Genesis 49:25. We have discussed the correlation of Joseph's blessing in Targum Onqelos with the blessing of his father, Jacob, in Genesis 27. Both the MT and Targum Onqelos note the use of "dew" (טל; טלא); it is necessary to take a closer look at the use of "dew" in the MT and how Targum Onqelos choose to follow it.

"Dew," טל, occurs approximately thirty times in the Old Testament. Nearly all of these references consider dew a gift from Yahweh, and this gift involves or implies life. Yahweh gives fertility to the land; without dew and rain there is no fertility.[58] During certain seasons in Palestine, most notably the long, hot summer, it is only the dew that provides a certain amount of moisture for plants. The summer dew is as necessary for life as the winter rain.[59] Conversely, the lack of dew, or the withholding of dew, is considered to be a curse or a punishment. The *Theological Dictionary of the Old Testament* states: "The dew is thus linked indissolubly with the order of creation, with fertility and God's blessings. It is therefore natural for the promise of dew to be included in blessing formulas, and conversely, for the absence of dew to be threatened in curse and punishment formulas."[60] This is shown in the references and usages of טל in the MT of the Pentateuch. In Genesis 27:28 Jacob's blessing from his father states: "May God give you the dew of heaven," but Isaac's words to Esau in verse 39 read more like a curse: "Behold, away from the fatness of the earth shall be your dwelling, and away from the dew of heaven on high." Targum Onqelos follows this closely with טלא and then adds the same language to Jacob's blessing of Joseph in 49:25. He appears to be following the blessing formula of Moses in Deuteronomy 33:13, 28. In verse 13, Moses' blessing of Joseph includes "with the choicest gifts of heaven with the dew," which is again connected to the blessing of Jacob in verse 28, "whose heavens drop down dew."

There are only four other references to dew in the Pentateuch. While these are not found within the context of blessings or curses, each one reflects the theme of life. In the Song of Moses in Deuteronomy 32, Moses is speaking of his teachings, the words of his mouth. "May my teaching drop as the rain, my speech distill as dew, like gentle rain upon the tender grass, and like showers upon the herb." Moses certainly considers his words and teachings to be those of God, and it is these words that bring life to the people of Israel, just as rain and dew bring life to the earth.

The other references to dew in the MT (Exod 16:13–14; Num 11:9) are used in the context of the manna the Lord provides the people of Israel on their wilderness journey. While dew is not the main referent in these

---

58. In Ugaritic texts dew is the gift of Ba'al.

59. See the detailed discussion of the significance of dew for ancient Near Eastern societies in general, and for the writers of the Hebrew Bible in particular, by B. Otzen, "If tal," in Botterweck, Ringgren, and Fabry, *Theological Dictionary of the Old Testament*, 5:323–30.

60. Otzen, "If tal," 325.

passages, it does play an important part. Exodus 16:13–14: "In the evening quail came up and covered the camp, and in the morning dew lay around the camp. And when the dew had gone up, there was on the face of the wilderness a fine, flake-like thing, fine as frost on the ground." Numbers 11:9: "When the dew fell upon the camp in the night, the manna fell with it." Dew is the vehicle by which the Lord delivers his blessing of manna to the Israelites. The dew from above leaves the manna, which sustains the lives of the people of Israel—the bread of life. In each pentateuchal usage of dew in the MT, dew (טל) is closely related to life, either as that which gives life or that which brings the life-giving substance.

Beyond the Pentateuch, the MT uses dew in connection with resurrected life. Targum Onqelos would have been familiar with these references. Especially we note Isaiah 26:19: "Your dead shall live; their bodies shall rise. You who dwell in the dust, awake and sing for joy! For your dew is a dew of light, and the earth will give birth to the dead." This is one explicit reference to bodily resurrection in the Old Testament, and dew is used prominently. There is also the idea of restoration of Israel and remnant theology connected to dew. These concepts also have a new life or resurrection context—Zechariah 8:12, notably: "For there shall be a sowing of peace. The vine shall give its fruit, and the ground shall give its produce, and the heavens shall give their dew. And I will cause the remnant of this people to possess all these things" (see also Mic 5:6–7). There are other connections in this passage from Zechariah with the Joseph blessing of Genesis 49. Also, from the Psalms, 110:3 reads: "Your people will offer themselves freely on the day you lead your forces on the holy mountains; from the womb of the morning, the dew of your youth will be yours." Psalm 110 is understood as having messianic significance and being connected to restoration and resurrection. With his knowledge of these passages in the Old Testament Scriptures, why did Targum Onqelos choose to strengthen the connections with the addition of dew in Genesis 49:25? If it was his intention to point to Joseph as a death-and-resurrection figure, why does he forgo the opportunity to do so explicitly?

The way in which Targum Onqelos has dealt with the Joseph blessing in Genesis 49 connects Joseph with the patriarchs. It helps to explain the "bones" of Genesis 50:25 and Joseph's insistence that his bones be returned to the promised land of Canaan when God "remembers" his covenantal people. A closer examination of "bones" (עצם) in the MT is in order, as well as a look at Targum Onqelos's corresponding translation.

The Hebrew עצם occurs 123 times in the MT in one form or another. It is considered to be a primary noun—not derived from a verbal root.[61] One way in which "bone" is used in the MT is as a designation of relationship. The first occurrence of this is in Genesis 2:23, as Adam identifies his new wife, Eve, with these words: "This is at last bone of my bone and flesh of my flesh," and Targum Onqelos follows, rendering גרם. This usage is seen again as Laban greets Jacob the first time in Genesis 29:14: "You are my bone and my flesh." However, Targum Onqelos chooses קריבי, "kinsman," in this instance.[62]

Another, more significant use of bones in the MT is one that points to health and life, and conversely dying and death. Both uses are prevalent, but not in the Pentateuch. Examples of dying and death are common to Job (Job 2:5; 4:14; 19:20; 30:17, 30), Psalms (Pss 22:14; 31:11; 102:6), Lamentations (Lam 1:13; 4:8), and the prophets (Jer 20:9; Amos 6:10; Hab 3:16; Mic 3:2–3). We see examples of health and life just as frequently in Proverbs (Prov 3:8; 15:30; 16:24) and Isaiah (Isa 38:13; 66:14), with language referring to the "refreshment," "flourishing," and "health" coming to or being in the bones.

On two occasions bones are referred to as being unclean (Num 19:16, 18) and being used as a means of desecration (2 Kgs 23:14). However, one of the more intriguing uses of bones is found in significant texts with resurrection or life overtones. The first example takes place in Exodus 12:46 as Moses receives instructions concerning the first Passover and as the Israelites observe it, preparing to exit Egypt. A very explicit command concerning the Passover lamb is delivered to Moses: "and you shall not break any of its bones." The Passover angel of death is certainly a life-and-death issue, and it is the blood of the Passover lamb on the doorposts and lintels that preserves life. Later, the Christian church identified Christ as the Passover

---

61. See the detailed discussion on the language and use of bones in the ancient Near East and in the writings of Scripture in particular by K. M. Beyse, "עצם 'eṣem," in Botterweck, Ringgren, and Fabry, *Theological Dictionary of the Old Testament*, 11:305–9.

62. Other examples of "bone" designating relationship include Judg 9:2; 2 Sam 5:1; 19:13, 14; 1 Chr 11:1.

Lamb whose blood rescues from death and whose bones were not broken on the cross (John 19:32–37).

In 2 Kings 13:21 there is an example of bones connected to resurrection. Elisha, the prophet, has died and been entombed. Later, due to fear of marauding Moabites, a group sent out of the city to bury a man threw his body into Elisha's grave, and "as soon as the man touched the bones of Elisha, he revived and stood on his feet." Again, in Ezekiel 37, where the prophet is shown the valley of the dry bones and then is called on to prophesy over the bones—when he does he witnesses the bones coming together, and then the breath of life enters them. Again, bones are seen in reference to life and new life, restoration, and even resurrection. Levenson writes:

> The dead bones are the people of Israel, who, living in exile after the great destruction at the beginning of the sixth century B.C.E., have given up hope: "Our bones are dried up, our hope is gone; we are doomed" (v 11). The restoration of those bones to life—the LORD's giving them sinews, then flesh, skin, and finally the breath of life— indicates that God will open the graves of Ezekiel's audience and restore them to the land of Israel, so that they may once again lie upon "[their] own soil" (vv 13–14). What Ezek 37:1–14 presents, in short, is a vision of resurrection that is then decoded as a prediction of exceedingly improbable historical events that the God of Israel will soon miraculously unfold.[63]

Finally, it is important to consider one other usage of bones. The first example is found in Genesis 7:13: בעצם היום הזה, literally "in the bone of that day." The verse is a reference to Noah and his family entering into the ark. Most English translations render this as "On the very same day." The *Theological Dictionary of the Old Testament* explains: "Since bones are 'man's most durable part—his core, so to speak, עצם takes on the meaning 'self,' as in the formula בעצם היום הזה, 'on this very day' (Genesis 7:13; etc.)."[64] They refer to this as a secular use or secular sense, which is still incorporated in modern Hebrew. Targum Onqelos choose to render all of these cases as

63. Levenson, *Resurrection and Restoration*, 157.

64. Beyse, "עצם ʿeṣem," 305.

an idiom, using the word בכרן. The LXX also translates in like manner: εν
τη ημερα ταυτη. This formation is chiefly found in the Pentateuch, with
two examples in Ezekiel and one in Joshua (Gen 7:13; 17:24; Exod 12:16, 41,
51; Lev 23:14, 21, 28, 29, 30; Deut 32:48; Ezek 2:3; 40:1; Josh 5:11).

This appears simple enough, but the explanation given by Beyse does
not adequately explain or address why עצם was chosen or how this Hebrew
idiom came about.[65] Why is this particular idiom used when there are other
phrases more commonly available? It helps to note the context in which
this word is used. All of these texts have significant import to the Hebrew
people beyond the rest of Scripture.

As mentioned before, Genesis 7:13 is referencing Noah and his family
entering into the ark that they might be saved from the water of the flood.
Genesis 17:24, 27 are references to the Old Testament covenantal mark of
circumcision. This marked the people of Israel as belonging to the Lord,
and if one was not circumcised, he was to be "cut off" from God's people.
Exodus 12:16, 41, 51 are all verses in connection with the Passover, as is also
Joshua 5:11. Leviticus 23:14, 21, 28, 29, 30 are in the context of the various
festivals and feasts the Israelites are called on to observe—verse 14, Day of
Firstfruits; verse 21, Festival of Weeks; verses 28–30, the Day of Atonement.
Deuteronomy 32:48 is the foretelling of Moses' death. Ezekiel 2:3 is the call
of Ezekiel into the prophetic ministry, and Ezekiel 40:1 is his vision of the
new temple. In every example there are implications of life.[66] Given the
other usages of bones in the MT, it seems more than coincidental that this
idiom was chosen for these particular texts.

There is one further use of בעצם to be examined. In Exodus 24, Moses,
Aaron, Nadab, Abihu, and seventy of the elders of Israel ascend Mount
Sinai, where they see God and eat and drink in his presence. This has
been an intriguing text for Old Testament scholars. In verse 10 of this
account, there is a description of the pavement under the God of Israel's
feet: "a pavement of sapphire stone, like the very [בעצם] heaven for clear-
ness." Targum Onqelos renders the בעצם with וכמחזי. This is a peculiar

---

65. Joosten notes: "Idiomatic expressions also relate more directly to metaphors when
their meaning is linked to the metaphorical meaning of one of its components. The semantic
analysis of idioms, even when they are well understood, is often rather involved, however"
("Translating the Untranslatable," 61).

66. With the possible exception of Deut 32:48, where the death of Moses is foretold.

usage, unique in all of Scripture. If one considers the common connections between Exodus 24 and Isaiah 25, where Isaiah prophesies that the Lord of hosts will prepare a rich banquet for all people on "this mountain," and then the fact that this is followed by another explicit resurrection text, "And He will swallow upon this mountain the covering that is cast over all peoples, the veil that is spread over all nations. He will swallow up death forever; and the Lord God will wipe away tears from all faces, and the reproach of His people He will take away from all the earth, for the Lord has spoken" (Isa 25:7–8), it would seem there is a deeper meaning in the usage of בעצם, and from this the Hebrew idiom developed.

TARGUM ONQELOS AND THE RESURRECTION

It is noticeable that Targum Onqelos does not remove or significantly change any of the verses of the MT Hebrew Joseph narrative that provide us with the motif of death and resurrection. The major subthemes we have examined in detail as constituting the substantial architecture of the death-and-resurrection motif remain intact in Targum Onqelos. Nowhere are they modified. This is an important point, inasmuch as the Targum has shown that it is quite capable of altering the Hebrew and of omitting biblical notions, wording, and expressions it deems inappropriate. The "translational" aspects of Targum Onqelos, therefore, retain and confirm the thrust of MT. At the same time, the specifically exegetical, interpretational elements in Targum Onqelos seem not to introduce explicit reference to death and resurrection. Here it should be recalled that Targum Onqelos is not an expansionist targum like Neofiti or Pseudo-Jonathan. Rather, it is by nature reserved and reticent, preferring to hint obliquely rather than to spell out in full the implications of a verse. That it retains in its entirety the key Hebrew death-resurrection motif is therefore telling.

Considering the historical context of 100–135 CE, there are possibilities that, taken together, may provide an answer.[67] First, the spiritual condition of the "grassroots" Jewish populace in Palestine and beyond may have influenced his decision to keep life and resurrection themes implicit in the text. The general population of Second Temple Judaism was inundated with

---

67. The later Babylonian revision held to the same basic patterns of Proto-Onqelos.

pseudepigraphal literature.[68] From what has survived to our day and even from what is referenced in other literature, we see very strong resurrection and eschatological elements. The rabbinic traditions of Targum Onqelos's day had their own resurrection and eschatological views, in part due to the destruction of the second temple in 70 CE by the Romans, but they were not as pronounced as those noted in the general population. Targum Onqelos may be showing a concern that the spiritual direction of the general populace of Palestine was far too resurrection and eschatologically minded, and feared that making explicit references in his translation would only serve to fuel these flames. Or, it is also possible he felt a responsibility to bring these two sides together and reunite the fractured Jewish scene. Considering the amount of apocalyptic literature that centers on Joseph, these scenarios are not unlikely.

There is also the possibility that Targum Onqelos and the rabbinic tradition of his day were concerned that any emphasis on a death-and-resurrection motif in the Joseph narratives would stand in the way of or deemphasize their efforts to set up Joseph as a moral and ethical example for the Jewish community in the midst of the Hellenization of Palestine. There is evidence within Targum Onqelos's translation that demonstrates a trend toward enhancing Joseph's image and emphasizing his godly qualities. Any explicit effort focusing on Joseph as a death-and-resurrection figure would likely have taken precedence over Joseph as a moral and ethical figure, especially considering the spiritual climate of the day. The general population would most likely have found a death-and-resurrection motif far more attractive than a moral and ethical example, and given the focus of the rabbis, a moral and ethical figure would be easier to manipulate.

Finally, Targum Onqelos found himself in the midst of one of the most difficult historical times in Jewish history. Israel remained under the control of the Roman occupiers, the temple had recently been destroyed (70 CE) by these same forces, and as a result, the Jewish population of Jerusalem and Palestine was in disarray as many Jews were displaced from their homeland, scattered in a far-flung diaspora. In addition, the major Jewish sects of Pharisees and Sadducees continued their long conflict. With the destruction of the temple, the Pharisees were placed in the leadership role,

---

68. Charlesworth, *Old Testament Pseudepigrapha*.

and they were definitely in favor of a moral and ethical treatment of the Old Testament text. Bringing even more confusion into this chaotic situation was the existence of a new, fast-growing religious sect, later to be called Christians. This religious group had its roots in Judaism and was gaining momentum as it brought over converts first from the Palestinian Jews and then from those who had been scattered in the diaspora. The Jewish religious leaders of Targum Onqelos's time appear to have realized the need to make a clear distinction between Jews and Christians as well as provide a united front in the face of this new threat. Previous to the destruction of the temple, they had already expelled the Christians from its courts. They had begun efforts to normalize the canon of the Hebrew Scriptures and to begin to deal with Christian exegesis, which was based primarily on the LXX texts available at the time.[69] They also adhered to the scroll as their method for recording sacred Scripture, while the Christians and much of the rest of the world were transitioning to the codex.[70] A clear line of demarcation was forming between the two religious groups.

A great challenge faced by the rabbinic school of Targum Onqelos's day in regard to life, death, and resurrection was a man known by the name of Jesus. The Christians believed that Jesus was the Messiah promised in the Old Testament Scriptures, who, although crucified, dead, and buried by the Romans, rose from the dead. This death and resurrection of Jesus formed the main tenet of their religious belief system and was the apologetic they used to convince the general Jewish population that the promises of the Hebrew Scriptures found their fulfillment in Jesus. This reality, set within the context of the other challenges of Targum Onqelos's time, especially within the grassroots, Second Temple eschatological climate, provided a significant threat to the organized, official religion of the Jews,

---

69. The Hebrew canon is generally considered to have been normalized between 90 and 110 CE. For discussions of the various scholarly opinions on canon and its final definition, see J. C. VanderKam, "Revealed Literature in the Second Temple Period," in *From Revelation to Canon: Studies in the Hebrew Bible and Second Temple Literature* (Leiden: Brill, 2000), 1–30; L. M. McDonald and J. A. Sanders, eds., *The Canon Debate* (Peabody, MA: Hendrickson, 2002). The version of Aquila represented a thoroughgoing attempt by Jewish authorities to produce a Greek version of Scripture that was as close to the Hebrew as was possible. It is often described as a literal translation. While this version would have proved useful to Jews in debates with Christians in questions about "the original text" of Scripture, it is not entirely clear that anti-Christian concerns were paramount in its creation. See Dines, *Septuagint*, 87–91.

70. L. Hurtado, *The Earliest Christian Artifacts* (Grand Rapids: Eerdmans, 2006), 43–94.

represented by the rabbis. If Targum Onqelos had made specific life, death, and resurrection connections in his translation, it is difficult to know how this may have fueled the situation.

With all of the challenges facing the rabbinic school of thought, Targum Onqelos may have been compelled to avoid any explicit reference to life, death, and resurrection, especially in an official rabbinic writing. To do otherwise may very well have compromised an already messy situation. It may even have provided support to the new and dangerous cult of Christianity. Targum Onqelos still understands the need to be true to the holy text of the Torah. Therefore, Targum Onqelos avoids explicit references to life, death, and resurrection in the Joseph narratives, while choosing to preserve these themes in an implicit way, as we noted in detail in the discussion of Joseph's blessing.

CONCLUSION

Targum Onqelos proves to be quite useful in understanding some of the more difficult sections of the MT of the Joseph narratives. This is most clearly seen in the blessings of Genesis 49. Targum Onqelos also preserves the downward/upward movement of the MT and generally remains true to the consistent doubling of words and text. As we consider the overall tone of Targum Onqelos in these narratives and how Joseph is used to provide a moral and ethical example for the Jewish community with glimpses of life themes throughout, and as we compare this to the LXX's use of Joseph as a salvific character, a more dramatic approach, one question remains. Who is closest to the MT intent of these narratives? Both of these aspects are part of Joseph's character and are present in his narrative, but the question of how Second Temple Judaism could have spawned both the rabbinic movement and the Jewish apocalyptic movement, both using Joseph as a key example, remains baffling.[71]

A close examination of Targum Onqelos and its approach to the text shows that the writer takes seriously the notion that Scripture presents itself as a unified theological narrative and therefore reads the text in

---

71. J. D. Levenson, *Creation and the Persistence of Evil* (Princeton: Princeton University Press, 1988), 33. For an in-depth discussion of this history, see N. Gillman, *The Death of Death: Resurrection and Immortality in Jewish Thought* (Woodstock, VT: Jewish Lights, 1997); Levenson, *Resurrection and the Restoration*.

such a way that the thrust of the Hebrew original is never lost, but only stands out more clearly. Targum Onqelos helps us see that reading the text as a unified narrative is both possible and, when undertaken with proper respect for the Hebrew, cogent and persuasive. Targum Onqelos also allows the Hebrew to speak, such that the death-and-resurrection motif is not crowded out by the incidental problems and difficulties. The targum acts as a filter for these problems and difficulties. The hearer/reader, instead of getting preoccupied with (for example) Joseph's naming of his son Manasseh, is provided with answers to questions that permit them to get to the essentials of the text without distraction.

8

The Second Temple "Resurrection" of Joseph

Why does Joseph tend to fade from the pages of Scripture? The Joseph narratives provide the longest section of Genesis (fourteen chapters, Gen 37–50), and Joseph receives more verbiage than any other figure in Genesis. After such an impressive beginning, we hear comparatively little about Joseph after the record of his burial (Josh 24:32). The references to his descendants classify them as Ephraimites and, occasionally, as the tribe of Manasseh, but Joseph's name is neither mentioned nor attached. There appears to be a distinct separation of Joseph from the people of Israel. This may be in part due to how Joseph separated himself in the land of Egypt; yet, it seemed that this rift had been healed, as evidenced by the care taken by Moses and the people of Israel in claiming his bones and taking them along as they exited Egypt. This care continued as Joshua carried them through the conquest of Canaan and interred them only when the nations were driven out and the land of Canaan had been apportioned.

However, Joseph was not entirely overlooked. There are clear references to his descendants, "the house of Joseph," in texts such as Judges 1:22, 23, 35; 2 Samuel 19:20; 1 Kings 11:28; Amos 5:6; and Obadiah 18. More importantly, he reappears in the Psalms. While mention of him is brief in Psalms 78:16 (a somewhat negative evaluation, certainly of his progeny); 80:2; and 81:6 (both strong and positive evaluations), a quite different picture of Joseph emerges in Psalm 105:16–23. These verses leave the reader in no doubt that the whole of Joseph's story was acted out entirely under divine guidance at every turn. God invoked a famine and "sent" Joseph (Ps 105:16–17): although he ended up as a slave, and endured cruel sufferings not recorded in Genesis (Ps 105:17–19), he was proved to be a true prophet and became master of Pharaoh's house (Ps 105:19–22). Thus Israel came into Egypt (Ps 105:23). The date of this psalm is uncertain; but it is not uncommonly placed in the Persian period, at the beginning of Second Temple times, when Israel's fortunes were at last reviving.[1] The psalmist feels able to accord a prophetic status to Joseph: we should note not only the element of suffering (characteristic of many prophets), which the poet describes in graphic detail, but also the link he is able to establish with Abraham, Isaac, and Jacob-Israel, named earlier in the psalm (Ps 105:9–13). Throughout their wanderings, God had protected them, warning kings: "Do not touch my anointed ones: and do my prophets no harm" (Ps 105:15). Joseph, for the psalmist, belongs firmly in their company, and at a key watershed in the history of the nation.

EXILIC AND POSTEXILIC BIBLICAL REFERENCES

Whatever the date of Psalm 105, in the period of the exile the figure of Joseph had come again to prominence in the preaching of Ezekiel. First, Ezekiel's evocation of the Joseph tradition is particularly significant, given its present canonical placement immediately following the prophet's famous vision of the valley of dry bones (Ezek 37:1–14). In that vision, dead, dry bones come to life: they are revivified, and they represent "the whole house of Israel" (Ezek 37:11).[2] Joseph, in the prophet's teaching, stands for the old Northern Kingdom of Israel. In 37:16 Ezekiel is instructed to "Take a stick and write on it, 'For Judah and the people of Israel associated with him'; then take another stick and write on it, 'For Joseph (the stick of Ephraim) and all the house of Israel associated with him.'" It is interesting that Joseph is a specific replacement for Ephraim (also Ezek 37:19). Then Ezekiel is instructed to bind the two sticks together to show that the people, the house of Israel, will be one once again. The divided kingdom will be no more when the Lord restores them from exile, gathering them in the land of Israel. Ezekiel also references Joseph in 47:13 and 48:31. Both follow the vision of the new temple, a heavenly, eschatological temple, as is evidenced by the glory of the Lord, which fills it (Ezek 43:2; 44:4), as well

---

1. On all this see especially F.-L. Hossfeld and E. Zenger, *Psalms 3: A Commentary on Psalms 101–150* (Minneapolis: Fortress, 2011), 62–74.

2. On these passages, see W. Eichrodt, *Ezekiel: A Commentary*, trans. C. Quin (London: SCM, 1970), 505–15; J. Blenkinsopp, *Ezekiel* (Louisville: John Knox, 1990), 170–78; L. J. Greenspoon, "The Origins of the Idea of Resurrection," in *Traditions in Transformation: Turning Points in Biblical Faith*, ed. J. Halpern and J. D. Levenson (Winona Lake, IN: Eisenbrauns, 1981), 247–321; L. C. Allen, *Ezekiel 20–48*, Word Biblical Commentary 29 (Nashville: Thomas Nelson, 1990), 181–96.

as the inclusion of foreigners who are circumcised in flesh and heart—
believers (44:6–7). Ezekiel 47 speaks of the division of the land into tribes
once again, with Joseph receiving a "double portion" (47:13), and 48:30–35
lists the names of the gates of the city, and "Joseph" is used again. As with
the new-temple, the new-land, and the new-city vision, there is also a
place for the foreigners who will share in it as an inheritance (47:21–23).[3]

The present, canonical placing of references to Joseph within the final
form of Ezekiel's book is suggestive. We must be careful not to make too
much of it; but we may note that Ezekiel's concern with the double portion to be granted Joseph (Ezek 47:1) is perhaps to be related to another,
probably postexilic, text, preserved in 1 Chronicles 5:1–2, which records
how Reuben, Jacob's eldest son, forfeited his birthright, which was then
legally transferred to Joseph. Joseph thus legally acquired the birthright
and the double portion of Jacob's inheritance that birthright automati-
cally entailed.[4]

Joseph's presentation in the MT of Genesis as a death-and-resurrection
figure is not explicitly brought before us in these passages from the Psalms,
Ezekiel, and the Chronicler, and one can only speculate what influence
the traditions that informed the Genesis narratives might have exercised
on these other Hebrew compositions. The latter do, however, testify to a
growing awareness of Joseph's importance in exilic and postexilic times,
and serve to pave the way for the increased attention paid to Joseph in
postbiblical writings. James Kugel describes the resurgence of interest in
Joseph among Jews of the later Second Temple period:

> The last parts of what was to become the Hebrew Bible were prob-
> ably written in the second century before the common era. Even
> before that time, however, texts had begun to be written which
> in one way or another sought to interpret and explain points in
> Israel's sacred literature, and it is in these works that the figure of
> Joseph attains a new prominence. For, with the "geopolitical" asso-
> ciations of Joseph now a distant memory—and, along with them,

---

3. Joseph is also included in the Psalms: 77:15; 78:67; 80:1; 81:5; 105:17.

4. For detailed discussion of the textual and legal problems in these verses, see S. Japhet, *I and II Chronicles: A Commentary* (London: SCM, 1993), 132–33.

the regional issues that his name had represented—what was foremost was the Joseph of the Genesis narrative. Here, among all of
Israel's illustrious ancestors, Abraham, Isaac, Jacob and the rest,
it was Joseph who had received the lion's share of attention; and
what figure in that book might better serve as the raw material for
a lesson in virtue?[5]

PSEUDEPIGRAPHAL AND OTHER WRITINGS

While the name of Joseph begins to show up with increased frequency in
the biblical text—Chronicles makes use of "Joseph" in its numberings and
lists (1 Chr 2:2; 5:1; 7:29); Zechariah mentions "the house of Joseph" in 10:6;
and there are other Second Temple texts that seem to allude or reference
Joseph by theme and vocabulary (Neh 5:5; the bulk of Daniel; etc.)—the
greatest resurgence is noted in the pseudepigraphal writings. Not only
are there entire documents devoted to Joseph, such as Joseph and Aseneth,
the Prayer of Joseph, and the History of Joseph, but there are many others
that devote considerable time to him—Testaments of the Twelve Patriarchs,
Jubilees, and Genesis Rabbah. There are also many references to Joseph
in other intertestamental writings such as Ben Sira, 1 and 4 Maccabees,
Pseudo-Philo, the Sibylline Oracles, and Wisdom of Solomon. In addition,
Artapanus writes on Joseph, fragments of which still remain, and Philo
devotes extensive time to him, as does Josephus in his Jewish Antiquities.
While each account and allusion has its own perspective and agenda in
regard to its view of Joseph,[6] it is still relevant to consider the question of
why Joseph enjoyed such a resurgence of popularity.[7]

---

5. Kugel, In Potiphar's House, 18.

6. See chap. 9.

7. For more on the view of Joseph in post-OT writings see Niehoff, Figure of Joseph. Kugel
notes: "It is truly only in the corpus of extrabiblical Jewish writings known as the apocrypha
and pseudepigrapha of the Hebrew Bible that one encounters such a 'rehabilitated' Joseph.
But if the change was long in coming, it was nonetheless striking" (In Potiphar's House, 18). For
different scholarly approaches to the growth of interest in Joseph in later Second Temple times,
see E. S. Gruen, Heritage and Hellenism: The Reinvention of Jewish Tradition (Berkeley: University
of California Press, 1998), 73–109; M. Niehoff, "New Garments for Biblical Joseph," in Biblical
Interpretation: History, Context, Reality, ed. C. Helmer (Atlanta: Scholars Press, 2005), 33–56; J. J.
Collins, "Joseph and Aseneth: Jewish or Christian?," Journal for the Study of the Pseudepigrapha
14 (2005): 97–112; R. A. Kugler, "Joseph at Qumrân (I): The Importance of 4Q372 Frg. 1 in

It is important to note that while I will make a case that the resurgence
of Joseph's popularity was caught up in his role as a death-and-resurrection figure, these extrabiblical writings do not necessarily dwell on this.
One exception would be the Testaments of the Twelve Patriarchs, which
makes strong allusion to this characteristic.[8] However, this text must be
approached with caution for several reasons. (1) There is almost unani-
mous agreement that this collection of writings referred to as Testaments
of the Twelve Patriarchs in its present form was produced by Christians
in the second and third centuries CE. (2) It is widely agreed that the collection was fashioned out of preexisting traditions of Jewish origin. This
is easily seen in the Testaments of Levi, Judah, and Naphtali, although the
extent of Jewish material in the separate testaments is contested. (3) From
the second century CE onwards there is abundant evidence that some
Christians in various places made a point of collecting, preserving, and
transmitting Jewish apocryphal and pseudepigraphal texts. They were
motivated in this because they perceived those texts as confirming at various points the antiquity of the Christian gospel. Therefore, (4) in the case
of the Testament of Joseph, it might be argued that it was preserved by
those who saw it as providing evidence for a death-and-resurrection motif
deriving from ancient times. If this is the case, we have in our possession
a document whose author read the narrative of Joseph in a manner somewhat similar to what I am advocating. The Testament of Joseph shows
that the patriarch could be understood as a death-and-resurrection figure
from ancient times. In addition, since the language of the Testaments is
Greek, it may be that the biblical text underlying the Testament of Joseph
is the LXX, or a form of it. The LXX might be revealed in the Testament of
Joseph as a version that could also be read with reference to Joseph as a
death-and-resurrection figure.

Most extrabiblical writings, however, hold to a more rabbinic understanding of Joseph and thus emphasize his holy and righteous actions. This
allows for Joseph to be viewed and used as a moral and ethical example

---

Extending a Tradition," in *Studies in the Hebrew Bible, Qumran, and the Septuagint Presented to
Eugene Ulrich*, ed. P. W. Flint, E. Tov, and J. C. VanderKam (Leiden: Brill, 2006), 261–78.

8. T.Jud. 25.1; T.Jos. 1.2–7, where the downward/upward movement is evident; T.Jos. 19.
Note also Ben Sira 49:15, which seems to connect the idea of Joseph's bones being transported
to the land of Canaan with Enoch's assumption into heaven.

for the people, although it is interesting to note the rabbinic sources frequently referencing resurrection in their writings. For whatever purpose, this resurgence of Joseph in Second Temple literature, along with other resurrection figures such as Enoch and Elijah, does give one pause.

TALMUDIC RABBIS

The rabbis during the talmudic era were focused on more than the moral and ethical alone. They also focused on resurrection as they wove this expectation into the expectation of restoration to the land. To the rabbis, resurrection without the restoration of Israel, including its renewed adherence to Torah, was incomprehensible.[9]

The concentration of the rabbis on the Torah in contrast to the apocalyptic with its eschatological resurrection is interesting, as both groups held strongly to an understanding of resurrection. For the rabbis, this teaching had to be based in the Torah in order to be valid, and yet there are no explicit resurrection texts in the Pentateuch. This was not seen as a difficulty: "No passage lacks the resurrection of the dead, but we lack the capacity to interpret properly."[10] Those who denied the resurrection of the dead were denied this resurrection: "And why so much? A Tanna taught: He denied the resurrection of the dead. Therefore he shall have no share in the resurrection of the dead. For all the measures [of retribution] of the Holy One (blessed be He!) operate on the principle that the consequence fits the deed."[11] Again: "If someone should say to you, 'Is it possible the Holy One (blessed be He!) will resurrect the dead?' say to him, 'It has already happened. He has already resurrected the dead through Elijah, through Elisha, and through Ezekiel in the Valley of Dura.'"[12]

The belief in the resurrection of the dead by the rabbis at the time of the exile had long been entrenched, and any who denied such a resurrection were considered outside the community. This belief was rooted in the Torah, and a return to the Torah at the time of the Babylonian exile

---

9. Levenson, *Resurrection and Restoration*, 229.

10. Midr. Sifre Deut 306.

11. b. Sanh. 90a.

12. Midr. Lev Rab 27:4.

enhanced it. Levenson shows how this belief in the resurrection of the dead tied into a national resurrection or restoration:

> It is possible, of course, to interpret this language of the joyful awakening of the dead and the destruction of death itself as only metaphorical for the restoration of Israel and the establishment of its collective security. Even so, one has to concede that Daniel 12 did not so interpret it, and if the author(s) of Isaiah 24–27 had thought resurrection literally impossible, their choice of it as a metaphor for the national resurrection that they fully expected was highly inappropriate and self-defeating.[13]

As Levenson points out, the expectation of the resurrection of the dead was a weight-bearing beam in the edifice of rabbinic Judaism.[14]

We have already discussed Joseph in relation to the LXX and the targums earlier. The question is, Why did such a prominent Old Testament figure as Joseph all but disappear from view following Joshua 24:32? An equally important and more intriguing question is, Why is the figure of Joseph suddenly resurrected in the Second Temple era?

WHY THE "RESURRECTION" OF JOSEPH?

As illustrated in Ezekiel, the destruction of Jerusalem and Solomon's temple changed the focus of Jewish thinking. No more talk of the Northern Kingdom and the Southern Kingdom, for both had been taken into exile, the northern tribes to Assyria (712 BCE) and the southern tribes to Babylon (597–586 BCE). The tribal distinctions were blurred, for now there was only Israel, and she was in exile. This reality had a profound effect on the people, not only as they contemplated their new political reality, but especially as they struggled to determine their religious identity. Since Abraham, they had looked on themselves as a people set apart, with whom the Lord had covenanted. As they possessed the promised land of Canaan, they began to think of themselves in an intimate relationship with this Holy Land. When David moved the capital to Jerusalem and Solomon built and dedicated the

---

13. Levenson, *Resurrection and Restoration*, 214.

14. Levenson, *Resurrection and Restoration*, x.

temple, the nation of Israel saw its identity in relation to a Holy Land, a Holy City, and a holy place of worship. All of these pointed to them as a holy people set apart by a holy God. Even when the kingdom was divided and the enemy forces had overrun the vast majority of the country, the people of Israel dwelling in Jerusalem lived with an attitude that nothing could defeat them and no one could breach their walls—they had been promised, covenanted, and set apart—they were the Lord's special people.

In this attitude was their understanding of their God. Since the Lord had promised to dwell with them and had shown his presence at the dedication of the temple, they came to believe that the Lord would not dwell anywhere else. In spite of the warnings of the prophets, they continued in their myopic ways. When the Lord delivered Jerusalem from the Assyrians by destroying Sennacharib's army (Isa 37:36–38; 2 Kgs 19:35–37), it only strengthened this attitude of denial.

Then came the first fall of Jerusalem (597 BCE), and many were taken into exile, yet the city still stood and the temple was intact. But when Ezekiel, in exile in Babylon, received word of the destruction of the Holy City and the temple as well, everything changed (Ezek 33:21). This change is illustrated in the nature of Ezekiel's prophecy. Ezekiel's words seem to prefigure some of the concerns of later apocalyptic literature, and his visions sometimes make use of the kind of symbolism that features in later apocalyptic texts. In texts such as these and other writings, the Israelites began to reflect deeper eschatological concerns. Their writings also exhibit more references to the afterlife and especially the bodily resurrection.[15]

They had not totally forgotten Joseph, nor was the death-and-resurrection motif of his character discovered for the first time. My thesis suggests that Israel had always had a basic understanding of the afterlife and a sense of the resurrection of the dead, which the attentive reader of the Joseph narratives could discern.

---

15. D. Flusser notes two Jewish approaches: "Two Jewish approaches to the end of days: one found in Jewish apocalyptic literature, the other in the writings of the rabbinic sages. Both describe the world to come in fundamentally similar terms: it will be a post-historical era, the time of a new creation, the resurrection of the dead and the great day of judgment; in the end of days, a new Jerusalem will be established, in which God himself will construct a new and everlasting temple." See Flusser, *Judaism of the Second Temple Period*, vol. 1, *Qumran and Apocalypticism* (Grand Rapids: Eerdmans, 2007), 207.

Joseph became a focal point for renewed theological reflection on the theme of new life springing forth out of the old; of a glorious revival of things that had seemed to be finished, dead beyond recall; and of the mysterious ways of the Almighty in bringing such things to pass in situations that human beings had regarded as offering no hope. Along with Enoch and Elijah, Joseph was the figure most looked on as the people contemplated death and resurrection. The multiple submotifs of death and resurrection in the Joseph narratives made him a dominant figure. Even as the Israelites dealt with exile and the return, the book of Daniel and other Second Temple writings with their death-and-resurrection tones continued to point them to Joseph.[16]

CONCLUSION

The people of Israel struggled with the loss of the land and the destruction of Jerusalem and the temple; they also struggled with their loss of identity. This led them to their holy writings, and they became known as "the people of the Book." The advent of the synagogue and the teaching houses during this time is not anachronistic to the point. The people were searching fervently for an identity, but rather than establish a completely new persona, they returned to that which they knew and had known. In seeing themselves as the people of the Book, they also searched out historical, biblical heroes of the faith to provide hope and examples for their children.

Considering the plight of the exile and the location in the land of the Babylonians, they also struggled to understand their future, both physical and spiritual. Once more, they discovered the answers in the Torah and the prophets. That which they set aside, perhaps even forgot, as they lived in the shadow of the temple became of most crucial importance. Eyes were fixed with hope on the coming of the Messiah with apocalyptic fervor and eschatological hope. Deliverance and restoration were the desires, but even these themes could not be separated from the desires of salvation and a bodily resurrection, as noted by Levenson:

The differences between the striking tale of the resurrection of the Shunammite's son in 2 Kings 4 and the resurrection of the dead as

---

16. Daniel mirrors the majority of the same death-and-resurrection submotifs as Joseph.

envisioned in Second Temple and rabbinic Judaism must not be minimized. The former is a specific episode of limited scope; its subtle and manifold resonances with the larger story of Israel do not suggest (at least not directly) a context of national restoration, a key ingredient in the Jewish expectation of resurrection. ... There is, nonetheless, a lesson to be learned from this tale about the expectation of resurrection that will first appear much later. It is simply that long before the apocalyptic framework came into existence, the resurrection of the dead was thought possible—not according to nature, of course, but through the miraculous intervention of the living God.[17]

The afterlife, the final location of the faithful, moved to center stage, but only over the course of time. Resurrection found its place within a larger vision not of the continuation of the world but of its redemption.[18]

Out of the past, Joseph was resurrected as a central figure in this new context. I propose that it is the structure of his narratives and the life of his character that recommended this restoration. The continual downward/upward movement in the Joseph narratives is obvious to even a casual reader/hearer, and the more subtle death-and-resurrection motif and its multiple manifestations has its effect.[19] Joseph, along with Enoch and Elijah, became a focus. Joseph, however, demonstrates both aspects of death and resurrection. Enoch and Elijah did not taste death, only immediate transport into heaven. Joseph and his life clearly exhibit death in its downward movements and resurrection as the Lord continually lifts him up. Precisely because of this, Joseph was resurrected into a new life of prominence among the Second Temple people of Israel.

---

17. Levenson, *Resurrection and Restoration*, 131–32.
18. Levenson, *Resurrection and Restoration*, x.
19. See chap. 5.

9

Joseph, "The Adopted One": The Use of Joseph

The figure of Joseph slipped into obscurity for a relatively long period of time, but when he was resurrected in the Second Temple era he enjoyed immense popularity. The story of Joseph and his character in the Joseph narratives were compelling enough to bring about renewed interest. There was and continues to be something about his condition and the circumstances of his life that intrigue readers, who are drawn in and finds themselves identifying with his situation. The character of Joseph can be identified with on several levels, and the stand-alone quality of the Joseph narratives lends to the dramatic environment. These fourteen chapters have encouraged many to adapt them into varying formats.[1] In the context of Second Temple times as well as the climate of third-century BCE Alexandria, Egypt, it is no wonder that Joseph and his story became popular.[2] Why did it take so long? How does such an engaging figure as Joseph fall into disuse?

Another facet of Joseph's resurgence is the various ways in which he was used. There is no question concerning his popularity in the Second Temple times, but there was far from any uniformity. Joseph was adopted by many groups and individuals, but for a variety of reasons and purposes. In order to use Joseph for their purposes, some adaptations were required. We have explored some of these adaptations as we looked at the text traditions of the MT, the LXX, and Targum Onqelos. If we consider the MT to be a close representation of the original Hebrew text that preserves the intended sense of the narrative—and there is good reason and evidence to do so—then a close examination of the LXX and Targum Onqelos shows efforts to enhance, polish, and change Joseph's character, while at the same time accurately holding to the sense of the received text. While these efforts are subtle and do not negate the original character, they do reveal efforts taken to support agendas.

---

1. By way of example see Lang, *Joseph in Egypt*.
2. See chaps. 6, 8.

PHILO

Individuals have used Joseph to prove their argument and augment their position. One such individual is Philo. Philo does not always portray Joseph in a positive light. There is no doubt that he is less taken by Joseph's righteous character and salvific actions than most. Why this is so is not clear, but Philo does not give Joseph the credit and praise that others heap on him. There is, however, one area on which Philo focuses.

Philo refers to Joseph as the "political man." Indeed, he introduces his treatise on Joseph as βιος του πολιτικου,[3] "A life of the statesman." He then continues by referencing Joseph's early training as a shepherd as a good beginning for a statesman:

> Yet he began to be trained when he was about seventeen years old in the principles of shepherding which corresponds closely to those of a statesman. I therefore think the poets are accustomed to call kings "shepherds of the people" for someone successful in shepherding is also likely to be the best king since he has been taught care of the noblest flock of living creature, man, through the charge of flocks which deserve less. (*Life of Joseph* 2)

Philo continues to press his point as he refers to Joseph's success in managing Potiphar's household and then his career as second in command of all Egypt. Philo is obvious in his desire to portray Joseph as a prime example of statesman or politician. Little is known about Philo's personal life, although it appears that he would have preferred to live a quiet life centered in study and writing. We do know that he was part of an active political family, and though he would have preferred to avoid the profession, he did become somewhat active and participated in the Jewish embassy to Gaius is 39–40 CE.[4]

It appears that Philo needed a good Jewish role model to advance the political position of the Jews. Joseph provided the best example. We can also postulate that Philo's ambivalence, even distaste, for the political role led to his less than positive view of Joseph.

---

3. Niehoff, *Figure of Joseph*, 54.
4. Niehoff, *Figure of Joseph*, 59.

JOSEPHUS

Another prominent historical figure who sought to adopt Joseph was Josephus. Due to the similarity of their names, Josephus was immediately attracted to the character and story of Joseph. Josephus even saw his personal life story in the light of the biblical Joseph. In many aspects they are similar, and Josephus emphasizes these similarities in his paraphrasing of the text.

Josephus has a dual purpose in focusing on the figure of Joseph. The first, as mentioned, is due to the similarity of name and life circumstances with his own. Josephus finds correlations in the dreams of Joseph, as he had also shown ability to foretell the future, allegedly based on a dream; in the events of Joseph's familial relations, which he sees in light of his relationship with the coleaders of the Jewish revolt; the jealousy shown toward Joseph reminds him of the jealousy he believes has been demonstrated toward him; and Joseph's service in a foreign country mirrors Josephus's own work for the Romans.[5]

This leads us to the second purpose for which Josephus adopts Joseph. Josephus notes that many contemporary Egyptian historians wrote with strong anti-Semitic voices, showing influence from distorted historical accounts of the Israelites in Egypt.[6] So, unlike Philo, Josephus focuses not on Joseph's statesman-like qualities, but rather on his relations with the people of his adopted land.

> He thus asserts that despite contemporary accusations the Jews are not to be considered rebellious by nature. Their leaders, so argues Josephus now, are also capable of a conciliatory policy. It thus emerges that Josephus' portrait of Joseph in Egypt reflects to a certain degree concerns of a diaspora writer. In anticipation of

---

5. Niehoff, *Figure of Joseph*, 90, 92, 95; *Jewish War* 2, 350–352. By way of example: "But wonderful it was what a dream I saw that very night; for when I had betaken myself to bed, as grieved and disturbed at the news that had been written to me, it seemed to me, that a certain person stood by me, and said 'O Josephus! Leave off to afflict thy soul, and put away all fear; for what now grieves thee will render thee very considerable, and in all respects most happy; for thou shalt get over not only these difficulties, but many others, with great success. However, be not cast down, but remember that thou art to fight with the Romans'" (*Vita* 42). Also see *Jewish War* 3.8. W. Whiston, trans., *The Works of Josephus* (Lynn, MA: Hendrickson, 1980).

6. Niehoff, *Figure of Joseph*, 107–8.

certain prejudices, he highlights Joseph's humane decrees as a governor. More specifically, he presents him as the kind of leader that the Romans might wish to have encountered in Judaea prior to the revolt.[7]

Joseph's connection with the Egyptians allows Josephus to provide an apology for Judaism against the false reports and accounts.

In both of these agendas, Josephus sees in Joseph a type of his own life. He uses Joseph not only as an apologetic for the Jews, but also as an apology for himself.

A DRAMATIC NARRATIVE

The Joseph narratives are structured in such a way as to lend themselves to dramatic purposes. This is not only the case for the Second Temple era, but also for all ages thus to follow.

> In Joseph, people recognized their religious, moral and political ideals. As they heard and read the biblical story anew, exposing themselves to it and absorbing it in the archaic, "intensive" way, a multi-layered mental image was built up—and in the hands of creative authors that image took on a live of its own. To understand why this should be the case we have to remember that in literary history the Joseph story ranks with the *Odyssey* and other ancient legends as a canonical model story that supplied authors with archetypal scenes and plots to imitate, elaborate, and allude to.[8]

Although Lang focuses on the seventeenth and eighteenth centuries CE, he aptly describes the role Joseph and his narrative play in the minds of the people. It requires little editing to amend the Joseph narratives in a way as to adapt them to the stage, and so it was done, providing examples of virtue, forgiveness, piety, moral and ethical purity, and strong leadership.

---

7. Niehoff, *Figure of Joseph*, 109.
8. Lang, *Joseph in Egypt*, 9–10.

CONCLUSION

On one level, this adoption and use of Joseph can be viewed in a complimentary way. He is a hero in most depictions and is looked on as one to
emulate. Where he appears to be lacking, various translators and para-
phrasers have inserted information into the story that generally enhances
the figure of Joseph, encouraging the building up of his character. Not only
this, but many sources and various individuals have adopted Joseph and
his narrative to support their agendas. Most of this is basically true to the
text, while others take more liberties. Joseph is viewed as a man for all eras
and ages—a man for all seasons.

The difficulty in this kind of adulation and adoption lies in the lack of
faithfulness to the text. Again, while the changes may be minor, perhaps
only an intensification of an already-existing dramatic moment, these
variants turn the reader's focus away from the original intended message
of the narratives. The LXX in its focus on the salvific character of Joseph
has not departed from the Hebrew writings, and yet, this intensifying of
a particular theme results in the softening of the original, desired theme.

The MT as it has come down to us today can be read showing Joseph
in the guise of a death-and-resurrection figure. The evidence supporting
this claim, which we have assembled here, is cumulative and impressive.
The key downward/upward movement in the narrative, which so strongly
supports the notion of death and resurrection, proved central to other biblical texts, such as Isaiah 25–26; Ezekiel 37; and Daniel 12.

10

Traveling Bones: Death and Resurrection

As we near the end of the Joseph narratives, there is a strange and unusual turn of events. Joseph, having lived 110 years, is approaching death and so addresses his brothers: "I am about to die, but God will visit you and bring you up out of this land to the land that He swore to Abraham, to Isaac and to Jacob." Then, Joseph makes the sons of Israel swear, saying: "God will surely visit you, and you shall carry up my bones from here" (Gen 50:24-25). While the desire to be buried with one's ancestors in one's country of origin is nothing new in the pages of Scripture, there are several things that set this request apart.[1] First, Joseph has distanced himself from his Hebrew background and adopted the way of the Egyptians. Second, Joseph makes it clear that God will surely visit them and return them to the land of Canaan, and when he does, they are supposed to take his bones with them up from Egypt. Third, Joseph does not speak of his body or of his person in general. He specifically speaks of his bones being carried up. Thus, we see the same language employed in Exodus 13:19 as Moses and the Israelites are leaving Egypt: "Moses took the bones of Joseph with him, for Joseph had made the sons of Israel solemnly swear, saying, 'God will surely visit you, and you shall carry up my bones with you from here.'" And, again, in Joshua 24:32: "As for the bones of Joseph, which the people of Israel brought up from Egypt, they buried them at Shechem, in the piece of land that Jacob bought from the sons of Hamor, the father of Shechem." This burial takes place after the land of Canaan has been possessed and divided among the tribes, but again, "the bones of Joseph" is specific.

BONES IN THE MASORETIC TEXT

An examination of the references to bones in the MT is in order. Much of this has already been discussed in chapter 7, but a brief recap may prove helpful. The Hebrew word עֶצֶם, "bones," occurs 123 times in the MT, with

---

1. Jacob makes Joseph swear to bury him with his fathers in Gen 47:29-31.

the most common usage pointing to health and life and, conversely, death and dying. While this usage covers the preponderance of cases, it is not used this way in the Pentateuch.[2] Common to the Pentateuch, beginning with Genesis 2:23, we see עצם being used as a designation of relationship.[3] This is a common theme, with further examples in Genesis 29:14; Judges 9:2; 2 Samuel 5:1; 19:13–14; and 1 Chronicles 11:1. What is most surprising is the rarity of bones referenced to as unclean. Only in Numbers 19:16, 18 is this referenced, although in 2 Kings 23:14 we do note bones being used as a means of desecration.[4]

The use that is most useful for our consideration in the discussion concerning the bones of Joseph is those texts with strong overtones of death and resurrection. Because these texts are extremely significant to both the restoration and resurrection belief of the Hebrew people, they must be taken seriously in any discussion of death and life, or even death and resurrection. It is easy to understand the death component in regard to bones, but what is generally overlooked is the life and resurrection or even the restoration aspect.

In Exodus 12:46, Moses receives explicit instructions concerning the treatment of the lamb whose blood was spread on the doorposts and lintel in order that the angel of death might pass over and spare the lives of those dwelling in the house. While the lamb is to be roasted and eaten, none of its bones shall be broken. This was clearly seen by the New Testament writers as foreshadowing Christ on the cross—the Lamb of God who rescues from sin and death. John 19:36 states: "For these things took place that the Scriptures might be fulfilled: 'Not one of His bones will be broken.'"

Next, in 2 Kings 13:21, the bones of Elisha play an important role in the resurrection of a dead body. When a group of Israelites are about the task of burying a man, they encounter a group of Moabite bandits. In their haste to return to the safety of the city they throw the body into the first convenient grave, that of Elisha the prophet: "As soon as the man touched

---

2. This usage is common in Job, Lamentations, Psalms, Proverbs, and the Prophets.

3. Genesis 2:23: "This is at last bone of my bone and flesh of my flesh."

4. Numbers 19:16: "Whoever in the open field touches someone who was killed with a sword or who died naturally, or touches a human bone or a grave shall be unclean seven days." Second Kings 23:14: "And he broke in pieces the pillars and cut down the Asherim and filled their places with the bones of men."

the bones of Elisha, he revived and stood on his feet." Once again, bones
and life/resurrection are intimately united.

Nowhere else is this connection more clear than in Ezekiel 37. Here we
read Ezekiel's vision of the valley of dry bones. He is called on to prophesy
to these dry bones, and as a result the bones come together, and the breath
of life enters them. In reference to this vision, verses 12–13 read: "Thus
says the LORD God: Behold I will open your graves and raise you from your
graves, O my people. And I will bring you into the land of Israel. And you
shall know that I am the LORD, when I open your graves and raise you from
your graves, O my people." Regardless of how one views this vision and its
fulfillment—a prophecy of the restoration of Israel from Babylon, or speaking of the bodily resurrection from the dead, or perhaps both—there is no
escaping the theme of life, new life, and resurrection connected to bones.
Levenson writes, "If resurrection were thought ludicrous, or impossible
even for God, then it would be a singularly inappropriate metaphor for
the national renewal and restoration that Ezekiel predicts, and the vision
in Ezek 37:1–10 could never have succeeded in its goal of overcoming the
hopelessness of the audience."[5]

All of these examples answer the question of how the Israelites considered bones in general and how they viewed the bones of Joseph in particular. Due to the gravity of the texts and the contexts in which bone language
is used, the reader may be encouraged to give consideration to possible
patterns, mindsets, and understandings. The biblical text attaches specific
importance to the usage of עצם, and the event of Joseph's bones being carried to Egypt is particularly unique.

THE BONES OF JOSEPH IN SECOND TEMPLE LITERATURE

In Second Temple literature, the subject of traveling bones is revisited, but
always in the greater context of Joseph's bones. In Jubilees the account of
Joseph's bones is expanded as the writer not only mentions the oath made
to carry Joseph's bones to Canaan, but also that the Egyptians refused to
allow them to be returned immediately to Canaan, a reference to their
sacred quality to the people of Egypt, and also that the king of Canaan was

---

5. Levenson, *Resurrection and Restoration*, 161.

more powerful than Pharaoh and refused to allow entry into his territory.[6] However, when Egypt went up to fight the king of Canaan, it is written that the children of Israel took all the bones of the children of Jacob—except for Joseph's bones—and buried them at Machpelah. "And the king of Egypt went forth to fight the king of Canaan in this forty seventh jubilee in the second week in the second year. And the children of Israel brought forth the bones of the children of Jacob, all except the bones of Joseph. And they buried them in the field in the cave of Machpelah in the mountain" (Jub. 46:9). This account is interesting in that bones are specifically referred to in the context of Joseph and his bones. Other places referring to burial, even that of Jacob himself (Jub. 45:13-15), who is carried to Canaan for burial, do not refer to bones. Rather, in the case of Jacob, he slept with his fathers and was buried.[7]

The Testaments of the Twelve Patriarchs also includes the account of Joseph's traveling bones.[8] The Testament of Joseph says: "You shall carry my bones along with you, for when you are taking my bones up there, the LORD will be with you in the light, while Beliar will be with the Egyptians in the dark" (T.Jos. 20.2). It is interesting that four of the other testaments of the patriarchs also refer to their bones being carried to Canaan—Simeon, Dan, Naphtali, and Benjamin. Of particular interest is the account in the Testament of Simeon:

> They placed him in a wooden coffin in order to carry his bones up to Hebron; they took them up in secret during a war with Egypt. The bones of Joseph the Egyptians kept in the tombs of the kings, since their wizards told them that at the departure of Joseph's bones there would be darkness and gloom in the whole land and a great plague

---

6. The date of the final form of Jubilees is to be placed at some point around the middle of the second century BCE. A convenient survey of scholarly opinions may be found in M. Segal, "Jubilees, Book of," in The Eerdmans Dictionary of Early Judaism, ed. J. J. Collins and D. C. Harlow (Grand Rapids: Eerdmans, 2010), 844.

7. Jubilees 49:13-14 does speak of bones as it lays out the restrictions on how to treat the lamb sacrificed for Passover. Contrary to the NT, it connects the mandate not to break its bones to the observation "because no bone of the children of Israel will be broken."

8. On the debate concerning the origin of the Testaments of the Twelve Patriarchs, see above, page 256, to which may be added the detailed discussion in Schürer, History of the Jewish People, 3.2:767-81, with discussion of date at 774-75 (first quarter of second century BCE for the Semitic background of the Testaments).

on the Egyptians, so that even with a lamp no one could recognize his brother. (T.Sim. 8.2–3)

The transportation of the bones of Joseph continued to carry great importance, as these later writings indicate. We also see a possible reason for Joseph's bones not being buried in Canaan soon after his death. Apparently, the Egyptians also placed great meaning on his bones, as they did for all their kings.

Kugel, in his book *In Potiphar's House*, takes up the topic of Joseph's bones but from a different angle.[9] Kugel, tracing various mishnaic sources, along with Jubilees and the Testaments of the Twelve Patriarchs, speaks of Joseph's "inaccessible bones." The focus of this motif is that Joseph's bones are difficult either to find or to access. A large amount of rabbinic tradition grew up around these perceived issues in the biblical text. While we will not go into any detail concerning this, it is appropriate to note these traditions because their existence points to the import placed on Joseph and his bones. It also illustrates how essential it was that the bones of Joseph be located and transported to Canaan. One particular issue in these traditions that is germane to our discussion is, Why were the bones of Joseph not taken up to Canaan immediately upon his death? The MT seems to indicate that Joseph knows that the interment of his bones will take place only when the Lord "visits" the people of Israel (Gen 50:25). While it is common to see Joseph in the role of the prophet in this account as he proclaims that the Lord will surely visit them and bring them out of the land of Egypt and up to the land of Canaan, there may be practical considerations as well.

Jubilees (46:9) speaks of the border between Egypt and Canaan being closed because of ongoing conflict between the two nations. The Testament of Simeon (8.1–3) mentions that the wizards of Pharaoh had foreseen a plague of darkness descending on the land of Egypt if Joseph's bones were removed. Kugel also points to the tradition from the Mishnah, which basically states: "Since Joseph was the greatest of the brothers, his good deed in burying his father could not be properly rewarded until someone greater than himself, Moses, could come along and bury him."[10] Each of these

---

9. Kugel, *In Potiphar's House*, 125–55.

10. Kugel, *In Potiphar's House*, 129–31, 149.

explanations is a plausible attempt to deal with this peculiar reality, but there is another thought that should be considered.

Ben Sira records an important list of biblical heroes in his writing. Each is referred to in relation to one or more of their heroic deeds. In 49:15 he treats the biblical hero Joseph: "There has not been another man like Joseph, yea, his remains were taken care of."[11] Kugel states: "Clearly, the one element in the whole long Joseph narrative that Ben Sira has found worthy of comment is the fact that Joseph's bones are specifically mentioned in connection with Moses and again in the book of Joshua."[12] Another translation of Ben Sira's "Praise of the Fathers," 49:15 is: "Was there ever a man born like Joseph? And his bones are taken care of." Niehoff writes: "In this stichos Joseph's uniqueness is established on the basis of his bones being carried back to the Holy Land. This is presumably highlighted also in view of Enoch's transfer to heaven."[13] Harl, in *La Genèse: La Bible d'Alexandrie*, points to another way in which this short verse from Ben Sira may have been understood. Rather than "and his bones were taken care of," she points to a tradition that "his bones are visited":[14] "Le *Siracide*, qui a donné à Joseph le titre de 'chef de ses frères,' dit: 'ils visitèrent ses ossements,' probablement pour signaler un culte du tombeau de Joseph à Sychem (selon Jos 24, 32; Si 49, 15)."[15]

If the bones of Joseph became the object of veneration after they are interred at Shechem, how much more so in Egypt immediately following his death? The Egyptians were accustomed to venerating their pharaohs and other leaders in death. How could they not do the same for the one who had delivered them from certain death by famine? And if this indeed was the case, the Egyptian people, both common and noble, would have been reluctant to allow Joseph to be buried in Canaan following his death.

---

11. Ben Sira makes only two references to bones in fifty-one chapters of text. In 46:12, speaking of the judges, he states: "Let their bones flourish/sprout out of their place, and let the name of them that were honored be continued upon their children." In 49:10, referencing the twelve prophets: "May their bones flourish out of their place." These are clearly life/resurrection texts in relation to bones.

12. Kugel, *In Potiphar's House*, 129.

13. Niehoff, *Figure of Joseph*, 50.

14. This may come from understanding the MT as indicating "When the LORD visits you, visit me."

15. Harl, *La Genèse*, 318.

It is only when there arose a new king in Egypt who did not know Joseph (Exod 1:8) that Joseph's bones were forgotten, thus freeing the Israelites and Moses to carry them out when the Lord visited them.

TRAVELING BONES

There was great importance attached to the return of Joseph's bones to the promised land of Canaan. As has been pointed out, there is too much attention placed on this event in both biblical and extrabiblical sources to dismiss it as an insignificant peculiarity of the text.

Joseph is embalmed on his death and placed in a coffin. The Hebrew word used for coffin is ארן, which may also be translated as "box" or "ark." It is the same word used to identify the ark of the covenant.[16] This draws an interesting picture for the reader of the exodus. In the beginning, the people of Israel are led out of Egypt by the ark of Joseph's bones. Eventually, they are led by two arks—Joseph's bones and the ark of the covenant (Exod 25:10–22). This continues until Joseph's remains are buried at Shechem in Joshua 24:32. Day in and day out, the bones of Joseph are displayed prominently before the people, and this continues for more than forty years. It is no wonder that these bones become of special importance for Israel.

PATRIARCHAL TO TRIBAL

One possible explanation for the necessity of Joseph's bones remaining in Egypt until the Lord visits the Israelites and brings them out and up to Canaan is the historical transition from the patriarchal to the tribal era.[17] In many ways, Joseph is a bridge figure between these time frames. Joseph's bones must to be buried in Canaan because he is the last of the patriarchs, as alluded to by his blessing, and all patriarchs are interred in the land promised to Israel in the covenant. Even Jacob, who died in Egypt, was brought to the family burial cave at Machpelah by Joseph to be buried with his fathers (Gen 50:4–14). The possible reasons Joseph was not immediately interred like his father have been discussed earlier, but it may also

---

16. This is not the same word used in reference to Noah's ark. תבה, "ark," as in Noah's ark, is only used in one other context in Scripture. In Exod 2:3 it is the word translated as "basket," as in Moses' basket of bulrushes.

17. Targum Onqelos translates "visits" as "remembers," possibly in an attempt to provide continuity with Exod 2:24.

hold true that the reason had an historical/theological dimension.[18] The delay may have had as much to do with the necessity to close the chapter on one era and open the pages to a new era.

Arguments in favor of the explanation for this late transport of Joseph's bones include Jacob's first blessings, which include Manasseh and Ephraim as a replacement for the tribe of Joseph. It is the two sons of Joseph who become half tribes—receiving the double portion—but Joseph is not referred to as a tribe. He is distinguished and set apart from his brothers. He is also the recipient of one of the two pieces of patriarchal land in Canaan, the mountain slope/shoulder of ground at Shechem.[19] Later, Joseph is buried in this place (Josh 24:32). None of the bones of the other sons of Jacob are carried to the land of Canaan, according to the biblical text, because they are the first of the tribal era, while Joseph bridges the two.[20]

Also in support of this argument, note that Joseph's bones are not buried until the land of Canaan has been possessed. It is immediately following the division of the land among the tribes that Joseph's remains are buried at Shechem. It appears to indicate the end of an important era and the beginning of something new.

A strong argument against this theory is the place of Joseph's grave. If he is the last of the patriarchs, why is he not buried in the cave of Machpelah—the patriarchal burial plot? As time progresses, the Israelites speak of their fathers as Abraham, Isaac, and Jacob—Joseph is not included. Another troubling reality is that Joseph does not receive the blessing of the messianic line; that blessing goes to Judah. Even Joseph's mother, Rachel, is not buried at Machpelah (Gen 35:16–20; 48:7), although she was Jacob's favorite wife. Rachel has a grave apart from the patriarchal cave with its covenantal lineage. Scripture tells us that the cave of Machpelah contains the remains of Abraham and Sarah, Isaac and Rebekah, Jacob and Leah (49:29–32).

---

18. See chap. 10.

19. The cave of Machpelah purchased by Abraham was the other (Gen 48:22).

20. The Testaments of the Twelve Patriarchs and Jubilees do clearly state that the bones/bodies of all the brothers were to be taken to Canaan, but this is nowhere indicated in the biblical record.

JOSEPH'S CONFESSION

One of the great difficulties with the life and the character of Joseph is his adoption of the Egyptian way of life. While this was thrust on him due to his slavery and imprisonment, and especially as he assumed the position of second in command of all Egypt, Joseph never appears to have relinquished this way of life and rejoined his family in Goshen. Following his successful deliverance of the land and the people from the throes of famine, he has the opportunity to return to his ancestral roots, customs, and culture, yet he does not appear to do so. In fact, the naming of his son Manasseh, "for God has made me forget all my hardship and all my father's house" (Gen 41:51), appears to be Joseph's divorce decree. Jacob is not pleased by this naming, as is indicated by the crossing of his hands and his giving the firstborn blessing to Ephraim instead (48:14–19). Jacob recognizes the decree Joseph has made, and their relationship is never the same. The level of trust between the two suffers, and Jacob requires Joseph "to swear" an oath that he will bury him in Canaan because he does not trust Joseph's pledge (47:29–31). Joseph has become an Egyptian, forsaking his Hebrew heritage.

As Joseph approaches his death, why does he make his brothers swear to carry up his bones from Egypt to be buried in Canaan? Could it be that even though Joseph has chosen to live as an Egyptian, in death he wants to be a Hebrew? The theory proposed is that this request of Joseph takes the form of a confession. In the end he does the right thing and forsakes the pagan life and the pagan country of Egypt in order to return to his homeland, his people, and his family. This confession also includes his reentry into the covenantal people, so he uses covenantal language as he speaks to his brothers. "And Joseph said to his brothers, 'I am about to die, but God will visit you and bring you up out of this land to the land that He swore to Abraham, to Isaac and to Jacob'" (50:24). In death, Joseph does not desire to be an Egyptian; he wants to return to the people of Israel. Joseph confesses by making his brothers swear to take his bones home.

COMPLETING THE CYCLE

In light of the general thesis of this writing—the recommendation that Joseph be viewed as a death-and-resurrection figure—the third argument for the purpose accomplished by Joseph's traveling bones is the strongest.

When Joseph's bones are buried by Joshua at Shechem, it signifies the completion of another cycle of Joseph's journey—another death-and-resurrection cycle.

Joseph being sold into slavery into the land of Egypt is the first portion of one of the manifestations of the death-and-resurrection motif of Scripture. "Going down to Egypt," an evil and pagan land, is a kind of death. The upward movement that accompanies it is "going up to the promised land." Although Joseph does return to Canaan to bury his father, Jacob, he never dwells there again until his burial. When Joseph's bones are returned to Canaan to dwell, it is a completion of a death-and-resurrection cycle. Joseph's journey might very well be an example of the same journey embarked on by the people of Israel.

By means of his bones, Joseph also participates in another manifestation of the death-and-resurrection motif, going down into the water/ drowned and being brought up out of the water/new life. Joseph's bones do this twice. First, when Moses parts the Red Sea, the people of Israel go down into the waters along with the bones of Joseph and come up on the other side. As the waters crash in on the Egyptians, drowning them, the Israelites experience new life as they have been rescued from certain death. Second, when Joshua parts the waters of the Jordan River (Josh 3:14–17), the people of Israel, along with the bones of Joseph, go down into the waters and up to the other side. In this scenario, the other side is the promised land—another way to speak of life and salvation in the courts of heaven. Joseph's bones go through this downward/upward movement once again.

There are also other manifestations of the death-and-resurrection motif evident in the traveling bones, namely, the submotif of separation and reunion as Joseph's bones are returned and reunited with his homeland, along with exile and return from exile as Joseph, who was exiled to Egypt because of his brothers' jealousy, finally returns.

Considering all the downward/upward movements in the life of Joseph and how they have pointed to a death-and-resurrection motif, it is appropriate that his bones continue this pattern. There is a distinct sense of completion and accomplishment surrounding these traveling bones, and the people of Israel feel a strong sense of duty to bring the cycle full circle. Their leaders, Moses and Joshua, are faithful in seeing Joseph's final words carried out. I would suggest that the Israelites saw the bones of Joseph in the same way they viewed Joseph and his life. He was the one who led the Israelites from death to life. First, as he provided salvation from the famine, and now as his bones return them to the promised land.

CONCLUSION

While it is tempting to adopt one of these explanations to the exclusion of the rest, it is more likely that all three explanations are true to one extent or another. However, in light of all that has preceded this discussion, I am of the opinion that the most significant and most revealing is to view this journey of Joseph's bones as another important death-and-resurrection cycle that helps cement this death-and-resurrection reality in the minds of the people of Israel. In light of the MT use of bones in life-giving situations, it seems that this understanding is most fitting and consistent. When Joseph makes his request—his confession—to have his bones carried out of Egypt, he is fulfilling the role of a prophet. He foresees that the Lord will visit his people and they will be brought up from their slavery, brought up to the promised land, delivered up from their enemies, and given new life in a new place. Out of the pit of darkness, despair, and death, the people will be lifted out and raised up to this new life in the new, promised land. It is only proper that Joseph's bones lead the way.

Conclusion

Using the biblical hermeneutic of reading Scripture as a unified theological narrative produces several important results. First, such a reading allows one to identify the various biblical motifs that weave their way through the entirety of the biblical narrative. These motifs not only show the unity of the narrative, but they also bear witness to a unified theological message. Conversely, these motifs show the unity of the narrative as they connect all Scripture—Genesis to Revelation—into one story. In the identification of these motifs comes the recognition that there are various characters, events, and even geographical locations that serve as the crossroads for a multitude of motifs. It is these characters, events, and locations that help demonstrate the faith, beliefs, and theological perceptions of the Hebrew people.

Second, employing this hermeneutic with the Joseph narratives distinguishes the foci of the various submotifs examined here. The LXX, while replacing the majority of the Hebrew narrative doubling, incorporates more dramatic phrases, using word choices that enhance the plot of the Joseph story as it draws the hearer to Joseph's salvific role without negating the death-and-resurrection character. Targum Onqelos maintains the literary nuances of the Hebrew but goes to obvious lengths to improve Joseph's character so that he might be used as a righteous example of a moral and ethical figure without denying or negating the death-and-resurrection character of the MT. The departures of the LXX and Targum Onqelos from the MT served specific needs and agendas. In the process, while they have not denied or negated the death-and-resurrection message, they have obscured it for many readers along the way. Reading the Joseph narratives as a unified theological narrative and seeing their place in the whole counsel of the biblical story recaptures and uncovers the motif that defines the character and place of Joseph in the larger narrative of Scripture.

Thus, the final, larger result of employing this hermeneutical method is the revelation of the death-and-resurrection motif of the Joseph narratives and Joseph's role as a death-and-resurrection figure. The intertwining of the downward/upward movement with the various manifestations of death and resurrection provides strong evidence in support of Joseph's original role in the Scriptures. The development of these various manifestations over the course of time and in the larger context of the entirety of Scripture helps explains the resurrection of this role in Second Temple Judaism. Thus, signposts are provided reminding us of Joseph's importance as a death-and-resurrection figure in ancient times as well as in Second Temple Judaism.

IMPLICATIONS

Reading Scripture as a unified theological narrative reveals the various biblical motifs. When these motifs are discovered and their unifying features identified, the reader develops a greater appreciation for the complex way in which the whole of Scripture has been artfully tied together. Such an understanding not only provides important information for academic biblical scholarship, but it also produces practical theological information useful for faith communities. In addition, it points to the inadequacies of some older, well-known discussions of the Joseph narratives that have focused on the historicity of the text, with the result of collapsing the world of the text and the world in front of the text into the world behind the text.

In regard to Joseph and his character, the implications are also significant. Employing this hermeneutic within the Joseph narratives allows its proper relationship to the rest of the biblical text to unfold. While Joseph has historically been used, adopted, and even abused by various sources in order to support agendas, with this new reading, Joseph can once again assume his unique position. Uncovering the biblical motifs reveals Joseph's true character—that which was portrayed by the received text. Joseph is not primarily a moral and ethical example, an excellent statesman, or a salvific character. While each of these accurately expresses some aspects of the Joseph narratives, my thesis has attempted to show that the death-and-resurrection theme is pervasive in the Joseph material to such a degree that Joseph may properly be understood as a death-and-resurrection figure. Such a view carries with it the implication that scholars might need to change their focus somewhat, not only with regard to Joseph, but also with respect to understanding Hebrew thinking on the afterlife more generally.

This book has given detailed reasons for arguing that the scholarly methods and procedures promoted by Alter, Childs, and Levenson in particular offer better readings overall of the narrative than those that preceded them. My conclusions in this book provide additional support for several of Levenson's observations, while at the same time expanding the discussion.[1] I have built on the work of these and other like-minded scholars to argue that a unified theological narrative reading offers the most comprehensive understanding of the account of Joseph in relation to the Hebrew Bible. Furthermore, a unified theological narrative approach to the Joseph narratives opens up the possibility for a clearer explication of the Joseph story as it appears in the LXX, Targum Onqelos, and other postbiblical Jewish texts.

BROADENING THE DISCUSSION

The hermeneutic proposed here is essentially literary in character and in many important respects stands in continuity with other literary approaches to the Bible: the name of Robert Alter, for example, has featured prominently in this book.[2] Looking at the narrative as a whole that contains a unified theological message allows for a higher view of the text and incorporates the whole into the discussion. When it is no longer permissible to deal with the text strictly in a piecemeal fashion, there is less opportunity for difficult portions of Scripture to be obscured. Engaging every portion of the text can only broaden the discussion as biblical scholars wrestle with these sections and consider their place in the whole.

There is also greater opportunity for the entire faith community to engage in the discussion. The growing divide between academy and the church and synagogue may be bridged with this unified theological

---

1. Levenson, *Death and Resurrection*.

2. Compare also the well-known approach to the scriptural text adopted by N. Frye, *The Great Code* (Toronto: University of Toronto Press, 2006).

narrative. A discussion that incorporates the entire text while identifying biblical motifs is more than an academic exercise. It produces fruit that is helpful, practical, and insightful for both communities. This book has come to several smaller, useful conclusions, which, taken as a whole, lead to the larger conclusion in support of Joseph as a death-and-resurrection figure.

Finally, it is important to emphasize that I am not offering a totalitarian interpretation of the Joseph narratives. As noted, assuming these narratives as a key component within a unified theological narrative reading focuses on the strong death-and-resurrection character. However, there are other possible interpretations. Many of my results depend on the insights of earlier scholarly work, and I have acknowledged that no one school of thought or scholarly interpretation exclusively has the answer to all issues raised by the Hebrew text studied here, while pointing to significant and clearly discernible benefits of the unified theological narrative's approach as diminishing or removing interpretive problems that some other methods seem unable to address. In many instances I have been able to provide here valuable independent support for those insights, approaching the text using a method different from that employed by earlier researchers. In addition, what I have done is to demonstrate, and demonstrate systematically, that the unified theological narrative approach can be and is coherent, and casts light on the narratives in a way that other approaches have not done. It is my hope that the discussion will be ongoing and that the work of this book will provide additional grist for the theological milling of the whole of Scripture.

Bibliography

Ackroyd, P. *Exile and Restoration*. Philadelphia: Westminster, 1968.

Alexander, P., trans. *The Aramaic Bible*. Vol. 17A, *Targum of Canticles Translated, with a Critical Introduction, Apparatus, and Notes*. Collegeville, MN: Liturgical Press, 2003.

Allen, L. C. *Ezekiel 20–48*. Word Biblical Commentary 29. Nashville: Thomas Nelson, 1990.

Alter, R. *The Art of Biblical Narrative*. New York: Basic Books, 1981.

———. *The Art of Biblical Poetry*. New York: Basic Books, 1985.

———. *Genesis*. New York: Norton, 1996.

Anderson, G. "Joseph and the Passion of Our Lord." Pages 198–215 in *The Art of Reading Scripture* Edited by R. B. Hays and E. Davis. Grand Rapids: Eerdmans, 2003.

Anderson, G. A. *The Genesis of Perfection*. Louisville: Westminster John Knox, 2001.

Barr, J. *Holy Scripture: Canon, Authority, Criticism*. Oxford: Oxford University Press, 1983.

———. "The Synchronic, the Diachronic and the Historical: A Triangular Relationship." Pages 1–14 in *Synchronic or Diachronic? A Debate on Method in Old Testament Exegesis* Edited by Johannes C. De Moor. Leiden: Brill, 1995.

Barton, J. *Reading the Old Testament: Method in Biblical Study*. Louisville: Westminster John Knox, 1998.

Bauckham, R. *Bible and Mission: Christian Witness in a Postmodern World*. Grand Rapids: Baker Academic, 2004.

———. *Jesus and the Eyewitnesses*. Grand Rapids: Eerdmans, 2006.

———. *The Testimony of the Beloved Disciple: Narrative, History and Theology in the Gospel of John*. Grand Rapids: Baker Academic, 2007.

Bergmann, C. D. *Childbirth as a Metaphor for Crisis*. New York: de Gruyter, 2008.

Biblia Hebraica Quinta. Stuttgart: Deutsche Bibelgesellschaft, 2015.

Blenkinsopp, J. *Ezekiel*. Louisville: John Knox, 1990.

Botterweck, G. J., H. Ringgren, and H-J. Fabry, eds. *Theological Dictionary of the Old Testament*. Grand Rapids: Eerdmans, 2004.

Bowman, John. *The Samaritan Problem*. Pittsburgh: Pickwick, 1975.

Bremmer, J. N. *The Rise and Fall of the Afterlife*. London: Routledge, 2002.

Brown, F., S. R. Driver, and C. A. Briggs. *A Hebrew and English Lexicon of the Old Testament*. Rev. and corrected ed. Oxford: Clarendon, 1968.

Brueggemann, W. *Genesis: A Bible Commentary for Teaching and Preaching*. Atlanta: John Knox, 1982.

———. *Theology of the Old Testament*. Minneapolis: Fortress, 1997.

Buber, S., ed. *Midrash Legah Tob*. Lvov. 1878.

Byron, J. *Slavery Metaphors in Early Judaism and Pauline Christianity*. Tübingen: Mohr Siebeck, 2003.

Carr, D. M. *Writing on the Tablet of the Heart. Origins of Scripture and Literature*. New York: Oxford University Press, 2005.

Charles, R. H. *Apocrypha and Pseudepigrapha of the Old Testament*. 2 vols. Oxford: Clarendon, 1913.

Charlesworth, J. H., ed. *The Old Testament Pseudepigrapha*. 2 vols. New York: Doubleday, 1983–85.

———. *Introduction to the Old Testament as Scripture*. Philadelphia: Fortress, 1979.

———. *Old Testament Theology in a Canonical Context*. Philadelphia: Fortress, 1985.

Childs, B. S. "Karl Barth as Interpreter of Scripture." Pages 30-39 in *Karl Barth and the Future of Theology: A Memorial Colloquium Held at Yale*

Divinity School January 28, 1969. Edited by D. L. Dickerman. New Haven: Yale Divinity School Association, 1969.

———*Old Testament Theology in a Canonical Context*. Philadelphia: Fortress, 1985.

Chung, Y. H. *The Sin of the Calf: The Rise of the Bible's Negative Attitude toward the Golden Calf*. New York: T&T Clark, 2010.

Coats, G. W. *From Canaan to Egypt: Structural and Theological Context for the Joseph Story*. Catholic Biblical Quarterly Monograph Series. Washington, DC: Catholic University of America Press, 1976.

Collins, J. J. *The Bible after Babel: Historical Criticism in a Postmodern Age*. Grand Rapids: Eerdmans, 2005.

———. *A Commentary on the Book of Daniel*. Hermeneia. Minneapolis: Fortress, 1993.

———. "Joseph and Aseneth: Jewish or Christian?" *Journal for the Study of the Pseudepigrapha* 14 (2005): 97–112.

Daley, B. E., SJ. *The Hope of the Early Church: A Handbook of Patristic Eschatology*. Peabody, MA: Hendrickson, 2003.

———. *The World of the Early Christians*. Collegeville, MN: Liturgical Press, 1997.

Davies, J. *Death, Burial and Rebirth in the Religions of Antiquity*. London: Routledge, 1999.

Davies, W. D. *The Territorial Dimension of Judaism*. Oakland: University of California Press, 1982.

Davis, E. F. *Getting Involved with God: Rediscovering the Old Testament*. Lanham, MD: Cowley, 2001.

———. *Proverbs, Ecclesiastes and the Song of Songs*. Louisville: Westminster John Knox, 2004.

———. *Scripture, Culture and Agriculture: An Agrarian Reading of the Bible*. Cambridge: Cambridge University Press, 2008.

De Troyer, K. "The Hebrew Text behind the Greek Text of the Pentateuch." Pages 15–32 in *XIV Congress of the International Organization for Septuagint and Cognate Studies. Helsinki, 2010*. Edited by M. K. H. Peters. Atlanta: Society of Biblical Literature, 2012.

Dever, W. G. *What Did the Biblical Writers Know and When Did They Know It? What Archaeology Can Tell Us about the Reality of Ancient Israel.* Grand Rapids: Eerdmans. 2001.

Dines, J. *The Septuagint.* Understanding the Bible and Its World. London: T&T Clark, 2004.

Driver, D. R. *Brevard Childs, Biblical Theologian.* Grand Rapids: Baker Academic, 2010.

Driver, S. R. *Introduction to the Literature of the Old Testament.* Edinburgh: T&T Clark, 1898.

Eichrodt, W. *Ezekiel: A Commentary.* Translated by C. Quin. London: SCM, 1970.

———. *Theology of the Old Testament.* Philadelphia: Westminster, 1961.

Eissfeldt, O. *The Old Testament: An Introduction.* Translated by P. R. Ackroyd. New York: Harper & Row, 1965.

Flesher, P., and B. Chilton. *The Targums: A Critical Introduction.* Waco, TX: Baylor University Press, 2011.

Flusser, D. *Judaism of the Second Temple Period.* Vol. 1, *Qumran and Apocalypticism.* Grand Rapids: Eerdmans, 2007.

Fohrer, G. *Introduction to the Old Testament.* London: SPCK, 1968.

Fokkelman, J. P. "Structural Reading on the Fracture between Synchrony and Diachrony." *Jaarbericht van het Voorziatisch-Egyptisch Gezelschap (Genootschap) Ex oriente lux* 30 (1989): 123–36.

Fraser, P. M. *Ptolemaic Alexandria.* Oxford: Oxford University Press, 1972.

Fretheim, T. E. *The Pentateuch.* Nashville: Abingdon, 1996.

———. "The Reclamation of Creation: Redemption and Law in Exodus." *Interpretation: A Journal of Bible and Theology* 45, no. 4 (1991): 354–65.

Frye, N. *The Great Code.* Toronto: University of Toronto Press, 2006.

Fung, Y.-W. *Victim and Victimizer: Joseph's Interpretation of His Destiny.* Sheffield: Sheffield Academic Press, 2000.

Gieschen, C. A. *Angelomorphic Christology: Antecedents and Early Evidence.* Leiden: Brill, 1998.

Gillman, N. *The Death of Death: Resurrection and Immortality in Jewish Thought*. Woodstock, VT: Jewish Lights, 1997.

Greenspoon, L. J. "The Origins of the Idea of Resurrection." Pages 247–321 in *Traditions in Transformation: Turning Points in Biblical Faith*. Edited by J. Halpern and J. D. Levenson. Winona Lake, IN: Eisenbrauns, 1981.

Greidanus, S. *Preaching Christ from Genesis*. Grand Rapids: Eerdmans, 2007.

Grossfeld, B., trans. *The Aramaic Bible*. Vol. 6, *The Targum Onqelos to Genesis: Translated, with a Critical Introduction, Apparatus, and Notes*. Edinburgh: T&T Clark, 1988.

Grossman, J. "Different Dreams: Two Models of Interpretation for Three Pairs of Dreams." *Journal of Biblical Literature* 135, no. 4 (2016): 717–32.

———. *Heritage and Hellenism: The Reinvention of Jewish Tradition*. Berkeley: University of California Press, 1998.

Gunkel, H. *Genesis*. Macon, GA: Mercer University Press, 1997.

———. *The Legends of Genesis*. New York: Schocken Books, 1964.

Hamilton, V. P. *The Book of Genesis*. 2 vols. Grand Rapids: Eerdmans. 1995.

Haran, M. *Temple and Temple Service in Ancient Israel*. Winona Lake: Eisenbrauns. 1985.

Harl, M. *La Genèse: La Bible D'Alexandrie*. Paris: Éditions du Cerf, 1994.

Hays, R. B. *The Conversion of the Imagination*. Grand Rapids: Eerdmans, 2005.

———. *Echoes of Scripture in the Letters of Paul*. New Haven: Yale University Press, 1993.

———. *The Faith of Jesus Christ: Narrative Substructure of Galatians 3:1–4:11*. Grand Rapids: Eerdmans, 2002.

Hays, R. B., and E. Davis, eds. *The Art of Reading Scripture*. Grand Rapids: Eerdmans, 2003.

Hayward, C. T. R. *Divine Name and Presence: The Memra*. Lanham, MD: Rowman & Littlefield, 1981.

Horowitz, H. S., and I. A. Rabin, eds. *Mechilta D'Rabbi Ismael*. Jerusalem, 1970.

Hossfeld, F. L., and E. Zenger. *Psalms 3: A Commentary on Psalms 101–150.* Minneapolis: Fortress, 2011.

Howell, J. C. *The Beatitudes for Today.* Louisville: Westminster John Knox, 2005.

———. *Conversations with St. Francis.* Nashville: Abingdon, 2008.

Humphreys, W. L. *Joseph and His Family.* Columbia: University of South Carolina Press, 1988.

Hurtado, L. W. *The Earliest Christian Artifacts.* Grand Rapids: Eerdmans, 2006.

Jacob, B. *Das Erste Buch Der Tora Genesis.* New York. Ktav Publishing, 1934.

Japhet, S. *I and II Chronicles: A Commentary.* London: SCM, 1993.

Jellicoe, S. *The Septuagint and Modern Study.* Winona Lake, IN: Eisenbrauns, 1989.

Jenson, P. P. *Graded Holiness: A Key to the Priestly Conception of the World.* Sheffield, UK: Sheffield Academic Press. 1992.

Jenson, R. W. *Canon and Creed.* Louisville: Westminster John Knox, 2010.

———. *Ezekiel.* Grand Rapids: Brazos, 2009.

———. *Song of Songs.* Louisville: Westminster John Knox, 2005.

Johnson, W. S. *Crisis, Call, and Leadership in the Abrahamic Traditions.* New York: Palgrave Macmillan, 2009.

Johnston, P. S. *Shades of Sheol: Death and Afterlife in the Old Testament.* Downers Grove, IL: InterVarsity Press, 2002.

Jones, L. G. *Theology and Scriptural Imagination: Directions in Modern Theology.* Malden, MA: Wiley-Blackwell, 1998.

———. *Why Narrative? Readings in Narrative Theology.* Eugene, OR: Wipf & Stock, 1997.

Jonge, M. de. *Jewish Eschatology, Early Christianity, and the Testaments of the Twelve Patriarchs.* Leiden: Brill, 1991.

———. *The Testaments of the Twelve Patriarchs: A Study of Their Text, Composition, and Origin.* Leiden: Brill, 1953.

Joosten, J. "Translating the Untranslatable: Septuagint Renderings of Hebrew Idioms." Pages 59–70 in *"Translation Is Required": The Septuagint in Retrospect and Prospect*. Edited by R. Heibert. Leiden: Brill, 2010.

Kaminski, C. M. *From Noah to Israel: Realization of the Primaeval Blessing after the Flood*. New York: T&T Clark, 2004.

Kaminsky, J. S. *Yet I Loved Jacob: Reclaiming the Biblical Concept of Election*. Eugene, OR: Wipf & Stock, 2007.

Kleinig, J. *The Glory and the Service: Worship in the Old Testament*. Fort Wayne, IN: Concordia, 2004.

Knierim, R. *The Task of Old Testament Theology: Method and Cases*. Grand Rapids: Eerdmans, 1995.

Knoppers, G. *Jews and Samaritans: The Origins and History of Their Early Relations*. Oxford: Oxford University Press, 2013.

Koehler, L., and W. Baumgartner. *The Hebrew and Aramaic Lexicon of the Old Testament*. Rev. ed. 5 vols. Leiden: Brill, 1994.

Kugel, J. L. *In Potiphar's House: The Interpretive Life of Biblical Texts*. Cambridge: Harvard University Press, 1990.

Kugler, R. A. "Joseph at Qumrân (i): The Importance of 4Q372 Frg. 1 in Extending a Tradition." Pages 261–78 in *Studies in the Hebrew Bible, Qumran, and the Septuagint Presented to Eugene Ulrich*. Edited by P. W. Flint, E. Tov, and J. C. VanderKam. Leiden: Brill, 2006.

———. *Testaments of the Twelve Patriarchs*. Sheffield: Sheffield Academic Press, 2001.

Lang, B. *Joseph in Egypt: A Cultural Icon from Grotius to Goethe*. New Haven: Yale University Press, 2009.

Lee, J. A. L. *A Lexical Study of the Septuagint Version of the Pentateuch*. Atlanta: Society of Biblical Literature, 1983.

Lessing, R. *Jonah*. Concordia Commentary Series. St. Louis: Concordia, 2007.

Levenson, J. D. *Creation and the Persistence of Evil*. Princeton: Princeton University Press, 1988.

———. *The Death and Resurrection of the Beloved Son: The Transformation of Child Sacrifice in Judaism and Christianity.* New Haven: Yale University Press, 1993.

──────. *The Hebrew Bible, the Old Testament and Historical Criticism.* Louisville: Westminster John Knox, 1993.

──────. *Resurrection and the Restoration of Israel.* New Haven: Yale University Press, 2006.

Levine, L. I. *The Ancient Synagogue: The First Thousand Years.* New Haven: Yale University Press, 2000.

Longacre, R. E. *Joseph: A Story of Divine Providence.* Winona Lake, IN: Eisenbrauns, 2003.

Louth, A. *Discerning the Mystery: An Essay on the Nature of Theology.* Oxford: Clarendon, 1983.

Luther, M. *Luther's Works.* American edition. Vol. 6. St. Louis: Concordia, 1965.

Luzzato, S. D. *Ohev Ger.* 2nd ed. Krakow, 1895.

MacDonald, John. *The Theology of the Samaritans.* London: SCM, 1964.

Maher, M., MSC, trans. *The Aramaic Bible.* Vol. 1B, *The Targum Pseudo-Jonathan: Genesis.* Collegeville, MN: Liturgical Press, 1992.

Martin-Achard, R. "Resurrection (OT)." Pages 680–84 in vol. 5 of *The Anchor Bible Dictionary.* Edited by D. N. Freedman. New York: Doubleday, 1992.

McDonald, L. M., and J. A. Sanders, eds. *The Canon Debate.* Peabody, MA: Hendrickson, 2002.

McNamara, M., MSC, trans. *The Aramaic Bible.* Vol. 1A, *Targum Neofiti 1: Genesis.* Collegeville, MN: Liturgical Press, 1991.

Menn, E. M. *Judah and Tamar (Genesis 38) in Ancient Jewish Exegesis.* Leiden: Brill, 1997.

Moberly, R. W. L. *The Bible, Theology, and Faith: A Study of Abraham and Jesus.* Cambridge: Cambridge University Press, 2000.

──────. "Living Dangerously: Genesis 22 and the Quest for Good Biblical Interpretation." Pages 181–97 in *The Art of Reading Scripture.* Edited by R. B. Hays and E. Davis. Grand Rapids: Eerdmans, 2003.

———. *The Old Testament of the Old Testament*. Eugene, OR: Wipf & Stock, 2001.

———. *Old Testament Theology: Reading the Hebrew Bible as Christian Scripture*. Grand Rapids: Baker Academic, 2013.

———. *Old Testament Theology: The Theology of the Book of Genesis*. Cambridge: Cambridge University Press, 2009.

———. *Prophecy and Discernment*. Cambridge: Cambridge University Press, 2006.

———. "What Is Theological Interpretation of Scripture?" *Journal of Theological Interpretation* 3, no. 2 (2009): 161–78.

Moo, D. J. *Major Cities of the Biblical World: Alexandria*. Nashville: Thomas Nelson, 1985.

Munnich, O. *Le texte du Pentateuque grec et son histoire*. Paris: Éditions du Cerf, 2001.

Nickelsburg, G. W. E. *Resurrection, Immortality and Eternal Life in Intertestamental Judaism and Early Christianity*. Cambridge: Harvard University Press, 1972.

Niehoff, M. *The Figure of Joseph in Post-biblical Jewish Literature*. Leiden: Brill, 1992.

———. "New Garments for Biblical Joseph." Pages 33–56 in *Biblical Interpretation: History, Context, Reality*. Edited by C. Helmer. Atlanta: Scholars Press, 2005.

Noth, M. *A History of Pentateuchal Traditions*. Englewood Cliffs, NJ: Prentice-Hall, 1972.

Pirson, R. *The Lord of the Dreams: A Semantic and Literary Analysis of Genesis 37–50*. London: Sheffield Academic Press, 2002.

Pritchard, J. P. *Ancient Near Eastern Texts Relating to the Old Testament*. Princeton: Princeton University Press, 1954, 1969.

Rad, G. von. *Genesis: A Commentary*. Philadelphia: Westminster, 1961.

Rahlfs, A., ed. *Septuaginta*. Stuttgart: Deutsche Bibelgesellschaft, 1935.

———. *A Study of the Biblical Story of Joseph (Genesis 37–50)*. Leiden: Brill, 1970.

Redford, D. B. *A Study of the Biblical Story of Joseph (Genesis 37–50)*. Leiden: Brill, 1970.

Rendsburg, G. A. *The Redaction of Genesis*. Winona Lake, IN: Eisenbrauns, 1986.

Rendtorff, R. *The Canonical Hebrew Bible: A Theology of the Old Testament*. Leiderdorp, Germany: Deo, 2005.

Rosenburg, R. *The Concept of Biblical Sheol within the Context of Ancient Near Eastern Belief*. Cambridge: Harvard University Press, 1981.

Saldarini, A. J. *Pharisees, Scribes and Sadducees in Palestinian Society: A Sociological Approach*. 2nd ed. Grand Rapids: Eerdmans, 2001.

Salvesen, A. "The Role of Aquila, Symmachus, and Theodotion in Modern Commentaries on the Bible." Pages 95–112 in *Let Us Go Up to Zion: Essays in Honour of H. G. M. Williamson on the Occasion of His Sixty-Fifth Birthday*. Edited by I. Provan and M. Boda. Leiden: Brill, 2012.

Samely, A. *The Interpretation of Speech in the Pentateuchal Targums*. Texte und Studien zum antiken Judentum 27. Tübingen: Mohr Siebeck, 1992.

Sarna, N. M. *The JPS Torah Commentary: Genesis*. Philadelphia: Jewish Publication Society, 1989.

Schniedewind, W. M. *How the Bible Became a Book: The Textualisation of Ancient Israel*. Cambridge: Cambridge University Press, 2004.

Schürer, E. *A History of the Jewish People in the Time of Jesus Christ*. 5 vols. Revised and edited by G. Vermes, F. Millar, and M. Goodman. Edinburgh: T&T Clark, 1987.

Segal, A. F. *Life after Death: A History of the Afterlife in Western Religion*. New York: Doubleday, 2004.

Segal, M. "Jubilees, Book of." In *The Eerdmans Dictionary of Early Judaism*, ed. J. J. Collins and D. C. Harlow. Grand Rapids: Eerdmans, 2010.

Seitz, C. *The Character of Christian Scripture: The Significance of a Two Testament Bible*. Grand Rapids: Baker Academic, 2011.

Seters, J. van. *Prologue to History: The Yahwist as Historian in Genesis*. Louisville: Westminster John Knox, 1992.

Smelik, W. *Rabbis, Language, and Translation in Late Antiquity.* Cambridge: Cambridge University Press, 2013.

Smith-Christopher, D. L. *A Biblical Theology of Exile.* Minneapolis: Fortress, 2002.

Speiser, E. A. *Genesis.* Anchor Bible. Garden City, NY: Doubleday, 1983.

Sperber, A. *The Bible in Aramaic.* Vol. 1, *The Pentateuch according to Targum Onkelos.* Leiden: Brill, 1959.

Spronk, K. *Beatific Afterlife in Ancient Israel and in the Ancient Near East.* Kevelaer, Germany: Butzon and Bercker, 1986.

Steindorff, G. *The Religion of the Ancient Egyptians.* New York: G. P. Putnam's Sons. 1905.

Steiner, F. "Enslavement and the Early Hebrew Lineage System: An Explanation of Genesis 47:29–31; 48:1–16." Pages 33–54 in *Anthropological Approaches to the Old Testament.* Edited by B. Lang. Issues in Religion and Theology 8. Philadelphia: Fortress, 1985.

Steinmann, A. *Daniel.* Concordia Commentary Series. St. Louis: Concordia, 2008.

Steinmetz, D. *Calvin in Context.* Oxford: Oxford University Press, 1995.

———. *Luther in Context.* Grand Rapids: Baker Academic, 1986.

———. *Reformers in the Wings.* Grand Rapids: Baker, 1981.

Stemberger, G. *Der Leib der Auferstehung.* Analecta Biblica 56. Rome: Pontifical Biblical Institute, 1972.

Syrén, R. *The Blessings in the Targums: A Study on the Targumic Interpretations of Genesis 49 and Deuteronomy 33.* Abo, Sweden: Abo Akademi, 1986.

———. *The Forsaken First Born: A Study of a Recurrent Motif in the Patriarchal Narratives.* Sheffield: Sheffield Academic Press, 1993.

Sysling, H. *Tehiyyat Ha-Metim: The Resurrection of the Dead in the Palestinian Targums of the Pentateuch and Parallel Traditions in Classical Rabbinic Literature.* Tübingen: Mohr Siebeck, 1996.

Theodor, J., ed. Genesis Rabba acc. to *Bereshith Rabba.* 1965.

Thompson, M. M. *Colossians and Philemon*. Grand Rapids: Eerdmans, 2005.

———. *1–3 John*. Downers Grove, IL: InterVarsity Press, 1992.

Tigay, J. H. *The JPS Torah Commentary: Deuteronomy*. Philadelphia: Jewish Publication Society, 1996.

Toorn, K. van der. *Scribal Culture and the Making of the Hebrew Bible*. Cambridge: Harvard University Press, 2007.

Tromp, N. J., MSC. *Primitive Conceptions of Death and the Netherworld in the Old Testament*. Rome: Pontifical Biblical Institute, 1969.

VanderKam, J. C. "Revealed Literature in the Second Temple Period." Pages 1–30 in *From Revelation to Canon: Studies in the Hebrew Bible and Second Temple Literature*. Leiden: Brill, 2000.

VanGemeren, W. A., ed. *The New International Dictionary of Old Testament Theology and Exegesis*. 5 vols. Grand Rapids: Zondervan, 1997.

Vawter, B. *A Path through Genesis*. New York: Sheed & Ward, 1956.

Weiss, I. H., ed. *Sifra debe Rab*. Vienna, 1862.

Wellhausen, J. *Die Composition des Hexateuchs und der Historischen Bücher des Alten Testaments*. Berlin: G. Reiner, 1899.

Wenham, G. J. *Genesis 16–50*. Word Biblical Commentary. Dallas: Word Books, 1994.

Westermann, C. *Genesis 37–50: A Commentary*. Minneapolis: Augsburg, 1986.

———. *Genesis: An Introduction*. Minneapolis: Augsburg Fortress, 1992.

Wevers, J. W. *Notes on the Greek Text of Genesis*. Atlanta: Scholars Press, 1993.

Whiston, W., trans. *The Works of Josephus*. Lynn, MA: Hendrickson, 1980.

Whybray, R. N. *The Making of the Pentateuch: A Methodological Study*. Sheffield: Sheffield Academic Press, 1987.

Wright, C. J. H. *The Mission of God: Unlocking the Bible's Grand Narrative*. Downers Grove, IL: InterVarsity Press, 2006.

Würthwein, E. *The Text of the Old Testament: An Introduction to Kittle-Kahle's Hebraica*. Oxford: Basil Blackwell, 1957.

Subject and Author Index

Subject Index

Author Index

Scripture Index

Old Testament

New Testament